The Bureaucrats of Buenos Aires

The Bureaucrats of Buenos Aires,

1769–1810: Amor al Real Servicio

SUSAN MIGDEN SOCOLOW

DUKE UNIVERSITY PRESS

DURHAM AND LONDON

1987

©1987 Duke University Press
All rights reserved
Printed in the United States of
America on acid-free paper ∞
Library of Congress Cataloging in Publication
Data appear on the last printed page of this book.

"No hay prenda mas apreciable en el Hombre, que el amor al real servicio, sus desvelos tareas y fatigas, a tan digno objeto, en media de los mayores obstáculos, tiene un alagueño aspecto."

Letter of Francisco de Viedma to the Crown Cochabamba, 5 June 1778 (AGI, Buenos Aires 144)

"fue oficio siempre de mucha estimación, y se le llamaron ilustre, y con razón, por que la materia de su ejercicio es de las mas importantes por serlo tanto la hacienda, nervio y musculos de la Monarchia, y asi al paso de esta importancia y de los riesgos y cargas deben ser favorecidos y distinguidos estos Ministros."

Letter of Félix de Casamayor, Antonio Carrasco, and José Maria Romero to Viceroy Rafael de Sobremonte. Buenos Aires, 24 April 1806 (AGNA, Hacienda, Legajo 61, Expediente 1580, IX-33-7-3)

"Su genio franco, su desinteres, y la banagloria conque puede lisongearse su memoria de no haber reportado mas premio ni luero en su empleo que su corto sueldo . . . no les permitieron formar caudal, ni ahorros algunos."

Petition of Antonio de la Peña referring to the estate of his grandfather, Juan de Vilanova, chief customs inspector of the Viceroyalty of Río de la Plata. Buenos Aires, 1813 (AGNA, Pertenencias Extrañas, Tomo 2, Número 11, IX-15-2-10)

Contents

Tables and Figures

Acknowledgments

ALTHOUGH I AM OF COURSE responsible for this work, I wish to thank those friends and colleagues who have helped along the way. Adela Harispuru and Judy Sweeney worked on copying Argentine materials. Silvia and Ora Waisman provided friendship and good cheer. Ann Twinam, Gary Miller, Lyman Johnson, John TePaske, Herbert Klein, Jacques Barbier, Mark Burkholder, and Zacarias Moutoukias, each in their own way, made research and writing a pleasant and rewarding endeavor. The staffs of the following archives and libraries also deserve mention: Archivo General de la Nación Argentina, Archivo de la Provincia de Buenos Aires, Archivo General de Indias, Archivo General de Simancas, Biblioteca Nacional de Madrid, Real Academia de la Historia (Madrid), Archivo Histórico Nacional (Madrid), the Library of Congress, and the Emory University Library. And special thanks to María Antonia Colomar and Pilar Lázaro of the Archivo General de Indias for their never-failing good humor and patience. This manuscript was typed and retyped by Patsy Stockbridge, a most faithful stalwart.

I have been generously supported in this research by the National Endowment for the Humanities, the U.S.-Spanish Joint Committee for Educational and Cultural Affairs, and the Emory University Research Committee.

My husband, Dan, has continued to provide love, encouragement, patience, understanding, and compassion in all that I have undertaken. Without his support neither this book nor much else would have been accomplished. My children, Ari and Josh, have proved to be good "troopers," forgoing a mother from time to time to have a historian. To them, in the hope that their lives prove to be as fulfilling and enjoyable as mine is, I dedicate this book with love.

Paris
June 1987

Glossary of Terms
and Monetary Units

abogado en el consejo real: licensed lawyer
academia de ambos derechos: practice of both civil and church law
administración: the administrative section of a government agency
administración general: local office of the Royal Tobacco Monopoly
administrador: administrator
administrador general: chief official of a local branch of the Royal Tobacco
    Monopoly
administrador principal: chief administrator
Aduana: Customs Agency
agente fiscal: a lawyer who assists the crown attorney
agregado: ancillary personnel
agregado con sueldo: salaried adjunct personnel
albacea: executor of an estate
alcabala: sales or excise tax
alcaide: overseer of customs collections
alcalde de crimen: junior judge for criminal cases in the Audiencia
alcalde de segundo voto: second municipal magistrate and vice-mayor
alcalde provincial: provincial magistrate
alguacil mayor: constable of the town council
almacenes generales: general storehouse or warehouse
altiplano: high plains of the Andes
amanuense: scribe; copyist
apoderado: proxy
archivero: record keeper
asentista para la conducción de azogues: crown contractor for the shipment
    of mercury

asesor: legal advisor or counselor to a government agency

asesor de reales rentas: counselor for the Royal Monopolies

asesor general or *asesor de gobierno:* viceroy's legal counselor; crown's attorney

asesor letrado: legal counselor

asesor y auditor de guerra: viceroy's legal advisor for civil and military affairs

Audiencia: High Court of Justice

auditor de guerra: military legal advisor

auxiliar: assistant

ayuda de cámara: valet

ayuda de costas: financial grant

caballerizo: head groom

cabildo: town council

cabildo abierto: open town council meeting called in cases of emergency

cadet: cadet; military school student

caja or *caja real:* provincial treasury

caja principal: principal treasury office

caja subordinada: branch treasury office

canciller: chancellor

canciller registrador: recording chancellor

canónigo: canon of a cathedral

capitan general: commander-in-chief of a military district

carrera de oficinas: bureaucratic career

cartas cuentas: annual accounts

casa del asiento: headquarters of the English slave trade

casa de dirección: headquarters

causas: lawsuits

cédula or *real cédula:* royal decree

celador de fábrica: factory supervisor

chantre: church choirmaster

cobro y distribución de caudales: collection and disbursement of royal funds

colegio: secondary school

comandante de marina: navy commander

comerciante: wholesale merchant

comercio libre: free trade within the Spanish empire

comisaria de la Santa Inquisición: office of the Holy Inquisition *comisario:* delegate; deputy

comisario de guerra: commissary-general of the army

comiso: confiscation of contraband

comissión de limites: boundary commission to determine the demarcation between Spanish and Portuguese areas

composición (de tierra): granting of a land title

consulta: written report

contador or *contador oficial real:* accountant

contador de diezmos: accountant in charge of tithes

contador de dinero: accountant in charge of cash funds

contador de resultas: junior accountant charged with resolving accounts

contador de retasas: junior accountant charged with reassessing accounts

contador de tributos: junior accountant for Indian tribute

contador entretenido: one waiting to be promoted to an accountant's post

contador factor: accountant in charge of sequestered property

contador general: chief accountant of the Real Renta de Tabacos

contador interventor: auditor

contador mayor: chief accountant of the Tribunal de Cuentas; chief comptroller

contador mayor de ejército: chief accountant for army accounts

contador ordenador: junior accountant (like all government positions, this one could rank from first [primer] to sixth [sexto]

contaduría: accounting section of a government agency

contaduría de cuentas: office of the regional chief comptroller

contaduría de diezmos: Bureau of Tithe Accounts within the Royal Treasury

contaduría de ejército: Bureau of Army Accounts within the Royal Treasury

contaduría de propios y arbitrios: Bureau of Municipal Accounts

contaduría general: General Comptroller of Royal Tobacco Monopoly Accounts

corregidor: chief officer of a rural administrative district

criollo, criolla: a Spaniard born in America

decano: dean; highest-ranking official at that rank; i.e., *contador mayor decano*

decreto de oficio: resolution

defensor: counsel for the defense

dependencia: branch agency

dependiente: clerk employed in a branch agency

dependiente de resguardo: minor clerk in the coast guard

depositario de Indias: depository of funds from the Indies

depositario general: municipal treasurer

despacho oficial: office for conducting official business

dirección general: office of the Tobacco Monopoly responsible for overseeing the agency's offices throughout the viceroyalty

director general: director-general of the Tobacco Monopoly

donativo: a contribution, forced loan, or gift

entretenido: aspirant to a bureaucratic office

escribanía: all offices relating to notary services

escribanía de cámara de la Real Audiencia: official notary of the High Court of Justice

escribanía de real hacienda y minas: official notary of the royal treasury and the king's mines

escribanía pública de número or *escribanía de registro:* public notary services

escribano: a notary

escribano actuario: notary taking part in legal proceedings

escribano de gobierno: government notary

escribano del Rey or *escribano real:* the king's notary; the royal notary

escribano mayor del virreynato: chief notary of the viceregal government

escribano público de número: one of a certain number of public notaries

escribiente: scribe

escribiente auxiliar: scribe's aid

eslingajo: charges for storing goods in the customs warehouse

español: a Spaniard; a white

esquina: corner apartment

estanco: shop licensed to sell tobacco products

expedientes: legal proceedings

fábrica de nuevas labores: experimental tobacco products factory

fabricante de polvillo: snuffmaker

factor oficial (real): royal treasury agent

fiador: bondsman

fianza: bond

fiel: inspector

fiel estanquero: licensed tobacconist

fiscal: crown attorney of the Audiencia; prosecuting attorney
fiscal del crimen: prosecuting attorney in criminal cases
fiscal de lo civil: prosecuting attorney in civil cases
fondo de Temporalidades: funds from the sale of ex-Jesuit property
fuero militar: special exemption from civil justice granted to the military
funcionario: bureaucrat
gente decente: well-born people of Spanish descent
gentiles hombres: gentlemen-in-waiting
gobernacion: political district
gracias: royal grants or concessions
gracias al sacar: legal exemption
gratificación: supplementary allowance for expenses
guías: customs house permits
habilitación: preparation; process of receiving financial backing
hacedor: steward; manager
hacienda or *Real Hacienda:* Royal Treasury
hojas de servicio: personnel service records
información de legitimidad: proof of legitimacy
instrucciones: official guidelines
instrumento: legal document
intendente: chief administrator of a large district or intendancy; intendant
intendente de policia: intendant of police; police commissioner
interino: interim position
interventor agregado: adjunct comptroller
interventor de fábrica: factory supervisor
jefe superior: chief
juez de bienes de difuntos: probate judge of the local court
junta: a committee or government board
junta de real hacienda: treasury board supervising royal finances in a
    district
junta superior de real hacienda: Superior Board of the Royal Exchequer;
    Special Committee for Fiscal Affairs
legajo: file or docket
letrado: lawyer
letras primeras: primary school instruction
ley de consolidación de bienes: Law of Expropriation of Church Wealth
libranza: bill of exchange

libro de méritos y servicios: personnel records

libro manual: account book

libro mayor: ledger

limpieza de sangre e hidalguia: proof of purity of blood and nobility

maestra: master craftswoman

maestre de campo: military officer of a rural district

maestro mayor: master craftsman

mandas forzazas: mandatory bequests of small sums of money to different
   church funds that were included in all wills drawn up in the period

mariscal de campo: general commanding a division

mayordomo: steward

mayordomo de fábrica: overseer of construction

media anata: tax equivalent to a half-year's income paid by most government bureaucrats

memoria: memorandum book

mercader: retail merchant

meritorio: unsalaried employee

mesa: department within an agency

ministro: a minister or royal official of substantial rank; chief of the Royal
   Hacienda

ministro contador: chief accountant

ministro principal: chief administrator

ministro tesorero: chief treasurer

mozo de oficio: office boy

número, de: a regular or statutory position

oficial: clerk in a government agency

oficial cuarto: fourth-ranking clerk

oficial de contaduría: clerk in the accounting section of a government
   agency

oficial de libros: bookkeeper

oficial de pluma or *oficial escribiente:* clerk-scribe

oficial de retasas: reassessment clerk

oficial entretenido: clerk in training

oficial interventor de fábricas: production auditor

oficial primer or *oficial mayor:* first clerk; chief clerk

oficial quinto: fifth-ranking clerk

oficial segundo: second-ranking clerk

oficial sexto: sixth-ranking clerk
oficial tercero: third-ranking clerk
oficios vendibles y renunciables: salable posts
oidor: judge of an Audiencia
oidor honorario: honorary Audiencia judge
oposición or *oposiciónes:* public examinations
orden general: general regulation
papel sellado: paper marked with a government stamp
pariente: a blood relation
patria chica: fatherland; native district
peninsular: a Spaniard born in Spain
platense: from the Río de la Plata
plumista: scribe
porteña, porteño: one born in Buenos Aires
portero: doorman
pragmática: royal ordinance
procurador: solicitor
procurador general: attorney general
producto de eslingajo: charges for storing goods in a customs warehouse
producto de guías: charges for documenting legally imported goods
promotor fiscal: district attorney
propietario: owner
proprios y arbitrios: taxes and rents paid to the town council
puro: cigar
quinto oficial de libros: fifth-ranking bookkeeper
ramo: branch of royal revenue; fiscal account
ramo de comisos: royal revenue derived from confiscated goods
ramo de sisa: royal revenue from local tax on trade
ramo municipal de guerra: municipal account for defense
ramo particular: one of the branches of royal revenue earmarked for special use
Reales Cajas: Royal Accounts Office (synonymous with Real Hacienda)
Real Hacienda: Royal Treasury
Real Renta de Tabacos: Royal Tobacco Monopoly
receptor: tax collector or receiver
receptor de alcabala: collector of the excise tax
receptor de penas de cámara: collector of court fines

receptor del ramo de carretas: collector of the tax on wagon trains

receptor de real derecho de sisa: collector of the royal tax on internal trade

regidor: town councilman

reglamento: rules governing agency conduct

relación de méritos: résumé (literally "a narration of excellence")

relator: an officer of an agency or court whose job it is to prepare legal briefs

repartimiento de bienes: forced sale of goods to Indian communities

resguardo or *resguardo de mar:* coast guard; branch of the customs agency charged with policing the waters

residencia: judicial review at the end of a high official's term of office

sagrados canones: church law

saladero: meat-salting plant

sección de escribientes: scribe department; secretarial pool

secretaría de cámara: viceroy's secretariat

secretario: secretariat

segundo amanuense: second-ranking scribe

sindico procurador general or *procurador sindico general:* municipal official charged with representing the town council before official agencies; attorney general

sisa: tax on certain products of internal trade

situado: royal subsidy

sobrestante: tobacco factory inspector

subalternos: subordinates

superintendencia: large governing district encompassing several intendancies; superintendency

superintendente (general): financial administrator of a large district, often coterminous with a viceroyalty

supernumerario: a supernumerary, one who occupies a temporary or unauthorized extra position in a government agency

tasador de costas: appraiser of legal fees

Temporalidades: government agency that administers property formerly belonging to the Jesuits

teniente: lieutenant; assistant

teniente asesor or *teniente letrado:* assistant legal counselor

teniente general: lieutenant general

teniente visitador or *teniente de visitador:* assistant inspector *tercenista principal:* chief wholesale tobacco agent

tesorería: the treasury section of a government agency

tesorería de reales cajas: the treasury section of a branch royal treasury

tesoría general de exército y Real Hacienda: General Treasury of the Army and Royal Exchequer

tesorero: treasurer

tesorero general: chief treasurer

tesorero oficial real: official royal treasurer

título: title of office; letter of appointment

tomas de razón: registry

tornaguías: landing certificates

Tribunal de Cuentas: chief auditing agency; Court of Audit

tribunal de visita: court of official inquiry

vacantes mayores: vacant high-ranking church positions whose income devolves back to the crown

vecino: inhabitant

veedor: inspector

visitador de tabacos: tobacco inspector

visitador general: an individual named to conduct an official inquiry into the conduct of a government agency

vista: customs inspector

vista primero: chief customs inspector

Monetary Units

doblón: worth 4 pesos

escudo de vellón: worth 1,000 reales de vellón

maravedi: a Spanish coin of small value

peso: silver unit worth 8 reales de plata or 20 reales de vellón or 272 maravedis

peso escudo or peso fuerte: worth 10 reales de plata

1. Introduction

THIS BOOK IS, IN MANY WAYS, a companion piece to my earlier study of wholesale merchants in late colonial Buenos Aires.[1] Both books are tentative attempts to answer the larger question of the development of society in viceregal Buenos Aires. As such, they are also contributions to the general literature on the eighteenth century in Spanish America and the effect of the Bourbon reforms on local societies. They are two pieces in the larger puzzle of the formation, aspirations, and way of life of the late colonial elite.[2]

It is only fitting that a volume on the bureaucrats follow one on the merchants, for the internal imperial reorganization that resulted in the creation of the Viceroyalty of Río de la Plata reflected and encouraged both the mercantile and administrative functions of the city. Just as the extension of "free trade" to the city in 1778 transformed an illegal port into a prosperous commercial center, so the founding of the viceroyalty two years earlier changed Buenos Aires from a growing regional center to the primary city in the area. To a large extent these two urban activities—mercantile and bureaucratic—have continued to dominate the present-day "queen of the Plata."

Among the most important of the Bourbon reforms enacted to revive the Spanish colonial empire in the eighteenth century was the administrative reorganization and division of the Viceroyalty of Peru. Carving up the once unified viceroyalty, between 1717 and 1778 two new viceroyalties (that of Río de la Plata and that of New Granada) and one captaincy-general (Caracas) emerged. This reorganization, with military, financial, and administrative objectives, involved more than simply drawing lines on a master map. As new political units were delineated, government institutions were replicated in each administrative center, new institutions were created, and others were disbanded. The avowed aim of the institutional and geographical realignment that followed the dismemberment of the Lima viceroyalty was to make colonial agencies more responsive to the defensive needs of the Spanish crown and more economically productive for Spain.

Perhaps the region that profited most from the Bourbon reforms was the newly created Viceroyalty of Río de la Plata. Although a period of expansion had begun in the littoral area adjoining the city of Santa María de los Buenos Aires before 1776, the creation of the viceroyalty, and the inclusion of the silver-producing province of Upper Peru within this viceroyalty, dramatically increased the pace of economic grown in the area.[3] Viceregal organization and reorganization were not without problems—(witness the strife between Viceroy Nicolás del Campo, Marqués de Loreto, and Superintendent Francisco de Paula Sanz)[4]—but the elevation of Buenos Aires to a viceregal capital, combined with the increased legal trading activity of its port decreed by the so-called Free Trade Act of 1778, marked a new and prosperous stage for both the capital city and its surrounding areas.

The late eighteenth century also marked an unprecedented growth of bureaucracy throughout Spanish America. As Bourbon reformers undertook what they believed to be far-reaching changes in the administration of their New World colonies, new departments, monopolies, and offices were created, administrative units were redrawn, and a more dynamic model of the government bureaucrat, or *funcionario*, was introduced into the Spanish dominions. In many areas these reforms produced bitter conflicts, for the bureaucratic newcomers, often bright young men from Spain close to the power center or the metropolitan court, were much resented by the older creole establishment, which was fast losing power.[5] Even in regions that had been peripheral to the empire, the extension of a stronger Spanish government, albeit a government that aimed to provide better services to local citizens, was frequently resented. Paradoxically, one region of the Spanish American empire that welcomed the growth of local bureaucracy would also be the first area to successfully rebel against this bureaucracy.

The Bourbon reforms were more than piecemeal attempts to improve defense, curb the power of the Catholic Church, and tax new fiscal resources. The reforms, especially those pieces of legislation passed between

1775 and 1785, hoped to restructure both the bureaucracy of the New World and the administration of the royal colonies. They coupled fiscal reform with administrative reform and a restructuring of the entire bureaucracy. As such they represented a new view of government and the role of civil servants in providing this government.

In many ways Buenos Aires was a tabula rasa on which the Spanish government could draw its conception of the ideal bureaucracy in America. As both a developing area, one with a relatively simple social system devoid of either a powerful local aristocracy at one end of the social scale or masses of Indians on the other, and an area without a large entrenched bureaucracy to undermine the reforms, Buenos Aires could serve as a proving ground for many bureaucratic restructurings and reforms. Moreover, Buenos Aires, to the degree that it was on the geographical periphery of the Spanish American empire, also represented the redistribution of power toward that periphery that took place at the end of the eighteenth century. The inclusion of the silver-producing area of Alto Perú within the Viceroyalty of the Río de la Plata reflects this late Bourbon redistribution of power. The fact that the viceroyalty's capital city, Buenos Aires, was the fastest-growing city in the entire Spanish colonial world is another indication of the emergence of this area. Although the Viceroyalty of the Río de la Plata was a Bourbon creation, the extent and success of the bureaucratic, fiscal, and economic changes that the Bourbons attempted to institute in their colony affected not only immediate developments but continued to reverberate through Independence and into the nineteenth century.

Many scholars have written on the Bourbon reforms. Much of this work has concentrated on the reform legislation itself or on the extent to which the Bourbon kings (especially Charles III) were influenced by French physiocratic ideas in drawing up their new programs.[6] Of late some excellent scholarship has examined the local effect of specific reforms and fiscal policies in Spanish America,[7] and scholars are now looking at the agents of these reforms within specific colonial settings.[8] That is the aim of this study—an inquiry into the professional careers and personal connections of the bureaucrats of colonial Buenos Aires.

This creation of bureaucracy within a fairly limited period of time made the subsequent institutional history of Buenos Aires somewhat unusual. Within ten years the bureaucracy of Buenos Aires was transformed from a traditional institution, staffed by a small group of officeholders who had purchased their positions, into a modern, salaried bureaucracy. Another unusual feature of the Bourbon bureaucracy, not only in Buenos Aires but throughout Spanish America, is that the rapid growth of the 1770s and 1780s was followed by a period of relative stagnation. Nevertheless, the bureaucrats of Buenos Aires represented an attempt by a colonial power in the late eighteenth century to provide its colony with a "modernizing" civil service.

This study while concentrating on the lives of Buenos Aires bureaucrats is set against the backdrop of Bourbon reforms. The problem of the effect of these reforms on colonial bureaucrats is a complex one, for the scholar must look at the legislation that created various agencies, the socioeconomic impact of these new agencies in the local milieu, and the internal structure of the bureaucracy to understand how both the institutions and the bureaucrats themselves fit into colonial society.

This study begins with an overview of the development of the Bourbon bureaucracy, its multiple agencies, and functions. Chapter 3 discusses the alternate paths that an aspiring young man could attempt to follow to enter the bureaucracy; chapter 4 discusses patterns of advancement, both theoretical and real, that were present for those who had successfully entered the civil service. Issues of salary, retirement policy, and retirement benefits are discussed in chapter 5, for these issues, part of the definition of a modern bureaucracy, are crucial in understanding the level of satisfaction that a bureaucrat experienced. Also important to our comprehension of the way that the bureaucrats fitted into the local society are the matters of personal ties, marriage, and family, all of which are considered in chapter 6. The extent to which the crown was successful in weeding out corruption and scandal among its civil servants, an issue related, in the crown's eyes, to the existence of ties to local creole society, is the subject of chapter 7. Finally, the concluding chapter attempts to correlate the case of Buenos Aires with other Bourbon bureaucracies and with the Weberian model of bureaucracy and to glimpse the result of Independence on this cadre of civil servants.

The institutions and bureaucrats included in this study are the viceroy and his secretariat, the intendant and his secretariat, the Royal Audiencia (High Court), the Tribunal de Cuentas (Royal Auditing Agency), the Real Hacienda (Exchequer), the Real Renta de Tabaco (Royal Tobacco Monopoly), the Aduana (Customs Service), the Correo Real (Royal Postal Service), and the commissions, juntas, and special governing boards that came under these agencies. I have specifically excluded local agencies such as the Cabildo (Town Council) and the Consulado (Board of Trade) because these agencies were composed of local people (overwhelmingly merchants) who held an elected office for a stipulated period of time.[9] It is the career bureaucrat rather than the merchant holding a local part-time post who is the object of this study.

With few exceptions this book does not deal with the stars of the Spanish bureaucratic world. There is no José de Gálvez, no Viceroy Revillagigedo. Only the few men fortunate enough to serve as viceroys or superintendents even approached this level of power, fame, and public recognition. Even the viceroys themselves tended to look upon Buenos Aires as an inferior posting, second to Lima or Mexico City. Rather than the stellar members of the Bourbon bureaucracy, the bureaucrats under study here represent the average member of an expanding corps of funcionarios. These were people who might have entered government service full of dreams and schemes, planning illustrious careers that would culminate in a position of power back in Spain, but whose reality often proved to be much reduced. Although by definition any book that deals with the bureaucrats of colonial Spanish America is concerned with an elite, this study does not limit its scope to those who held high rank within the local bureaucracy.

The variety of sources consulted reflect the complex nature of this study. First, this book looks at the development of a full-blown colonial bureaucracy in Buenos Aires and the role of these agencies in the colonial world. Here the sources are rather straightforward—royal decrees and *instrucciones* (official guidelines) setting up a variety of agencies, specifying their duties and responsibilities. Second, this study seeks to find out who were the men who entered the colonial bureaucracy. What were their aspirations and experiences, their victories and defeats? To answer these questions a variety of prosopographic sources were used. Specific issues such as origin, education, recruitment, promotion, marriage and kinship patterns, and client-patron relations were studied through working with internal agency reports, personnel files (*fojas de servicio*), viceregal correspondence, wills, parish records, and royal orders. In addition, the relationship of the bureaucrats to *porteño* (Buenos Aires)[10] society and the eventual disenchantment with colonial government were examined, as were the related issues of bureaucratic expenditures and corruption. Did bureaucrats represent the central government, identify with local interests, or evolve particular self-interests divorced from both Spain and Buenos Aires? Here agency accounts, legal proceedings against bureaucrats, notary records, and the proceedings of lay religious organizations were helpful. All these aspects of the bureaucracy and its servants are essential to understand the theoretical role that the reformed bureaucracy was to play in the colony, the reality experienced by these bureaucrats, and the effect of both bureaucracy and bureaucrats in setting the stage for independence.

2. The Leadership: Viceroys and Intendants

AMONG THE HOST OF MEN who eagerly flocked to the city of Buenos Aires hoping to advance their respective careers in the imperial bureaucracy, a small group arrived already wearing the mantle of high government authority. These men, the eleven viceroys sent to the region from 1776 to 1810 and the three intendants who arrived during the viceregal period, were the most visible agents of a new policy that aimed at improving government, strengthening military security, and developing the economy of the area. The institution of the viceregal system in the La Plata area, coupled with the naming of the first intendant the next year, was to be a public manifestation of the new role of the area and of the new type of bureaucrat who would now be charged with governing and administering the colony.

Prior to the creation of the viceroyalty, Buenos Aires had been the seat of one of three *gobernaciones* (political districts) in the area (the other two were the Gobernación de Tucumán, created in 1549 with its seat in Santiago del Estero until the end of the seventeenth century and then in Salta; and the Gobernación del Paraguay set up in 1593 with its capital in Asunción).[1] The Río de la Plata gobernación was carved out of the Paraguayan jurisdiction in 1617. Although Buenos Aires was not officially declared the capital of the district until 1695, from 1618 it served as the official residence of both political and church authorities in the area. From 1618 to 1778 the district was administered by a series of thirty-six governors, several of whom had purchased the office.[2] These men, who frequently also had the title of *capitan general*, served an average term of a little over four years. Nominally under the jurisdiction of the viceroy of Peru, the governor was the highest-ranking official in the region, exercising powers of government, justice, and war; he was also in charge of the local branch of the Real Hacienda and nominally controlled all royal officials in his jurisdiction.[3]

Although appointed directly by the king, the governor was theoretically under the domain of the viceroy of Peru. The viceroy in Lima could and did make interim appointments to the governorship, but only the king could issue a regular appointment. Once in office the distance from Buenos Aires to Lima allowed the local governor to exercise a large degree of autonomy.

In addition to his administrative duties, the governor was also the chief military figure resident in the area, the captain general. This military role, plus the strategic importance of Buenos Aires as a buffer to Portuguese expansion, produced an overwhelming preference for the choice of military men as governors. Although nonmilitary men had been named governor of Río de la Plata early in the eighteenth century (up to 1714 the position could be purchased by civilians for a generous donation or *donativo*), from 1742 to 1777 the post was held by military men named to the job because of supposed leadership abilities. The last three governors, Pedro de Cevallos (1756–66), Francisco de Paula Bucareli y Ursua (1766–70), and Juan José de Vértiz y Salcedo (1770–77), proved to be most competent in both their civilian and military duties.

In 1777 Pedro de Cevallos returned to the Río de la Plata at the head of a military expedition charged with again ousting the Portuguese from Côlonia da Sacramento across the river. Cevallos also carried a royal *cédula* (decree), issued on 1 August 1776, that created the Viceroyalty of Río de la Plata and named him first "viceroy, governor, captain general, and superintendent general of the Royal Exchequer" for the area. The newly created viceroyalty included the provinces of Buenos Aires, Paraguay, Tucumán, Potosí, Santa Cruz de la Sierra, and Charcas, as well as the province of Cuyo. The 1776 cédula not only enhanced the powers of the chief government official of the area, it also greatly enlarged the geographical domain under his command.[4]

Like all other viceroys named to this position throughout Spanish America, Cevallos, the first viceroy of Río de la Plata, was given wide-ranging administrative duties. The viceroy, serving as local representative of the king, was the chief administrative, religious, and military officer of the realm. All other government agencies fell under his jurisdiction. Empowered by the crown to protect its interests in the area, the viceroy was in charge of organizing military defense, overseeing the collection of taxes, tithes, and tribute, supporting the Catholic Church, and implementing new policy directives received from Spain.

From its creation in 1777 to its demise in 1810, the Viceroyalty of Río de la Plata was governed by a series of eleven viceroys (including three who received temporary appointments), all of whom had a military background.[5] With the exception of three brief periods of interim Audiencia (high court) rule, none of which lasted more than four months, the military tradition inaugurated during the latter governors' terms continued unabated in the Río de la Plata. Indeed, continuity between the days of the governorship and those of the viceroyalty was provided not only by the continued choice of military men to head the royal bureaucracy but also by the very men chosen. The first two viceroys, Cevallos and Vértiz, had both seen previous service as governors of the area and were therefore well acquainted with the particular problems, as well as the local personalities, present in Buenos Aires.

While much of the bureaucratic superstructure was created or enlarged under the first two viceroys, it was under their successor, Nicolás del Campo, Marqués de Loreto, a man who had never served in the area prior to his appointment as viceroy, that two major bureaucratic modifications occurred—the Audiencia was put into place and the Intendancy of Buenos Aires was expanded into a Superintendency. The creation of these two institutions so close on the heels of the establishment of the *platense* (Río de la Plata) viceroyalty had the effect of limiting the newly enlarged powers of the chief administrator. The Audiencia, created in 1783 but not fully functioning until 1785, placed a high court of justice within the same city as the viceroy, thereby creating greater potential for conflict than with the distant Audiencia of Charcas.

Even more than the Audiencia, the Intendancy (later Superintendency) of Río de la Plata served as an institutional limitation on the powers of the viceroy.[6] In 1777 an intendant was named for the Buenos Aires region. With the enactment of the Real Ordenanza de Intendentes in 1783, the newly promoted superintendent was given control of the Royal Exchequer within a jurisdiction as large as that of the viceroy. This shearing of fiscal power from the chief administrative official, the ambiguities of jurisdiction in financial, military, and judicial matters, and personal incompatibility eventually led to the disestablishment of the Superintendency in Buenos Aires and elsewhere in Spanish America. From 1788 to 1804 Buenos Aires, in fact, had neither intendant or superintendent; the post of "Superintendente general subdelegado de la Real Hacienda" was instead held by the viceroy. In 1804 the post of intendent was reestablished in Buenos Aires, but the original wide charge of the office was greatly reduced. The intendant was now clearly subordinated to the viceroy in all areas, and further jurisdictional disputes were avoided.

A growing bureaucracy both enhanced and limited a viceroy's actual power, although the image perceived by platense subjects was one of limitless control, for above all the viceroy was the representative of the Spanish king. In fact, the power of viceroys differed greatly, affected by their personalities, political acumen, and ability to coexist with (or perhaps skillfully manipulate) their bureaucrats and the local elite. In addition, all viceroys were limited by their tenure of office, which in the case of Buenos Aires averaged just over two years. While the office of viceroy provided continuity, individual viceroys were rarely on the scene as long as exchequer officials, Aduana clerks, or local churchmen.

The majority of the men who served as viceroy were army officers, although the last two viceroys—Liniers and Cisneros—had earned their military expertise in the Royal Navy. All had seen combat early in their careers; the early viceroys, Cevallos, Vértiz, Loreto, and Arredondo, served in the Italian and Portuguese campaigns during the War of Austrian Succession (1743–48) and in earlier battles against the English in Menorca and Gibraltar during the War of Jenkins's Ear (1739–48). Later viceroys were veterans of the many battles against the English that occupied Spanish forces from 1762 to the end of the eighteenth century.

To a man, the viceroys were from solid upper-middle-class families, often the sons of Spanish military officers or government bureaucrats. At least four were born to the lesser titled nobility, but in each case the title was an eighteenth-century creation, and the young man in question, as second or third son, did not stand a strong chance of inheriting it. All at the age of fourteen to eighteen were encouraged to begin a military career, enlisting as cadets in a Spanish regiment. After approximately five years, like other aspiring military men, the future viceroys received their first regular appointments, usually as *teniente* (lieutenant). Indeed, for the majority the first twenty years of their respective military careers while successful were hardly exceptional. After years of service in Spain and/or North Africa, the turning point came when these future viceroys were sent to the American colonies as officers within the military bureaucracy. Each man then spent approximately eighteen years in the New World, progressing from lieutenant-colonel to teniente general, and moving up within the military or military/civilian bureaucracy. The average candidate for viceroy was approximately sixty years old. (The oldest viceroy was del Pino who was seventy-two at the time of his nomination; the youngest was Cisneros who was named viceroy at the age of fifty-three.) The two posts that most frequently served as direct stepping stones to a nomination as viceroy were governor of Chile or of Montevideo. In addition, the subinspectors of the viceroyal troops were generally favored as interim viceroys. By the time they were named viceroys, all these men held the rank of at least *mariscal de campo* (field marshal), and all but two had accumulated on-the-scene experience in the American colonies.

All but two of the platense viceroys were Spanish-born. The exceptions were Viceroy Vértiz, a creole born in Mérida, Yucatán, while his father had served as governor of the area, and Santiago de Liniers, born in Niort, France, the son of a French military officer, Jacques, first count of Liniers. Nine viceroys were from southern or eastern Spain (four were born in Andalucía, one in Murcia, and one in Cataluña), while only three were from the central districts (one each from Old Castile, Extremadura, and León). The preference for Andalucíans is often associated with José de Gálvez's term as minister of the Indies, but two of the four Andalucíans served long after Gálvez had left office.

Though all had military experience, all but one also had extensive bureaucratic experience with the military. To the degree that military forms and organization were increasingly transferred to the civilian bureaucracy under the Bourbon rulers, military experience was valuable in all aspects of the viceroy's duties. Nonetheless, because no viceroy had come from a legal or purely bureaucratic background, they were often at a disadvantage when dealing with these aspects of the civil machinery. No viceroy could vote in Audiencia decisions, for example, for none was a *letrado* (lawyer). In general, all viceroys were overly dependent on the legal advice that their *asesores* (legal advisers) supplied, sometimes allowing these advisers to dictate general viceregal policy. Most were also similarly limited in day-to-day dealings with their own bureaucracies. In contrast to the viceroys, intendants, such as Francisco de Paula Sanz, had a stronger bureaucratic background and wider experience in day-to-day administration, including the arts of compromise, employee relations, and budgeting. Too many viceroys, coming from a tradition of strong centralized command, tended to ignore these finer points while governing. Instead, they frequently dictated impossible orders and relied on intimidation to manage even their closest associates. In reading their *memorias* (memoirs), one also sees that the majority of the platense viceroys were happiest when engaged in dynamic active tasks, such as overseeing Patagonian exploration or planting colonies in the Malvinas.[7] The mundane, day-to-day business of running a large viceroyalty—the correspondence, review of bureaucratic procedures, lawsuits, and minor snafus—provided neither excitement nor satisfaction to these men.

One important experience, shared by all but two viceroys, was prior training in the New World. In keeping with the reforms of Charles III and his attempts to create a body of men knowledgeable about (although not necessarily sympathetic with) the New World, these men had spent from seven to thirty-one years in America before becoming viceroy and had frequently served in the Río de la Plata itself. When they assumed the post of viceroy, only two lacked firsthand knowledge about the major strengths and weaknesses of the colony. It is probably not accidental that these two viceroys were the Marqués de Loreto, who had a rather acrimonious term of office, and Baltasar Hidalgo y Cisneros, the viceroy ousted by the *Cabildo Abierto* (open Town Council meeting) of May 1810. Unfortunately, once in office no viceroy was able to travel to areas of the viceroyalty that he had not previously seen in order to increase his knowledge of the land he governed. While previous service in the area produced men well versed in local problems (especially military ones), few Spaniards who had ever been to the area were eager to be named platense viceroy. To those who had served as governor of Montevideo or Chile, the viceroy's post might be considered an advancement, but for the ambitious courtiers back in Spain any government appointment to this part of the world was the equivalent of banishment. Indeed, some of the viceroys themselves, in spite (or perhaps because) of long service in the area, begged to be returned to Spain. Poor health was the usual pretext.

Many of those who would later become viceroys, arriving in the New World with new ranks and increased salaries, well on their way to a successful career or at least assured that they had risen to the middle ranks of their respective military services, found themselves at last able to afford a wife and family. It is not surprising, therefore, that in spite of the difficulties in receiving royal permission to marry local women, four of the viceroys married criollo women while holding military office.[8] Already high-ranking military officers at the time of their marriage, they uniformly married the daughters of local military men, men who had frequently served in government before the founding of the viceroyalty and were closely tied through marriage and kinship to the porteño elite. It is difficult to determine the degree to which these marriages helped further their careers, for while the family and kin they thus acquired provided important local connections, these families did not wield power back in Madrid where decisions as to career advancement and naming of the viceroys occurred. The marriages, nevertheless, seem not to have hindered promotion. There is also a suggestion that marriage to a local woman became less of an obstacle to viceregal appointment in the later decades of the period. Before 1795 no man married to a local woman was chosen viceroy. From 1795 to 1807, with the exception of Gabriel de Avilés who held office for two years while his wife waited in Peru, all viceroys were married to porteñas.

Marriage to local women linked these men to certain groups or clans within porteño society.[9] Regardless of steps taken to insure objectivity, it could only benefit local citizens to have their brother-in-law or niece's husband serving as viceroy. And while three of the four viceroys who married local women had married into military families, all of these families had branches engaged in commerce. Being related to a viceroy produced different benefits for different individuals, ranging from military promotion to preferential treatment in commerce.

Three of the platense viceroys—Pedro Melo de Portugal, Joaquín del Pino, and Fernando Rafael de Sobremonte—had also served as provincial intendants in the Río de la Plata area before being named viceroy. Melo had spent two years as intendant of Paraguay, ten years before his viceregal appointment. Del Pino, by contrast, was a military man with wide bureaucratic experience in the area. From 1773 to 1790 he was governor of Montevideo. Then he was transferred to La Plata, where he served as intendant of La Plata and president of the Audiencia of Charcas until 1795. After a further stint as captain general of Chile, del Pino became viceroy in 1801. Even more impressive was the experience of del Pino's successor, Viceroy Fernando Rafael de Sobremonte. Sobremonte, a young military officer, had come to Buenos Aires after five years in Puerto Rico. He secured an appointment as secretary of the viceroyalty under Viceroy Vértiz and with Vértiz's recommendation was named intendant of Córdoba in 1783. From 1783 to 1797 Sobremonte was a model intendant. In 1797 he moved to the post of sub–inspector-general of regular troops and militia within the viceroyalty and from there to viceroy in 1804. Unfortunately, Sobremonte's performance as viceroy was quite different from that as intendant. Faced with the British invasion of 1806, Sobremonte rather ignominiously chose to flee to Córdoba under the pretext of raising fresh troops. While direct bureaucratic experience as intendant or governor did not always have a positive effect on the actual performance of a viceroy, it is not surprising that two of the three viceroys who had previously served as intendants were married to local-born women.

In addition to their wives, viceroys were often accompanied by kin— sons, brothers, nephews, and cousins who they employed either officially or extraofficially in their task of governing. Viceroy Loreto employed his nephew as the viceregal secretary, successfully placing him on the government payroll. Viceroy Joaquín del Pino used his son Ramón as an unofficial conduit between himself and office seekers.[10]

Both governors and viceroys also surrounded themselves with personal attendants who served a variety of roles within the viceroy's household and were paid from his private purse. Most viceroys employed four to six pages, a *caballerizo* (head groom), a *mayordomo* (steward), and an *ayuda de cámara* (valet) in their retinue. At least one governor also included a private secretary and a chaplain in his household staff.[11]

Caballerizos and mayordomos as well as ayudas de cámara were usually older men from lower social strata who were making a career out of service to one individual and had been in his employ for several years. The latter group of servants had been picked up by the viceroy over many years and tended to display a diversity of birthplaces in both Europe and America. The pages, on the other hand, were usually recruited by the viceroy right before leaving for Buenos Aires; their origin correlates closely with the location of the viceroy before his departure to take on his new duties. In addition, extra pages were sometimes recruited in Buenos Aires when needed. Pages were usually young men who hoped that personal service would lead to more permanent government employment. In fact, in the closing months of their terms of office, almost all viceroys were busy attempting to place some of those who had served as either pages or amanuenses in clerkships.

Pedro Melo de Portugal, appointed viceroy in 1795, brought nineteen servants in his personal entourage: a private secretary, a steward, an equerry, three pages, a maître d'hôtel, two valets, a wardrobe master, a cook and a pastrycook, an ironing woman, a lackey, a groom, a footman, a pastry-cook's helper, and two cook's assistants. The overwhelming majority of these servants were single men; the only female was an ironing woman. The private secretary and the pastrycook were married, although both had left their wives behind in Spain. All the viceroy's servants except for one free black who served as the cook's assistant were white (*español*), although only the eight highest-ranking servants merited the use of the honorific title of "don." The servant group was also overwhelmingly Spanish-born, with thirteen of the fourteen *peninsulares* coming from the northern sections of the country (four were natives of Madrid, while the rest hailed from small towns in Asturias, Galicia, León, and the Basque regions). Three of the viceroy's servants had been recruited locally, but they (the ironing woman from Côlonia, the footman from Asunción, and the black cook's assistant from Buenos Aires) were clearly the least prestigious members of the household. In addition, two servants, brothers serving as maître d'hôtel and valet, were natives of Parma. Two other servants, the private secretary and the steward, were also related to each other, father and son. They were clearly the most crucial individuals in Melo de Portugal's establishment.[12]

Viceroy Marqués Gabriel de Avilés arrived in Buenos Aires in 1799 after previous military service in Spain, Peru, and Chile. His personal retinue consisted of twelve men: a private secretary, a chaplain, a caballerizo and his assistant, a mayordomo, two gentlemen-in-waiting (*gentiles hombres*), four pages, and an ayuda de cámara. Only one of these men was a Spaniard, the mayordomo Manuel Fernández de Arredondo. All others, including the three Luzuriaga brothers, were American-born, either Peruvians or Chileans who had come to Avilés's attention during his service in these areas. In addition, two porteño-born pages were added to Avilés's retinue after his arrival in Buenos Aires. The porteños and the three Luzuriagas remained in Buenos Aires after Avilés's departure, the latter, instead of seeking government positions, choosing to become local merchants.[13]

No information on the specific salaries paid to the individual members of a viceroy's retinue has been uncovered, but the personal account books of Viceroy Loreto show an average monthly expenditure for household salaries of 134 pesos.[14] The viceroy was also expected to provide clothing and shoes for his pages and for any members of his retinue who wore livery. Food and board were also supplied by the viceroy. In return, members of the household were required to give good and faithful service to their master.

Salaries for members of his retinue were only one of the myriad expenses that a viceroy was expected to cover out of his own pocket. Personal-expenses incurred in touring the countryside or in military campaigns were also charged to the viceroy. Loreto's personal account books provide still more detailed information on the nature and amount of personal expenses incurred in governing the Río de la Plata. In addition to salaries, clothing, and food the viceroy also paid for household improvements, furniture, dishes and silverware, straw and oats for his mules, a carriage and the mules themselves, illumination of his residence, and re-tining copper cooking pots. Periodical donations to local charities (in Loreto's case usually the Casa de Niñas Huérfanas), religious expenses for special masses and processions, costs of special ceremonies celebrating the ascension of a new king or the queen's birthday, and token gifts to Indians who had ventured into Buenos Aires, as well as ransom for white settlers, medical bills, and laundering of clothing and tablecloths, all figure prominently in these accounts. Over a six year period (March 1784 to April 1790) Loreto's expenses ranged from 668 to 3,878 pesos per month. The average month's expenses totaled 1,289 pesos. Of this average only 31 pesos per month were used by the viceroy as pocket money.

The creation of the Viceroyalty of Río de la Plata not only enlarged the jurisdiction and scope of the chief official, it also greatly increased his salary. Before 1777 governors earned salaries that varied according to their prior experience and military rank, ranging from 6,000 to 12,000 pesos per year.[15] With the founding of the viceroyalty, the viceroy's salary was established as 20,000 pesos per year, approximately one-third of that paid to the viceroys of Mexico and Peru but more than any other official within his jurisdiction received. While governors had received indirect salary supplements in the form of "perquisites, fees and gifts," at least one zealous viceroy refused to accept these tributes finding them "an old-fashioned practice" without "legal origin."[16] In addition, the viceroy, like many other public officials, was subject to an income tax (the *media anata*) and to payments into the retirement (*montepío*) fund. In addition, 8,000 pesos were held back from each year's salary to be held on deposit until the final verdict of the viceroy's *residencia*[17] (judicial review).

Whether the new salary was adequate to cover expenses is difficult to determine. According to Loreto's accounts, it had cost him 12,964 pesos to come to Buenos Aires, and while there he incurred an average of 15,468 pesos of expenses per year. Loreto was able, nevertheless, to send a total of 34,142 pesos back to Spain, suggesting that he received income from other sources. Vértiz, as both governor and viceroy, complained bitterly that his low salary coupled with the expenses incumbent upon him forced him to live in constant debt:

> In order to maintain the honor of this position, it has been necessary to contract personal debts and obligations to fulfill the duties I must undertake. I want to give an account of my conduct to God and to my king, [for I have been] forced to banish all types of comforts from my house, including those of a fine table. My poor luck is that I live dependent on only my salary, from which I must pay for my table, a secretary, and other servants, including a lawyer, who in addition to serving as the crown's attorney (*asesor de gobierno*) I need to help me fulfill my public obligations. . . . As the salary that has been assigned to me is insufficient, it has become indispensable that I live in debt. You can only imagine the pain this causes someone who has never before experienced need.[18]

No similar complaints from viceroys have been unearthed after 1780.

Whether or not their salaries provided sufficient recompense to cover all expenses and provide a modest profit, viceroys were often forced to borrow funds for short-term expenses. For small loans one could turn to members of one's retinue. Viceroy Avilés, for example, twice borrowed money from Miguel de Lastarria, his personal secretary.[19] But these sources did not suffice for larger expenses, such as the cost of undertaking the trip to Buenos Aires or installation in the new city. For loans to cover these expenditures, none of which were reimbursed by the Real Hacienda, viceroys turned to merchants both in Spain and in Buenos Aires.

Lending funds to the viceroy provided an important point of entry into government circles for a few select merchants, access to an important new client, political influence, and even personal friendship. The Marqués de Loreto, for example, borrowed money from the merchant José González de Bolaños and later purchased goods and slaves from him. Manuel de Basavilbaso, another merchant who shared the viceroys interest in the Casa de Niñas Huérfanas, also frequently sold goods to Loreto.[20] The Marqués de Avilés borrowed money from the merchant José Blas de Gainza to cover the expenses of his trip from Chile to Buenos Aires. Gainza, who greeted the viceroy on behalf of the Consulado, soon became the viceroy's best friend in Buenos Aires and was named as one of the viceroy's executors (*albaceas*) in case the viceroy was to die in Buenos Aires. While Avilés was forced to leave Buenos Aires before his residencia could be undertaken, Gainza was named as the viceroy's *apoderado* (proxy).[21]

In locating a source of ready cash those viceroys with strong local ties, that is, those married to local women, had a decided advantage. But since having a viceroy as a debtor was also highly advantageous to an ambitious merchant, no viceroy found himself unable to borrow funds whenever they were needed. Indeed, some merchants used their connections with the bureaucracy to reach the viceroy. Gainza, for example, established a close relationship with Viceroy Loreto through his son-in-law Matias Bernal, an aide to Intendant Fernández, who had moved to a post in the Royal Treasury. This connection no doubt helped Gainza approach the viceroy with his initial loan offer.

Up to the English invasion of 1806 the viceroy who created the most controversy among the civilian and ecclesiastical bureaucracy was, without doubt, the aforementioned Marqués de Loreto. Part of Loreto's problem was that he had the ill fortune to follow Cevallos and Vértiz, two men who were well acquainted with the region through their prior service as governors. Loreto was also named viceroy just as the newly revised intendant code was being put into effect. He perceived (rightly) that the post of superintendent would limit his viceregal powers and came to resent both the reform and the man chosen for the new position. But perhaps the major part of Loreto's difficulties can be ascribed to his personality, for by all accounts he was a difficult man to deal with, deeply suspicious and irascible.[22]

Loreto's first run-in was with Francisco de Paula Sanz, a man who had been in Buenos Aires as director general of the Real Renta de Tabaco since 1777 and was the first superintendente general of the Real Hacienda. Sanz had taken office in 1783 during the Vértiz viceroyalty. Although Viceroy Vértiz had been opposed to the new ordinances, he was willing to cooperate with Sanz, and the superintendency met with initial success.[23] Sanz was in many ways the complete opposite of the new viceroy, Loreto. Described as "benevolent, affable, and a lover of this city,"[24] Sanz was a close friend of several of the city's outstanding merchants. The relationship between Loreto and Sanz was always difficult, but things worsened after the denouement of the Ximénez de Mesa scandal in 1785.[25] Loreto seems to have held Sanz personally responsible for the Aduana chief's embezzlement or at least to have blamed Sanz for not unearthing this scandal earlier.

Full of personal bitterness toward the superintendent, Loreto chose to translate his resentment into a series of legal battles about the jurisdiction of the new office. Their first confrontation, over the extent of the superintendent's legal power to curb the illegal sale and slaughter of cattle, soon gave way to a dispute over Sanz's licensing of imports of Portuguese tobacco and slaves. Argument over the superintendent's right to publish proclamations enforcing public hygiene and his power to impose a new tax on cattle followed. Although early skirmishes were won by the superintendent, Loreto was eventually able to ally himself to the Buenos Aires Cabildo (over the right of the superintendent to establish a lottery) and the Audiencia (over the question of whether the Tribunal de Cuentas should be allowed to move to a new building). Bombarded with letters from both Sanz and Loreto that reflected important questions of jurisdiction as well as petty day-to-day squabbles, Antonio Valdés, secretary of state for war, finance, commerce, and navigation of the Indies, abolished the superintendency in 1788.[26] Both the viceroy's implacable enmity and the superintendent's tactlessness had convinced the crown that the new system could not work.

Sanz was not the only bureaucrat who incurred Loreto's wrath. By 1785 Loreto also began to pursue Ignacio Flores, the Quito-born first intendant of La Plata, who had been named to the post by the creole viceroy,

Vértiz, and was in turn choosing a large number of native-born men as sub-delegates within his intendancy.[27] Appointment by Vértiz itself put Flores in an uncomfortable position because Loreto's general suspicions of others were especially directed at those who had enjoyed Vértiz's favor. In addition, Loreto feared that Flores, exercising power in a remote region of the viceroyalty, was alienating Europeans by preferring creoles. Loreto again allied with an Audencia (this time the Audiencia of Charcas) to remove the intendant.

From his surviving account books, replete with monies paid to the church for special masses and devotions, there is no doubt that Viceroy Loreto was, like many other colonial bureaucrats, a religious man. But his faith did not prevent him from pursuing churchmen who had offended him with the same fervor that he went after civil bureaucrats. His relationship with Manuel de Azamor y Ramírez, the bishop of Buenos Aires, was always difficult. The viceroy also became embroiled in a dispute with the ecclesiastical Cabildo over the election of a new provisor, forcing the aged *canónigo* (canon) Baltazar Maciel into exile in Montevideo. In this last case the viceroy seems to have suffered remorse, for whem Maciel died soon after being forced to leave Buenos Aires, Loreto himself paid 161 pesos 7-1/2 reales for a series of masses for the churchman's soul.[28]

Viceroys could find their relationships strained because of jurisdictional conflict, the checks and balances of other institutions such as the church or the Audiencia, or personality difficulties. Nonetheless, viceroys could always fall back on years of precedence, which the institution itself had amassed since the sixteenth century. This was not true for the other central bureaucratic position in Buenos Aires, that of intendant or superintendent. This post was clearly an eighteenth-century, Bourbon creation and as such represented an attempt to personify the Bourbon desire for reform in a single individual.

The restructuring of colonial government through the transfer of the intendant system to America began in the Río de la Plata area in 1777. In that year Manuel Ignacio Fernández, the intendant general of the army who had accompanied Cevallos to Buenos Aires, was appointed intendant of the army and exchequer for the new viceroyalty.[29] According to the terms of the royal cédula that defined the new position, the intendant was put in charge of all exchequer affairs, as well as the economic dimension of managing the army.[30] He was also to oversee agriculture and commerce within the area. In Buenos Aires the intendant was also charged with heading his own bureaucracy, which like the intendant himself was to be separate and independent from that of the viceroy. Like the viceroy, the intendant could write directly to the authorities back in Spain.

Five years later the Ordinance of Intendants restructured the intendant system throughout the Viceroyalty of Río de la Plata. The Ordinance of Intendants for Buenos Aires, published in January 1782 and distributed throughout the viceroyalty the next year, created multiple intendancies within the viceroyalty and elevated the intendant in Buenos Aires to the rank of superintendent.[31] The superintendent, in addition to guiding those agencies charged with justice, general administration, finance, and war within the Buenos Aires district, was also to serve as the chief financial officer of the entire viceroyalty. He would provide, it was hoped, a uniform, effective fiscal policy. He alone of all the intendants continued to report directly to Madrid.

The redefinition of the intendant post into the more powerful position of superintendent was soon accompanied by a personnel shift. By March 1783 Fernández, the original intendant who had been promoted to superintendent was rewarded with a position on the Council of the Indies. He was replaced in Buenos Aires by Francisco de Paula Sanz. For the next five years Sanz served as superintendent general, frequently quarreling with the viceroy, the Audencia, and the Cabildo. In May 1788, partly as a result of the never-ending fractiousness between Loreto and Sanz, which was seriously damaging the government's ability to conduct business, and partly in keeping with the empire-wide decision to abandon the new structure of government, which separated the executive powers of the viceroy from any financial powers, the Superintendency of Río de la Plata was dissolved. All powers of the superintendent were now transferred to the viceroy, although the regional intendants continued to function much as before.

The dismantling of the Superintendency in effect shifted a series of duties to the viceroy. In assuming the role formerly held by the superintendent, the viceroy was not only to oversee all financial practice and policy throughout the viceroyalty, he was also to serve as intendant for the city and province of Buenos Aires. These duties soon proved overwhelming. In 1799 some of the original duties related to public works and the maintenance of order in the city, which had fallen under the jurisdiction of the superintendent, were turned over to a new government official, the *inten-dente de policía* (intendant of police), who was clearly subordinate to the viceroy.[32] While relieving the viceroy of some work, this did not provide a final solution.

After much discussion in Madrid, article 10 of the New Ordinance of Intendants was enacted in 1803, recreating and redefining the post of inten-dant in Spanish America. Although the local intendant enjoyed much the same power as his provincial peers in his jurisdiction outside the city of Buenos Aires, within the capital the intendant's powers were severely lim-ited.[33] This reflected a determined attempt on the part of the crown to pre-vent a repetition of the viceroy-superintendent dissension that had so hindered effective government.

The intendant-superintendent post, which essentially went through three stages in the Río de la Plata, was held by three men, each identified with a different point in the institution's metamorphosis. Nevertheless, there were certain commonalities between these men. Two of the three in-tendants were civilians (unlike the viceroys), although all had had wide-ranging experience in the area before their respective nominations. All were native-born Spaniards, and none were married at the time of their service in Buenos Aires. Although Francisco de Paula Sanz was clearly the most beleaguered of the intendants, his predecessor Manuel Ignacio Fernández had also run into personality problems with another bureau-crat, José Vicente Carrancio, *asesor de reales rentas* (legal adviser to the royal monopolies).[34] Until the intendant position was made clearly subsidiary to the viceroy in 1803, the position was a difficult one, marred by constant jurisdictional conflicts. Nonetheless, at least Fernández and Sanz took their duties seriously, traveling to Montevideo and other outlying districts to monitor royal interests. During those periods when the intendancy system was in effect in Buenos Aires, the incumbents served for a longer average term (over six years) than the viceroys.

The salary paid to the intendant clearly reflected the importance of the position in royal eyes. From the creation of the position in 1778 until he left office in 1783, Fernández's salary was set at 8,000 pesos, second only to that of the viceroy. Fernández later convinced the crown to give him an increase of 2,000 pesos per year.[35] As superintendent, Sanz's salary was set at 10,000 pesos. This compared quite favorably to the 6,000 pesos being paid to the provincial intendants under his command.[36] The reestablished intendancy taken over by Domingo de Reynoso was clearly a far less important position, and his salary of 5,000 pesos per year reflected the fact that, although still one of the chief bureaucrats in the city, the post had been shorn of much responsibility. Nevertheless, Reynoso's salary again compares favorably to that being paid to provincial intendants whose pay had been reduced, as a wartime emergency measure, to 4,000 pesos. Reynoso was not happy with this small differential; he appealed unsuccessfully to the crown to grant him a raise before even taking office, claiming that 5,000 pesos was inadequate to maintain a dignified standard of living, especially in Buenos Aires.[37] Buenos Aires, he argued, had the highest cost of living in all South America.

Intendants, like viceroys, often found it necessary to borrow from local merchants. Francisco de Paula Sanz, for example, borrowed almost 14,000 pesos from José González de Bolaños in 1785, money he had still failed to repay in 1798.[38] One can only surmise how much an individual intendant's or viceroy's total indebtedness amounted to and how funds were tapped to repay these loans.

By law all governors, intendants, and viceroys were subject to the residencia after they had left office. This review involved more than the actions of just the viceroy; it also included all high-ranking bureaucrats appointed by the viceroy and "his advisors, secretary, dependents, and servants."[39] Nevertheless, in the surviving residencias taken for the platense viceroys and superintendents, little negative information on their conduct was ever unearthed.[40] Instead merchants, bureaucrats, and other citizens called to testify usually rehashed local problems already known to the authorities in Spain. Even the most negative residencia, that of Viceroy Loreto, uncovered little that directly reflected poor performance on the part of the viceroy himself.

Residencias, in addition to being rather time-consuming, also tended to impose a financial burden on the chief administrative official in question. First, all viceroys and intendants were to leave a bond (*fianza*) behind, a bond not repaid until the conclusion of the proceedings. This rather large sum of money (4,800 pesos in the case of Viceroy Loreto) was extracted at the very same time that the viceroy and his family were incurring the expenses of preparing their return to Spain.[41] The costs of the residencia, including the salaries of the judge, *alguacil mayor* (chief constable), and *escribano* (notary), plus the paper, copying costs, and paper taxes, were paid by the viceroy himself. These expenses ranged from over 3,800 pesos in the del Pino residencia to over 7,000 pesos for Loreto. Any fines levied against the viceroy were of course another addition to the costs incurred.

While not without their problems, the men who served in these top administrative positions in the Río de la Plata were fair to middling in overall quality. Well-paid, loyal civil servants, the viceroys and intendants tried to provide the best government they were capable of creating. But although the most visible representative of the Spanish Bourbon imperial policy in Buenos Aires, viceroys and intendants were only one aspect of the new bureaucracy being put into place in the last decades of the eighteenth century. How was this new bureaucracy created by the Bourbon reforms, and who were the men who filled positions in an enlarged administration?

3. Growth of the Bureaucracy

THE CREATION OF THE VICEROYALTY of Río de la Plata was a momentous event for the inhabitants of Buenos Aires. The decision to separate the southern domains of the Viceroyalty of Peru into a new jurisdiction that included the provinces of Alto Perú, Paraguay, Chile, the Banda Oriental, Charcas, Tucumán, and Buenos Aires was essentially a strategic one. It reflected and in turn encouraged the growing importance of this previously neglected area of Spanish colonization. For those living in Buenos Aires, the anointing of their city as a viceregal capital of the same rank as Lima, Mexico City, and the more recently elevated Bogotá produced euphoria and pride.

Buenos Aires had always been a commercial center, a city forced to depend on its links to the outside world to prosper. From the end of the sixteenth century, the days of the second founding of the city, it had been clear to the inhabitants of this tenuous community that its location and lack of attractive mineral resources or Indian populations made trade the only viable solution to the basic problem of survival. Usually this trade consisted of contraband shipments: goods coming from Europe, slaves from Africa, and agricultural products from Brazil, to be exchanged for the silver of Upper Peru, and a few agricultural and extractive products from the Paraguay-Paraná basin. Illegal trade had allowed Buenos Aires to survive and grow fitfully during the seventeenth and early eighteenth centuries; legal and extralegal trade would continue to provide a major source of prosperity after 1778.

Buenos Aires was more than just a trading town. It was also an administrative city that, since the beginning of the seventeenth century, housed a governor and a rudimentary bureaucracy charged with governing the Spanish areas on the southern flanks of the Portuguese empire in America. Much like its commercial functions, its administrative role had fallen to the city almost by default—it was the largest, indeed in many senses it was the only, Spanish settlement in the area. Like commerce, administration had grown slowly but gradually from the seventeenth century on. Both administrative and commercial roles were well established before the founding of the platense viceroyalty, but both would prosper and grow as these late Bourbon reforms changed the dimension of the city's presence in the Spanish colonial world.

During the seventeenth and the first half of the eighteenth century, governors were aided in their duties by a rudimentary bureaucracy befitting a poor, underpopulated zone of the Spanish empire. An Audiencia had been created in Buenos Aires in 1661 and installed in 1663 but was disbanded eight years later because of supposed political inefficiency.[1] (The Audiencia had perhaps been too efficient in curbing local contraband, resulting in a flood of complaints from the local citizenry to the crown.) In addition, the city housed a small branch treasury office, the Cajas de Reales Cuentas.

The growing presence of royal agencies, which was to accelerate after the founding of the viceroyalty, actually began in the middle of the eighteenth century. In an early attempt to improve government and military defense of a region fast becoming vital to the Anglo-Spanish rivalry, three new gobernaciones, subordinate to that of Río de la Plata, were created.[2] The expulsion of the Jesuits from Spanish dominions also led to the creation of a new government office, the Junta Provincial de Temporalidades, charged with administering ex-Jesuit property under the supervision of the governor of the province.[3] In addition to new provinces created under the jurisdiction of the governor of the Province of Buenos Aires, an increased number of government offices were put in place in Buenos Aires during the decade before the founding of the platense viceroyalty, including the Contaduría de Cuentas and the Correo set up in 1767 and the Real Renta de Tabaco established in 1775.

While the fiscal bureaucracy was growing from the middle of the eighteenth century on, after the creation of the Viceroyalty of Río de la Plata in 1776 and the arrival of the first viceroy, Pedro de Cevallos, in 1777, the number of bureaucratic agencies mushroomed. Within five years of the founding of the viceroyalty, Cevallos and his successor set up two additional branches of the Real Hacienda—the Junta de Diezmos (1777) and the Aduana (1778). In addition, the Reales Cajas (Royal Accounts Office), which had originally been founded in 1605, was expanded and renamed the Tesorería y Contaduría de Real Hacienda. To improve the overall financial administration of the viceroyalty, a new division of government, a *junta de hacienda* (treasury board), was created at the time of the founding of the platense viceroyalty and expanded to a *junta superior de real hacienda* (Superior Board of the Royal Exchequer) by 1782. The junta superior, composed of the chiefs of the major fiscal agencies of the viceroyalty, was charged with looking after the management of the treasury, providing uniform justice in all financial matters, and supervising military expenditures.[4]

The growth in the number of bureaucratic agencies that began with Cevallos continued with his successor, Viceroy Vértiz. Under Vértiz first the Intendancy system and then the Superintendency was introduced into the Río de la Plata, creating a new agency to oversee justice, the treasury, war, and general administration.[5] A subagency of the Exchequer, the Contaduría de Propios was put in place to review Cabildo accounts throughout the viceroyalty. The Audiencia was also reestablished in 1783, partially in response to requests begun in 1770 to improve judicial administration. Although the creation of new agencies slowed considerably after 1785, further atomization of existing agencies continued. For example, a separate Resguardo was created under the Aduana in 1794. The same year also saw the belated creation of a Consulado, which although not a government agency did enjoy semiofficial status.

Because many government agencies had branch offices in the cities of the interior, bureaucratic growth was felt throughout the viceroyalty, but it was especially in the city of Buenos Aires that this growth was most marked. As new agencies were created and existing institutions enlarged their jurisdiction, the number of government employees grew.

From 1767 to 1785 the civil bureaucracy headquartered in Buenos Aires expanded from four agencies employing fourteen men to ten agencies and commissions with a work force of more than 125. Most of this growth had occurred in the years after 1776. In 1778, for example, the total number of bureaucrats in Buenos Aires stood at thirty-five (See table 3.1.) The very next year this number had more than doubled as the new viceroyalty welcomed an enlarged staff. By 1785 this number had grown even more, with

Table 3.1   Number of Bureaucratic Positions in Buenos Aires, 1767–1810

Agency	Year						
	1767	1778	1779[a]	1785[a]	1790[b]	1803[c]	1810
Viceroy (Governor) and Secretaria[1]	3	6	6	6	8	15	17
Superintendent and Secretaria[1]	–	–	–	7	8[2]	–	–
Real Audiencia[1]	–	1	–	12	15	19	17
Tribunal de Cuentas	3	6	20	23	23	37	26
Real Hacienda	6	6	20	23	18	27	22
Aduana	–	6	14	20	24	28	27
Tabacos	–	5	17	20	23	26	25
Correos	2	5	5	6	9	9	9
Propios y arbitrios[3]	–	–	–	5	3	–	–
Temporalidades[4]	–	–	–	4	3	3	–
Total	14	35	83	126	134	164	142

[1] Including legal staff.
[2] Superintendent position not included.
[3] Independent agency from 1783 to 1791; then joined to Tribunal de Cuentas.
[4] Independent agency from 1783 to 1798; then joined to Real Hacienda.
Sources: (a) AGNA, Contaduría de Buenos Aires, Registros de empleados, IX-9-3-10. (b) *Guía de forasteros en la ciudad y virreynato de Buenos Aires: Para el año de 1792* (Buenos Aires, 1791). (c) José Joaquín de Araujo, *La guía de forasteros del virreynato de Buenos Aires para el año de 1803* (Buenos Aires, 1908). All other totals have been reconstructed from a variety of sources including *títulos* (letters of appointment), *hojas de servicio* (personnel records, pay records, and internal agency accounts).

the civil bureaucracy totaling 126. Growth continued at a much slower rate until the early years of the 1790s. (See table 3.2.) In 1790 the salaried bureaucratic corps only totaled 134. The European wars of the 1790s forced the Spanish crown to seek new sources of funding. This produced continued slow growth in the numbers of bureaucrats in Buenos Aires as agencies charged with collecting revenues for the crown increased their staffs. Indeed, the porteño bureaucracy reached its apogee in the years right around the turn of the century. But the first decade of the nineteenth century only worsened Spain's problems. The English invasions of Buenos

Table 3.2 Growth Rate of Porteño Bureaucracy, 1767–1810

Years	Number of bureaucrats at beginning and end of each period	Average increase per year (in percentages)
1767–1778	14–35	8.69
1778–1779	35–83	137.14
1779–1785	83–126	7.21
1785–1790	126–134	1.24
1790–1803	134–164	1.57
1803–1810	164–142	−2.84

Formula: $r = m(\frac{X_n}{X_t} - 1)\ 100.$

Aires coupled with the Napoleonic invasion of Spain brought bureaucratic growth to a standstill. By 1810 a bureaucratic corps that seven years earlier had 164 members now numbered only 142.

While all agencies constantly requested increases in the number of their personnel, overall the growth and subsequent decline of numbers was achieved through expansion and retraction of entry-level rather than upper- and middle-management positions. A new position as *quinto oficial de libros* (fifth bookkeeper) or *segundo amanuense* (second scribe) was relatively inexpensive to create and provided jobs for hard-working young men, eager to please their superiors with the fine quality of their work. Agencies were always pleased to have more hands toiling at account books or copying correspondence and records. When faced with overwhelming cries for increased personnel, the crown also showed itself more ready to create entry-level or clerk positions than the more expensive middle- or upper-management posts.

Given these conditions of expansion and retraction, how did the bureaucracy grow in terms of levels of appointment? The following table (3.3) analyses all bureaucratic posts in terms of the level of salary and administrative importance. Important government posts, those of upper or middle management in an agency, were uniformly those that paid more than 1,000 pesos per year. Included in these groups were the heads of all agencies, the administrators, chief accountants, treasurers, judges, and legal advisers responsible for running the local bureaucracy. Those posts that paid 1,000 pesos or less were positions in the rank and file of the lower administration.

Nonetheless, with the exception of the years before the founding of

Table 3.3   Distribution of Bureaucratic Posts by Salary, 1767–1810

	1767	1779	1785	1790	1803	1810
HIGH-SALARY POSTS						
Agency or office						
Viceroy	1	2	3	3	4	4
Intendant	–	–	2	1	–	–
Audiencia	–	1	6	7	8	8
Tribunal de Cuentas	1	6	6	6	16	10
Hacienda	3	4	4	5	6	5
Aduana	–	3	3	4	5	5
Tabacos	–	5	5	6	5	5
Correos	1	1	1	1	1	1
Propios	–	–	1	1	–	–
Temporalidades	–	–	2	1	1	–
Subtotal	6	22	33	35	46	38
LOW-SALARY POSTS						
Agency or office						
Viceroy	2	4	3	5	11	13
Intendant	–	–	5	7	–	–
Audiencia	–	–	6	8	11	9
Tribunal de Cuentas	2	14	17	17	21	16
Hacienda	3	16	19	13	21	17
Aduana	–	11	17	20	23	21
Tabacos	–	12	15	17	21	20
Correos	1	4	5	8	8	8
Propios	–	–	4	2	–	–
Temporalidades	–	–	2	2	2	–
Subtotal	8	61	93	99	118	104
Total	14	83	126	134	164	142
% High	43	27	26	26	28	27
% Low	57	73	74	74	72	73

the viceroyalty when the area was run by a skeleton bureaucracy, there is surprising consistency in the ratio between upper-level management and staff. For each high-ranking bureaucrat, the government agencies employed three men as clerks or as other ancillary personnel. In addition, the ratio of bureaucrats to total population appears to have been greater for

Buenos Aires than for other viceregal capitals such as Mexico City, the bureaucrats did not represent a particularly large segment of the city's inhabitants.[6]

At the same time as the bureaucracy increased in size, the crown sought to endow its agencies with more rationally structured organizations, carefully delineating power, position, and duties within each institutional hierarchy. This restructuring combined with growth to affect all branches of government, including those agencies that had existed in a truncated form before 1776 as well as those created afterward.

The model of the "new" bureaucrat and the "new" bureaucracy was most clearly articulated by the Ordenanza de Intendentes. In addition to creating the Superintendency of Buenos Aires and seven subsidiary intendancies, the ordenanza spelled out the duties of several groups of public employees. Agencies such as the Real Hacienda were restructured. Furthermore, a governing board, the junta superior de Real Hacienda, was created. This junta was to provide the mechanism by which the intendant in conjunction with Audiencia officials would oversee fiscal policy. The Ordenanza de Intendentes also attempted to create new mechanisms to collect revenues from traditional sources by creating agencies such as the Contaduría de Propios y Arbitrios (Bureau of Municipal Accounts).

One agency already in place, although in a modified form, before the founding of the platense viceroyalty was the Tribunal de Cuentas, a court of audit charged with reviewing accounts and initiating legal proceedings in cases of fraud. It is an ideal branch to examine in depth for it reflected many of the changes in personnel, job responsibility, and employment policies that were adopted by all government agencies during the viceregal period. Growth in the number of employees and jurisdiction was not limited to the Tribunal de Cuentas, but the pattern found there was similar to that of other agencies. Furthermore, the Tribunal de Cuentas stands as an example of the continuing bureaucratic inefficiency and frustration that plagued most branches of viceregal administration in spite of increased staff. (See Appendix D for other agencies.)

The first step in establishing financial autonomy for the Río de la Plata had come in 1767 when the king, Charles III, issued an instrucción governing the creation of a Contaduría de Cuentas in Buenos Aires.[7] From its founding in 1767 the Buenos Aires Contaduría de Cuentas audited all royal accounts generated in the provinces of Buenos Aires, Paraguay, and Tucumán. In 1776 the districts of Mendoza and San Juan were added to the jurisdication of the Buenos Aires office.[8] Four years later, with the introduction of the intendancy system into the Río de la Plata, the Contaduría de Cuentas was transformed into a Tribunal Mayor (or Tribunal de Cuentas) responsible for verifying the accounts of the entire viceroyalty. Minor changes in the jurisdiction of the Tribunal took place during the next thirty years, but for all intents and purposes the Tribunal remained as outlined in the Ordenanza de Intendentes.[9]

The Tribunal de Cuentas, in its new expanded form, experienced a growth in personnel designed to complement its additional responsibilities. At the time the Contaduría de Cuentas was set up, three men, one *contador mayor* (head accountant) and two *oficiales* (clerks) were dispatched to Buenos Aires.[10] In 1779, complying with the Royal Order of 7 October 1778, which reorganized the Río de la Plata bureaucracy, Viceroy Guirior of Peru transferred seven bureaucrats (two contadores mayores and five *subalternos* [junior officials]) to the Buenos Aires Tribunal.[11] In addition, the Buenos Aires superintendent, Manuel Ignacio Fernández, moved three oficiales from the Royal Treasury staff and added seven more junior positions.[12]

The increased number of employees made it necessary to rationalize and reorganize the duties of Tribunal staff. In 1779 the intendant drew up a new *reglamento* (rules and regulations) outlining the internal structure of the expanded Tribunal de Cuentas.[13] All salaried employees below the rank of *contador ordenador* (middle-level accountant), so-called *individuos subalternos,* were divided into three *mesas* (departments) that were charged with specific accounting tasks. Within each mesa bureaucrats were ranked according to position. The largest department, that responsible for reviewing the annual accounts of the Real Hacienda, was staffed by six men, ranging from *oficial primero* (first clerk) to *oficial sexto* (sixth clerk). The second department, in charge of auditing army accounts, employed only two oficiales. The third department was responsible for the Cabildo accounts (*propios y arbitrios* [ways and means]) and all other so-called *ramos particulares,* monies collected for specific ends. This department employed four oficiales. In addition, two low-ranking employees were charged with general bookkeeping and copying tasks and another was to serve as the agency's *portero* (doorman-receptionist).

In spite of increased staff and internal reorganization, the agency was chronically unable to complete auditing accounts within what the crown considered a reasonable period of time. Like its sister agencies throughout the Spanish empire, the Tribunal had difficulties keeping to a satisfactory work schedule and continued to fall increasingly behind. As early as 1784 the total staff of twenty proved unable to handle the amount of work charged to them. When goaded by the viceroy and intendant to speed up their "final balancing of accounts," the Tribunal requested that it have more paid employees.[14] The viceroy agreed that the Tribunal's employees were overworked and forwarded the Tribunal's request to Spain, where it was eventually turned down.

By 1789, awaiting a reply from the crown to their request for increased staff, the three contadores mayores turned to their subordinates, the contadores ordenadores and oficiales, to aid them in their final accounting, but this informal granting of powers to lesser bureaucrats was curtailed by the king who reprimanded the contadores mayores sharply, telling the viceroy to "make the contadores mayores understand that in accordance with the Laws of the Indies it is their job, and not the job of others, to review, audit, and settle all accounts."[15] In another attempt to increase manpower, the *contador de propios y arbitrios,* a treasury official, was loaned to the Tribunal as supernumerary contador mayor. The addition of one more contador mayor did little to alleviate delay, although he and three other staff members of the contaduría de propios y arbitrios were incorporated into the Tribunal staff in 1791.

By 1794, still faced with the continued problem of unaudited accounts, the Tribunal, this time with the backing of the Junta Superior de Real Hacienda, submitted another plan calling for new positions to the secretary of state for finance. Although the Tribunal's plan was not approved in its entirety, the crown did create two new clerkships.[16]

The infusion of additional manpower on the junior level did not alleviate the Tribunal's accounting problem, for as mentioned above only the contadores mayores could give final approval for all work done. By 1796 the age and physical health of the three contadores mayores de número had further slowed the Tribunal's work, for all three were "sickly" and "unable to attend to their daily work because of their advanced age." (Their average age was sixty-two.) In still another attempt to speed up the auditing process, the king, advised of the "considerable delay which the accounts are suffering, and the large number of daily matters that are not being attended to by the Tribunal," gave Viceroy Melo one of two requested additional supernumerary contador mayor positions.[17]

Two years later the crown, after additional consultations with the local

Tribunal, the Junta Superior de Real Hacienda, and the Contador General de Indias, finally reorganized the Tribunal, creating new divisions and shifting and adding personnel.[18] The Tribunal was to be staffed by twenty-eight men, including two *contadores de resultas* (junior accountants for resolving accounts) and ten contadores ordenadores. The crown also took advantage of the reorganization to change the pay scale with the agency, reducing the annual salary of top and middle management to finance the explosion in condator ordenador posts.

Nevertheless, these extra officials proved unable to overcome the Tribunal's tardiness. In March 1799, shortly after entering office, Viceroy Avilés requested a general statement of the finances of the viceroyalty. In reply he was told that the Tribunal de Cuentas, "from the year 1780, in which it was established, to the present time, has been unable to close out the accounts for any five-year period, nor even for a single year."[19] The Tribunal's unaudited accounts had grown from 112 in 1786 to 210 in 1791 and now stood at 618.[20] The Tribunal blamed the Real Hacienda and other offices for failing to send complete accounts, a truthful although one-sided explanation of the problem.

The Real Hacienda was not the only institution that delayed the Tribunal's completion of its appointed tasks. Viceroys and intendants were not above also citing a supposed lack of "required exactness" in the auditing procedures that were followed by the Tribunal, thus also slowing remission of accounts back to Spain.[21] Any slight modification of the format followed by the Tribunal in auditing accounts automatically produced grounds for the agency involved to challenge the Tribunal's power, delaying the transmission of completed paperwork and surplus funds to Spain.

These tactics coupled with the Tribunal's perpetual shortage of competent officials exacerbated the situation and fed royal frustration. In a letter of 26 September 1800 the Spanish crown warned the viceroy that "these types of complaints should stop" for they just added to the Tribunal's "most notable delay in the dispatch of its duties." In a rare display of emotion the minister continued:

> realizing the possible problems of judicial cognizance produced by the present most extraordinary circumstances, circumstances that make it crucial to find the shortest route to solve the problem; knowing how many means are feasible to those who serve His Majesty, especially when there is an urgent matter at hand; and stressing the attainment

of this most desirable goal (which should be most important to that august body), nothing, nothing, nothing should be allowed to serve as an obstacle.[22]

The wartime financial needs of the government were too urgent to allow continued haggling and delay in concluding accounts. Indeed, the crown became more desperate for funds; it increasingly berated its colonial bureaucrats for using "frivolous pretexts" in delaying accounting and remission of funds. But the continued tarriance with which accounts were dispatched from Buenos Aires to Madrid prove that although royal patience was growing short, the Tribunal would not, or could not, be moved. Local bureaucrats failed to respond to Spain's urgent call and did not dramatically increase the return of royal revenues to the Peninsula.

The continued inability of the Tribunal to fulfill its duties, coupled with the pressing royal need to have an accurate report of finances in the Río de la Plata, finally led the crown to name a special *visitador general* (general inspector) to review all branches of the Royal Hacienda, including the Tribunal. Diego de la Vega arrived in Buenos Aires in 1803 charged with "reforming and rearranging a Tribunal de Cuentas[,] . . . which instead of having been given all the help it has requested to finish the final accounting of its multitude of back accounts, has made progress in almost nothing."[23] De la Vega proceeded to again reorganize the Tribunal, creating a large division dedicated to *cuentas rezagadas,* old unaudited accounts, which had continued to accumulate. Here four ordenadores and eight oficiales were charged with catching up on the agency's work. How successful these men were is difficult to determine. By 1810 new economies had forced the Tribunal to cut back on ten members of this temporary staff.

In addition to manpower problems, interagency jealousy hampered the Tribunal's efficiency. The Tribunal's chief adversary, not surprisingly, was the agency it was created to police—the Real Hacienda. Although the Tribunal de Cuentas and the Royal Hacienda were in theory to work together, these two agencies frequently squabbled over matters ranging from questions of procedure to those of jurisdiction. Constant bickering between the Tribunal and the Real Hacienda marred their relationship from the start, doing little to make the Tribunal's performance more efficient. These disagreements, which usually occurred when a modification had been made in existing procedure or when a slightly different transaction presented itself, ran the gamut from minor problems to major flare-ups. The Tribunal had been in arrears in its work ever since its establishment. As the work load grew, so did the haggling over Real Hacienda's presentation of accounts. In 1791, for example, the *ministros principales* (chief administrators) of the Real Hacienda and those of the Tribunal engaged in a long debate over how certain charges were to be recorded in their account books.[24] A disastrous attempt to institute double-entry bookkeeping further complicated the Tribunal's schedule and put them even further into arrears.[25]

Frustrated by the Real Hacienda's delays and harassed by crown demands that accounts be audited and dispatched to Spain, the Tribunal was not above seeking local retribution. This exacerbated the tension between the Reales Cajas and the Tribunal, further slowing the transaction of fiscal business, and inconvenienced both the citizenry at large as well as other government officials. The Tribunal proved especially adroit at using its power to create situations in which minor bureaucrats associated with the Reales Cajas suffered. Francisco Díaz y Orejuela, third oficial of the Contaduría General de Propios y Arbitrios, for example, had been tapped for special assignment as a representative of the Royal Exchequer in the second round of Spanish-Portuguese boundary demarcation negotiations. Shortly after finishing this assignment, Díaz concluded all business that he had been handling, presented his accounts, and prepared to leave Paraguay. Because of the expense of undertaking his return journey to Buenos Aires, he appealed to the Reales Cajas for an advance of six months' salary, pointing out that this was a customary procedure followed by all those bureaucrats dispatched to the demarcation commission. But what to Díaz was a simple request turned out to be far more complicated. Because Pedro Medrano and Antonio de Pinedo, *contador* (accountant) and *tesorero* (treasurer) of the Reales Cajas, had supported Díaz's request, officials of the Tribunal de Cuentas joined together to block payment. They claimed that it would be "most prejudicial to the Royal Exchequer" and would furthermore contradict the Royal Order of 11 November 1790, which forbade any new payment from the Reales Cajas without express royal order. In vain Díaz argued that this was not a new payment and that as a member of the demarcation commission he was under special royal provision. Tribunal members held firm to their first interpretation and instructed Díaz to request any advances from the Reales Cajas of Paraguay.[26]

Constant fractiousness between these two agencies not only caused delays that inconvenienced government personnel, it also seriously hampered the implementation of royal policy. In 1803, for example, when asked by the Tribunal to submit the accounts of the *mayordomo de fábrica* (overseer of construction) of the cathedral, the Real Hacienda questioned the Tribunal's very right to review these papers, arguing that this was the duty of the diocesan prelates. An earlier request for accounts in 1800, this time for accounts clearly within the Tribunal's purview, elicited a bitter complaint from the Real Hacienda officials as to the style of address and manner in which the Tribunal had asked for these papers.[27] Behind most of these disagreements was an ever-smoldering resentment and power struggle between the officials of the Real Hacienda and their supervisors, the officials of the Tribunal de Cuentas. Although questions of jurisdiction and of etiquette were always decided in favor of the Tribunal, local treasury officials consistently attempted, at the least, to delay the Tribunal's audits.

Shortly after his arrival, visitador general De la Vega realized that he was faced with the nearly impossible task of investigating a bureaucracy, both in Buenos Aires and the interior, that was firmly entrenched and had much to lose.[28] His distrust in the local bureaucracy is reflected in the fact that even before he arrived on the scene, he ordered the dismissal of two of the Tribunal's chief accountants. But he trusted the rank-and-file employees of the Tribunal and used four of them to staff his six-man *tribunal de visita* (court of inquiry).

In addition, the viceroy was less than supportive. The visitador general quickly concluded that Viceroy Joaquín del Pino was more interested in providing his protégés with lucrative positions than with improving the exchequer's administration. The visitador general's enemies lost no time in obtaining a royal order limiting his review to only the Buenos Aires Tribunal de Cuentas.[29] While de la Vega was able to draw up a new code for the Tribunal (the Instrucción para el Tribunal de Cuentas de Buenos Aires of 23 October 1805), his presence in Buenos Aires set off a new round of squabbles between the Real Hacienda and the auditing agency. In addition to the instrucción, de la Vega was also instrumental in convincing the crown to issue the Royal Order of 27 October 1805, which again tackled the problem of bringing the Tribunal's accounts up to date. The king now ordered all employees of the Tribunal to hire and pay for additional help out of their own pockets, if necessary, to complete the Tribunal's work.

The chief officers of the Real Hacienda, in addition to limiting de la Vega's power to audit their books, soon convinced the king to stop Ramón de Oromí, one of the new contadores mayores, from checking their accounts (on the pretext that de la Vega was the son-in-law of Rufino de Cárdenas, *administrador general* [chief official] of the Buenos Aires Real Renta de Tabacos). Oromí, for his part, voiced opposition to de la Vega, while Juan Andrés Arroyo and Pedro José Ballesteros, the two contadores mayores dismissed by de la Vega, attempted to discredit both the visitador general and Oromí. Two contadores de resultas were pressed into emergency service as acting contadores mayores, but one of them, Juan José Ballesteros, brother of the temporarily discredited Pedro José, was far from a disinterested party. Internal chaos ensued.

By 1807, in an attempt to restore the Tribunal de Cuentas to its previsitador general stage, both Arroyo and Pedro José Ballesteros were reinstated as contadores mayores de número, and Oromí was demoted to contador mayor supernumerario. Still the larger matter of the Tribunal's right to demand the accounts of the Real Hacienda was not resolved. As late as July 1810 both the Tribunal and the Real Hacienda addressed long letters to the provisional government, attempting to win support for their respective positions. Not only were earlier accounts still outstanding, but the Tribunal had still not concluded its preliminary review (partially because it still lacked complete accounts) of finances for 1805, 1806, 1807, 1808, and 1809.[30]

Regardless of inefficiency and internal squabbling, the Tribunal's growth, similar to the numerical growth of all branches of royal bureaucracy in viceregal Buenos Aires, provided new career opportunities for a host of men. By 1810 a branch of the government that had consisted of three men as late as 1775 now employed four contadores mayores (plus two honorary contadores mayores), six contadores ordenadores or contadores de resultas, eight oficiales, an *archivero* (record keeper), a *contador de retasas* (reassessor), two *oficiales de retasas* (reassessment clerks), and one *oficial de libros* (bookkeeper). In addition, an escribano, one *escribiente interino* (interium amanuensis), and a portero also worked at the Tribunal. The Tribunal also housed a number of *meritorios,* unpaid assistants or trainees, who joined the Tribunal in hope of accruing merit and eventually being rewarded with a salaried post.

In addition to the major governmental agencies—Tribunal de Cuentas, Real Hacienda, Aduana, and Secretaría—the bureaucratic organization of the viceroyalty also featured a number of juntas, high-ranking standing committees charged with providing bureaucratic and fiscal guidance in questions concerning the day-to-day administration of specific branches of colonial government. Among the more important juntas were the Junta Superior de Real Hacienda, which oversaw the functioning of the treasury; the Junta Provincial de Temporalidades, which was to keep check on the activities of Temporalidades; and the Junta Superior de Propios y Arbitrios, set up to review municipal finances. All of these juntas had been created by the Ordenanza de Intendentes, and the superintendent of Buenos Aires originally sat as presiding officer on these various boards. After the Superintendency was disbanded in 1788, this position was taken by the viceroy. In addition, the regent and the *fiscal de lo civil* (prosecuting attorney) of the Buenos Aires Audiencia were also permanent members of these boards. Total membership on any one junta usually varied from six to eight individuals, with other members drawn from the leadership of the civil, military, and religious bureaucracy. The contador mayor of the Tribunal de Cuentas, for example, served on the Junta Superior de Propios y Arbitrios; the *chantre* (choir-master) of the cathedral and the *asesor general* (legal counselor) of the viceroy's Secretaría were permanent members of the Junta Provincial de Temporalidades.

The Junta de Almonedas, for example, was a specialized junta created to supervise public auctions held under the jurisdiction of the Real Hacienda. This junta consisted of six members, five bureaucrats drawn from the offices of the viceregal administration and one escribano. Two of the five bureaucrats on this commission, one *oidor* (judge) and the fiscal de lo civil, represented the Audiencia. The asesor general of the viceroyalty was another member of the commission, as were the chief accountant and the treasurer of the Buenos Aires Reales Cajas. Four of these bureaucrats—representatives of the Audiencia and the Real Hacienda—also sat on the Junta de Diezmos, another specialized agency set up to oversee the collection of tithes. This junta was larger and more important than the Junta de Almonedas, for in addition to the aforementioned four bureaucrats, the intendant and the regent of the Audiencia sat on the board. The Junta de Diezmos also employed an escribano and two officers, entitled *hacedores*, who served as stewards or managers of tithe collection. Although the collection of tithes had been transferred from religious to secular hands, at least one priest also served on this junta.

The proliferation of special juntas empowered to oversee agencies or special jurisdictions quickly produced a small group of overworked bureaucrats. All juntas were by definition to be composed of the best, most-qualified, most-experienced, and highest-ranking bureaucrats. Although the porteño bureaucracy had increased greatly, those individuals who filled the highest criteria were in short supply. As a result, the same men were called upon repeatedly to serve on many juntas, while still attending to their principal job, that of supervising an agency or administering justice. The case of Pedro Medrano is instructive. Medrano, who had begun his career at age twenty-one in the Río de la Plata as a contador with the 1755 Cevallos military expedition, gained wide experience in both accounting and military finances in the Reales Cajas and the Contaduría de Ejército (Bureau of Army Accounts). By 1790 Medrano had reached the position of *contador mayor de ejército* (chief accountant for army accounts). He also served on the Junta Superior de Real Hacienda, on the Junta Superior de Aplicaciones, on the Junta de Diezmos, and the Junta de Almonedas, in addition to being a member of the governing board of the Montepío de Ministros de Justicia y Real Hacienda. Even if these groups met less frequently than theoretically stipulated (usually once a week), Medrano and other bureaucrats like him were being asked to fulfill an almost impossible variety of tasks in the time available to them. Little wonder that both juntas and agencies were often slow in meeting basic obligations.

In theory the juntas drew their manpower from a variety of agencies in order to provide a system of checks and balances among agencies. No one agency fully staffed a junta that had jurisdiction over its procedures. Nevertheless, the Audiencia and the Real Hacienda usually provided a majority of junta members, thus strengthening the power of these two institutions within the colonial bureaucracy. Paradoxically, at the same time as the viceroy was consolidating power in the platense viceroyalty, royal government was increasingly being transformed into government by committee. Whether the junta system produced greater efficiency is somewhat doubtful, but it clearly produced lively, even acrimonious debate. As a result of the close overlap between the members of one junta and another, personality conflicts that had developed in one setting were often transposed to another, further limiting the efficiency of the juntas.

Regardless of their success of their internal composition, all the juntas employed a skeleton staff consisting of an escribano and/or contador who also functioned as secretary of the junta proceedings. In addition, each junta employed as relator a lawyer charged with providing legal counsel to the junta. Frequently, one man held the relator post in several agencies and juntas at the same time. Manuel Mariano de Irigoyen, for example, served as relator of both the Audiencia of Buenos Aires and the Junta Superior de Real Hacienda. These posts, like those of asesor general, were most desirable for they could serve as an important entry into the higher echelons of the judicial bureaucracy for lawyers who chose careers in government service. As those who practiced law in Buenos Aires tended to be native-born and American-trained, these two routes proved to be the principal way in which a handful of creoles achieved important judicial positions.[31] Irigoyen, for example, after serving as relator in Buenos Aires, was named oidor of the Audiencia of Chile in 1800.

Escribano positions in the juntas, as well as in other government agencies, were also an important point of entry for creoles, although unlike the asesores or relatores, one did not progress from the rank of escribano to more exalted jobs. An escribano also often combined several duties, serving in an agency or as *escribano público de número* (public notary) at the same time as he held one or two junta appointments. Such was the case of Pedro Velasco who in addition to being the *escribano actuario* (acting notary) in the *despacho oficial* (office) of the Real Hacienda was also the escribano of the Junta Superior de Real Hacienda and the Junta de Diezmos.

Both the intendancy system and the multiplicity of juntas created by the Ordenanza de Intendentes sought to rationalize and expand royal revenues. One of the targets for financial reorganization if not outright expropriation of funds was the church, increasingly viewed by the Bourbons as a source of much-needed liquid capital. The transfer of fiscal responsibilities for ecclesiastical funds from the hands of the church to those of the state also affected the careers of another group of colonial bureaucrats—laymen employed by the church. The problems created by jurisdictional changes are well illustrated by the experiences of two bureaucrats linked to the church, the first a salaried clerk in the Contaduría de Diezmos (Bureau of Tithe Accounts) and the second the owner of the post of treasurer of the Santa Cruzada.

Although the Junta de Diezmos oversaw the collection of tithes throughout the viceroyalty, a small agency, the Contaduría de Diezmos, was charged with both the local collection and the viceregalwide accounting of tithes. Outside of Buenos Aires collection of tithes was usually auctioned off to the highest bidder. Individual tithe collectors were expected to turn over their funds to the closest Reales Cajas together with an accounting of tithes collected in each district. In addition, accounts were also to be presented to the contador de diezmos, whose function was analogous to that of an accountant of the Tribunal de Cuentas specially charged with checking tithe accounts, although he was employed by the Tribunal de Cuadrantes, a section of the ecclesiastical bureaucracy. Headquartered in the cathedral, alongside the ecclesiastical Cabildo, the contador de diezmos was therefore an administrative position within the church hierarchy, akin to other clerical jobs such as "clerk in charge of the collection of the ecclesiastical subsidy." These positions, initially outside the civil bureaucracy, provided employment to a group of men much like those who entered the lower ranks of the viceregal administration. But because of the changing relationship between church and state that marked the late Bourbon reforms, men employed in these semiecclesiastical clerical jobs often found themselves in a most perilous position.

Such was the case of Damián de Castro, a native of Córdoba in Andalucía who arrived in Buenos Aires shortly before the founding of the viceroyalty. Castro arrived with letters of recommendation to his fellow countryman, Juan de Osorio, an established shopkeeper of the city. Shortly after his arrival, Castro found employment as an unpaid trainee in the church's Tribunal de Cuadrantes working with tithe accounts. He held this position for the next twelve years, from 1776 to 1788, no doubt also taking on odd jobs for retail merchants such as Osorio on the side in order to survive. His dedication finally paid off in 1788 when Andrés del Pedregal, another Buenos Aires merchant, renounced his post as contador de diezmos. Castro was named to the newly opened salaried post in an interim status and was serving as such when the *real cédula* (royal order) of 22 July 1792 arrived in Buenos Aires. The cédula, part of the general royal plan to divert church funds more directly into the hands of the royal government, called for the office of contador de diezmos to be disbanded and the duties to be taken over by one of the contadores of Reales Cajas. Castro, an employee of the church, was deprived of his new post after more than sixteen years of service. Instead, he found himself picking up odd clerical assignments from the bishop while petitioning for entrance, again as an unpaid trainee (meritorio), into the Tribunal de Cuentas.

Transference of the diezmo accounts to Reales Cajas pleased neither church nor secular officials. The former resented their loss of power and influence, while the latter, already overworked, did not welcome additional duties. Within three years a new real cédula reversed the 1792 law, re-establishing the contaduría de diezmos in its earlier state and reappointing Castro to his previous position. But Castro had learned a bitter lesson in 1792, and although he resumed the job of contador de diezmos, he also spent the next three years using his personal connections, reputation for hard work, and his work as meritorio to join the Tribunal de Cuentas. By 1798 he was again in the Tribunal, this time employed as an oficial. By 1803 he had progressed to the post of contador ordenador and by 1810 was the *primer* (first) contador ordenador of the Tribunal.

The Spanish crown, realizing the chaos that could ensue from the growth of the Buenos Aires bureaucracy, took pains to limit the authority of the various new agencies being put into place and to also delineate the authority of any particular officeholder with his agency. Both the reglamentos drawing up agencies and the power of the viceroy and the intendant were to be used to assure that no individual attempted to usurp special power. In the powerful Tribunal de Cuentas, for example, the authority of its chief official, the contador mayor, was limited by several provisions of the 1779 tribunal reglamento.[32] First, in nearly all matters pertaining to the hiring or firing of personnel, he had to consult with the intendant before acting. Second, detailed reports following general guidelines set by the intendant were to be submitted by the contador mayor to the intendant every year. In addition, no contador mayor had the right to alter "in any way" any royal orders but was only to "observe and make them observed by all His Majesty's subjects."

To insure that a contador mayor did not tamper with established procedures, he was not only to be scrutinized by the intendant, but those bureaucrats serving under him were encouraged to be on guard against any intentional or unintentional deviation. Clerks were in fact charged with reporting any "innovation or mistake" made by the contador mayor to their respective chief clerk who in turn was to point out the error to the contador. This system, therefore, called for lines of communication and control from both ordinates and subordinates, but no evidence has been found that any fifth clerk ever availed himself of this opportunity to correct the Tribunal's chief officer.

Clearly established lines of bureaucratic communication and uniformity of bureaucratic procedures were goals close to the heart of Enlightenment political and administrative thinkers. In the case of the Tribunal de Cuentas this policy reflected in regulations that forbade any Tribunal employee, including the chief officer himself, from communicating directly with any Tribunal in Spain or from sending secret letters to any government agency in the motherland. All correspondence from the Buenos Aires Tribunal de Cuentas had to pass through the hands of the viceroy or intendant. To insure that the agency functioned efficiently, no Tribunal employee, including the contador mayor, could leave his post without express royal permission.

In addition to bureaucratic professionalization and increased efficiency, the Bourbon reforms also aimed at increasing state revenues by eliminating the leasing of government tax revenues to private individuals. In their attempt to generate greater revenues, the Bourbons increasingly placed the administration of a series of government monopolies directly into the hands of royal officials. Included among those taxes that were transferred from private to public hands throughout the empire during the 1760s were those on tobacco and playing cards and sales taxes (*alcabalas*). In addition, gunpowder and salt monopolies also reverted back to the state.

One of the major problems facing all royal agencies at the time of the creation of the platense viceroyalty, a problem that became more acute as individual agencies grew, was the rather mundane issue of space. Buenos Aires, a city never famous for its sumptuous structures, had few buildings suitable for government offices. In addition, the city's population had been growing since the middle of the century causing whatever space available to be put on the market for a premium price. Furthermore, a shortage of trained artisans and the scarcity of wood and other building materials tended to make new construction relatively expensive.

1 Fort
   Viceroy's residence
   Secretariat
   Real Audiencia
   Real Hacienda
2 Tribunal de Cuentas
3 Real Renta de Tabacos, Casa de Dirección

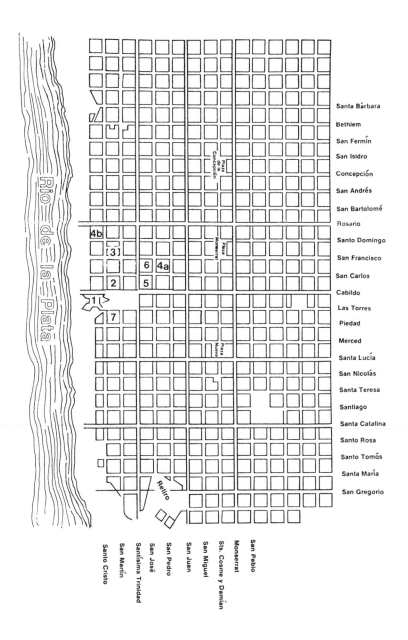

Río de la Plata

Santa Bárbara
Bethlem
San Fermín
San Isidro
Concepción
San Andrés
San Bartolomé
Rosario
Santo Domingo
San Francisco
San Carlos
Cabildo
Las Torres
Piedad
Merced
Santa Lucía
San Nicolás
Santa Teresa
Santiago
Santa Catalina
Santo Rosa
Santo Tomás
Santa María
San Gregorio

Plaza de la Concepción

Plaza Monserrat

Plaza Nueva

Retiro

Santo Cristo
San Martín
Santísima Trinidad
San José
San Pedro
San Juan
San Miguel
Sts. Cosme y Damián
San Pablo
Monserrat

Location of Government Offices in Buenos Aires

4a   Aduana headquarters 1778–85 (Ranchería)
4b   Aduana headquarters 1785–1810
5   Administración de Correos
6   Administración de los Pueblos de Misiones
7   Real Consulado

Several government agencies were located in the fort on the city's central plaza. Here, in addition to the viceroy's residence, were the Secretariat, the Real Audiencia chambers, and the offices of the Real Hacienda. But the space available in the fort was inadequate for the growing bureaucracy. The Spanish crown was nonetheless loath to spend its money erecting new buildings to house the expanded bureaucracy. As a result several important government agencies were forced to rent local residences and convert them into offices.

Local property owners, especially those who owned large buildings suitable for this conversion, realized the escalating value of their real estate and wasted no time in demanding handsome, even exorbitant, rents from the crown. The Aduana, for example, had originally been interested in renting a building belonging to the merchant Vicente de Azcuenaga, the *casa del asiento* (former headquarters of the English slave trade) located on Santo Domingo between Santo Cristo and the river, (present-day Calle Belgrano between Balcarce and Paseo Colon), but the rent being requested (3,000 pesos per year) was deemed exorbitant by the intendant. Instead, the Aduana first occupied a building known as the Ranchera located on the corner of San José and San Carlos (present-day Calles Peru and Alsina), which had previously belonged to the Jesuits and was nominally the property of the Guaraní Indians. Although the rent was only 500 pesos per year, within five years the administratador was lobbying for a reconsideration of the Azcuenaga property, which the merchant's heirs had decided to offer for the much reduced rent of 1,700 pesos per year. The Azcuenaga house had two distinct advantages. First, it was closer to the river and the major commercial establishments of the city and would cut the time that merchants' clerks had to spend far from their shops. In addition, the building provided greatly increased office and living space for the administrador, the contador, and the *vista* (customs inspector). With this in mind, the administrador, supported by Superintendent Francisco de Paula Sanz, was able to effect a change in Aduana location. On 23 October 1783 Sanz authorized the administrador to sign a lease with Azcuenaga's estate, and two years later, after substantial modifications had been made to the building, the Aduana began to function from its new quarters. No change in the Aduana's location would be made until after Independence.[33]

In their attempt to find relatively inexpensive offices, government agencies often found themselves situated in less than ideal space. The Tribunal de Cuentas, for example, chose to rent a house located on the main plaza, between Santo Cristo and San Martín (present-day Avenida H. Yrigoyen between Balcarce and Defensa), which was available for an annual rent of 450 pesos.[34] The building, although centrally located, was far from satisfactory because the archive and other rooms of the building were subject to "much humidity," causing documents to suffer extensive water damage. Tribunal officials were able to convince Superintendent Sanz to consider relocating the Tribunal to a drier building that they planned to purchase from Temporalidades. But Viceroy Marqués de Loreto was adamantly opposed to any change in the Tribunal's physical location, citing cost, destruction of documents during the process of moving, and the distance of the proposed site from the Real Audiencia as the reasons for his stance.[35] Sanz and the Tribunal tried to convince Loreto of the need for relocation, but the removal of Sanz from the Buenos Aires superintendency in 1788 dashed all Tribunal plans.

Like other royal agencies, the Real Renta de Tabaco showed great reluctance to purchase the buildings that it occupied, preferring instead to rent from local inhabitants on a yearly basis. Initially, the Real Renta de Tabaco leased its headquarters (*la casa de dirección*) from Isidro Lorea, a local merchant.[36] After nine years the Renta was finally given permission to purchase the building. The Fábrica de Nuevas Labores, set up in 1785, occupied quarters rented for 576 pesos per year. Permission was eventually given to purchase some buildings and warehouses used by the Renta. Nonetheless, from time to time the Renta was forced to rent additional warehouses along the waterfront when their regular space became too constricted. Faced with increasing bureaucratic expenses, the crown showed itself not only unwilling to rent suitable office space for the royal administration, but also ever more hesitant to repair any quarters already occupied. Upkeep of government buildings also proved to be a formidable expense and one which the crown attempted to avoid as long as possible. Here the crown was torn between its desire to economize and the need to keep the government offices in a barely presentable state.

The building that gave the crown the most trouble was the Royal Fort, which housed the viceroy's palace. Not only was it necessary to provide the viceroy with quarters befitting his rank, but the fort, because of faulty construction, had to be constantly refurbished. By 1802 that section of the fort occupied by the viceroy had fallen into such disrepair that the viceroy ordered major work done on the roof and walls of the palace, the kitchen, and the secretariat, as well as repainting.[37] Although not happy to be faced with such large expenses, the crown approved the outlay of more than 13,500 pesos, warning the viceroy to be more prudent with repairs in the future. While willing to cover this large expense, the crown also increasingly forced the viceroys to pay for other repairs. For example, although repair of windows, glass, and lanterns in the viceregal residence had always been charged to the royal treasury and covered with funds collected under the *ramo de sisa* (revenue from a local tax on trade) in 1792 Viceroy Arredondo was told that he, and not the royal coffer, was responsible for covering this expense.[38]

Starting approximately ten years before Buenos Aires became a viceregal capital, and continuing through a period of bureaucratic reorganization that accompanied the intendancy reforms, the size of the bureaucracy in place in the capital city experienced unprecedented growth. Not only was the number of government agencies located in Buenos Aires greatly expanded, but the total number of bureaucrats increased more than tenfold. Bureaucratic reorganization continued through the remaining years of the viceroyalty, but later changes tended to be internal adjustments as the crown and local policymakers attempted to improve organization and make government a more efficient generator of income for the crown coffers. The numbers of agencies within the colonial bureaucracy and the numbers of positions available within each agency mushroomed from 1776 to 1783, but after this major period of growth and internal expansion bureaucratic growth slowed dramatically. While many agencies found their numbers increasing from a staff of two or three to a staff of ten or twelve during the early viceregal period, in general only one or two new positions were created in each agency after this initial growth.

In theory the growth of the Buenos Aires bureaucracy and the transfer

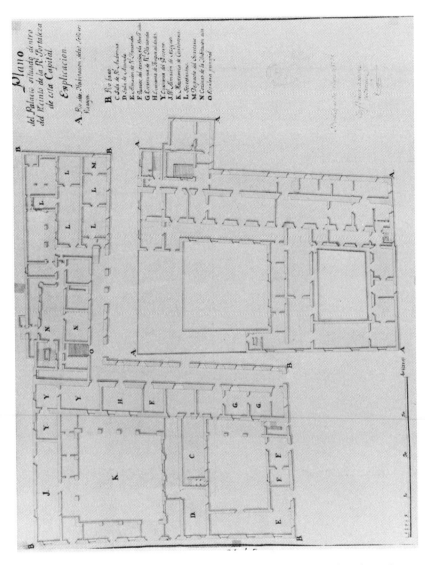

Floor Plan of the Palace, Showing the Offices of the Real Audiencia, Viceroy's Secretariat, and Real Hacienda

of posts from the sphere of purchased office to that of salaried bureaucrat created multiple opportunities for the educated and ambitious to serve the crown while advancing their personal careers. The question of who responded to these new opportunities and how realistically their ambitions could be fulfilled is discussed in the following chapters.

4. The Bureaucrats: Recruitment and Appointment

THE CREATION OF THE VICEROYALTY and its attendant new bureaucracy opened a host of new positions for those seeking employment as civil servants. These jobs coupled with the crown's avowed aim to professionalize its bureaucracy resulted in new patterns of recruitment, which developed as the enlarged government staffs took form.

While the numbers of agencies and bureaucrats grew markedly from 1750 on, the eighteenth century also witnessed a gradual change from the practice of outright purchase of office or appointments to a system of appointing salaried full-time bureaucrats. This reform, which strove to change the very nature of bureaucratic appointment, began under Ferdinand VI and was continued by Charles III. Throughout Spanish America the goal was the creation of a loyal, honest group of civil servants, dependent on the crown and the bureaucratic system for promotion and power. Nonetheless, the transformation from purchased posts to salaried ones was gradual and uneven. Throughout the eighteenth century some spheres of government service continued to be supplied by men who had purchased their jobs directly or indirectly from the Royal Treasury.

From the creation of the gobernación of Buenos Aires until the middle of the eighteenth century, the crown had sold either office or appointment to office to all the major and minor offices in the small local bureaucracy, including the post of governor; treasurer, contador and *factor* (agent) of the Buenos Aires Reales Cajas; and all *escribanía* (notary) posts. The latter were sold as *oficios vendibles y renunciables* (salable positions) and usually included a provision allowing the purchaser to resell or bequeath the post. These offices, frequently purchased from the crown in public auction, were governed by a complex set of laws controlling the transfer of property and subsequent crown profit.[1]

Reales Cajas posts were never sold as renounceable offices. Instead of selling the office, the crown sold the appointment, a legal nicety that also prevented these positions from becoming inheritable property.[2] Upon the death of a treasury official, the crown reappointed another bureaucrat. The crown also maintained the fiction that these were salaried posts by providing token yearly wages and collecting a full media anata.

The most important posts were purchased by local merchants and military men. While holding an important government post added luster to a man's accomplishments, the individual in question already occupied an important social and economic position within the city before taking office. Office tended to serve as an additional wise investment, an attempt to diversify economic holdings.

In Buenos Aires, as in other parts of the Spanish colonial empire, need for new sources of funds, coupled with the long tenure of officeholders, also forced the crown to sell *futurario* posts, the right to hold a bureaucratic post upon the death of the actual incumbent. Nevertheless, by the middle of the eighteenth century, the desire to reestablish strong centralized control over her colonial possessions and to improve colonial finances forced the crown to begin bureaucratic reform.

The first signs of reform occurred in the treasury. The first treasury post was transformed from a purchased to a salaried appointment in 1757 when Domingo Valverde *oficial segundo de la contaduría de Marina* (second clerk of the Bureau of Navy Accounts) in Cádiz was named to replace the late Antonio de Artueta as *contador oficial real* (royal accountant) of the Buenos Aires Reales Cajas.[3] The decision to forgo sale of office in the hope of eventually realizing greater profits through improved bureaucrat efficiency and honesty was an expensive transition. Not only was Artueta replaced by an experienced bureaucrat, but the costs incurred in this transformation were considerable. In 1740 Artueta had bought the post for a payment of 4,000 pesos *fuertes*, plus an additional fianza of 30 *ducados* (42 pesos 4 reales). In return for holding this office, he received a yearly salary of 3,500 *maravedíes* (less than 13 pesos) and paid a media anata of 1750 maravedíes (less than 6-1/2 pesos).[4] A total of 4,049 pesos entered the treasury, while only 13 pesos per year in expenses were incurred. By comparison, Valverde paid nothing to the crown in the form of a direct purchase price. He was promised a salary one hundred times greater than that paid to Artueta (350,000 maravedíes or approximately 1,287 pesos) and in return paid a media anata of 175,000 maravedíes (approximately 643 pesos). Because the amount of the required bond was related to salary, the fianza required of this salaried employee was also one hundred times greater than that requested from the previous purchaser. The crown therefore received a total of 4,893 pesos from Valverde, while incurring yearly expenses of 1,287 pesos. Royal revenue was immediately reduced by 11 percent in appointing a bureaucrat rather than selling the office; in each subsequent year salary expenditure would be ninety-nine times greater than before. Over a fifteen year period a purchased contador oficial post would generate approximately 3,811 pesos, while the same position as a salaried post would cost the crown 18,662 pesos.[5] Clearly, the Bourbons envisioned a massive improvement in revenue collection to offset net losses of this magnitude.

The majority of individuals hired by the porteño bureaucracy from 1776 on were true salaried employees, not individuals who had purchased their posts from the Royal Treasury.[6] The creation of a cadre of professional, salaried bureaucrats was posited on the belief that salaried bureaucrats would prove more interested in efficient administration and less apt to concentrate on reaping huge personal profits from government service. In addition, it was hoped that these new bureaucrats, because of their professional interest and training, would be more disinterested, more consistent, and less fractious in carrying out royal policy. Viceregal government was instituted in Buenos Aires by a Spanish crown that had since the middle of the eighteenth century been slowly but eagerly pursuing a policy of reestablishing royal authority at the expense of entrenched colonial elites.[7] In the case of this new capital city the task was made easier by the fact that, compared to other areas in Spanish America, no group or individual in the earlier bureaucracy was well entrenched or particularly powerful.

As agencies and numbers of bureaucrats grew, the crown sought to rationalize government, while applying an empirewide policy aimed at severely limiting sale of office and completely abolishing the sale of appointment to office. Preexisting institutions were incorporated into the new system, and their personnel either dismissed or placed on a salaried basis. The separate office of Protector de Indios, for example, was consolidated into the duties of the *fiscal* (crown attorney) of the Real Audiencia in 1784. Juan Gregorio de Zamudio, a local-born man who had held the appointment to this post since 1745 was repaid his purchase price and dismissed from royal service.[8] The post of factor of the Reales Cajas was also discontinued, but its purchaser was consolidated into royal service. José Zenzano, the *escribano de gobierno* (government notary), was accorded the same treatment; his position was incorporated into the viceregal Secretaría, and he was named *escribano mayor del virreynato* (chief notary of the viceroyalty).[9]

Although the "new" bureaucrat was the model, the crown could not dismiss all those who had purchased their posts at an earlier date. This was especially true in the Real Hacienda where Reales Cajas posts had been sold for considerable sums of money. Instead, a system by which the "old" bureaucrats were replaced by the "new" ones only upon retirement of the former was adopted. The reasons for adopting this more gradual policy were many. Wholesale replacement of the agency's leadership would have left the Reales Cajas bereft of staff members who could have provided administrative continuity. In addition, such a policy would have also involved unwanted expenditures of liquid capital, for the crown would have had to purchase these posts back from their owners. No doubt the crown was also aware that dismissals of "old" bureaucrats would have produced long legal proceedings, not unlike those following Bucareli's attempt to replace the chief Reales Cajas bureaucrats. Therefore, reorganization and expansion of the Reales Cajas did not produce an entirely new leadership. Men, such as Martín José de Altolaguirre, who had inherited purchased offices continued to work in the Reales Cajas long after reorganization, although they were eventually replaced by royal appointees.[10]

From the middle of the eighteenth century not only did the number and type of bureaucrat posted in Buenos Aires gradually begin to change, but the duties of those previously employed in the city were greatly expanded. María Josefa Aldao, widow of Juan Manuel de Labarden, the governor's *auditor de guerra* from 1761 to his death in 1777, presented the following testimony on her husband's duties:

> The duties and obligations of this job have grown notably since my husband took office. First came the Royal Cédula of 15 October 1754, which ordered that the Auditor de Guerra attend all meetings where sale and *composición* (title) of land was dealt with. Then he was obliged

to go to the meetings of the Junta de Real Hacienda, meetings that took place much more frequently than that in the past. He had to go to meetings dealing with the business of the Contaduría de Cuentas, and a royal order also obliged him to attend meetings of the military montepío. He was also required to attend all meetings of Temporalidades, including municipal, provincial, and appellate sessions. All of these duties have become part of the job of auditor de guerra, in addition to the infinite number of consultative, contentious, political, and government matters that he had to attend to. . . . He had to eventually employ an amanuense, especially for all the business dealings with Temporalidades. . . . He was also required to travel, like when he was called by the Governor Don Pedro de Cevallos upon his return from Misiones, to the siege and conquest of Côlonia da Sacramento . . . and later to help pacify the uprising in the city of Corrientes. . . .[11]

Government employment was clearly becoming a full-time job. By the 1760s the type of men who sought and were awarded posts as government officials changed markedly; no longer was government office purchased by a merchant seeking to diversify his experience or an exmerchant who had decided that bureaucracy was also a lucrative field. Although the change was not sudden, it was constant in all branches of the bureaucracy; increasingly, royal officials were chosen from among those who had prior government or military rather than commercial experience. In addition, the reforming zeal of Charles III and Charles IV changed the outward connections between the mercantile and the bureaucratic groups. Openly allowing government officials to use merchants as *fiadores* (bondsmen) was increasingly discouraged.[12] Close public friendships between bureaucrats and merchants became more circumspect. Public officials were admonished to be impartial and free of any compromising ties:

> Treasury employees will abstain in the future from accepting powers of attorney when paying out the salaries of third parties, or when paying delayed credits; neither will they treat with agents of communities or agents of private individuals, and they will be punished whenever it is discovered that in person, or through a third party, they have taken part in any treaty, contract, or agreement which is in any way related to the Royal Treasury.[13]

Government officials no doubt continued to engage in dubious but profitable deals with merchants, but much greater care was now taken to conceal these relationships from public view.

This change in the kind of men recruited into the bureaucracy occurred on all levels of the bureaucracy beginning gradually before 1777 and gaining strength after that date. Before the founding of the viceroyalty and the institution of the Ordenanza de Intendentes, for example, the fiscal bureaucracy of Buenos Aires had been small and depended on tax farming to actually collect many of its revenues. Posts such as *receptor de alcabala* (excise tax collector), *receptor del real derecho de sisa* (collector of the royal tax on internal trade), or *receptor del ramo de carretas* (collector of the wagon tax) were auctioned off to the highest bidder or, failing any interested party, assigned to a local citizen with the promise of a fixed salary. In general, those who served as tax farmers close to Buenos Aires, whether on a voluntary basis or not, tended to be local shopkeepers, retailers, and *estancieros* (ranch owners). These men, both Spaniards and porteños, were theoretically pure of blood, literate, and generally considered to be dependable, responsible citizens. Shopkeepers and lesser merchants welcomed the guaranteed income that these appointments gave them; in addition, although the posts brought sometimes onerous duties, the bookkeeping skills needed were not unlike those used in everyday commercial transactions. While these minor positions did not bring a great deal of influence or prestige to the shopkeepers, neither did they hinder those who sought local respectability and recognition.

In addition to other reform the government also sought to replace tax farmers with salaried bureaucrats. This change was not always easy to accomplish, especially when the tax farmers were prepared to fight for the loss of these lucrative contracts. Benito González de Rivadavia, for example, a local lawyer who had inherited one of the two perpetual town councilman positions and the posts of *depositario general* (municipal treasurer) and *juez de bienes de difuntos* (probate judge) of the Cabildo from his father-in-law, also served as diocesan treasurer of Santa Cruzada funds. In 1784, already employed as provisional asesor general of the Intendancy, he was appointed to the newly created Junta de Real Hacienda. Although no doubt an honor, the appointment was also a pretext to force Rivadavia to return the collection of Santa Cruzada monies to the civil bureaucracy. Rivadavia, nonetheless, was not willing to surrender quietly the private economic gains realized as treasurer of the Santa Cruzada in the name of more efficient fiscal management. Instead, he refused to turn over his office without just compensation, skillfully arguing that 12,000 pesos was a fair price for this position. Rivadavia's stubbornness allied to his knowledge of the laws of the realm convinced the viceroy that he had little alternative but to award this sum to him. Although Francisco Cabrera, the contador of the Real Hacienda, strongly argued against the payment, the viceroy's decision was approved in a Royal Order dated 5 November 1790.[14] The need to rationalize financial administration and place it firmly in the hands of the state could produce handsome profits for those "older" bureaucrats willing to fight to protect their investments.

Powers of tax collection were, nonetheless, gradually removed from local tax farmers and placed in the hands of the official bureaucracy. The creation of an organized bureaucracy did not necessarily mean the loss of a government position for all tax farmers; some were given the opportunity to become full-time members of the colonial bureaucracy, continuing their previceregal positions with a new or revised agency. Such was the case of Manuel de la Colina y Escudero, a *mercader* (retail merchant) who decided to forego commerce in order to join the Aduana bureaucracy as receptor del real derecho de sisa, a post he had previously held before the creation of the viceroyalty.[15] But recruiting ex-tax farmers into the bureaucracy was relatively rare. In general, especially at the lower ranks of bureaucracy, growing professionalization created employment opportunity for a host of "new" men.

Prior to the expansion and professionalization of the Buenos Aires bureaucracy, local bureaucrats had limited official responsibilities and therefore employed few ancillary personnel. Indeed, clerkships seem to have been filled by the same men who served as clerks in mercantile operations. Oficiales came and went, few serving in an agency for any length of time, for clerkship did not yield any professional advancement within an agency. Clerks recognized that continued employment in a government office would never lead to amassing the needed capital to eventually purchase a major government position.

The professionalization of the local bureaucracy transformed bureaucracy into a lifetime career. Most bureaucratic posts were henceforth to be awarded to those who had demonstrated the requisite level of education and who had entered the bureaucracy at a low rank, slowly advancing into the higher reaches of administration. A clear professional ladder with clear-cut lines of internal agency authority and advancement was established through which an eager, ambitious, and talented young man would theoretically make his way. As the crown strove to create a skilled professional group to administer the viceroyalty, training and prior service increasingly became the prerequisite of bureaucratic office.

The growing professionalization of the bureaucratic, although less than uniform, was consonant with the twin goals of Bourbon policy—centralization of royal authority and rationalization of government. A trained group of salaried government bureaucrats, men who had served the crown for long periods of time, apprenticing within bureaucracy and moving methodically through its ranks, would be creatures of royal policy, dependent on the crown for economic and professional survival. Men who had entered the bureaucracy in their youth as low-level clerks and who had spent years slowly inching up the ladder of the internal agency hierarchy would be obedient to their superiors and to the crown, for their very careers depended on this obedience. The slow progress through the bureaucratic ranks would produce agency leaders who were experienced and knowledgeable in the benefits of complying with royal policies instead of young men who had purchased their office and could rashly ignore its responsibilities. In theory at least the whims of fortune and economic power that had allowed the wealthy to purchase bureaucratic leadership were to be replaced with a system in which public office would go to the most talented and hard-working. Under these new laws of rational government, the bureaucrat of viceregal Buenos Aires could expect to be rewarded for years of excellent service, ability, skill, and dedication with career promotion.

In general, three different types of training were useful for entering a bureaucratic career. To aspire to the highest ranks in the Spanish colonial bureaucracy, that is appointment as governor, viceroy, or intendant, a prior career in some branch of the armed services was almost indispensable. Every viceroy and intendant named to serve in the Viceroyalty of Río de la Plata during the late eighteenth century had come into the bureaucracy from the military. The general Bourbon tendency to appoint military men, especially those who had some bureaucratic experience within the military, was strengthened in the Río de la Plata because of the overwhelming military and strategic importance of the zone. Clearly, the crown believed that tried and true military officers were most capable of giving and taking orders, of providing dynamic leadership, and of realizing the importance of military strategy in the governing of colonial areas.

For those seeking the highest offices of the realm who lacked military experience, still another type of training could be useful. This was a legal (or legal cum clerical) education. Legal training was the sine qua non of appointments to the Audiencias, the high courts whose power in theory could rival that of a viceory or governor. Lawyers were also employed in a host of lesser positions as asesores (legal counsel) in almost every major government agency. Several gifted young creoles were trained as lawyers, and it was perhaps at the rank of asesor that the participation of the American-born in the colonial bureaucracy was most important. It should be noted, however, that asesores were usually not permanent employees but were rather adjunct staff. As such their salaries were neither large nor assured. Several lawyers, therefore, supplemented their regular incomes with asesor posts or held several of these positions at the same time. Nevertheless, this type of government service could serve a lawyer as experience prior to an Audiencia post. Occasionally, men trained as lawyers came to head government agencies such as the Secretaría, but this was rare.

The last but most common training was the most vague. This was training for the *carrera de oficinas* (bureaucratic career). A young man seeking to enter the bureaucracy via this route had to have completed at least primary education and be knowledgeable in arithmetic, grammar, philosophy, and perhaps accounting. With this background he entered the bureaucracy as an apprentice, hoping to advance up the professional ladder. The most ambitious no doubt continued their education through reading of "works on ancient and modern politics, both Spanish and foreign; [works on] natural law and the law of nations, civil economy, treaties of commerce and navigation and universal history, and some [books] on travel and observations on the laws and customs of each nation." [16] Although there is some indication that entrance into apprenticeship became increasingly difficult during the later years of the viceroyalty, even at the beginning a civil servant could not advance without general knowledge of the laws, decrees, and forms involved in the daily business of his agency. In general, those who entered the carrera de oficinas hoped to rise at least to positions of middling importance and power in the local colonial bureaucracy.

As each agency was created or expanded, top- and middle-level personnel were usually transferred from agencies in Spain, Lima, or other parts of the empire to Buenos Aires. Because the Viceroyalty of La Plata had previously been part of the larger Viceroyalty of Peru, *limeño* (native of Lima) bureaucrats were preferred, for they were the most conversant with the major problems and responsibilities to be tackled in Buenos Aires. For example, five men, ranging from *contador mayor decano* (senior head accountant) to a *contador entretenido* (temporary accountant), were transferred to the Tribunal de Cuentas from the Lima agency and joined by only one Spanish-based bureaucrat. The same pattern can be seen in the naming of the first Audiencia judges five years later. Of the five Audiencia positions created in 1783, two (regent and oidor) were filled by men transferred from Lima (Manuel Antonio Arredondo y Pelegrín, who had previously been oidor there, and José Cabeza Enríquez, who had served as *alcalde de crimen* [junior judge]); two (both oidors) by men transferred from Charcas (Alonso González Perez, who had also been oidor in Charcas, and Sebastian de Velasco y Munguía, who had previously been a low-ranking official in the same court); and one (fiscal) by a man moved from Chile (José Márquez de la Plata, who served previously as fiscal de lo civil in Santiago).[17] While there seems to have been a preference for men with prior American experience in the Tribunal de Cuentas and the Audiencia, other agencies were staffed primarily with bureaucrats transferred from the Peninsula. Four of the top five officials in the Aduana were sent from Spain, as were the top three bureaucrats in the Real Renta de Tabaco.[18] For most of these bureaucrats transfer to Buenos Aires was accompanied by a substantial promotion in rank and a rise in salary. Such was the case of Francisco Ximénez de Mesa, promoted from head of the Alcaldia de Tabasco in New Spain to administrador general of the Buenos Aires Aduana and granted a salary of 2,500 pesos per year.

Even more positions were created on the lower level of bureaucracy, for all new and enlarged agencies need a complement of clerks and scribes to conduct the more tedious aspects of everyday business. Here, too, men were transferred from Lima, but more frequently local recruitment was used. For the few months while a new agency was being created or enlarged, several clerkships would open up, and eager candidates could apply for appointment. A host of young men, both Spanish-born and porteño, sought positions, but those generally favored for appointment had some degree of influence either in Spain or more likely in Buenos Aires. Especially prominent in filling these positions were young men who had arrived in Buenos Aires as part of the Cevallos military expedition.[19] New openings continued to be created under Viceroy Vértiz, although the pace slowed considerably, and again young men with some influence or connections received preference in appointment. By the beginning of the term of Viceroy Loreto, however, there was a marked decline in the creation of new openings. Prospective candidates for clerkships increasingly found themselves unable to enter directly into government service. Instead, they were increasingly channeled into a traineeship program where as meritorios they waited for an opening in the ranks. By 1783 virtually every agency in the platense viceroyalty had begun to accept eager young men as voluntary trainees, who persisted in their dream of someday holding a paid position in the bureaucracy.

Every department of viceregal bureaucracy, whether it was founded before or after 1776, was headed by an individual who held the title of *secretario* (secretary) or *director* (director). This is not to suggest that all of these positions were of equal importance, prestige, or salary, for there was a clear hierarchy within the colonial bureaucracy. The contador mayor of the Tribunal de Cuentas, for example, was a far more important position to hold than that of director of the Real Renta de Tabaco, for in addition to salary and jurisdictional competence, the latter reported to the former who in turn reported to the viceroy.

Below each agency head were a small group of middle-level bureaucrats, called either contadores mayores or contadores ordenadores. These men oversaw the work of the clerks or oficiales, the office staff of each agency department. In general, numbers of oficiales varied from agency to agency, but the overall tendency during the viceregal period, as we have seen, was for this staff to increase in size. In addition to a hierarchy among government agencies, there was a descending order established within each section of an individual agency. Clerkships, for example, ranged from oficial primero (head clerk) to fifth or sixth clerk. In theory a young bureaucrat entered government at the lowest level (i.e., sixth clerk) and then progressed up the status ladder, ending his career as oficial mayor (chief clerk) or better. The years served at each step were to bring increased knowledge and experience, preparing the young man for positions of greater responsibility.

Legal proof of holding a government position was awarded by a título or legal title to that job. Títulos themselves could be temporary, interim, substitute, or permanent, depending on the job under consideration; they were issued by departmental heads, viceroys, imperial officials in Spain, or in the case of an exalted few, by the crown itself. Department heads routinely had the power to name the lowest-level bureaucrats, the porteros and scribes. Most middle-level clerks and accountants were also named through a process of local appointment and royal confirmation; they were granted temporary títulos by the viceroy, títulos which were then approved and made permanent by the crown's ministers. Agency heads, on the other hand, were usually named directly by the crown.

There was also a difference in the official mechanism employed in naming individuals of differing ranks to their positions. In general, only the highest-ranking officials in any branch of the royal bureaucracy received their appointment by royal cédula; all others were appointed via a less formal royal order. In 1778, for example, when the expanded Real Renta del Tabaco was put into place in Buenos Aires, of the fourteen individuals confirmed of appointment to positions only four, the respective heads of the *dirección general* (general headquarters), *contaduría* (accounting), *tesorería* (treasury), and the *administración* (local administration) sections, received royal cédulas confirming their positions.[20]

A growing literature on the role of the bureaucrat, in part a reflection of the new emphasis on a national bureaucracy, had begun to appear in eighteenth-century Spain. These manuals, directed toward an enlarged professional corps of government employees, provided general instruction on how to best fulfill the duties of office. They are, of course, an invaluable insight into the ideals of bureaucratic conduct and performance.

One of the earliest of these manuals for bureaucrats, written to help clarify their responsibilities and obligations, was Antonio de Prado's *Reglas para oficiales de secretarias*.[21] As the title indicates the book was directed specifically at those who were employed in secretariats, but the general advice and attitude reflected therein was relevant to all bureaucrats. Most important was the clear conviction that being a government bureaucrat was a profession, a calling to which one could honorably dedicate one's life. The goal of this profession was a dual one: service to the king and to the public. One achieved excellence in the profession by combining science with experience, the major touchstones of the Enlightenment world view. The end result of successful service was usefulness to both king and public.

The call to provide good public service was stressed throughout Prado's manual, and the way in which it was phrased suggests that Spanish bureaucrats were well aware of the haughty treatment that the public in general and office seekers in particular had often received from bureaucrats and the need to remedy the problem.

> Charity and human sociability . . . demand . . . that we provide a courteous treatment for even the poorest office seeker, keeping in mind the ups-and-downs, and the inconveniences that as a general rule accompany all job hunting, even when the candidates have all those requirements that make them commendable for the position; because truthfully, it is still tyrannical when someone who cannot give any comfort to the individual who needs it instead promotes that individual's suffering, offering nothing more than the harshness of a rigid demeanor and hostile or even harmful words, depriving the poor candidate of the small comfort that he could receive in finding out, to the degree that it's permitted, something about his request. This defect is known to all of us, but we have not corrected it, doubtlessly because of the bad influence of our motives and the overweaning pride that having deprived the deserving of jobs gives us.[22]

Most of Prado's work served as an instruction sheet on how to draw up various types of correspondence that were under the jurisdiction of the Secretaría. Because of its practical nature, information on the form and purpose of *ordenes generales* (general regulations) *decretos de oficio* (resolutions), instrucciones, títulos, and cédulas is included, as is a description of the various types of *consultas* (written reports) that occupied the secretary. Instructions on the roles of various bureaucrats within the Secretaría were also contained in the manual, especially instructions for the oficiales primeros and subalternos. Everything was to be put in writing, and all work was to be approved by the oficial primero before a final draft was prepared.[23] Although oficiales spent most of their time drawing up official documents, care was also to be given to arranging papers and *legajos* (files) so that they were easily accessible when needed.[24] Indeed, much stress was given to the duties that should occupy oficiales when they were not busy with their "daily affairs." During such free moments they were to dust all legajos and then review old and new cases carefully, "as if they were trying to memorize them," so that if called upon to locate various papers, they would be able to put their hands on them immediately.[25] The ability to find documents easily was mentioned as the cause of "much joy"; the inability to locate papers had caused "most bothersome unpleasantness." [26] Clearly, the first state of affairs was preferable and within the control of the office personnel.

Prado also endorsed the idea of employing *entretenidos* (aspirants) in secretariat offices. These young men were to be used "according to their assiduity and their talent for the job." Entretenidos were viewed as being most useful in the task of registering *instrumentos* (documents), a task that many oficiales viewed as "most onerous and objectionable." [27] Entretenidos, those who "have been brought up among the papers," were to be preferred for appointment whenever an oficial opening occurred. According to Prado, many excellent secretarios had begun as unpaid trainees.[28]

Far more all-encompassing and more detailed in specific information was Angel Antonio Henry's *El oficinista instruido*. Published in Madrid in 1815 by Henry's son, the original manuscript was written several years earlier. Both the junior and senior Henrys drew on their experience in the Spanish postal administration to compose a manual and dictionary aimed at members of the government bureaucracy, regardless of their rank and years of service. The volume was addressed to "high-ranking ministers and ambassadors down to the last meritorio or entretenido" and aimed at improving the conduct of all civil servants.[29] Although we cannot judge the effect of Don Angel's treatise, the manuscript presents interesting insights into the behavior, temperament, and duties of the ideal civil servant. Information is also provided on professional requisites and entrance into government service. Above all, the goal of the book was to encourage the formation of a group of civil servants who combined "talent, knowledge, and study" in optimum proportions.

As mentioned above, the book deals with civil servants at all levels, and presents a helpful taxonomy of the general organization of the Spanish bureaucracy in the late eighteenth century. All civil servants were divided into six principal categories: secretarios, contadores, *administradores* (administrators), tesoreros, oficials and all other lower-ranking bureaucrats (including meritorios, escribientes, and porteros).[30] At least for the first four categories the taxonomy was based strictly on function, with each function demanding special talent. Secretarios were those who dealt with issues of policy and government affairs; as such the object of their concern was "everything that pertains to the management or governing of an agency." They were, therefore, concerned primarily with "writing or having written, forming or dictating all the paperwork related to governmental duties and attending to public and confidential matters in [their] office." Because of the very nature of their work, reserve and secrecy were much-valued personal qualities.[31] Contadores were responsible for "taking charge of all accounting of the income and outlays of the section of accounts to which they have been assigned" and therefore were to spend their time keeping a variety of ledgers in which the "incoming monies, expenditures, and funds on hand" were registered. In this branch of government absolute compliance with the established forms and rigorous cross-checking to see that all forms were signed by the competent authority was vital. Administradores had less specific duties, for they were charged with "administering, directing, governing, and guiding the fulfillment of the goals for which the administrative sections of the particular agency had been set up."[32] As such they combined the duties of secretaries and accountants and added the larger dimension of interaction with the public. Lastly, the treasurers handled actual disbursement of funds. In this branch of the bureaucracy, purity and integrity were stressed, as was a practical knowledge of the "management of funds, ledgers, papers, and government contracts."[33]

The popular conception of skills needed to enter the bureaucracy was a knowledge of writing and arithmetic (or more delicately stated "to write a good hand and make fine figures"). As a result, Henry complained, the bureaucracy was full of men who had come into offices and had maintained themselves there for years without understanding the workings of the organization nor its reason for existing.[34] These men were mindless drones, "subjected to formula and models" or, worse yet, incompetents who "capriciously scorned old ways of doing things simply because they were old."[35]

Luckily, there was also a group of bureaucrats who realized the complexity of their tasks, stood ever ready to learn from those in superior positions, and had the good sense and "judgement, steadiness, and skill" to make intelligent decisions. Instead of just knowing rudimentary arithmetic, these exemplary civil servants understood the principals of "good accounting and calculations." Instead of just having a fine hand, they also had acquaintance with Spanish grammar and spelling, knew perhaps a smattering of French and Latin, and were knowledgeable in "the art of thinking or logic." All talented oficials wrote in a "large and clear hand with ease and rapidity" but most important of all understood the principals of "debts and credits," the underlying basis of the Spanish administration.

For Henry as for Prado, the goal of all bureaucrats, indeed the goal of the entire bureaucracy itself, was twofold: to serve the state and the public. The most efficient manner to obtain these goals was through the use of an orderly, methodical system in which a bureaucrat or groups of bureaucrats were entrusted with specific tasks. This specialization revolved around the physical separation of different duties—in any agency the secretariat was to be apart from the contaduría, which in turn was separate from the tesorería. In addition, each transaction within a section was to be handled by an official (and his respective aides) charged with a specific mesa. Instinctly mixing duties and functions would result, warned Henry, in disorder and confusion, impeding an agency's ability to reach its goals.[36] Furthermore, only in these agencies in which each employee clearly knew his responsibilities could there be the necessary harmony on both the group and individual level.

Oficiales and subalternos composed the two lower-ranking groups of bureaucrats who labored beneath secretaríos, contadores, administradores, and tesoreros. The oficiales or clerks were salaried employees with a fixed position whose duties consisted of "providing immediate help and aid to the secretary or accountant and working under their orders and direction in everything having to do with the duties and affairs of the department."[37] Using the analogy of the human body, Henry described the relationship of the oficiales to those above them thusly: "The *jefes* (superiors) . . . are the head, the oficiales are the arms and hands."[38] Because they actually did much of the day-to-day work of their offices, oficiales were expected to be skilled, versed in their specific duties, punctual, neat, well organized, and ready to help. The oficiales in turn had still another group of workers below them, the subalternos (including escribientes, meritorios [also referred to as entretenidos], within the office itself, and *porteros y mozos de oficio* (doormen and office boys) at the door. These underlings were all charged with

> exactness in fulfilling all orders that are given to them, good performance in all duties that are entrusted to them, loyalty and keeping of office furnishings, care in their personal grooming and dress, punc-

tuality and willingness to serve superiors and bureaucrats in whatever they are instructed to do regarding their obligation, fetching and delivering all messages and papers that are brought to them, and helping in whatever has been prepared to them and they are able to do.[39]

Clerks were encouraged to "give pleasure" to their superiors while taking care to treat their *dependientes* (subordinates) well. They were instructed to keep their chiefs informed of all matters "but never voice opposition to their decisions."[40] Chiefs were nonetheless warned that subalternos were not their servants. Among themselves oficiales were to treat each other as "compañeros y amigos," with the highest-ranking oficial (oficial mayor) being especially careful to treat those below him with consideration and attention.[41] All oficiales, regardless of rank, were to be reserved and prudent. Respectful treatment of all coworkers was especially important for the continued existence of internal harmony, a most desirable quality for people who "have to always be together, seeing each other every day."[42] They were also charged with trying constantly to increase and perfect their knowledge of their tasks, paying attention to details as seemingly unimportant as "which is the best paper, the best pen, the best ink" while also understanding the theoretical implications of their duties. According to Henry, this knowledge and skill should be rewarded by promotion (oficiales were also to be ambitious), although in a less than perfect world Henry was forced to admit, "usually just antiquity and the habit of being in the office . . . is seen as being the same as accruing merit."[43] In addition to intelligence, oficiales needed "certain personal traits, like correct conduct and prudence, devotion to work, the desire to please others and to be useful, tractability and subordination, a sense of honor and good judgment, discernment, steadiness and skill, combined with a normal briskness and a prudent decision-making ability to keep work moving along, without getting confused or tied down." A good clerk, in short, was

> he who knows all these things, or tries to learn them as he should, without becoming vain or overly proud, because of the deep satisfaction and pleasure that he gets from being useful to the state in general, and to the office in which he works in particular. He who fulfills all his duties and obligations well and is aware of the true underlying order that should be present in everything relating to royal service and service to the public.[44]

Furthermore, this exemplary oficial was to have ambition, for "from the day he enters this rank, he should not content himself to remain among the ranks of the trainees, knowing at the end of thirty years just as much as he knew in school at the age of fourteen."[45]

Treatment of the general public was also one of the major duties of the oficiales in any office, and again high ideals for their behavior were delineated. "Treat the public attentively and courteously, with affability and moderation, willing to perform all those services and kind acts for them that are within your means and jurisdiction, but without compromising yourself or harming the king's interest."[46] Oficiales were enjoined to show respect not only in their daily dealings with the public but in their correspondence. Here a balance between "affectation of style" and "the extreme opposite . . . writing to all, even to their superiors, as if they were writing to their most intimate friends" was required. Above all, clerks were charged with treating all their office duties with dignity and decorum.

The last group of bureaucrats found in government offices were the meritorios, unpaid trainees who usually entered service in their early adolescence with the hope of eventual promotion to clerk or "even agency head, if luck brings them to this point."[47] Although the meritorio system had come under harsh criticism, Henry defended it vigorously. Others attacked the system because it had been abused; meritorios were overworked by the oficiales who routinely passed all their work to these young men. Acknowledging that this abuse should be stopped, Henry nevertheless saw the meritorio system as the most effective way of forming young men for the civil service. Under strict control of superiors who would control the "indiscretion, levity, and general inconsiderateness of youth," the system's merits included the fact that it saved the king from paying salaries to those who were not yet productive workers; it provided a way of acquiring "judgment and discretion, knowledge and good principles"; and because they were anxious to impress their superiors, it produced work of a high quality. Furthermore, Henry believed that in general, those who had entered government service through this route had become excellent clerks, in part because they had been trained "since childhood, the age at which everything makes a stronger and more durable impression."[48] Childhood was, furthermore, the right season to learn and to work.

In order to benefit from this period of training, a relationship akin to that of a father to his son had to be created between the regular government bureaucrats and the meritorio. In return for their protection the meritorios were to demonstrate to their superiors that they were capable of "blind obedience, respect, flexibleness, dedication and love for their job, continuous help, the greatest amount of care, cleanliness and curiosity for what they are doing, few distractions, great discretion, and enormous amounts of reserve and secrecy." Indeed because of their youth, it should be easier to train them "from the very beginning to become accustomed to displaying regular conduct, both in the office and outside, correct procedure, civility, and to be a model for the whole world."[49] Meritorios had always to be aware that receiving a regular appointment was not automatic, that to receive a salary one had to truly deserve it, and that any agency was free to prefer someone who was not a meritorio but who showed natural capacity and good conduct over them for promotion.[50]

While published manuals provided general advice on the performance of various bureaucratic posts, specific internal instructions or reglamentos carried not only detailed information on the duties of government agencies, but also on the day-to-day work load of the bureaucrats employed therein. Part of the plan to rationalize the colonial bureaucracy, these reglamentos codified each agency's guidelines for training, conduct, personnel reports, and promotion. To create and perpetuate a loyal corps of well-trained bureaucrats, all agencies were to provide on-the-job training and opportunity for advancement up the bureaucratic ladders. The reglamento also outlined the responsibilities of each bureaucrat and detailed general office conduct. Little of the working of the government agencies was to be on an ad hoc basis. Instead, minute regulations, drawn up to govern each agency, were to be followed by all concerned.

Procedures established for all agencies were similar. An in-depth look at the reglamento of the Tribunal de Cuentas will serve as an example of the training, duties, and professional lives of rank-and-file government officials.

With the exception of the doorman, who was not in line for advancement within the Tribunal, the agency's clerks were to be rotated to a different department every two years.[51] The aim of this rotation was twofold— to better determine which clerks were most competent and to give each oficial the opportunity to become familiar with a full-range of the Tribunal's work. Underlying this training system was the belief that the agency was "the most appropriate seminary to develop useful subjects for the ministerial career." [52] To further aid in the training of these future civil servants, the contador was charged with "inspiring, always in everyone, not only the desire to carry out their respective duties, but also the honorable ambition to acquire as much training as they can to achieve a complete knowledge of the Tribunal." [53] Because "nothing is usually more powerful than the good example of superiors," the contadores were instructed to place their desks so that they could observe all the activities of the clerks under their supervision and in turn be observed by these aides. The contador was also to make sure that the oficiales came to work every day, dressed in a manner befitting their importance, and treated the public in a manner that would lead to "the widespread estimation of all people and a universal appreciation of their services."

Although the contador was to divide the clerks into departments as outlined by the intendant, he could, after consultation with the intendant, temporarily switch an individual from one department to another because of work load. Special care was to be taken, when moving a clerk from one department to another, to make sure that all documents had been returned to their proper place. In addition, no clerk working in one department was to extract papers from another section without asking permission from the chief clerk and leaving a written note explaining what had been moved. The problem of missing documents was clearly a serious one, and the intendant reminded the Tribunal staff that "much trouble and loss of time occurs when we cannot find what we need." [54] To the same end of maintaining some sort of clerical order, all employees were to carefully file their papers before leaving the office, thus avoiding the doorman's inadvertently moving documents or spilling ink on them.

The oficiales primeros of each department, as the heads of their respective sections, were to oversee that section, reporting periodically to the contador mayor. By the fifteenth of January each section head was to present a written report outlining the status of the accounts under his care. The contador, in turn, was to use this information to present an annual report of the Tribunal's work to the intendant. The contador was also to include in his annual report a secret report on the "conduct, application, and hard work" of each clerk, information that would later be entered into the *libro de méritos y servicos* (personnel records). [55] These progress reports were to be consulted before deciding to promote an oficial whenever a vacancy occurred. Candidates put forward for promotion by the contador mayor (three candidates were usually suggested for each opening) were to be those individuals deemed most deserving because of talent and hard work, not those with most seniority or highest rank. So strongly did the intendant believe in the promotion of the most capable that he stressed that "no oficial should think that he has the right to be promoted solely on the basis of seniority."[56]

Although promotion was theoretically to be on merit, a clerk's general demeanor weighed heavily in a favorable report. Among specific prohibitions oficiales were forbidden to chew tobacco during office hours, for this forced them to "get up from their desks at any moment, leaving this work unattended."[57] Personal toilette, while neat and clean, was not to approach "profusion"; lack of moderation of any type was considered odious.

The contador, in consultation with his most trusted oficial mayor, was also to undertake spot checks of all work, looking for omission or delays. If such a problem were discovered, the contador was to speak privately to the oficial in question. Those who failed to mend their ways after one warning were to be reported to the intendant who could make the second correction "more public." The contador and the three oficiales mayores were also charged with generally overseeing all the Tribunal's operations and with making sure that everything was done with "method and regularity."[58] It was most important to avoid any disputes between Tribunal employees; personal quarrels were to be kept to a minimum, and employees were encouraged to treat each other as friends, both in and out of the office. Only through harmonious dealings with each other could one preserve one's "honor, good public opinion, and fortune." Lack of rancor among bureaucrats also made it easier for any agency to accomplish its missions.

Another interesting set of rules was contained in the Ordenanzas de Aduana drawn up by Intendant Manuel Ignacio Fernández in February 1779.[59] This reglamento spelled out how ships were to land and be loaded and unloaded in Buenos Aires and Montevideo, the collection of Aduana duties and alcabala taxes, and the role of all members of the Aduana bureaucracy in fulfilling these tasks. It also detailed what books were to be kept by whom and the manner in which frequently adjusted accounts were to be passed on to the Buenos Aires superintendent. It included as well admonitions to incumbents in positions deemed to be most crucial to the successful operation of the Aduana. For example, the position of *vista,* a post full of lucrative pitfalls, was described in the following words:

There is no doubt that the job of vista should be considered to be one of the most sensitive ones in the Aduana, and therefore should only be held by a person who has great knowledge about commerce and is of known loyalty. He will have to swear to serve the office well and faithfully in front of the superintendent, with the understanding that if any case of fraud or misconduct is found against him, he will be punished in an exemplary fashion, and all his property will be confiscated by the Royal Treasury.[60]

Still another reglamento, the *reglamento de los dependientes* (staff rules) of the treasury of the Royal Hacienda, submitted in 1779, detailed the salary and working conditions of its six oficiales.[61] All clerks were to work seven hours per day. The only holidays granted these men were to be those designated "days of strict observance." (Men employed in agencies concerned with the administration of justice also enjoyed "Tribunal holidays," which were specifically forbidden for these treasury bureaucrats.) Furthermore, oficiales were to answer all questions, even those that were impertinent, with "kindness, care, and good manners," being careful to deal with the public in a manner that would not discredit their office. All oficiales were to be dressed during office hours in "the most decent dress," both to preserve their own integrity and as a sign of respect for the public. Failure to obey the treasurer, their immediate chief, or to "inspire in their fellow workers the necessary dedication to work in order to complete, in the shortest time possible, the backlog of work" could result in dismissal by the intendant. When a vacancy occurred, the treasurer was to suggest candidates to the intendant, who in turn undertook an official inquiry as to the conduct and application of those employed as oficiales and meritorios. The individual named to the vacant position was to be the most deserving candidate, he who had displayed the greatest degree of talent, loyalty, and usefulness to the crown, not always he who had the longest length of service.

Regardless of government regulations and published manuals, the actual conduct of government officials in Buenos Aires occasionally seems to have fallen short of the ideal. In 1789 the demeanor of the junior officers of the Tribunal de Cuentas was described as follows: "the scandalous conduct of most of the bureaucrats consists of standing around talking to each other and smoking in all of their offices. They even stand around and smoke in the Archive, running the risk that some spark from the end of their cigarettes, given the frequent winds that blow up in this country, will catch some of their papers on fire without their even knowing about it."[62] But even when officials were fined for "disrespect and lack of subordination," "lack of obedience and respect, setting a bad example, and scandalizing everyone else," they usually continued to work in the same office, rarely being demoted or removed.[63]

Even in agencies not plagued by problems of conduct, the rational division of work, so carefully spelled out in reglamentos and other internal documents, was rarely the reality. Three years after his agency was set up the administrator of the Aduana described the actual duties of his staff as follows:

> The chief clerk of the accounting section is in charge of weekly and monthly statements and is at the present time also filling the post of head accountant because of the latter's temporary indisposition . . . the chief clerk of the treasury section is not doing this job at all, but is rather employed full time in the accounting section. Speaking frankly, he is truly the accountant. As he is in charge of the principal account book, he liquidates all the accounts, and he checks all vouchers. . . . The supernumerary, who has a very large handwriting, has been working on the reference guidebook, without physically being able to undertake anything else. Another supernumerary is busy with the daily permit clearances and returning permits and is helped in these duties by a salaryless trainee who is also in charge of keeping the official registry up-to-date and writing whatever the accountant gives him. The second clerk in the treasury section has been assigned, since the beginning of this year, along with the cashier of the same section, with managing the cash, pressing for payment, transferring funds to the treasury, and keeping internal accounts. The second oficial has also been in charge of the principal treasury book and of taking care of whatever else comes up. Still another supernumerary, who has beautiful handwriting and the most promise of any clerk employed in the Aduana, has been involved in all the emergency requests involved in setting up this agency. In addition, no one else has touched the treasury account books of 1779 and 1780. . . . Finally, another unpaid trainee is working with me, usefully employed in copying whatever has to be done and is now busy finishing up a copy of the accounts of 1780.[64]

After 1777 there were several ways in which one could receive appointment to a government agency. Initially, during the years when agencies were being expanded from their earlier and smaller form to their viceregal form, posts were filled by bureaucrats drafted from the same agency in other parts of the empire and by men in other government agencies in Buenos Aires. At the time the viceroyalty was founded the meritorio system was put into place to train a group of young men who would theoretically move into lower-ranking bureaucratic positions as men in lower positions advanced up the agency's hierarchy.[65] The system of internal promotion within an agency did not replace drafting of bureaucrats from other agencies but rather existed side by side with it. Especially at the higher ranks of bureaucracy the crown usually preferred to appoint from outside the agency; the contadores mayores of the Tribunal de Cuentas, for example, were usually men who had long service in other branches of government such as the Aduana or the Real Renta de Tabaco. In addition, not all low-ranking oficiales had come up through the meritorio system; young men, usually newly arrived from Spain, were sometimes able to transfer their past service to the crown or their connections into appointments as fourth, fifth, or sixth clerks, receiving preference over meritorios who had been waiting for two or three years for an official appointment to become available.

The continuation of a variety of recruitment patterns can be seen by examining the case histories of three oficiales who joined the Tribunal de Cuentas between 1790 and 1795. One man, Victorino de la Fuente, moved to the post of archivero after four years as meritorio in the Tribunal; another, Manuel Medrano, son of a high-ranking bureaucrat in the Reales Cajas, was named archivero after serving eight and a half years as meritorio first in the Real Hacienda and then in the Real Renta de Tabaco; the third, Bernardo Ledesma, was recruited for the Buenos Aires Tribunal by the viceroy after spending almost nine years as an oficial in the Montevideo Aduana.

Even after the creation of a more professionalized bureaucracy under the viceroyalty, those with exceptional influence at court could always receive preferential treatment in appointment and promotion. The most frequently stated reason for this treatment was *servicios contrahidos*, usually outstanding service given the crown by the father of the aspiring bureaucrat. In addition, extreme hardship could also be cited in pressing one's case, for one of the roles of the king was to provide justice to those deserving citizens whom fate had treated badly. But hardship never supplanted extraordinary service as the reason for special royal consideration.

Two examples of the same phenomenon, separated by more than eighty years, serve to demonstrate the lasting value of personal influence but also suggest that personal pleadings even by the most powerful local citizens were of decreasing value in achieving high office once bureaucratic professionalization took hold. In 1716 Alonso de Arze y Arcos was named contador oficial real futurario of the Buenos Aires Reales Cajas, an important position in the small imperial bureaucracy then in place in the city. Alonso, age twelve, was the son of the late Coronel Don Alonso de Arce y Soria, a military man who had served the crown for forty years in Flanders and America. The elder Arce had been named governor and captain general of Buenos Aires in 1714, after paying 19,000 pesos to the Royal Treasury, but had died within four months and three days of taking office. His widow then successfully appealed to the crown for her son's appointment citing "the immensely helpless situation in which I find myself . . . with four children and two grandchildren, without any type of income whatsoever that could help maintain us, 2,000 leagues away from our homeland, and with the legal obligation to repay 16,000 pesos in debts that my husband undertook in order to pay 19,000 pesos to the Royal Treasury."[66] Doña Claudia's plight and the desire to prevent her defaulting on these large debts in conjunction with her late husband's "celebrated service to the crown" won an important bureaucratic position for her son.

In 1797 Tomás Antonio Romero, loyal servant to whom the crown was indebted for his role as *asentista para la conducción de azogues* (official contractor for the shipment of mercury) (1779–1789), attempted to use his personal connection to have his son, José María, named *comisario de guerra*. Although Romero was a merchant rather than a high-ranking military officer, there can be no doubt of his influence both in Buenos Aires and Spain.[67] Nevertheless, the best appointment that he could wrangle because of "services undertaken to the benefit of the Royal Treasury" was that of oficial supernumerario (temporary clerk) in the local Reales Cajas.[68]

The porteño elite believed firmly that the king should dispense individual justice by awarding bureaucratic posts, even though this attitude clashed with the new royal goal of bureaucratic professionalism. Scores of requests for preferential placement in a bureaucratic post, no matter how minor the position, were sent to the Spanish crown by the wives and sons of those who had served the crown or by loyal citizens down on their luck. Some requests met with a positive reply; others were turned down, but aspirants waited several years before receiving a definite reply. Thus the widow Isabel María de Castro y Herrera, whose husband had "suffered many setbacks in the Peruvian uprising including losing his life in the service of the king," requested that her son be helped in finding employment in "the profession of letters." [69] She received a favorable reply within two years, a royal order that directed the viceroy "to help this family, giving their oldest son a position proportionate with his circumstances and aptitude, or proposing him for some job when it becomes open so that he can enjoy a literary career." But as no immediate opening was in sight, Isabel de Castro and her son were forced to wait several more years for their much needed assistance.

A similar request was sent to the visitador general of the Real Hacienda, Diego de Vega, in 1804, this time from a young man named Miguel Tagle y Velasco. Tagle, the son of Don Pedro de Tagle and Doña Ignacia Velasco, told a sad tale, for his father, "many years ago, left this capital for the imperial city of Potosí to undertake some business, but since then we have had no word as to his whereabouts." Doña Ignacia and children were abandoned, and "like a true widow," she was left with "the heavy burden of having to feed and dress, only with the help of her own meager resources, not only her son, but two other daughters." Realizing her limitations but aware of her race and social position, Doña Ignacia had encouraged her son to study for a "career as a public notary," but Miguel had soon found that employment as a lowly escribiente in the office of a public escribano "produced so little in the way of income that instead of helping my mother, I have done nothing but waste my time." Now, at age twenty he hoped that the visitador, who was engaged in restructuring the Royal Exchequer office, would be able to find some "future with a pen paying an adequate salary" for him, but Vega's reply dissuaded him of any such possibility. [70] Like Tagle, most of those who hoped to receive preferential placement ended up disillusioned, for this placement was rarely awarded.

Porteños also requested appointment to government positions in order to redress admitted official mistakes (errors made, of course, by the king's agents and never by the king himself). But even when the government admitted that a citizen had been abused or otherwise treated unfairly, restitution was painfully slow in coming. Miguel Garcia de Tagle (no relation to the Tagle mentioned above), a porteño merchant, was kept waiting twenty-three years as he petitioned the court for a government appointment. Tagle had been the victim of Governor Francisco Bucareli's ire when in 1767 the governor, believing that Tagle was protecting Jesuit interests, arrested him, embargoed his property, and sentenced him to die.[71] Although he fled to a church haven and eventually evaded Bucareli's order, Tagle suffered greatly from these "unjust actions." His "business interests, his home, and his family" as well as his good name were all damaged, although a Royal Order of 19 February 1775 declared him to be innocent. That year Tagle began a long quest for appointment to a government post that would allow him to recoup his financial losses, a quest marked by repeated frustration but crowned by eventual success.

Tagle, although he had suffered financial setbacks because of the Bucareli episode, was still a man with some important friends and at least local influence. He first attempted to use his connections to request a royal license for transporting the *situados* (state subsidies) of Buenos Aires province, accompanying his request with a letter of recommendation from Eugenio Lerdo de Tejada, an important local merchant. Tagle was not chosen. Undeterred, Tagle continued to plead his case to the crown and in August 1781 was rewarded with a royal order directed to the Buenos Aires superintendente instructing that "a job corresponding to his aptitude and accomplishments" be found for Tagle in "compensation for his loss of fortune." No such job materialized, and Tagle again turned to the crown. In March 1790 another royal order sent to the viceroy requested that Tagle be given the post of administrator of the Thirty Indian Missions of Uruguay y Paraná. He waited patiently for four years for this position to be vacated by the incumbent, Diego Casero, but when Casero finally resigned, Tagle was shocked to find that Manuel de Cerro, not he, had been named to the job by the viceroy. Tagle again sent a petition to the crown, this one more bitter and desperate than those that had preceded it. Shortly after this letter was sent, Tagle finally received word that he had been named alguacil mayor of the Buenos Aires Audiencia. Royal confirmation of his título made clear that this was a special appointment, made to satisfy Tagle's claims for justice.[72] His Gracious Majesty was still willing to dispense special favors, but they were increasingly slow in coming, in part because they flew in the face of the Bourbon campaign to professionalize the bureaucracy.

The crown was hesitant to issue royal orders calling for placement in the bureaucracy through special appointment. Moreover, even people like Tagle who had successfully petitioned for a royal order giving them preference in appointment soon found out that this order was far from a guarantee of employment. In 1790, responding to the request for a list of "subjects in this district who are waiting with royal orders to be placed in a government job," Viceroy Arredondo forwarded a list of sixteen names to the secretary of the Indies.[73] Two of these men had been waiting for a post to open up since 1778.

In addition to special pleading to the crown, occasionally one could receive official appointment through the influence of powerful local bureaucrats. This was especially effective if the local bureaucrat not only had good connections in court but was willing to "go to bat" for those he believed worthy of appointment and promotion. Such a man was Pedro de Cevallos, who served as governor of Buenos Aires from 1756 to 1766 and as the first viceroy from 1777 to 1778. In 1763, for example, Cevallos used his influence to point out the mérito (merit) of Juan de Bustinaga and get Bustinaga appointed contador oficial real of the Buenos Aires Reales Cajas.[74] But increasingly, with the professionalization of the bureaucracy and the growing supply of capable bureaucratic hopefuls, this type of political pressure became more difficult for even the viceroy to exercise.

Another frequently employed method of recruitment into the colonial bureaucracy was serving in the personal retinue of an important official, such as an agency director or, better still, a viceroy.[75] At the end of the eighteenth century viceroys were still accompanied by trains of personal servants, including pages, lackeys, chaplains, and private advisors. While some of these individuals were family members, parientes, others were young men recruited in the cities of southern Spain shortly before sailing or in America. While in the viceroy's household, some of these men received special assignments that eventually allowed them to join the bureaucratic payroll in a temporary or permanent capacity.[76] Others worked as pages while at the same time being enrolled as meritorios in government agencies. This arrangement allowed them to earn some income while receiving the training necessary for official appointment. Ideally, by the time a viceroy had been replaced, members of his retinue would have successfully ensconced themselves in the lower rungs of the regular bureaucracy. But increasingly, as bureaucratic promotion slowed down in all agencies and the numbers of meritorio posts were limited or were sought by creoles, this form of bureaucratic recruitment proved to be less successful. In 1784 the Marqués de Loreto brought four pages with him from Spain to Buenos Aires. Three of them, Lorenzo Fuentes, Antonio González, and Bernardo Sánchez, succeeded in gaining meritorio appointments, but by the time of Loreto's departure in 1789 not one had achieved a regular appointment. Only in 1793 would Fuentes finally receive a regular position as *oficial tercero* (third clerk) in the Secretaría.

Nonetheless, for those desperate to enter the bureaucracy, official debts for prior service could sometimes evoke a positive response. The aforementioned Bernardo Sánchez, for example, had undertaken "some important commissions and requests" for the secretary of the La Coruña Intendancy in 1778 before becoming Loreto's page. Fifteen years later, Bernardo, now age sixty-six, was able to use proof of his La Coruña deeds to enter the Buenos Aires Real Renta de Tabaco as *oficial interventor de fábricas* (production auditor) and *auxiliar* (assistant) in the general accounting office. Although earning only 300 pesos per year, Sánchez received appointment in spite of rather unimpressive credentials (scant bureaucratic service or training) and kept the appointment even though his superiors viewed his work as substandard ("aptitude—limited; talent—the same; conduct—good; application—the same").[77]

While ambitious young men could and did join in the train of government bureaucrats coming from Spain in the hopes of advancing their careers, it was always more advantageous to be a blood relative of a bureaucrat. The careers of José Antonio de Bedoya and José Joaquín Urdaneta demonstrate this truism. In the 1778 census of Buenos Aires, Don Francisco Urdaneta, the newly arrived *contador general* (chief accountant) of the Real Renta de Tabaco, is listed as residing on the Calle de San José. Urdaneta, a forty-three-year-old recent widower, had come to the city with his six-year-old son, José Joaquín, and with two dependientes, José Antonio de Bedoya, age sixteen, and Juan Alirruciaga, age eighteen. In addition, two white male servants (most unusual for Buenos Aires, but probably brought from Spain) and two black male slaves completed the Urdaneta household.[78]

According to Bedoya's testimony, not only had he arrived with Urdaneta in 1778, but "from the very moment that we disembarked in Montevideo, and the state tobacco agency was established in that port and in Buenos Aires, I have worked incessantly in the general accounting division." Although Bedoya was not paid for his service (he was classified as a meritorio), he spent one-and-one-half years in Buenos Aires before being appointed to the Córdoba Renta de Tabaco as an oficial. After four years in Córdoba, Bedoya became ill ("gravely sick in the chest, spitting up blood through the mouth") and was sent to Montevideo for two months to recover.[79] Returning to the other side of the river, Bedoya was named *teniente visitador* (assistant inspector) in Córdoba, a post he held for eight-and-a-half years, and was then promoted to visitador. In these positions Bedoya was required to travel widely in the interior of the country, "during summer in the fierce heat of the sun and the continuous rains, during winter in the harsh cold of the mountains." So arduous was the travel that Bedoya's health suffered once again (this time the problem was hemorrhoids), and he was finally forced to request that he be relieved of "the task of riding around this district."

By 1799 Bedoya had served the crown for twenty-one years. He had traveled through the interior (Córdoba, Las Peñas, Tras la Sierra, Tulumba, and Santa Rosa) setting up more than eighty government tobacco shops (*estanquillos*), had been in charge of dismantling the Real Renta de Tabaco branch in Santiago del Estero, and had also overseen all operations carried out in the tobacco warehouse in Córdoba. He now petitioned the crown to be named administrador of the Córdoba Real Renta de Tabaco, a position vacated by the death of Rafael María Castellano. In addition to the desire for career advancement and his health problem, Bedoya was tired of the travel that kept him from his family for up to nine months at a time. As the father of nine children, he also hoped to improve his 700 pesos per year salary. (In spite of his progeny and his small earnings, Bedoya pointed out in his petition that he had contributed 100 pesos per year during the present war with France, "proof of his loyalty and love of his sovereign.") For Bedoya, in spite of his personal contact with Francisco Urdaneta, twenty-one years of service had only brought him to a low-ranking and low-paying job.

While Bedoya was struggling to survive in the provincial branch of the Real Rentas de Tabaco, his patron, Urdaneta, was progressing in Buenos Aires. By 1788 he was named *director general* (director-general) of the Real Renta de Tabaco, replacing Pedro Dionisio de Gálvez, who had been promoted to contador mayor of the Tribunal de Cuentas in Lima.[80] Two years later Urdaneta was successful in his request that he also be granted the same honors as members of the Tribunal de Cuentas of Castile.[81] Urdaneta's promotion had also produced a change in his marital status. On 16 February 1789 the director general de tabacos, born fifty-four years earlier in Maracaibo, took a second wife, María Angela González de Rivadavia, a native of Monfort de Lemus, Galicia, and niece of the prominent local jurist Benito González de Rivadavia. Among the several witnesses at this wedding were Joaquin de Yoldi, treasurer of the Real Renta de Tabaco, and Rufino de Cárdenas, administrador of the agency.[82] During the next six years María Angela bore Urdaneta one son and one daughter; at the time of his death in December 1794 she was again pregnant; another daughter was born six months later.

More interesting is the professional advancement experienced by José Joaquín, Urdaneta's son by his first marriage, for it provides an example of how parental influence could help move a young man in a bureaucrat career. In 1784 José Joaquín, age twelve, was sent to study in Spain. Returning in 1787 at age fifteen, he entered the contaduria section of the Real Renta de Tabaco as an unpaid meritorio. Although his father was the chief of this division at the time, it was not unheard of for a young man to serve as meritorio in the same agency that employed his father. To this point José Joaquín's career was not unlike that of Bedoya. But after only eight months and twenty days of meritorio service, José Joaquín, age sixteen, was promoted to the post of oficial segundo in the general administration section of the tobacco agency. Less than one-and-a-half years later, José Joaquín, now eighteen years old, was advanced to oficial primero of the same section. Unfortunately, his father's influence had limits, and at the time of the older man's death, José Joaquín was still in the same position. But even more interesting is the fact that after his father's death, José Joaquín never received any promotion within the local bureaucracy.[83]

Recruitment into the higher echelons of the judicial branch of government, especially into the Audiencia or high court, differed in several important respects from recruitment into the rest of the viceregal administration. While Audiencia regents, oidores, and fiscales earned salaries comparable to those of the various departmental administradores and directores, Audiencia judges, because of their legal training and the sanctity that surrounded this high court, enjoyed a level of prestige close to that of the viceroy himself. Unlike other offices, the judgeships were filled directly from Spain, although viceroys could use their position to influence the nomination of an asesor to an Audiencia post in another jurisdiction.

Table 4.1   Birthplace by Audiencia Rank of All Appointments to Audiencia of
Buenos Aires, 1783–1813

Rank	Born in			Total
	Spain	Buenos Aires	New World	
Regent	4 (1)*	0	0	5
Oidor	15 (1)*	2*	2 (1)*	21
Fiscal	5	1*	1 (2)*	9
	26	3	6	35

*Appointment made after Independence.
Source: Burkholder and Chandler, From Impotence to Authority: The Spanish Crown and the American Audiencias, 1687–1808 (Columbia, Mo., 1977), app. x, 190–91.

While other bureaucrats might be related to Spanish officials and might use court influence to obtain positions in Buenos Aires, none of the judges were related to other civilian, military, or ecclesiastical officials in the colony.

Legal training was always an essential prerequisite for Audiencia appointment, although degrees beyond that of bachiller (bachelor) were not required. Having completed university education, a candidate applied to the Spanish government for an Audiencia position, presenting a relación de méritos (résumé) that outlined his qualifications to assume the post.[84] Some applicants had prior experience as university teachers or had practiced law in Spain; others seemed to have entered the high court system directly. The usual first appointment was to a minor Audiencia (Charcas, Caracas, or Buenos Aires) as fiscal. After serving successfully in this first position, an individual could hope to progress up the judicial ladder, from fiscal del crimen (prosecuting attorney in criminal cases) to fiscal de lo civil to oidor and finally to regent, while also moving to different courts. If one were to construct a scale of New World Audiencia positions, they would run from fiscal del crimen in Charcas to regent of Mexico City; Buenos Aires appointments would no doubt be somewhere in the intermediate to low-intermediate range. But while lacking prestige within the entire panorama of Audiencia positions, to the local inhabitants of Buenos Aires an Audiencia post was a very important one indeed.

From 1783, the year of its creation, to 1813, the year of its dissolution, thirty-five appointments were made to the Buenos Aires Audiencia; these thirty-five appointments were given to thirty-two different individuals. (Five regents, twenty-one oidores, three fiscales, four fiscales del crimen, one fiscal de lo civil and one fiscal de hacienda were appointed during this thirty-year period.) Twelve of these appointments were made to men who never actually served on the local Audiencia, four because they chose more promising appointments that were made before they arrived in Buenos Aires and eight because their appointments were made after Independence had become effective in the area.

Of the first group of men named to the Buenos Aires Audiencia in 1783, two of the four oidores were high court novices, never having served on an Audiencia in either Spain or the New World.[85] Of those who would serve the court in the following fifteen years, another ten appointments would be given to new recruits, a clear reflection of the low rank of the Buenos Aires court within the Hispanic world. Yet not one of these entry positions was given to a porteño, although the city had a healthy population of lawyers, nor to an American-born. The first American-born man appointed to the Audiencia in 1798 was transferred to Quito before he arrived in Buenos Aires. The first creole actually to serve on the Buenos Aires high court was Manuel Dionisio de Velazco y Camberos, a native of Charcas, named to the post of oidor in 1804. This pattern reflects the success of the Spanish crown and its ministers of the Indies in reestablishing strong central control over the Audiencia.[86] Only in 1811 did the Spanish crown modify this policy and appoint three porteño lawyers to Audiencia posts; neither these men nor three of the other Americans named ever served because their appointments were made after Independence (see table 4.1).[87]

By the time the Audiencia of Buenos Aires was refounded (1783), the Spanish crown was pursuing a policy that systematically discriminated against creoles who sought appointment as local Audiencia judges.[88] But although denied success in their quest for high position in the local Audiencia, nomination to other Audiencias was not totally outside of the possibilities of porteño-born lawyers. José Pablo Conti, for example, after serving as *teniente asesor* (assistant counselor) in Charcas, was named oidor of the Charcas Audiencia in 1794. Much like the case of Peru,[89] it was not the appointment of creoles to the high court as much as the appointment of creoles to the high court in the district of their birth that the late Bourbon Kings opposed. For those who combined education, connections, luck, and ambition, appointment to crown attorneyships (*fiscalias*) or even to an oidor post could be the eventual reward.

The case of Manuel Martínez de Mansilla is a good example of how far a young man of talent and ambition could go, even if he began life in humble circumstances. Manuel was born in Buenos Aires on 22 September 1771 to Francisco Martínez, a Spanish-born provisions-dealer (*tratante*), and his porteña wife Juana Mansilla. Seven years later the servantless family could be found living in one of the more rural districts of the city.[90] Manuel received his secondary education in the local Colegio de San Carlos, but after six years of studying philosophy and theology in Buenos Aires the young man was sent to Spain to continue his education. In 1790 Manuel, age nineteen, enrolled at the University of Santiago. After three years of civil law and two of *sagrados canones* (sacred canons), Manuel was awarded a degree as bachiller in civil law and admitted to the *academia de ambos derechos* (practice of civil and church law) of the same university. The next two-and-a-half years were spent in establishing a minor career as a faculty member at the university and fulfilling the required two years of practice before entry into the bar. In 1797, shortly after receiving his titulo as *abogado en el consejo real* (lawyer licensed to practice in royal council), Manuel petitioned the crown for "permission to apply for a post of *corregidor* (district magistrate) or any other legal position filled by the crown." The following year, 1798, he was named *asesor y auditor de guerra* (legal adviser for civil and military affairs) of the Intendancy of Maracaibo in the Viceroyalty of New Granada. Here luck intervened, for in May 1799 an attempted uprising headed by sailors from two French ships was put down. Martínez, as asesor, took a leading role in prosecuting the hapless Frenchmen and was rewarded in 1804 with an appointment at age thirty-three as fiscal de crimen in the Real Audiencia of Santa Fé. For the next seven years, until the Bogotá revolt forced him to flee with the viceroy and other Audiencia ministers to Havana, Martínez undertook his fiscalia position with "precision, self-sacrifice, and dedication to his work," taking part in a total of 4,506 *expedientes* (proceedings) and *causas* (lawsuits).[91] He was about to request promotion or transfer to a more prestigious Audiencia when the wars of Spanish American independence upset his plans. But instead of throwing in his lot with any insurrection, this loyal son of Buenos Aires preferred "to see himself locked up in jail, dragging chains around, and then imprisoned in the bowels of the Bocachica Castle" rather than betray the royal trust.[92]

With the exception of the Audiencia all branches of government in Buenos Aires encouraged qualified young men to join their ranks as meritorios. Meritorios were unpaid trainees, apprentices who were amassing seniority or mérito in the royal service in the hope that the next salaried position open in the agency would fall to them. As the time spent as a meritorio in one department of government could not be transferred to another department, a young man requesting a position of meritorio in one agency was essentially betting that this branch of government would provide him the opportunity at earning a salary sooner than any other. Two factors could influence his choice—the rapidity with which salaried jobs opened up in an agency and the number of meritorios already in line for future openings.

The idea of serving an unpaid apprenticeship in the royal service seems to have been instituted in Buenos Aires with the founding of the viceroyalty. Two years later in 1778 meritorios could be found working in all major government agencies. In 1782 article 215 of the Real Ordenanza de Intendantes codified the appointment of all meritorios and set down qualifications for the post. Meritorios were to possess the "beautiful attributes of aptitude, talent, good conduct, application, and a good upbringing"; in addition, they ideally were to have had some basic mathematics, write a good hand, have "education and principles," and show "promise of learning and helpfulness in the future." Good birth was of course a basic prerequisite; applicants had to be legitimate children of racially pure Spanish parents. Additionally, family influence was often a help in getting a young man started as a meritorio.

One could begin meritorio service in any government agency relatively easily—by simply obtaining permission from the agency chief—but for this service to be valid, a formal *solicitud* (petition) had to be presented by the meritorio candidate. The nature of this solicitud and the accompanying documents were outlined in the Real Ordenanza de Intendantes and included proof of legitimate birth, usually in the form of a baptism record.[93] This formal declaration of desire to begin work, along with supporting documentation attesting to one's parentage and education, was submitted to the head of the agency in question. He in turn, after some discreet inquiries, furthered this application to the viceroy, who approved or disapproved the nomination. The viceroy's letter of appointment itself served as official permission to begin serving an apprenticeship. In addition, the viceroy, upon presentation of a formal petition and supporting documents, had the right to grant retroactive credit for meritorio service undertaken without the necessary documents.[94]

Article 215 was based on the 1779 reglamento of the Tribunal de Cuentas that established the procedure by which the contador mayor could name meritorios or entretenidos in that agency. The number of these positions was not fixed. Rather the intendant, after consultation with the contador mayor, was to decide how many meritorios could be named. Preference was to be given to the sons and nephews of military officers, although any Spaniard of legitimate birth (*persona decente*) residing in the city could make a request. Candidates for the position of meritorio were to display "good conduct, application, the necessary qualities that the honor of the career necessitates, and [to] be able to write well and correctly." Any meritorio who proved to be lazy, lacking in ability or general good conduct could be summarily dismissed by the contador mayor after prior approval by the intendant. The young man so returned to his home forfeited all rights to claim mérito in royal service.

From 1786 to 1812 the Tribunal de Cuentas of Buenos Aires kept a book in which copies of the application and acceptance letters for all successful contenders for the meritorio post were recorded.[95] There is no extant record of unsuccessful applications and therefore no way to determine the total number of young men who applied for entry into the Tribunal nor to examine which qualities were most sought by the contadores mayores who advised the intendant or viceroy on an individual's suitability. Nevertheless, analysis of the appointment of unsalaried employees does provide information on the background of the successful applicants and allows us to trace their progress through the channels of bureaucratic advancement.

In the twenty-six-year period under review, a total of thirty-nine young men were accepted as meritorios by the Tribunal. They were uniformly white, of Spanish background, and legitimate. All but five of the successful applicants were Buenos Aires-born. Age at time of entrance can be reconstructed for seventeen of the thirty-nine meritorios; the average age for these young men was almost twenty years. The youngest man accepted as meritorio was the fifteen-year-old son of a Real Hacienda employee; the oldest was the twenty-nine-year-old son of a deceased teniente colonel. The majority of these young men also made mention of some previous education, ranging from a vague reference to having "received instruction in penmanship" to having studied "philosophy, grammar, and theology" in the Colegio de San Carlos.

Reviewing the number of new meritorios admitted each year by the Tribunal, it appears that in general the Tribunal tried to appoint only one young man per year. Major exceptions to this pattern occurred in 1793–1794 when rumors that the Tribunal was about to expand its salaried staff increased the pool of applicants and the numbers accepted jumped to six for this two-year period; in 1799 when three young men—two sons of military officers and one son of the contador mayor of the Tribunal—entered the ranks of the meritorios; and in 1802–3 when after two years with no new meritorios, a group of eight was allowed to join the Tribunal. How closely the number of incoming meritorios reflects a growth in total number of applicants is difficult to determine. In addition, it is impossible to tell whether fluctuations in the numbers of new entries were the result of a conscious policy undertaken by the contadores mayores to limit the total numbers of meritorios found in the Tribunal at any one time. Certainly, it was to the advantage of the Tribunal to take advantage of as many young men who were willing to work for nothing as could be found, but perhaps the time and trouble involved in teaching these meritorios the techniques and procedures of the work could become counterproductive when too many meritorios were in the wings. No doubt there was also a self-limiting mechanism at work among the applicants themselves; young men who otherwise would consider an official career in the Tribunal changed their plans when confronted with a cadre of three or four meritorios already in line and sought employment in other branches of government.

No meritorio in any branch of the royal government wished to spend too many years waiting for a salaried position to open up. Being accepted as a meritorio was only the first step in what was hoped would be a successful bureaucratic career. Jockeying for position, several impatient young men resigned a meritorio position in one branch of the royal government and reenrolled in what they deemed to be a more promising agency. Some entered the Tribunal de Cuentas as meritorio after futile service in the Reales Cajas, the Real Renta de Tabaco, or the military. Others went in the opposite direction, applying for meritorio posts in the aforementioned agencies after meritorio service in the Tribunal de Cuentas or taking lengthy leaves of absence. To gain a foothold in the bureaucratic career a meritorio had to constantly weigh the risk of moving to another agency (and the possibility that a salaried position would open up in another agency sooner than in the agency where he was) against the certainty that in moving he had to start anew to accrue seniority. Anguish and frustration was a permanent part of a bureaucratic career even at this beginning step.

Given the ever increasing demand for meritorio posts, in spite of the lack of remuneration and the long wait before receiving regular appointment, there is some indication that the Tribunal attempted to limit the numbers of those entering civil service by making entry requirements more stringent. In 1805 the agency began to demand that all candidates pass a formal examination before beginning the apprenticeship. This test, which lasted two hours, examined the applicant on "penmanship, spelling, number writing, the principle rules of arithmetic, and other operations."[96] There was no noticeable drop in the number of young men entering the Tribunal as meritorios after the exam's adoption. While the examination might have improved the quality of entering candidates, there were still a plethora of young men eager to enter government service and more than willing to submit to any formal requirements.

The frustration attendant upon moving from the ranks of meritorio to that of escribiente, from nonsalaried to salaried employee, never halted the number of eager young men requesting that they be allowed to serve the king for free. To the contrary, indirect evidence suggests that although entrance requirements became more stringent, there was a constant supply of meritorio candidates. By the decade of 1800 a formal trial period ranging from two to eight months was also instituted before a candidate was officially declared to be a meritorio. This trial period before a trial period only prolonged the time that a candidate had to spend before achieving his first, often elusive, goal of earning a salary.

Because of incomplete data, it is difficult to determine the average length of time that a meritorio spent in place before being promoted to a salaried post. For those fourteen meritorios in the Tribunal de Cuentas for whom information is complete, an average of three years eight months was served in this introductory-level position. Moreover, the range of time spent as a meritorio varied from eight to fifty-four months. Clearly, fortune, in the form of how many meritorios were in front of you and how quickly regular positions opened up, played an important part in a young man's hopeful progress up the bureaucratic ladder.

Who were the young men so eagerly awaiting regular bureaucratic appointment? Although the information is incomplete, of the thirty-nine meritorios accepted by the Tribunal de Cuentas, we can determine fathers' occupation for twenty-five. Two occupational groups are heavily represented: sons of government employees, bureaucrats and military men, and sons (often orphaned sons) of the local elite. Sons of government employees made up the most prevalent group of meritorios, and many of them expressed a desire to follow in the profession of their fathers, serving the crown of Spain. Among this group of bureaucrats' sons, the majority were children of men employed in the Tribunal de Cuentas itself. Although an oft-repeated royal dictum prevented relatives from serving in the same branch of government, Tribunal employees hoped to obtain royal dispensations when their sons finished their apprenticeship. The desirability of having their sons enter a bureaucratic career seems to have been strongly felt, and several Tribunal bureaucrats entered more than one son in the ranks of the meritorios. Beginning as a meritorio, one could enter into a respectable profession, amassing useful knowledge, and also enjoying the advantage of training with your father. "Who," rhetorically asked Juan Andrés de Arroyo "could look after the training of a young man as well as his own father?"[97] In addition, it seems clear that some Tribunal employees encouraged their sons to enter the same office because of the help the latter could provide. "The second reason that I want my son to become a meritorio in the Tribunal," admitted the portero Juan de Canaveris, "is so he can help me in the many things I have to do daily in the Tribunal, including carrying papers to the chiefs, and other duties that come up, taking my place whenever it might be necessary."[98]

Meritorios whose fathers were already employed in the Tribunal ranged from sons of contadores mayores and contadores ordenadores through sons of the escribanos and porteros. Clearly, the rank of one's father was not as important as the fact that he worked in the Tribunal. He could provide information to aide aspiring meritorios. The fact that at least three Tribunal employees had more than one son accepted as meritorio suggests that many bureaucrats perceived their own careers as fitting ones for their sons to follow. A bureaucratic career was secure, honorable, and befitting the social position of an español.

The second group of people who hoped to send their sons into bureaucratic careers were members of the local elite who had experienced recent economic setback. Frequently, this setback had been produced by the death of the male parent, although this was not always the case. Geronimo Lasala, son of the late Juan Baptista Lasala, Knight of the Order of Santiago, and the late Agustina Fernández de Larrazabal, descendant of an illustrious family, applied to the Tribunal for a meritorio position. So did José Erezcano Azcuenaga, son of Agustín Antonio Erezcano, a rather unsuccessful local merchant, and María Eugenia Azcuenaga. Although young José was related to some of the city's most important mercantile families, they were either unable or unwilling to advance him in a business career.

It should be pointed out that several applicants belonged to both groups: for example, they were sons of local bureaucrats, either living or deceased, who were also experiencing economic hardship. The son of José Antonio Hurtado y Sandoval, contador mayor decano of the Tribunal, stated in his application that he had originally planned a military career, having served in the army since age fourteen as a cadet, but because of "lack of money" his father was unable to send him to his next post, Montevideo.[99] Domingo José de Oruna y Sostoa, nephew of the later ministro of the Reales Cajas of Montevideo, and Fermín Justo Indart, son of the late ministro of the Reales Cajas of Río Negro, also told tales of economic woe, appealing to the mercy of government officials who could too easily envision their families left in similar straits. For a few meritorios entering the Tribunal's bureaucracy was a social step upward, but for the majority it was either a step down or an attempt to hold on to the position that their parents had established.

There is a strong suggestion that while all agencies trained meritorios, certain socioeconomic groups encouraged their sons to seek out special agencies. Aduana meritorios, for example, differed somewhat from those joining the Tribunal de Cuentas. Many Aduana aspirants were sons of retailers and lesser merchants who were attempting to establish contacts in the Aduana and at the same time to further their children's careers. Other Aduana meritorios were new arrivals from Spain who sought out the sponsorship of an established bureaucrat within the organization, a native of the same region (patria chica). These young men not only worked alongside their patron but also lived under his roof.

High-ranking bureaucrats used trainee slots to control their dependientes, placing them in government service where they might provide free assistance to their master. Francisco Ximénez de Mesa, for example, brought a young man named José del Pozo with him when he was transferred to Buenos Aires. Ximénez de Mesa used his influence as administrador of the Aduana to place del Pozo, age fifteen, in a meritorio position. After Ximénez de Mesa's fall from power, del Pozo defended himself by pointing out that "I arrived at the end of 1779 under the protection of and in the company of Don Francisco Ximénez de Mesa who had brought me up in his home since I was three years old, and I had no other future but to follow him and to live with him."[100]

Although originally created to recruit clerks for the bureaucracy, for the young men who entered the meritorio system, it was a most unsatisfactory vehicle in which to begin government service. Of the thirty-nine meritorios who entered the Tribunal de Cuentas, for example, only ten eventually received appointment to a salaried position within the Tribunal. (Four others would find regular employment in other agencies.) Nevertheless, the Tribunal de Cuentas was viewed as being a good place to serve as meritorio. While not staffed by as many officials as either the Real Renta de Tabaco or the Reales Cajas, many of the clerks and contadores ordenadores of the Tribunal were called to serve on special assignments such as the *comision de limites* (boundary commission), thereby creating low-level openings for the eager meritorios. Approximately the same rate of entrance into government service held true for meritorios in other government agencies. Relatively few openings occurred in government bureaucracy after the early 1780s, and these positions were as likely as not to be filled in ways that circumvented the procedure established by the meritorio system.

Even once a bureaucratic appointment was granted, there was no guarantee that fate, fortune, or government reorganization would not result in a demotion back to meritorio. Promotion from meritorio to an interim or substitute position was even more precarious, with young men routinely finding themselves returned to nonsalaried status when a permanent nominee arrived on the scene. Lorenzo Fuentes's quest for a regular appointment illustrates the frustration experienced by those who arrived in Buenos Aires a few years after the period of major viceregal reorganization. Fuentes, a native of Burgos, arrived with Viceroy Loreto in 1784. Unable to find a salaried position in the local bureaucracy, he joined the Secretaría de Cámara as a meritorio while continuing as Loreto's page. Six years later Fuentes was finally named *contador interino* (interim accountant) of the Real

Renta de Tabaco in Potosí, but this advancement proved to be ephemeral. After incurring debts to finance his trip to Potosí, Fuentes served barely eight months before finding himself ousted by a new regular appointee.[101] His only alternative was to return to Buenos Aires, again taking up his position as a meritorio in the Secretaría. Two years later Fuentes petitioned the crown for appointment to the first position available in any government office, an exception to the rule that meritorios receive appointment in the same agency where they had accrued merit.[102] This request was granted, for even the court realized that nine years was a long time to wait for a job.[103] In 1793 Fuentes was finally named oficial tercero interino of the Secretaría de Cámara, an appointment confirmed the next year.[104]

From the beginning having a parent, *pariente* (relative), or patron in the local bureaucracy helped a young man gain an entry-level position in the bureaucracy. Up to 1785 these bureaucrats were able to place their sons directly into salaried positions. Thereafter, as the growth of the local bureaucracy slowed, they could only find nonpaying meritorio posts for their offspring. Antonio Marín, who has the dubious distinction of having served in the position of oficial primero of the Contaduría General of the Real Renta de Tabaco for twenty-six years (1778–1804), was able to place his son quite easily in a regular Aduana post in 1781. By 1787 Francisco Urdaneta, contador general of the Real Renta de Tabaco, could only enter his son in royal service as an oficial meritorio in his agency. Bureaucrats could sometimes use personal influence to have their sons enter government service as entretenidos rather than meritorios, that is as aspirants who were guaranteed a job as soon as it became opened, rather than young men who had the vague hope of a position. Even those who began as meritorios seemed to have an advantage over others with no local bureaucratic connections. In general, sons of bureaucrats spent less time as meritorios than did other aspirants. As mentioned earlier, young Urdaneta, for example, was promoted to oficial segundo within eight months and less than a year-and-a-half later was moved up to oficial primero.[105]

Children of bureaucrats also moved from positions as meritorios in one agency to meritorios in another agency far more frequently than did their peers, perhaps a reflection of parental advice based on inside information. Pedro Medrano, a bureaucrat on the scene before the founding of the viceroyalty who rose to the position of contador of the Real Hacienda, used his influence and knowledge to move his son Manuel from meritorio of Real Hacienda to meritorio of the Real Renta de Tabaco. Another son,

Martín José, was able to advance after only two months as meritorio of Real Hacienda into the position of *oficial quinto* (fifth clerk) of the treasury. When this too rapid advancement proved unpalatable to the crown, Medrano again used his local influence to place Martín José in the Tribunal de Cuentas as *oficial escribiente* (clerk-scribe).

Spaniards posted to the colonies were often accompanied by a retinue of younger brothers, sons, nephews, and cousins who, it was hoped, would find gainful employment in the colonial bureaucracy. While usually successful in finding meritorio slots for these parientes, movement into salaried positions was not guaranteed. Much seemed to depend on the relative importance of the bureaucratic sponsor himself; parientes of viceroys, Audiencia officials, and high-ranking members of the Tribunal de Cuentas were far more lucky in being named to regular positions than were the relatives of middle-ranking bureaucrats. Much also depended on the blood proximity of the prospective candidate; brothers and sons received line appointments more quickly than nephews and cousins.

The limited effect of relatives already placed in middle-level positions can be seen in the case of Manuel Obarrio Fernández. Manuel, born in Madrid on 11 August 1775, was the son of Ramón de Obarrio, a native of San Pelayo de Arcilla in Mondoñeda, Toledo.[106] After some schooling in Spain, young Manuel, age twelve, was sent to Santa Fé in the company of his godmother and aunt Doña Manuela Fernández de Obarrio, who had come to the La Plata area to join her husband, Rafael María Guerrero y Montañes, newly named tesorero of the Real Hacienda and administrador general of the Reales Rentas de Tabaco y Naipes for Santa Fé. Too young to begin bureaucratic service, Manuel was first enrolled in the local ex-Jesuit *colegio* (academy) until the end of 1788. A few days short of his fourteenth birthday, the boy, who had displayed "well-known skill and progress in writing and sums, a clear talent and an ease of understanding" began work as a meritorio in the office of the Contaduría de la Administración General y Factoría de Tabacos of Santa Fé.[107] Four years later, Guerrero decided that Manuel's chances of moving into a permanent position would be greatly improved if he relocated to Buenos Aires, so the young man, barely eighteen, was set to continue his mérito in the offices of the Buenos Aires Real Aduana. (Guerrero himself also managed to temporarily relocate himself in the capital city, claiming that his health problems necessitated the move.)

Clearly, placing Manuel in a regular position was taking longer than originally expected. It was also proving to be somewhat of a financial inconvenience for Guerrero. On 24 January 1794 Manuel Obarrio, now age nineteen, requested that he be placed in "one of the public offices of the capital, or any other within the kingdom, in whatever job his needs could be attended to." In order to be considered for a permanent position, he also formally filed a petition to "attest to my experience and service."[108] One of the pressing reasons that Manuel gave for being placed in a paying job was "the great expense [which I have been] to my uncle . . . how onerous it is for him to continue to sustain me in even the most reduced circumstances because he is burdened down by family."[109]

It should be pointed out that in addition to his relationship to Guerrero, Manuel Obarrio was the nephew of Don Miguel de Obarrio, a Knight in the Order of Charles III, *ex-diputado* (ex-deputy) from the Kingdom of Galicia, and director general of the Madrid Renta de Tabaco. Although both Guerrero and Obarrio lost no opportunity in mentioning this connection in their petitions to the viceroy, Obarrio's name failed to produce the desired results. In desperation Manuel decided to draft all future petitions himself, thus proving that "the petitioner has an acceptable handwriting" for a government post.[110] A ray of hope showed through when Manuel, because of inside information garnered through his uncle, found out that Miguel Goñi, oficial segundo of the Buenos Aires Real Renta de Tabaco administration, was about to be transferred to an interim post in the dirección general. Obarrio quickly petitioned the viceroy to be named either in an interim or permanent basis to the post being vacated by Goñi, again mentioning his prior service, his need, and his political connections.

Obarrio's request was forwarded to the Real Renta de Tabaco, first to the administrador general and then to contador. Their replies to the young man's request illustrates the paradox that aspirants to royal service no doubt encountered repeatedly. Within two days Francisco de Paula Saubidet, responding for the ailing administrador general, penned a most encouraging reply:

> The request of Don Manuel de Obarrio y Fernández has arrived exactly on time, for the accounting section of this agency finds itself in need of helping hands in order to carry on its functions. . . . Because of this situation it seems to make sense that he be used to replace those who are absent. Obarrio's candidacy is most opportune because not only is he well-known and worthy of consideration, but his hard

work and talent are praised by his present chief, the administrator of this Royal Customs House, and his penmanship is worthy of appreciation in any office. Therefore, I not only suggest that he be given a position in this office as his petition requests, but I beseech the junta to strengthen my case by including in its report to the Superintendency the reasons why we need him and also the usefulness that will result from his being admitted to this office.[111]

Unfortunately, Manuel José de la Valle, while supportive of Obarrio's nomination, pointed out the problem:

As the commission that His Excellency [the viceroy] has conferred on Don Miguel de Goñi cannot end until another opening commensurate with his seniority has been found, and he enjoys no other income except for that which this present job provides him, it will be necessary that Obarrio be told that the service that he plans to undertake will be without any salary and that he cannot be considered for a permanent position unless the abovementioned Goñi is promoted.[112]

While Obarrio could indeed be appointed in an interim basis to Goñi's slot, it could only be *sin sueldo* (without pay), for during the time when Goñi's slot was empty his salary was still being used. Obarrio nonetheless accepted the offer, for he realized that interim appointment was at least some advancement over meritorio. Three years later in 1797 he finally received a permanent post, that of oficial primero in the Administración General de Tabaco.[113]

Although family connections had not proved as useful as Guerrero and Obarrio had hoped, they did no harm in the two men's future careers. Guerrero's decision to move to Buenos Aires proved most felicitous, for in 1796, while still on health leave from Santa Fé, he was appointed contador ordenador of the Tribunal de Cuentas, a post he held until his death in 1805.[114] Obarrio, capable and with a more powerful location connection now that Guerrero sat on the prestigious Tribunal de Cuentas, moved from oficial primero of the Administración General de Tabaco to auxiliar in the Real Renta de Tabaco's Contaduría General in 1802, and in 1807 replaced Guerrero as contador ordenador of the Tribunal de Cuentas.[115] A year later he married María Josefa Lezica, daughter of Francisco de las Llagas Lezica, a minor member of one of the city's more powerful mercantile families.[116]

Although the goal of all bureaucrats was to hold the título to a regular government appointment, they were sometimes forced to settle for a less satisfying term of appointment as supernumerary. Supernumeraries were temporary officeholders, people who did not enjoy tenure in office. From the crown's point of view the existence of supernumerary positions was one way to introduce some flexibility into the problem of manpower allocation, for a supernumerary post could be set up far easier than a regular line position. Frequently, supernumerary appointments were used to temporarily dispatch a tenured bureaucrat from one agency to another. The same mechanism could also be employed to name military men to temporary civilian posts or to employ tenured bureaucrats when agency reorganization had rendered their posts redundant.[117] Although bureaucrats filling this post also earned only half of the line salary normally awarded to the position, a supernumerario appointment gave one a preferential position when a regular line post came open.

While government posts were increasingly filled by professional, salaried bureaucrats, important groups of bureaucrats continued to purchase their positions from the crown. (See Appendix E.) Foremost among these more traditional groups were the colonial escribanos, both those who were employed in government offices and those who ran the public notary services. A second important group of positions that continued to be sold at auction were the staff positions in the Audiencia. Both groups of positions were dominated by local-born men, although the escribanos were full-time professions while the Audiencia jobs tended to be purchased by merchants of middling rank who continued to maintain their commercial ties.[118]

Hispanic infatuation with the written word combined with notorious legalism to produce a never-ending stream of paperwork to be copied and certified by escribanos. Virtually every government department employed from one to three of them. Escribano posts were purchased from the crown, often with the stipulation that the position could be transferred or inherited in the future. While some individuals earned their major source of livelihood from the fees that they charged as government escribanos, others combined these positions with ownership of a public notary registry (registro de número).

The value of public escribanía posts had increased dramatically up to the founding of the viceroyalty. In 1727, for example, Francisco Merlo purchased an escribanía pública (notary public office) for 475 pesos.[119] By 1749 such posts were worth 600 pesos;[120] by 1762 they cost 1,300 pesos, and by

1774 an inexpensive escribanía sold for 3,500 pesos.[121] This clearly upward trend in the value of the notary office was of course a reflection of the growth of the jurisdiction and size of the city of Buenos Aires and its commerce. After 1776 rapid growth in the number of escribanías, coupled with the proliferation of government escribanos who siphoned off some of the work, depressed their value. An escribanía sold in 1779 brought only 1,025 pesos. The value of specific escribanías also reflected the reputation and amount of business of previous owners, with one escribanía, that of José Zenzano, clearly dominating the commercial transactions of the city.[122]

The auction price of an escribanía represented only part of the true costs involved in buying one of these positions. In addition to this principal cost, a successful bidder incurred additional expenses in taking formal title, in preparing transcripts of the purchase procedure, in paying the media anata due the crown, and in applying for confirmation of the post. These costs probably increased the true purchasing price by 25 percent.[123]

Government escribanías (the *escribanía de hacienda real y minas* [notary of the royal treasury], the *escribanía de cámara de la real Audiencia* [official notary of the high court] and the *escribanía mayor de gobierno y guerra del virreynato* [chief notary of the viceroyalty]) displayed a different value pattern during the eighteenth century. Initially, only one government escribanía was sold in Buenos Aires, that of hacienda real y minas. The position, worth 6,200 pesos in 1750 (that is more than ten times the value of a public escribanía), suffered a slight deterioration in value in the succeeding years. This was perhaps caused by the increasing use that the local government made of escribanos públicos, who often served as government or Cabildo notaries.

With the founding of the Audiencia, the press of legal business necessitated the creation of special escribanías de cámara, offices that it was believed would be extremely lucrative. Between 1785 and 1786 two such posts were created and sold, the first to José Zenzano at a specially reduced price of 8,000 pesos and the second to Facundo Prieto y Púlido at the rather inflated price of 14,000 pesos. But the expected revenues to be gleaned from the escribanía de cámara failed to materialize, and the price of these posts plummeted through the 1790s and 1800s, first to 9,725 (in 1791), then to 5,000 (in 1801), and still later to 4,000 (in 1806). The last government escribanía, that of escribano mayor de gobierno y guerra, held a constant value of 6,000 pesos throughout the period.

Although in theory escribanía posts were to be exercised by the purchaser, for a small fee the holder of an escribanía could also buy the right to name a teniente. In Buenos Aires all public escribanos seemed to have taken advantage of this *gracia* (special permission), using this assistantship to train sons and sons-in-law to carry on. All escribanías, both public and government, could for a price be declared oficios vendibles y renunciables, giving the owner of an escribanía the legal right to renounce his position and choose a successor. Successors thus named had to comply with all legal requirements for the posts and to purchase the position from the original owner or his estate at a price set by the superintendent or viceroy. In those cases where a successor had not been named or a presumptive successor chose not to take office, the post was again publicly auctioned to the highest bidder with the original owner or his estate reimbursed. Any profit that resulted from the increased value of the post was divided evenly between the original owner and the crown.

In the transfer of both public and government escribanías, a strong pattern of son-in-law replacing father-in-law emerges. This pattern is similar to the intergenerational continuity displayed by the Buenos Aires merchants who also passed on their businesses in the same way. In fact, in this branch of the local bureaucracy one consistently sees this type of successful two or three generation continuity. Both the ability to name a teniente and the power to renounce an office aided this transfer of position. Using the first prerogative, a son-in-law could be trained; using the second, a daughter could receive her share of her father's estate in the form of a position transferred to her husband.

Both public and government escribanos were employed by local government agencies. The escribanos' power was of a subtle nature, but their processing of documents could speed up or delay official business and the public's accessibility to any organ of government. Nevertheless, all escribanos were outside of the bureaucratic cadre and as such were not eligible for advancement to higher-level positions.

The sale of most public offices was a pro forma occurrence, fulfilling a series of legal and customary requirements before an office could be turned over to a new purchaser. Once the need to fill an office was established, the intendant, acting in conjunction with the Royal Exchequer, issued a decree calling for a public sale.[124] Thirty *pregones* (public proclamations by the town crier), required by law, followed under the aegis of the escribano of the Royal Exchequer, and a meeting of the Junta de Real Hacienda was convened to evaluate the post to be auctioned off and to establish a just minimum price. The intendant then issued another decree, setting the dates (usually three successive days) on which the post would be auctioned and making sure that public notices were posted around the city. On the appointed days all candidates would present themselves in front of the Royal Exchequer, and the auction held by the Junta de Almonedas would proceed. If no candidates were present, or if no acceptable offer had been made at the end of three days, the Junta de Almonedas and the intendant could either reschedule another auction or wait indefinitely to put the post up for sale again. If a successful bidder was present, the junta would certify the individual in question as having won the public auction.

Once a successful bid was made and accepted, the prospective candidate made his way to the Royal Exchequer where payment for the post was arranged, bonds (if required) were posted, and the media anata was paid. All those who obtained their public posts through auction were required to pay an additional twenty-one percent in media anata taxes, although these payments were greatly reduced for the first purchaser of an office. Antonio José de Escalada, for example, purchased the post of *canciller registrador* (recording chancellor) of the Buenos Aires Audiencia for 6,700 pesos but paid media anata tax of only 264 pesos, or 3.9 percent.[125] Once payment was received and a receipt issued, the successful bidder presented any required documentation as to his legitimacy, training, or prior service to the intendant, who passed these documents along for approval to his legal council (asesor). A provisional decree was then issued by the viceroy with the stipulation that within six years the appointment would have to be validated by a royal decree to remain in force.

This procedure was usually followed without any major problems, regardless of whether the post being auctioned was one of the staff positions of the Real Audiencia or a public escribanía. In general, from start to finish, that is from a successful bid to the issuance of a provisional título, a candidate could expect the process to take from two-and-a-half to four months. But when problems did arise, lengthy delays were usually encountered, in part because of the many agents and agencies—intendant, viceroy, Asesoría, Junta de Almonedas, and perhaps the Real Audiencia—involved in the auction process. The same was true of the transference of salable public offices. These transactions, although they did not include open bidding in public auction, were usually pro forma, but when delays occurred, formidable and time-consuming obstacles could be presented.

Such is the case of José Luis Cabral, who fought long and hard to obtain the *título de escribano público y del número* (title to the public notary's office), vacated by the death of Francisco Xavier Conget. On 13 July 1782 Cabral appeared with Rosalia Ramos, widow of the late escribano Conget, and drew up papers to be appointed Conget's successor.[126] Everything seemed in order. Conget, who had purchased his post in public auction for 3,510 pesos payable in three installments, had received his título from Governor Bucareli in July 1769. In 1774 Conget received permission from the crown (in return for a payment into the royal coffers) to transfer his office through the right of *renuncia* (renunciation). When he died in June 1782, the public renuncia that Conget had recorded in the registry of his fellow escribano, Eufrasio José Boyso, was still valid. In this document Conget stated that the escribanía post was now the possession of his wife, Doña Rosalia, who was free to transfer it to whomever she desired.

Renuncia y traspaso (renunciation and transfer) was of course the legal mechanism used to sell an office from one holder to another. According to law, the owner of the position was to receive half of the preestablished purchase price and the Royal Treasury the other half. With all the legal documents in order Doña Rosalia made arrangements to transfer her late husband's escribanía to José Luis Cabral, a *vecino* (resident) of Buenos Aires who had been born in the nearby town of San Isidro twenty-six years earlier. The legitimate son of Antonio Cabral and Ana Manuela Hernández, José Luis, although barely above the age of twenty-five, the legal age of majority, nevertheless, fulfilled all the legal criteria for the post.

During the week following the first filing of Doña Rosalia's request, Cabral presented the required documentation, including a copy of Conget's death certificate and his own birth certificate. By 18 July he was ready to request that the asesor general administer any needed examinations so that he could prove his knowledge of the profession he was about to undertake. The first hint of future delay came three weeks later on 13 August when José Antonio Hurtado, acting fiscal of the Audiencia and contador mayor of the Tribunal de Cuentas, advised Cabral to present his request to the viceroy, who had jurisdiction in questions of renuncia. Cabral followed this advice, and viceregal approval soon followed. Cabral was now ready to be examined on his knowledge, a test that was administered by the *asesor interino y procurador general* (temporary counselor and attorney general) of the city, Dr. Francisco Bruno Rivarola. On 28 June 1783, after an inexplicable delay of ten months, Cabral proved to Rivarola's "full satisfaction" that he had the "knowledge required to hold the position of escribano."

No price had yet been set for the escribano office that Cabral was trying to purchase. To this end on 11 July Cabral petitioned the Real Hacienda to undertake an "evaluation of the office." On 1 October two practicing escribanos, José Zenzano and José García de Echaburu, were named by intendant decree to evaluate the escribanía in question. After a month's delay Zenzano and García de Echaburu suggested that Conget's practice be sold for 1,500 pesos, an admittedly low sum but one that they felt was justified given the small number of *protocolos* and *autos* (judicial records and decrees) that Conget had handled and the general decadence that had be fallen this type of public office. To their evaluation, the two escribanos appended the valuations of two practices that had become vacant in the preceding years. Their figures seemed to confirm the wisdom of the evaluation that they now put forth.

By June 1784 the Real Hacienda had accepted the Zenzano-García de Echaburu evaluation and had forwarded the required papers to its media anata division. Media anata taxes were drawn up and paid, as was half of the purchase price and an additional 100 pesos, which was to serve as bond against future expenses to be incurred in gaining final royal approbation of the título. After waiting two years, Cabral seemed at last ready to take over the escribanía when another delay occurred. The Audiencia fiscal, reviewing the Cabral expediente, took exception to the valuation of 1,500 pesos previously accepted by all parties concerned. Fifteen hundred pesos was too little to pay for an escribanía, especially since escribano José Zenzano, the same man who had provided this evaluation to the government, had just sold his practice for 2,800 pesos. The fiscal, José Márques de la Plata, requesting a new valuation of the Conget escribanía, named another two escribanos, Pablo Manuel Beruti and Francisco Moreno Argumosa, to estimate "the true price, the price that the notary office gained over the years that Francisco Xavier Conget served the position."

On 22 July 1785 Beruti and Moreno Argumosa returned to the fiscal with their evaluation. The highest value that they were willing to assign to the Conget escribanía was 1,500 pesos, and this in their judgment was clearly an overvaluation. (At first they had considered a value of 1,300 pesos and then one of 1,025 before raising their estimate once again.) Why so low? Because, as they stated, the office had been vacant for three years without processing any papers or anything else that could be counted on to supply revenue to the new owner. The escribanía now consisted of little more than "notorial records in an archive," and copying old contracts provided only a minor portion of an escribano's revenue. Furthermore, the success and therefore the valuation of any escribanía depended on the "activity, intelligence, and trustworthiness of the escribano himself," and the late Francisco Conget, according to "the secret information that we have gathered about this case," was not noted for these qualities. Instead, Conget was infamous for handling the autos in his care with public indolence, a trait that did little to enhance the reputation of his escribanía. Cabral could at last take over the practice. First, of course, all agencies concerned, the fiscal, and the Real Hacienda had to approve the Beruti-Moreno Argumosa decision. On 22 September 1785 a title naming José Luis Cabral to the Conget escribanía was issued by the viceroy.

"Traditional" bureaucrats, that is those bureaucrats who continued to occupy purchased positions, also continued to collect fees for their services. Included in this group were the *escribano real* (royal notary), escribanos, and tasadores de costas. Legal advisers such as the fiscal of the Real Hacienda or the relator of a government agency were also entitled to charge fees for their services to private individuals, as was the alguacil mayor of the Real Hacienda.[127] Although it is impossible to calculate just how lucrative these positions were, their value probably varied greatly from post to post, with the auction price serving as a good indicator of the relative wealth of the position.

Audiencia staff positions, the so-called oficios subalternos, like the escribanías, were publicly auctioned to the highest bidder. Included among the oficios subalternos were the positions of *canciller* (chancellor), *tasador de costas* (appraiser of legal fees), *receptor de penas de cámara* (collector of court fines), *procurador* (solicitor), and alguacil mayor. The value of these jobs ranged from 800 to 7,000 pesos, with the highest-valued position that of canciller. Because these auctions were held locally, upper-class creoles, especially sons of merchants and military men, had ready access to these posts. Even after a royal cédula of 1789 changed receptor de penas de cámara and procurador posts to salaried ones, the original purchasers were able to maintain their positions.[128] Like escribanía positions, the numbers of porteños found in these ranks far exceeds the numbers found in any other part of government service.

Only one Audiencia staff post was never filled by auction, that of relator, which was specifically limited to men trained as lawyers. Here the posts were filled by *oposiciones* (public examination), and a token salary of 500 pesos per year was assigned to the job. Nevertheless, because the oposiciones were held in Buenos Aires, creoles again tended to monopolize this job.[129] Indeed, success in an oposición for a relator post could serve a talented lawyer as a first step in a successful legal career.

Another bureaucratic position that provided the possibility of professional advancement to young lawyers was a post in a despacho judicial, the law division attached to either the Secretaría de Cámara or the Secretaría de la Superintendencia. These despachos typically employed only one or two lawyers, as well as the same number of escribanos. Nevertheless, the legal position of asesor general to the viceroy or the superintendent was an important post and one opened to ambitious creoles.

For approximately fifty years preceding the founding of the viceroyalty, the asesoria general had belonged to two men, Florencio Antonio Moreyeras (1738–61) and Juan Manuel Lavarden (1761–77), both American-born lawyers. Their control of the position was so complete that Lavarden had no trouble naming his brother-in-law Antonio Basilio Aldao as interim asesor while he took a short leave of absence to recover from investigating an uprising in Corrientes. Governor Cevallos and Lavarden seemed to have enjoyed a close working relationship, cut short by the lawyer's death in 1777. For the next nine years, four different men filled the asesor's post; two served on an interim basis: one died within a year of taking office and one was promoted to oidor of the Cuzco Audiencia. Not surprisingly, the two who received only interim appointments were native sons married to local women; the two who were given regular appointments were Spaniards.

In 1786 Juan de Almagro de la Torre, a thirty-one-year-old native of Malaga, was named to the asesor's post left vacant by the promotion of Miguel Sánchez Moscoso. Almagro, who was a lawyer in the Real Audiencia of Seville and serving as *alcalde mayor* (district magistrate) of the Partido de Montalvo at the time of his appointment, restored stability to the Asesoría. Although he had several run-ins with the Buenos Aires Cabildo, for the next twenty-four years all viceroys received their legal advice from this man. In 1807 he was publicly denounced, along with Manuel Gallego, for "having been responsible for many abuses, having enriched himself extraordinarily, and being one of the first to flee during the 1806 British occupation thereby being responsible for the state of abandonment in which Sobremonte left this city." Nevertheless, he continued in office until 1810 when, in spite of voting for a compromise that would allow the Cabildo to govern the viceroyalty, he was forced to resign.[130]

Members of despachos judiciales were generally engaged in ironing out the legal niceties of policy. Nevertheless, because they were often called upon for legal opinions before a specific policy was implemented by the government, the asesores, as long as they enjoyed the support of the head of their institutions, could be influential and powerful figures. Indeed, a talented and clever lawyer called upon to give legal advice to the viceroy on the myriad subjects that were under the chief executive's aegis could hope to impress the leader with his sagacity and acumen. Ideally, the viceroy would remember the talents of his asesor when nominations were open for Audiencia positions. Indeed, the route from asesor to Audiencia was one that many lawyers, both creole and Spanish-born, attempted to follow with varying degrees of success. Miguel Sánchez Moscoso, asesor to Viceroy Loreto, was named oidor of the Buenos Aires Audiencia in 1786. Juan de Almagro de la Torre tried repeatedly to be awarded the honors of oidor on the Buenos Aires Audiencia or to be named to the position itself. He failed in both attempts, although he was eventually named *oidor honorario* (honorary judge) of the Audiencia of Charcas. (In requesting that he be given the honors of an Audiencia oidor, Almagro argued that his greater importance would aid him in carrying out his duties more easily and that the asesores of the other three viceroyalties [Mexico, Peru, and New Granada] already enjoyed this privilege. The crown delayed fifteen years in answering his request, which was rejected in 1805.)

Another avenue that was also used by creole lawyers to advance their careers both within and without the bureaucracy was part-time appointment as relator of one of the special juntas set up to oversee particular agencies or taxes. Juan Manuel Lavarden, *hijo* (junior), a porteño-born lawyer, served as relator of the Junta Superior de Aplicaciones and the Junta Provincial de Temporalidades in 1790. Lavarden, the son and nephew of lawyers, although failing to enter the permanent bureaucracy, soon became one of the most respected legal and literary figures in Buenos Aires.[131]

Some lawyers attempted to live by their wits, combining private practice with freelancing in government service whenever an opportunity presented itself. Such was the case of José Manuel Carvallo, who was appointed asesor of the newly created Tribunal de Protomedicato in 1799 and also served as administrador general interino of the Thirty Indian Mission Towns during Manuel Cayetano Pacheco's trip to Spain the same year.[132] Four years later Carvallo was named relator of the Junta Superior of Buenos Aires, a post created by the promotion of Manuel Mariano de Irigoyen to Audiencia oidor in Chile.[133]

Creole lawyers who obtained bureaucratic posts were by definition well educated. The majority had attended elementary and secondary church schools in Buenos Aires and at the age of about seventeen had been sent to Chuquisaca, Santiago de Chile, or even Lima to study law. They had returned to Buenos Aires soon after and generally entered into government service at about age twenty-three. Although university education was expensive, deserving sons of middle and lower-middle groups were sometimes able to find generous benefactors who would provide the needed funds. As a result lawyer-bureaucrats born in Buenos Aires demonstrated a multiplicity of occupational origins from sons of middle-level merchants to government bureaucrats. Escribanos on the other hand did not need any formal education, although many of them must have at least attended a school of *letras primeras* (primary instruction). In general, escribanos were sons of escribanos and had served a lengthy apprenticeship with their fathers before inheriting or purchasing their posts. No doubt most were aided by manuals that provided the most widely used legal *formularios* (formats).

The concentration of creoles, be they asesores generales or escribanos, in the despacho judicial section of the colonial bureaucracy was not accidental, for these were the positions that were filled locally, and no journey to the Spanish court was needed to get one of these appointments. The tendency for creoles to be found in purchased positions suggests that the native-born found it easier to amass capital than to establish bureaucratic connections. In essence those aspects of the Bourbon bureaucratic system that were carry-overs from the Hapsburg period were more supportive of creole bureaucratic pretension than the newer, more "modern" Bourbon reforms.

Almost all creoles who purchased offices were pure-blooded descendants of Spanish immigrants, but there were some interesting exceptions. The extent to which purchase of office provided mobility for nonwhites is reflected in the *gracias al sacar* (legal exemption) purchased by Juan José de Rocha, a public escribano, in 1797 that allowed him to be called "Don." Rocha, a mulatto, had put together enough capital to purchase an escribanía in 1792. "Although because of his office everyone generally calls him [by the honorific title] Don and many people realize that he is deserving of this title because of his personal circumstances, nevertheless, when he found out about the public Arancel of Gracias al Sacar, he was moved by a desire to have this privilege conceded by royal cédula."[134]

In Buenos Aires the Bourbon reforms did help to build a true bureaucracy in which appointment was based on merit and dedication. Although influence was always of help, in general the rules of first appointment were fairly universal. Another result of the Bourbon reforms in Buenos Aires was the replacement of a small number of local-born bureaucrats with a large number of Spanish-born ones. Moreover, the limited numbers of porteños who held government employment were heavily concentrated at the lower levels of the viceregal bureaucracy. The decreasing rate of expansion of the Buenos Aires bureaucracy, plus the ever-present corps of young men with some sort of connection to established bureaucrats, produced a situation in which it was increasingly more difficult for the native-born middle groups to find positions in the colonial bureaucracy. Increasingly in the decade of the 1790s, and markedly after the turn of the century, porteños were unable, even through appealing to those closely related to the viceroy, to obtain even the lowest posts in the local bureaucracy. Even appointment to unpaid training slots became more difficult for the native-born without strong bureaucratic connections.[135]

Regardless of the frustration associated with government employment, young men continued to seek entrance into the civil service. Indeed, even in the years after 1790, when for all intents and purposes the civil service had ceased to grow, there was no lessening of the number of eager candidates waiting to gain a permanent foothold in government offices. So desirable were these increasingly rare appointments that prospective candidates eagerly sought news of any possible opening, listening for rumors of ill incumbents, and then quickly petitioned the crown, careful to include claims based on even the most distant relatives to strengthen their cases. Most typical was the case of Andrés de Salazar, a native of Córdoba la

Llana, residing in Buenos Aires where he was trying rather unsuccessfully to establish himself as a merchant. In 1801 he petitioned the minister of finance asking to be named either contador de retasas ("the actual incumbent has been given up on by the doctors") or treasurer of the Montevideo Aduana. In support of his request Salazar cited the fact that his uncle Simón de Anda y Salazar had served first as a judge in the Manila Audiencia and later as governor of the Philippines and that his cousin Tomás de Anda was oficial primero of the Ministry of Justice's Secretaría de Estado y del Despacho de Gracia y Justicia.[136] Secure employment continued to tempt many young and not-so-young men who had found that the vagaries of Buenos Aires commerce did not always produce sought-after riches.

While the crown fought to professionalize its bureaucracy during the late eighteenth century, several paths of recruitment continued to exist for salaried posts, and purchase of some fee-producing offices was never suppressed. Increasingly, it was the Spanish-born who entered the salaried bureaucracy through influence, family connections, or special letters of appointment from the crown. Creoles also were able to find positions in the ranks of salaried officials, but they often met with more frustration than success. Those native-born who successfully used influence and/or the meritorio system to achieve appointment tended to be sons of either important local bureaucrats or merchants. The most effective mechanism for recruiting porteños into the bureaucracy continued to be the purchase of office, and as a result the native-born were overwhelmingly concentrated in the posts of escribanos and Audiencia personnel.

Once a young man had obtained some bureaucratic post, what did the future hold? What salary could he hope to earn? What promise of professional advancement could he plan for? The following chapter will discuss the realities of the bureaucratic career.

5. The Bureaucrats: Advancement

MUCH OF THE NEWLY EXPANDED bureaucracy was organized by the first intendant (later superintendent) of Río de la Plata, Manuel Ignacio Fernández. It was Fernández who worked out the organizational details of agencies such as Real Renta de Tabaco, the expanded Real Hacienda, and the Tribunal de Cuentas in a series of reglamentos. He envisioned an efficient bureaucracy, one in which competence and achievement were to be rewarded. In his 1779 reglamento for the Buenos Aires treasury Fernández, in outlining the procedure to be used in promotion, wrote that preference should always be given to the most deserving "without caring about his length of service *(antigüedad)*, but rather his talent, loyalty, and usefulness to royal service."[1]

In theory, therefore, talented, hard-working men should have been able to enter the local bureaucracy at a relatively low level, to progress based on merit, and to eventually achieve posts of importance in their respective agencies. But once begun in a bureaucratic career how fast did the officials really move through the ranks? What degree of internal mobility was indeed available, and what was the realistic possibility of beginning as a minor official and ending one's career in a position of responsibility and prestige? What effect did factors relating to personal achievement, factors such as talent and hard work, have on a bureaucrat's career? How did these qualities compare in importance with ascriptive factors such as birthplace, personal connections, and family influence?

To understand the degree to which individuals experienced professional mobility once they had successfully entered into the carrera de oficinas, it is necessary to look at specific agencies that functioned during the viceroyalty. Four of these agencies—the Tribunal de Cuentas, the Aduana, the Secretaría, and the Real Renta de Tabaco—provide good data on the careers of staff members during the period under consideration.

The Tribunal de Cuentas, the primary auditing agency of the viceroyalty, provides the best data for an analysis of mobility. In an attempt to rationalize the records on all civil bureaucrats, Charles IV required that all government offices draw up fojas de servicio, closely modeled on military service records, for each employee.[2] Close analysis of the fojas de servicio for the Tribunal at the midpoint in its development (1795) allows a more complete description of salary, age, marital status, and career advancement of its staff.[3]

In 1795 the Tribunal de Cuentas consisted of twenty-six employees, including nine meritorios who were unsalaried. As might be expected for those who received a wage, salaries were closely correlated with rank, although the greater variation of salary at the higher ranks (as reflected by the larger standard deviation from the mean) should be noted. (See table 5.1.) Age was also closely correlated with rank; while the average age for meritorios was over twenty-eight years, oficiales were almost thirty-six, and contadores ordenadores close to fifty. In general, advancement from one rank to another was a reward for long years of loyal service rather than for any premature genius.

Table 5.1   Salary, Age, and Marital Status of Tribunal Personnel, 1795

Rank	N	Average salary		Average age		Percent-age married
		Mean	sd	Mean	sd	
Contador Mayor	2	3,822.5	251	58	1.4	50
Contador Ordenador	4	1,310	376	49.7	7.5	75
Oficial	11	436.4	102.7	35.8	9.4	55
Meritorio	9	—	—	28.4	11.7	33
Total	26	1,607.7[a]	184.4[a]	37.1	9.3	50

Source: AGNA, Tribunal de Cuentas, Fojas de servicio del personal, IX-14-7-12; Tribunal de Cuentas, Títulos y nombramientos de Contadores Mayores, 1768–1812, IX-14-7-5.
[a]Mean and standard deviation calculated without meritorios.

Table 5.2   Time in Rank

Rank	Total years at that rank or equivalent	Total years in royal service
Contador Mayor	16.00	23.00
Contador Ordenador	12.19	18.86
Oficial	14.99	17.33
Meritorio	6.18	6.54
Total	11.69	14.21

Just how long that service was expected to last can be seen by analyzing the time in different ranks spent by the cohort of 1795 Tribunal employees. As the above table shows, the average Tribunal employee of the rank of contador ordenador or oficial had spent more than seventeen years in government service. (See table 5.2.) Not all the government service earned by Tribunal employees had been accrued in the Tribunal itself. Since the Tribunal had sought trained bureaucrats for its staff at the time of its first reorganization, several men had served clerkships in the Aduana or Reales Cajas. Interestingly, on the average oficiales had spent more time in rank than the more important contadores ordenadores. Clearly, at least some oficiales positions were staffed by men who lacked the talent to win promotion but who nevertheless clung to government employment.

Looking at the Tribunal's staff over the entire viceregal period the same pattern emerges. Of the forty-five men who worked as salaried employees below the rank of contador mayor in the Tribunal de Cuentas during these years, thirty-three failed to experience any major degree of professional mobility once in the Tribunal, that is, they failed to move from the rank of oficial to contador ordenador or from contador ordenador to contador mayor. And while twelve men (or 26 percent) did move to a higher rank within the Tribunal, only one individual was able to begin his career as an oficial and end it as contador mayor. This lack of mobility caused many men, especially those in the junior ranks, to request transfer to other government branches or more commonly to drop out of government service, either to return to Spain or to chance a mercantile career in Buenos Aires or the interior. Nevertheless, those who were unwilling to risk the unknown or who were willing to patiently wait for slow advancement were not rare. Eusebio Montaña, for example, spent six years nine months and twenty-seven days as *oficial cuarto* (fourth clerk) of the Tribunal before promotion to second contador ordenador; he served in this later post for another twenty-three years six months and eight days.[4]

Once the initial organization period had passed, and once the greatly expanded number of government positions were filled by men transferred from Peru, by locally born bureaucrats, or by newer recruits from the Peninsula, the possibility for advancement within the Tribunal slowed considerably. Promotion occurred only when additional positions were added, when a more senior bureaucrat was transferred, or more likely when he died. If the bureaucratic opening occurred at the middle rank (contador ordenador) or below, men already employed were moved along the career ladder.[5] The new position resulting at the bottom rung could be filled by either a meritorio, by a member of the viceregal retinue, or by a new Spanish arrival. But when the vacancy occurred at the agency's top rank, that of contador mayor, only rarely was a contador ordenador tapped for promotion. Instead, the viceroy tended to call upon men who had experience as high-ranking officials in other agencies, thus converting the position to a lateral rather than a vertical move for the new incumbent. Limited internal mobility coupled with the certainty that positions as contador mayor were reserved for outsiders caused a good deal of resentment among the loyal Tribunal staff.

While advancement was painfully slow for those of the rank of oficiales or above, meritorios found themselves spending years without pay hoping to gain entry into the bureaucracy. In 1795 the nine meritorios found in the Tribunal had been waiting an average of six years and two months in some government office. Of a total of seventeen young men who had entered the meritorio group in the preceding ten years, one had advanced to the lowest-ranking oficial position, seven were still in place, and nine had dropped out, seeking more promising opportunities elsewhere. Only four of the nine meritorios in the Tribunal in 1795 would eventually be promoted to oficial.

The high dropout rate among meritorios, a result of slow promotion along the bureaucratic ladder compounded by alternate, competing entry patterns into the paid bureaucracy, becomes even more important when we examine the origin of the meritorios and the salaried employees. In 1795 77 percent of the meritorios hoping for Tribunal jobs were porteños, while only 20 percent of those employed by the Tribunal had been born in Buenos Aires. The employment situation in 1795 was in no way atypical.

For the entire viceregal period, 84 percent of all meritorios were porteños, but only 25 percent of all salaried employees of the Tribunal de Cuentas were Buenos Aires-born (with another four percent born elsewhere in America). Clearly, the royal bureaucracy was not cut off to creoles, but the pool of local aspirants was far greater than the bureaucracy could absorb. Entry into even low-paying positions in the Tribunal was difficult for all, but for creoles it seemed to be especially frustrating.

Another important branch of colonial government, the Aduana, also provided few opportunities for clerks to advance to the higher administrative level. What made the Aduana unique among viceregal bureaucracies was the small number of individuals employed by this agency during the entire period under study. There was little promotion into or out of the Aduana and only the slightest movement between ranks by individuals within the institution. While an individual after many years of service might move from the rank of fifth official of contaduría to that of third or fourth official or while a clerk might progress from the less powerful tesorería division to the contaduría section, not one Aduana clerk ever occupied one of the five top administrative posts in the organization. Only the grossest malfeasance or death in office produced movement within this bureaucracy. Aduana officials were neither promoted to other agencies nor did they tend to leave the bureaucracy for other career opportunities. Unlike the Tribunal de Cuentas, there was one pattern within the ranks of the top Aduana administrators that was regularly repeated: that of promoting the contador, the number two post, to administrador. Nevertheless, movement at the top ranks was limited and resulted not from some rational program of promotion but rather from death or disgrace of the incumbent.

Furthermore, in the case of the Aduana entrance into the middle level of the bureaucracy was especially difficult for those already employed as oficiales. This lack of internal mobility was in part caused by a conscious royal policy. Not only at the time that the Aduana was officially established, but whenever a middle-level post became open, the crown intentionally named an individual from outside Buenos Aires to the post rather than promote a loyal clerk.

In addition, the static nature of Aduana positions was also caused by the longevity of the incumbents. During the viceregal period only one man, Juan Francisco Vilanova, held the position of *vista primero* (chief customs inspector), and only two men served as *alcaide* (overseer of customs collections). Employment within the Aduana for twenty to thirty years was not unusual; the abovementioned Vilanova, named vista primero in 1778, was still in the same position at the time of Independence thirty-two years later.

While few of the highest-ranking Aduana officials experienced promotions during their tenure in Buenos Aires, movement was even more restricted for the less important oficiales under them. Comparing oficiales employed in 1782 when the Aduana was reorganized with a list of employees in 1790, an interesting picture of the limited mobility at the clerkship level emerges. Of the seven salaried oficiales listed in 1782, six were employed by the Aduana in clerkships eight years later. Three of these men were still in the same job, while two others had been moved from one department to another. Only one had experienced some limited mobility; Francisco Marín, who had been named fifth oficial of contaduría in 1782 had been promoted to third oficial. In addition, one of the three meritorios found in the Aduana in 1782 had been promoted to fifth oficial de contaduría.

Even this limited degree of advancement was often tied more to personal connections than to disinterested accomplishment. An example of the influence of personal ties in a society that still honored client-patron relations is reflected in the rather dissimilar testimony about the state of the Aduana given by the administrador Francisco Ximénez de Mesa and his contador Nicolás Torrado. In their respective reports both men discussed the qualifications of their employees at great length, but here all similarity stopped. Ximénez de Mesa praised Miguel Obbes, supernumerary, as the most promising employee in his agency; Torrado, speaking of the same Obbes, accused Ximénez de Mesa of "exaggerating in the greatest degree the talents, capacity, and future of this young man." Furthermore, Torrado suggested the reason for Ximénez de Mesa's poor judgment; "there is no doubt that the administrador allowed himself to get too carried away because of his relationship to Obbes, that of godfather through marriage." On the other hand, Manuel Espinosa, a trainee who had been living and working with Torrado for over a year and a half, was not even mentioned by Ximénez.[6]

With such limited possibilities for advancement, why did Aduana employees persevere even at the lowest ranks? Unlike other agencies, why did the Aduana bureaucrats fail to petition the crown for promotion or at least a raise in salary? No doubt underlying their institutional loyalty was an excellent opportunity to supplement their earnings through the extralegal payments and favors that the Aduana provided. Nothing else can explain the tenacity with which the Aduana bureaucrats hung on to their low-paying jobs nor their general level of satisfaction while holding the same position for long periods of time. The crown itself suspected widespread corruption within the Aduana and refused to promote Aduana employees to other royal bureaucracies; the king had little desire to spread the Aduana disease to other agencies. The ability to supplement one's income was greatest, of course, among those fortunate enough to be in the central administration, but it was also found to some degree among all oficiales, especially among those who had worked their way to the post of oficial primero of an Aduana section.

The viceregal Secretaría was another agency that displayed a lack of rapid promotion, but here the frustration of its employees was expressed in repeated petitions to the crown. The essentially static nature of this bureaucracy can be seen by analyzing a list of nine Secretaría employees who signed one of these petitions requesting a raise in 1809.[7] These men composed the regular staff (those below the rank of secretario, excluding the legal advisers) of the combined Secretaría. They had served an average of 18.9 years in the Secretaría, and an average of 23.1 years in the royal bureaucracy. In addition, they had been in the same position in the Secretaría for an average of 12.9 years. Among their numbers was Matías Bernal, originally appointed to the Secretaría of the Superintendency by the first viceroy of Río de la Plata in 1777, and Juan Lustu, nominated by the second viceroy in 1778. One of the newest members of the Secretaría, an oficial tercero named Manuel Moreno, had been in the agency for nine years, six of them spent as a meritorio and three in his present position. He would later complain that the Secretaría was "run by inept and lazy superiors" and was in "such a state of indolence and delay that it offended the honor of the lesser bureaucrats who made up the staff."[8]

Another pattern of career immobility can be seen in the Real Renta de Tabaco. More than any other branch of the Buenos Aires bureaucracy, the Renta maintained close ties to its branches in the interior. This was perhaps a reflection of the clearly hierarchical nature in which the agency had been set up; all *administraciones generales* (regional offices) came directly under the Buenos Aires dirección general and its contaduría. There were no agencies or individuals that stood between the director general and his delegates in the cities of the interior. In addition, a specialized knowledge and similarity of concerns—the production and sale of tobacco products—reinforced these ties among all Renta employees. In recruiting and promoting its employees, the Renta, more than any other viceregal agency, practiced a system of geographical movement within its own ranks.

This geographical movement could be either into or out of Buenos Aires. Men who had worked for several years in Potosí, La Paz, or Lima were often transferred into the Buenos Aires Renta, just as those who had been employed locally were sometimes sent on permanent or temporary assignment to other branches of the Renta. Buenos Aires service was usually considered to be far more important and prestigious than work in lesser branch Rentas.

In general, individuals who had held relatively unimportant posts in Buenos Aires would be named to far more important positions at a far greater salary when transferred to the interior. Both title and pay were in effect used as inducements and as rewards for hardship service in the less desirable cities of the interior. Regardless of the length of time that they served outside of Buenos Aires, if they were again returned to the capital, both high-ranking position and salary were lost. Consider the case of Martín José de Goycoechea who after serving as oficial tercero of the contaduría of the Real Renta de Tabaco at an annual salary of 500 pesos was sent to La Paz as administrador general interino of the local Renta. Goycoechea spent four years and ten months in La Paz, during which time he earned a salary of 1,700 pesos per year (including the rent of his house and a 4 percent commission on the value of all *papel sellado* [stamped paper] sold by him); on his return to Buenos Aires, where he served as an assistant to the commission charged with arranging the contaduría papers for the de la Vega visita, his salary was reduced to 800 pesos. Goycoechea, anxious to advance within the Renta and perhaps desirous of regaining the independence and importance that serving as an administrador general afforded, again accepted an appointment outside of Buenos Aires seven years later. In 1802 he was sent as administrador general interino to Córdoba and in 1804 was transferred to the same post in Salta. While stationed in the interior, he earned 1200 pesos a year but was also able to successfully request a one-time supplement of 500 pesos for expenses. By 1805 Goycoechea was back in Buenos Aires, now a oficial segundo, but again earning only 800 pesos per year.[9] Willingness to accept transfer had not produced a meteoric career but rather slow steady progress up the bureaucratic ladder.

The relative inexperience of the men sent into the interior to serve as oficiales mayores, contadores, and administradores of local tobacco monopolies is striking. Antonio Cordero, for example, after barely seven months as oficial escribiente (oficial sexto) in Lima was named oficial mayor of the Administración General in Cuzco; Francisco Xavier de Aramburu after six-and-a-half years as meritorio and amanuense was sent as *contador interventor interino* (interim auditor) of the Administración General of Charcas.[10] In addition to their lack of experience, the youth of some of those sent into the interior merits a word. Goycochea was only thirty at the time of his appointment as administrador general interino in La Paz; Cordero was one year older when he was sent to Cuzco; and Aramburu was barely twenty-three at the time of his posting to Charcas. In general only young men, unmarried and in good health, were willing to serve even temporary appointments in the unhealthy and debilitating Andean area.

Although Buenos Aires employees were usually dispatched on temporary assignment in the interior, when the Buenos Aires Renta was short on manpower, bureaucrats stationed in the interior could be pressed into temporary service in Buenos Aires. In general, they greeted these assignments as a reprieve and worked actively to be transferred to Buenos Aires, even if only for a short time, in the hope that this would advance their careers. Fermin Sotes, age twenty-three and a native of the Rioja region of Spain, began his bureaucratic career as oficial tercera of the contaduría of the Potosí Mint in 1784. Initially, Potosi seemed a good place for a career, and Sotes moved rapidly from third oficial to second oficial, then on to the Potosí Aduana (1788) and the Potosí tobacco monopoly (1789). During his time in Potosí, Sotes married and began a family. Ever ambitious to advance his career, he then accepted appointment as teniente de visitador of the Resguardo for the Province of La Paz. Because this post required much traveling, Sotes left his wife and children in Chuquisaca for what he hoped would be a brief period. Arriving in La Paz, he soon realized that his new assignment would be slow to generate new opportunities for career advancement. By January 1791 Sotes voluntarily took leave, going to Buenos Aires to plead that he had "just reasons" for abandoning the *altiplano* (Andean highlands). Sotes "without royal confirmation, salary, nor any other form of payment" offered to work at the tobacco contaduría, which at the very time found itself, "because [of] some extraordinary events, with an overload of work." After serving without pay for two years in the Renta, Sotes was transferred, still earning only merit, to the Secretaría of the Superintendency where he worked for another several months before returning again to the Renta. The chance to remain in Buenos Aires, waiting for some salaried slot, was clearly worth any sacrifice. Unfortunately, by March of 1793 "the reasons for his remaining in Buenos Aires had ceased," and Sotes was ordered by the viceroy back to La Paz, this time to take on the job of contador interventor of both the Administración General and the Factoría of the tobacco monopoly. Faced with his impending departure from Buenos Aires, Sotes became gravely ill and was able to prevail upon Viceroy Arredondo to rescind his orders, allowing him to remain in the Buenos Aires tobacco monopoly as *plumista* (scribe).[11]

Two years later Sotes heard that the post of oficial primero of the Potosí mint had come open. Although he had succeeded in remaining in Buenos Aires, he had achieved little. He therefore decided the time was right to return to Alto Perú and began to push for this appointment. Unfortunately, in his haste to advance his career, he overlooked bureaucratic protocol. All requests for transfer or promotion were supposed to follow an established route, moving from the desk of the agency director to the Secretaría and then on to Spain. When Manuel Gallego, secretary of the viceroyalty, turned down Sotes's request for promotion, Sotes unwisely decided to persist.[12] Sotes appealed directly to Diego de Gardoquí, minister of finance, in Spain. Gallego, ever sensitive to any underling who attempted to by-pass his authority, made sure that Sotes's candidacy was roundly rejected.

While most government bureaucrats abhorred lengthy appointments to the interior, a certain group of hardy men welcomed appointments as corregidores to the Indian towns of the Andean region. Some of these men were also able to use corregidor posts and the forced sale of merchandise (*repartimiento de bienes*) to Indian communities to amass personal fortunes. Such a man was Antonio de Pinedo Montufar. Antonio, the son of Antonio Gaspar de Pinedo and María Josefa Montufar, was born in Madrid about 1725. As a young man he left Madrid for the Río de la Plata area, no doubt following his paternal uncle, Agustín, a military officer who was carving out a brilliant career for himself.[13] In 1747 Antonio was able to use his uncle's connections to purchase the position of corregidor de La Paz for 9,200 pesos.[14] While in Alto Perú he also served as *tesorero oficial real* (royal treasurer) of the branch Royal Treasury at Carabayo. Antonio de Pinedo prospered in Alto Perú; he married a local woman, Michaela de Bilbao, who bore him several children. None of these children survived infancy, and Michaela herself died soon after the death of her last born. Antonio began to search for a second wife and eventually decided on Rafaela de Pinedo, his porteña cousin whose late father had been so instrumental in Antonio's early career. Because the young woman was an orphan without a generous inheritance, Pinedo decided to dower her himself; he drew up a dowry worth 10,000 pesos before leaving Cochabamba on his way to Buenos Aires.

While in Buenos Aires to attend his wedding, misfortune overtook Antonio Pinedo in the form of an Indian uprising in La Paz. All of his investments in Alto Perú were wiped out, and he was left deeply in debt to several individuals who had supplied him with merchandise. In desperation Pinedo turned to the crown, requesting appointment as a Real Hacienda official in Buenos Aires. His timing was fortuitous, for Martín José Altolaguirre had been petitioning the crown to retire and supported Pinedo's appointment as his successor. In 1786 Pinedo was named treasurer of the Reales Cajas of Buenos Aires. Although the Buenos Aires post could not be as lucrative as that in Alto Perú, Pinedo clearly felt that as a married man he was compelled to provide his young wife with some financial security, for the promised dowry had also been wiped out in the Indian uprising. "I have been able to provide my wife, in case she survives me, an income sufficient for a widow, so that she will be maintained decently, as is befitting. This has been the main reason why I requested and gained the government position that I now hold."[15]

Another agency, somewhat atypical because of the special training that was required of its regular staff and the great prestige and power that accrued to its members, was the Real Audiencia. All of the Audiencia ministers had served the bureaucracy outside of Buenos Aires before this appointment, and all belonged to a specialized corps of mobile legal bureaucrats.

Table 5.3 presents available information on age at time of appointment and length of service. The group is divided by rank and by those who received royal nominations and those who actually came to Buenos Aires. Age correlates closely with rank. The post of regent, the highest position

Table 5.3   Age at Appointment and Length of Service

Rank	Age at appointment			Length of service in Buenos Aires	
	N of cases	x	sd	x	sd
Regent					
All appointed	5	54.2	12.76		
Those who served	4	52.5	14.06	8.02	6.35
Oidores					
All appointed	18	42.17	11.19		
Those who served	12	40.33	11.66	7.66	5.78
Fiscales					
All appointed	9	44.67	7.42		
Those who served	5	40.00	5.43	10.50	6.78
Total					
All appointed	32	44.95	11.05		
Those who served	21	42.57	11.60	8.24	5.83

Source: Burkholder and Chandler, *From Impotence to Authority,* 179–85, 190–209, 220–22, 224.

of any Audiencia, was clearly one that was obtained relatively late in life, after several years of prior Audiencia service. Surprisingly, oidores who served in Buenos Aires were only slightly older than the fiscales. Nevertheless, while only ten of fourteen oidores of Buenos Aires went on to more prestigious positions, all of the fiscales advanced.

Data on length of service in Buenos Aires also correlate well with age data. Of all judges on the Buenos Aires high court, the regents, men who were on the average past fifty when they came to the court, served the shortest length of time. Oidores, the middle group, were next. Fiscales stayed in office, on the average, almost three years longer than oidores. Indeed, it was through the tenure of fiscales that the Buenos Aires Audiencia received most of its continuity, although four individuals (Regent Benito Mata Linares, two oidores, Francisco Tomás Ansotegui and Sebastián Velasco, and the fiscal José Marqués de Plata) each sat on the court for more than fourteen years. At every rank the average age of those who served was lower than the average of all who received appointments, suggesting that older individuals, regardless of their rank, were somewhat reluctant to hazard the trip to a distant and newly created tribunal. The discrepancy between average age of those appointed and the subgroup that actually served is especially notable in the case of fiscales, suggesting that the trip was even less worthwhile for older appointees if their nomination was to a fairly unimpressive post and rank.

The type of rapid advancement that the viceregal bureaucrats hoped to experience was a reality for some in the transitional years between 1767 and 1778, but advancement slowed markedly once the viceregal bureaucracy was in place. Career biographies tell the same story repeatedly. Manuel Moreno Argumosa, for example, arrived in Buenos Aires in 1767 at age twenty-one. The young man from Santander immediately found a position as oficial quinto in the Reales Cajas at a salary of 200 pesos per year. Two years later Moreno was promoted to oficial cuarto, with a 275 peso salary, then oficial tercero (300 pesos), and by 1779 was serving as oficial quinto of the more prestigious Tribunal de Cuentas at 400 pesos per year.

Moreno clearly believed that he had a fine future in the Buenos Aires bureaucracy, and sometime before 1778 he encouraged his younger brother Francisco to follow him to Buenos Aires, where he entered the Reales Cajas as an escribiente.[16] In 1776 Moreno had also married; his spouse was Ana María Valle, daughter of the late Antonio Valle y Contamina, oficial mayor of the Reales Cajas, and María Luisa Ramos. But for Moreno, as for the majority of his peers, promotion, which had come so quickly and regularly in the proceeding years, virtually stopped in the years after 1780. Although Moreno tried serving on special commissions, requesting salary increases, and petitioning the crown for advancement or transfer, it was not until 1790, after thirty-two years of government service, that he was promoted to *sexto* (sixth) contador ordenador of the Tribunal.[17] The promotion had only occurred because of the death of the incumbent, Joaquín López.[18]

Although dedication to royal service and limited ambition were prized attributes of the successful bureaucrat, not all men who displayed ambition were successful in their quest to advance within the bureaucracy. Many, because of the politics of the moment or because of the perceived needs of their agencies, spent much of their professional lives working at the same job, their request for advancement unheeded. Such a case was that of José de la Barreda, a young man trained as an accountant who had originally come to Buenos Aires in Governor Vértiz's retinue. Barreda initially spent six years in the governor's Secretaría during Vértiz's tenure. Although temporarily replaced during the eight months of the Cevallos viceroyalty, when Vértiz returned to power as second viceroy of the Río de la Plata, Barreda was again appointed to what had now become the Secretaría de Cámara. Beginning in 1779 Barreda was oficial primero of this agency, a position that, although relatively well paid (1,000 pesos per year salary), left little room for advancement, for the secretario, the next position in the career ladder, was until 1790 a political appointment. In 1789 de la Barreda took advantage of the residencia of Viceroy Loreto to testify against Andrés de Torres, the viceroy's nephew and secretario.[19] Barreda was attempting to advance his career by ingratiating himself with Viceroy Arredondo, Loreto's successor, but his gambit failed. The next year Loreto, back in Spain, successfully used his influence at court to undermine Barreda's recent appointment as interim secretario.[20] Although the new secretary did not arrive in Buenos Aires for another three years, Barreda was demoted back to oficial primero. Unable to move within the Secretaría, in 1792 Barreda petitioned the crown to be considered for appointment as *tesorero general* (chief treasurer) of the Real Renta de Tabaco; his request was denied.[21] It is not clear how many unsuccessful requests for promotion and transfer were subsequently filed by Barreda, but in 1810 he was still serving as oficial primero of the Secretaría.

The ability to use personal and family connections in Spain to gain entry into the local bureaucracy always gave a clear advantage to those born and educated in the mother country. Nevertheless (like bureaucrats' sons who found it relatively easy to begin as meritorios but difficult to move into the regular salaried ranks), special appointment because of political connections was no guarantee of future rapid advancement within the local bureaucracy. Pasqual Cernadas Bermúdez, brother of the Charcas oidor, Pedro Bermúdez, arrived in Buenos Aires complete with a Royal Order of 16 April 1778 addressed to Intendant Fernández requesting that a bureaucratic post be found for the young man.[22] By 31 August 1780 Cernadas had been appointed oficial tercero of the Real Hacienda, but fifteen years later Cernadas had only risen to third official in the Tribunal de Cuentas.

Frustration with slow or nonexistent advancement and low salaries caused some bureaucrats to drop out of the profession altogether. Antonio Espinosa de los Monteros, for example, resigned as oficial escribiente in the Aduana contaduría section in 1791 after he had failed to receive a promotion for eight years.[23] Joaquín Belgrano resigned the same post in 1804 after failing to receive promotion for fourteen years.[24]

The fact that on the whole Buenos Aires bureaucrats experienced little career mobility did not mean that certain individuals failed to move quickly within the bureaucracy. In addition to cases of extreme immobility, such as the aforementioned José de la Barreda who spent the entire viceregal period, thirty-two years, as oficial primero of the Secretaría (with the exception of a brief nine-month period when he held the post of interim secretary), there are some cases of considerable career advancement. Justo Pastor Lynch, a porteño, went from plumista to administrador of the Aduana within the same thirty-two years. Manuel Medrano moved from meritorio in 1786 to first contador ordenador of the Tribunal de Cuentas by 1810. Even more startling is the progress of José Ortiz who moved from fifth oficial of the army treasury section of the Contaduría in 1784 to interim secretary of the Secretaría ten years later. Although there is no doubt that the men in question were competent and talented civil servants, in all these cases personal influence is clearly discernible.[25]

While many bureaucrats in all agencies spent years without moving others progressed from one agency to another, giving all appearances of making professional progress but actually standing still. Matías Bernal, for example, one of those who accompanied Pedro de Cevallos to the Río de la Plata in 1776, was named first oficial of the Secretaría of the Intendency (later Superintendency) under Intendant Manuel Ignacio Fernández. When Fernández left office in 1783, so did Bernal, but instead of returning to Spain he chose to remain in Buenos Aires. After four years without employment he was named oficial primero of the contaduría section of Real Hacienda, a post that he held for ten years. In 1796 the interim viceroy, Antonio Olaguer Feliú, found himself without an oficial primero in the Secretaría of the Superintendency General of the Real Hacienda and proceeded to name Bernal to the position that he had left thirteen years earlier.[26] Although the appointment occasioned some complaints from bureaucrats within the agency who felt they were in line for promotion, Bernal continued in the Secretaría until the May revolution.[27]

Promotion in all agencies was slow, but because of death, renuncia, or other unforeseen happenings, individuals did gradually move up in rank. But only once during the entire viceregal period did several events occur in tandem and create a relatively large reshuffling of bureaucrats within an agency. In 1800 three vacancies were suddenly created in the lower ranks of the Royal Treasury when Matías Bernal, the oficial primero of the accounting section of the Royal Treasury, resigned within months of the death of Pedro Moas, oficial primero of the treasury section of the same agency, and the disappearance of Felix Gallardo, third official of the accounting section.[28] This unusual combination of events allowed José Rodríguez de Vida, the meritorio with longest service in the Reales Cajas, to move up to oficial sexto, accounting section, while Vicente Aldana was promoted to oficial quinto, accounting section, and Antonio Luis Beruti became oficial sexto, treasury section.

The entire promotion system was also marred by the inability to transfer years spent in one branch of the royal bureaucracy to another branch when one had moved voluntarily to the new agency. For example, a man entering as an oficial in Real Hacienda did not receive any credit for prior employment in the Real Renta de Tabaco. Only those royal officials who had been transferred because of a decision by the viceroy, intendant, or king were able to transfer seniority, moving into positions that were laterally as important as those that they had come from. For all others this lack of transferability of prior service often produced a quandary and a gamble. An individual, after serving several years as a clerk in one agency, was faced with the decision of continuing in that same agency, awaiting promotion, or attempting entrance into a new agency where they might encounter a better chance of advancement. Choosing the latter course meant that the bureaucrat lost all merit previously accrued. This lack of transferability suggests that the Bourbons, while attempting to make their bureaucracy more efficient, did not encourage bureaucrats to move from agency to agency but rather tried to make moving across agencies difficult and unattractive.

For many the result of a career in the viceregal bureaucracy was dreary routine and advancing age. Ironically, this mind-numbing dedication could destroy any chances for advancement, even when an opening finally presented itself. Juan Lustu, who had been serving as oficial segundo in the Secretaría de Hacienda since 1778, should have been promoted to oficial primero in 1797 when Justo Pastor Lynch left the agency. The appointment went instead to another bureaucrat, in part because, according to Viceroy Olaguer Feliú, Lustu is "always kept busy with writing chores and because he is of a rather advanced age, lacking in the necessary knowledge, and incapable of fulfilling the duties of a first oficial."[29] According to the oficial tercero, ambitious young Luis Herrera Izaguirre, Lustu was considering retirement because of his infirmities. Herrera's report was overly sanguine; twelve years later Lustu was still working as the agency's oficial segundo.

Disbanding or reorganizing agencies often left the crown trying to find employment for those bureaucrats whose positions no longer existed. As the crown continued to pay the salaries of all bureaucrats who had received formal royal appointment, it was anxious to place these men in productive positions. Nevertheless, because fiscal restraints prevented the creation of new posts, from 1790 on the crown had to wait for openings to become available before it could place these already salaried individuals in new jobs. Juan Andrés de Arroyo, who lost his position as secretario of the Intendancy in 1792 because of bureaucratic reorganization, waited until 1799 to take his seat as contador mayor of the Tribunal de Cuentas. The crown sometimes succeeded in placing lesser-ranking bureaucrats in agencies as vaguely defined "salaried assistants." Such was the case of Francisco Díaz Orejuela, oficial segundo of the Contaduría de Propios y Arbitrios, who became jobless (but not salaryless) when the Propios was disbanded in 1801. By 1809 he was working in the Secretaría de Cámara as a so-called *agregado con sueldo* (salaried adjunct personnel).[30]

All promotion had increasingly become more difficult, but the most difficult was that between agency sections, (i.e., from oficial to contador). Regardless of their talent, performance, and patience, many oficiales found themselves in the situation described by Miguel Obes, oficial primero of the Aduana's treasury section. In a letter written in February 1810 Obes documented his thirty-one years of service in the Buenos Aires Aduana.[31] Although, as Obes wrote, "the nature and length of my services could not be any more praised," he had received neither promotion nor salary increase since entering royal service. He had in fact been turned down in his request for transfer to the Tribunal de Cuentas, as well as in his petition for a raise from 600 to 800 pesos. He was still earning 600 pesos per year, although now supporting a large family. Although a royal order issued in 1792 had recommended that he be promoted, nothing had happened for the last eighteen years. Obes summarized his career history as follows:

> since I adopted this career, perhaps because I so wanted to do the best job possible in carrying out my duties, perhaps because I was so young and full of hope because a new agency was being set up, I

fooled myself into thinking that I would one day be promoted to one of the top positions. In spite of this rather prudent idea, I have seen four administrators, the same number of accountants, and two treasurers pass through here in succession, without any of these job vacancies bringing me any promotion or advantage at all, for those named to these posts always came from the outside.

Lack of professional advancement occurred at all levels of the Buenos Aires bureaucracy. The crown did attempt to compensate for this professional stagnation for at least a small group of high-ranking individuals. Unable to promote high-ranking officials as fast as they might have desired, the Spanish crown began in the years following the assumption of Charles IV to the throne to award honorary positions to deserving public servants. Most frequently the honorary post was in an agency outside of Buenos Aires. This insured that the bureaucrat in question, while being honored with a new title and greater ceremony, did not meddle in the day-to-day affairs of the agency in question. Benito de la Mata Linares, regent of the Buenos Aires Audiencia, for example, was also *ministro honorario* (honorary minister) of the Council of the Indies.[32]

Likewise, bureaucrats posted in the cities of the interior were honored with membership in Buenos Aires agencies. The two most frequently awarded honorary posts were that of oidor of the Real Audiencia and contador mayor of the Tribunal de Cuentas. The crown began with contador honorario posts, granting two in the 1790s.[33] Only one honorary oidor title was granted up to 1802; from 1802 to 1809 at least three of these titles were issued by the crown.[34] Occasionally, local men received local honorary appointment, but this was rare. Such appointments tended to be used to reward only the oldest and most loyal civil servants and were to the less exalted Real Hacienda. Matías Bernal, a man who had worked as oficial primero in the Reales Cajas and secretary-accountant in the montepío, was named contador honorario of the Real Hacienda.[35]

Given this limited opportunity for advancement, why did the majority of government officials remain in the bureaucracy? In spite of frustration, staff bureaucratic positions brought with them a valued commodity, security.[36] In theory the crown could remove any government employee at any time, but this rarely occurred. The same right to remove incompetent employees was contained in the *Reglamento de dependientes de la tesorería* in 1779, which stated that the intendant could dismiss any bureaucrat who failed to fulfill his obligation, was disobedient to superiors, or failed to in-spire the necessary dedication to work among his fellow employees.[37] But subsequent royal cédulas limited this sweeping power by establishing com-plex formal proceedings to be followed before dismissal.

Once an individual had received royal appointment in the form of an official title, he enjoyed complete job security. He would only be dismissed in cases of the more horrendous misconduct, usually involving massive and blantant embezzlement of funds.[38] Even when bureaucratic reorganization made a position redundant, the incumbent continued to draw a full salary, perhaps the most important aspect of his job security. A bureaucrat with a regular paying position within an agency had that position for life. Al-though advancement might not come rapidly, incumbents were rarely fired, regardless of how inept their performance might be.

Occasionally, however, because of personal problems or the crusading zeal of a visitador, a middle-ranking bureaucrat could find his career shat-tered. Two such bureaucrats, both employed by the Real Renta de Tabaco, suffered the rare indignity of demotion, as close as a government bureau-crat could come to being openly dismissed. The first of these, Miguel Mar-qués de la Plata, arrived in Buenos Aires in 1787 in the company of his older brother José, newly appointed fiscal of the Real Audiencia. José, armed with a royal order requesting special placement for his brother, was able to use his influence to get Miguel placed as oficial entretenido in the Ad-ministración General of the tobacco monopoly and within two weeks named oficial primero of the accounting section of the same Administra-ción General. Less than two years later, Manuel José de la Valle, contador general interino, promoted Miguel to oficial tercero of the Contaduría General. Miguel, described as being of "well-known ability, unusual tal-ent, very exemplary conduct and most constant application," was clearly making record progress within the bureaucracy, due no doubt to a judi-cious mixture of his personal qualities and the influence of his brother.[39] Unfortunately, tobacco oficiales who had been patiently waiting for ad-vancement, and individuals within both the Real Renta de Tabaco and the Audiencia who resented Don José's high-handed tactics, appealed to the viceroy who in turn notified the king of the meteoric rise of Don Miguel. On 31 August 1790 a royal order decreed that the natural advancement pro-cess be reinstituted: "the position of third oficial must be given to the fourth oficial in the said Contaduría General and this man given the fifth clerkship in the same office." Miguel could be transferred to the rank of oficial but only to the lowest rung, that of fifth oficial.[40] Clearly, the royal prerogative, while willing to grant special consideration to Marqués de la Plata, did not believe the fiscal should be allowed to parachute his brother into a third oficial post, thereby upsetting a clearly established slow process of advancement.

The second case of demotion, that of Vicente Mariano de Reyna Vásquez, was in many ways more tragic than what had befallen Miguel Marqués de la Plata. Vicente Mariano, the porteño-born son of Vicente Reyna and María de Cáseres, had entered the bureaucracy in 1783 at the age of eighteen as a meritorio in the Contaduría General of the Real Renta de Tabaco.[41] Within nine months Reyna was promoted to the job of *oficial escribiente entretenido* (clerk-scribe in training) and granted a salary of 250 pesos per year. Six months later he received another promotion, this time to oficial escribiente (oficial quinto). Two years later he was again promoted to oficial quarto and after four-and-a-half years at this rank was named oficial tercero. Clearly, Reyna was moving along in the bureaucracy, although his progress was less than startling for a young man described as having "outstanding ability and talent," "most judicious conduct," and "consistent dedication."[42]

Reyna's outstanding talents seem to have been widely noted by his superiors, who occasionally called upon him to undertake special "commissions and charges," which he carried out with the highest intelligence. As early as 1783 Pedro José Ballesteros, the contador mayor supernumerario of the Tribunal de Cuentas, used Reyna, who was then employed as a meritorio, as an escribiente when faced with the task of "clarifying the smokescreen put up by the Director Don Pedro Dionisio Gálvez concerning the general accounts of the tobacco monopoly." Reyna, working in conjunction with Ballesteros and Francisco Urdaneta, contador general of the Real Renta de Tabaco, "toiled day and night for three months" helping to conclude the work at hand.[43] Again, in 1790 while employed as oficial quarto, Reyna, because he had demonstrated "a clear handwriting, correct conduct, and the circumspection needed to carry out the most important pursuits of Royal Service," was asked to aid Viceroy Loreto for a six month period.[44]

In January 1798, after seven years as oficial tercero, Reyna, who now had almost fifteen years of service in the Real Renta de Tabaco to his credit, received a major promotion. He was appointed contador interventor interino of the Renta's *almacenes generales* (general warehouses) and was given the task of paying all wages to those employed in the snuff factory located in the Renta's headquarters.[45] Although a temporary position, this was clearly a major career advancement, and Reyna's work seemed to please everyone. The assignment ended in 1802 when a new administrador was appointed, and Reyna returned to the accounting department of the Renta, where he was assigned the task of preparing five-year reports being drawn up for the visitador de la Real Hacienda, Diego de la Vega.

Although Reyna was soon complimented for having "fulfilled his duty in this difficult and delicate operation with intelligence and hard work," he was about to fall from bureaucratic favor.[46] De la Vega, undertaking a wide-ranging review of the Buenos Aires bureaucratic machine, soon encountered irregularities in the 1801 accounts of the almacenes generales. Reyna, a man who lacked strong family ties and political influence within the bureaucracy, was a perfect victim of the visitador's zeal. Unlike higher-ranking bureaucrats who successfully tussled with de la Vega, Reyna could command neither the power nor influence to challenge de la Vega's findings. Although he claimed to be innocent, in October 1803 Reyna was ordered to repay 2,309 pesos 2-1/2 reales to the Royal Treasury, the amount of the shortfall found in his accounts. The sum was to be taken in installments from Reyna's 600 pesos salary by discounting one-third of his annual salary until complete payment was made. But even worse than the fine was de la Vega's stricture, dutifully entered on Reyna's permanent employment records, that "the said Reyna, neither now nor in the future, is absolutely forbidden from taking on any job in the tobacco Renta, or in any of the other branches of the Royal Treasury in which he must manage any type of funds. . . . In case, because of future service, he is proposed for any job in the administration, it must only be a bookkeeping task."[47] Reyna, age thirty-eight, was a man destroyed, although he continued for at least another year to be employed in the Real Renta de Tabaco, working in the contaduría although officially listed as oficial de libros in the almacenes generales. The reaction of this once-exemplary civil servant is reflected in his personnel record. By 1804 "he had stopped coming to the contaduría office for 154 whole days and 86 half days making a total absence of 197 working days."[48]

De la Vega's visita, the most far-reaching inquiry undertaken during the viceregal period, also affected other bureaucratic careers. Charged in

1802 with reviewing all branches of the viceroyalty's Exchequer while also acting as contador mayor decano of the Tribunal, de la Vega was dispatched to Buenos Aires by the crown because of a long-simmering argument between the chief ministers of the Reales Cajas of Buenos Aires and the contadores mayores of the Tribunal, a dispute over who was ultimately responsible for the "bankruptcies, robberies, and poor investment of Royal Treasury funds."[49] The crown and the visitador sided with the treasury officials, blaming Juan José Ballesteros and Juan Antonio de Arroyo, newly named contadores mayores, for laxity in auditing and settling royal accounts and allowing a huge backlog of unbalanced accounts to mount up. Both men were immediately removed from their positions and forced into retirement by de la Vega. Although reinstated in 1807,[50] after they had repeatedly petitioned the crown and justified the Tribunal's state of affairs, the rapidity with which two proven government servants had fallen from grace made the precarious nature of the relatively secure bureaucratic career most evident. Nonetheless, because both Ballesteros and Arroyo enjoyed a degree of influence both in Buenos Aires and in Spain, they were eventually successful in annulling the visitador's verdict.

Because of the limited opportunities for advancement within the bureaucracy, competition for even minor advancement within the hierarchy was intense. Minor officials were extremely sensitive to their rank and ever on guard to prevent someone with less seniority from moving more quickly than they. In 1795 Lorenzo Fuentes, for example, successfully challenged the appointment of another bureaucrat as archivero interino of the the Secretaría del Virreinato.[51] Fuentes, who had arrived in the retinue of Viceroy Loreto, had spent ten years in the Secretaría de Cámara as a meritorio before receiving a regular appointment as oficial tercero. He very much resented the appointment of a relative newcomer, José Rebollar, who had served for only three years as *contador de dinero* (accountant in charge of cash funds) in the Cajas of Buenos Aires, to the archivero post. Although Rebollar was able to hold on to the position until 1797, Fuentes finally received the promotion he sorely felt was his due.

Although one aim of the Bourbon policy was a professionalization of the bureaucracy, personal connections, local politics, timing, luck, diplomacy, and ability all still played their roles in determining which few bureaucrats would experience career mobility. Still another factor was place of birth. Intendant Fernández, in his reorganization of the local bureaucracy, hoped that qualified creoles would play a role, albeit limited, in the expanding bureaucracy. In a letter written to José de Gálvez concerning the Real Ordenanza de Intendentes, the legislation that created many new positions, he commented:

> We are convinced that employing some local men with good handwritings and judgment in the lesser positions within the agencies, [employing] some able lawyers as assistant advisers to the Intendancies, and [using] some few other deserving subjects in other jobs, could be most useful although top officials or those in the most important posts should not serve in the city of their birth in order to avoid the problems that usually occur.[52]

Fernández's successor, Francisco de Paula Sanz, also believed that creoles had a role to play in the government bureaucracy, although he also subscribed to the view that they should not serve in their native provinces.

Given this somewhat guarded support for creole participation, did the bureaucracy provide equal career opportunities for native-born young men? To analyze the geographical origins of those who held bureaucratic posts during the viceroyalty, material was gathered on a sample of 158 individuals who served the colonial bureaucracy in some salaried capacity from 1776 to 1810.

As can be seen in the following table (table 5.4), creoles were by no means systematically excluded from the Buenos Aires bureaucracy. While far from the majority in any agency (and of course in the bureaucracy as a whole), some native-born men could be found in every government office in Buenos Aires. The only exception to this was at the rank of chief administrator; no porteño ever served as either viceroy or intendant, although one American, Juan José de Vértiz, did hold this leadership position.

While present in virtually every agency in Buenos Aires, native-born men were certainly not found in the same proportions in all agencies and at all ranks. The three agencies where porteños seemed to have a better chance of finding employment were the Real Renta de Tabaco, the Secretarías (where they comprised 38 percent of the employees), and the Aduana (where they comprised 35 percent). Conversely, the agency most resistant to employing native-born men was the Tribunal de Cuentas, followed closely by the Real Hacienda. Clearly, in the area of finance the crown showed a strong preference for bureaucrats born in Spain, assuming that

Table 5.4   Birthplace of Government Bureaucrats by Agency, 1776–1810

| Agency and rank | Birthplace | | | |
	Spain N	Buenos Aires N	Other America N	Total
Viceroy	10	–	1	11
Intendant	3	–	–	3
Total	13(93%)	–	1(7%)	14
Real Hacienda				
Ministro	3	1	–	4
Contador	4	1	–	5
Oficial	9	5	–	14
Total	16(70%)	7(30%)	–	23
Secretariats				
Secretary	5	1	–	6
Oficial	5	4	–	9
Legal advisors & escribanos	2	5	4	11
Total	12(46%)	10(38%)	4(15%)	26
Tribunal de Cuentas				
Contador Mayor	4	–	1	5
Ordenador	10	2	2	14
Oficial	9	4	–	13
Total	23(72%)	6(19%)	3(9%)	32
Aduana				
Administrador	4	1	–	5
Contador	6	1	–	7
Oficial	7	7	–	14
Total	17(65%)	9(35%)	–	26
Tabacos				
Administrador	3	–	1	4
Contador	4	–	2	6
Oficial	13	14	–	27
Total	20(54%)	14(38%)	3(8%)	37
	101(64%)	46(29%)	11(7%)	158

these men, devoid of local contacts, would be more honest in dealing with government funds.

If porteños fared only moderately well in obtaining government employment in their native city, men born in other cities of America fared even worse. While 29 percent of the bureaucrats contained in the sample were Buenos Aires born, only 7 percent came from other New World regions. But surprisingly, although few in number, some of the non-porteño Americans achieved relatively high positions in the local bureaucracy, especially in the Tribunal de Cuentas and the Real Renta de Tabaco. While no man born in Buenos Aires ever served as a contador mayor of the Tribunal de Cuentas, another American did achieve this honor; as many non-porteños as porteños reached the rank of contador ordenador. In the Real Renta de Tabaco no native of Buenos Aires ever served as administrador or contador, while a respectable percentage of other Americans were appointed to these positions. Clearly, few residents of other American areas were drawn to Buenos Aires. The few that came arrived with fairly high-level appointments, not in search of entry-level jobs. The crown seemed only too willing to use their talent, considering the non-native son to be more trustworthy than a man born in Buenos Aires itself.

Not only were the majority of bureaucrats born in Spain, but there was a strong positive correlation between Spanish birth and high bureaucratic rank. This is not to say that no Spaniards were found among the low-level bureaucrats in the city. Indeed, as can be seen in table 5.4, Spaniards were in a majority at every level of the salaried bureaucracy, including that of oficial. But while they represented 56 percent of the oficiales employed by all agencies, they were 60 percent of the middle-level accountants and 84 percent of the high-ranking agency chiefs. Conversely, the vast majority of native sons found in the bureaucracy were at the lower level. Indeed, while 32 percent of all Spanish-born bureaucrats held top-level positions in the Buenos Aires bureaucracy, only 7 percent of native-born bureaucrats could be found at the same level. Spanish policy did not exclude creoles; it rather concentrated them at the bottom of the bureaucratic heap.

For all individual agencies the same approximate relationship held true. In the Aduana, for example, of the twenty-six men identified as holding some position in the Aduana bureaucracy during the viceregal period, seventeen were Spanish-born. Again, as in all the bureaucracies established by the Bourbons after 1778, the correlation between rank within the bureaucracy and Spanish-birth was especially strong. The higher the position within the Aduana, the greater probability that the incumbent had been born outside of America.

Although the influence of the Andalucían José de Gálvez in obtaining bureaucratic posts for his fellow countrymen has often been cited in connection with the Spanish America bureaucracy, examination of the regional origin of high-ranking Buenos Aires bureaucrats named to posts during Gálvez's tenure as the secretary of state for the Indies does not reflect as strong a preference for men from the south as previously imagined.[53] Of fifteen high-ranking bureaucrats named to posts under viceroys Cevallos and Vértiz, for example, twelve were Peninsula-born.[54] Half of these men (six) were from Andalucía, but four of them, a surprisingly large group, were from Navarre. The third region to supply men was Galicia, which accounted for the remaining two individuals. Information gathered on the bureaucrats during the entire viceregal period indicates that these proportions remained fairly static; Andalucía followed closely by Galicia and the Basque region were the primary *patrias chicas* of Spanish-born bureaucrats.

Sketchy evidence on the socioeconomic background of the bureaucrats suggests that they were in the main members of the Spanish petite bourgeoisie. In the Aduana, for example, none of the bureaucrats were noble, and those who had any influence back in Spain usually had only tenuous connections. Some Spaniards, especially those who held posts in the Administración of the Aduana (administrador, contador, vista, or alcaide), had been promoted to the Buenos Aires Aduana after long years in the Spanish or American bureaucracy. A few had prior military service but usually as military bureaucrats rather than officers or soldiers. As in all other branches of the local bureaucracy, those in lesser positions tended to be younger, arriving in Buenos Aires with only a few years of prior royal service or, more likely, with letters of recommendation to a local high-ranking bureaucrat. Those few creoles who entered the Aduana bureaucracy came from similar backgrounds as their Peninsular counterparts; they were overwhelmingly the sons of *mercaderes* (retail merchants) or low-level *comerciantes* (wholesale merchants) who entered the Aduana after serving several years as meritorios. Again, as with the Tribunal de Cuentas, service as a meritorio did not guarantee that eventually a line position would be won, and young men from Spain seemed to be preferred over those porteños who had spent four or five years as meritorios.

Some porteño-born bureaucrats came from even more modest social backgrounds. In general, these individuals experienced less career mobility than the mainstream. Marcos Prudán, the son of José Prudán, a Buenos Aires shoemaker, entered the Real Renta de Tabaco and was posted to Corrientes where he served as *dependiente del resguardo* (subordinate in the coast guard).[55] Prudán, age twenty-two when he entered the bureaucracy, was tapped five years later by the de la Vega visita to serve as aide and scribe in a review of Paraguayan tobacco production and accounts. Returning to Buenos Aires in 1802, Prudán was put in charge of registering cigarette workers as they entered and left the factory. Soon after he was moved to the Buenos Aires contaduría, where he served as auxiliar. By the end of 1802 Prudán was again returned to Corrientes where he took up his original position. In 1806 he received word that he was to be transferred to Salta where he would work as *tercenista principal* (chief wholesale tobacco agent). During all these transfers, although his title was changed from dependiente de resguardo to a more prestigious *escribiente auxiliar* (assistant scribe), Prudán never earned more than the minimal salary of 180 pesos per year.

Whether or not creole birth influenced the attitude of a government official in considering promotion is difficult to determine, but there are indications that the issue never lay much below the surface. Charges of discrimination based on birthplace where hurled justly or unjustly in times of discord and stress. José Vicente Carrancio, a Spanish-born lawyer accused of being one of the parties involved in a lampoon scandal during the rule of Viceroy Vértiz, accused Vértiz's secretary, the creole Antonio Basilio Aldao, of discrimination against all Europeans. Carrancio blamed Aldao's implacable hatred of the Spanish-born for the "injustice with which I have been reviled."[56] Furthermore, Carrancio stressed Aldao's influence with the viceroy, the not unexpected result of holding a position of intimacy and importance in the running of the government. "With his influence" Aldao is able to "stir up or quell the docile temperament of the viceroy like the musician Timothy did with Alexander."

Although these charges against Aldao were never proven, Carrancio's complaints probably influenced Aldao's career. Officials in Madrid were only too anxious to react to any suggestions that creoles were guilty of favoritism. Aldao, a lawyer who had served as legal counsel for several government agencies during the 1760s (including asesor general and auditor de guerra during Cevallos's governorship, *síndico procurador general* [attorney general] of the Cabildo, *defensor* [counsel for the defense] of Temporalidades from 1767, and *promotor fiscal* [district attorney] of the Real Hacienda), was Vértiz's clear choice as secretario.[57] Indeed, Vértiz had nominated Aldao for the position, assigning him a salary of 2600 pesos per year. While Aldao occupied the secretary's chair on an interim basis awaiting royal confirmation, Carrancio's complaint arrived in Madrid. On 28 January 1779 the king, in a royal order addressed to Vértiz, rejected Aldao's nomination, although he was allowed to continue in office until a new secretary arrived in Buenos Aires.[58] Aldao was never again to achieve the same position of influence in the government. In 1785 Viceroy Marqués de Loreto, Vértiz's successor, complained in a letter to Gálvez that Aldao was now attacking his government because "the current authority does not follow his advice as in the past."[59]

The norm for bureaucratic advancement was to slowly move up the ladder of success within the confines of one agency. But this progression could only take one so far. In all agencies, but especially in the Tribunal de Cuentas and the Secretarías, top-ranking positions were usually awarded not to those who had come through the ranks but rather to bureaucrats who had first served in other government departments. The crown believed that these two agencies, because of their wide-ranging duties and the requirement that their leadership have a catholic knowledge of government, were best served by those who had firsthand experience in running one of the agencies to be overseen. While there is little doubt of the wisdom of advancing a man who had headed the Reales Cajas to the Tribunal de Cuentas (or the man who had directed the Real Renta de Tabaco to the head of the Superintendency), these individuals often proved to have vested interests linked to their former agencies that affected their performance in their new position. This pattern of parachuting in an agency's top administrators from other agencies rather than internal promotion also produced growing frustration among the ranks of the first oficiales. To continue to advance within the bureaucracy the oficiales primeros were forced to curry favor with the directors of other agencies and with the viceroy, for their only hope of progress became that of a lateral-vertical transfer, that is, appointment to a higher rank within another institution.

Nevertheless, a few individuals did work their way to high office in the platense viceroyalty. What was their method of bureaucratic advancement? What distinguished them from their fellow clerks who failed to be pro-

moted? Almost to a man they exhibited at least one of the following qualifications: they came to viceregal administration from a background in military administration, they were already in Buenos Aires by 1777, and/or they
were blood relatives of a local viceroy. So overwhelming were these patterns that a sample group of twenty high-level administrators (excluding
Audiencia judges) 60 percent filled one of these criteria while another 30
percent filled more than one.[60]

The preference for choosing bureaucratic leadership from among men
who had experience in the military bureaucracy should not be surprising,
given the military reasons underlying the creation of the Río de la Plata
viceroyalty and the continued importance of defense to the later Bourbon
monarchy. From 1715 on all governors of the province were men from military backgrounds, and each of the eleven viceroys who served in Buenos
Aires was a trained military man. Indeed, one of the more important duties
of the Buenos Aires viceroy was that of serving as captain general of the
Royal Army. It was only natural that these governors and viceroys when
choosing others to fill positions in their administrations would demonstrate a sympathy toward bureaucrats who, although they had not served as
combat soldiers, were at least acquainted with military procedure and military objectives.

Many men who would eventually become high-ranking officials first
arrived in Buenos Aires before 1777 as part of the military administration.
The years between 1770 and 1777, the years of heightened conflict between
the Spaniards and Portuguese in the Missions area recently vacated by the
Jesuits, had seen a sharp increase in the numbers of troops, expeditions,
military missions, and negotiating teams sent to the Río de la Plata. In
addition to soldiers, diplomats, royal envoys, and surveyors, each of these
missions had included at least one individual charged with keeping accounts and records. It was in this role that those who would later serve as
contadores and administradores first arrived in Buenos Aires.

The majority of high-level bureaucrats actually arrived in the area
under the auspices of military missions undertaken during the government
of Pedro de Cevallos, who first served as governor of Río de la Plata from
1756 to 1766 and was named the first viceroy of the area from 1777 to 1778.
When Cevallos sailed for Río de la Plata in 1776, he was accompanied by an
expedition of 116 ships carrying 19,000 troops, their officers, and officials.
In addition to being charged with setting up a new administrative unit in

the colonies, Cevallos was first to complete a military mission against the Portuguese in the Banda Oriental. Cevallos and his men arrived in the vicinity of Santa Catarina in February 1779, successfully engaging the Portuguese and ending their presence in the platense outpost of Côlonia da Sacramento.[61] Only then did Cevallos turn toward Buenos Aires and his civilian mission. Armed with royal orders creating a viceroyalty and fortified with additional orders to include Buenos Aires in the orbit of "free trade," Cevallos had a number of new departments to create and a number of new bureaucratic positions to dispense. In essence, while creating these departments and naming a full complement of staff, the viceroy showed an overwhelming preference for those who had accompanied him in past military exploits, especially in his choice for the highest-level positions.

The men chosen by Cevallos in 1777–78, although they had a fair amount of experience, were rather young for the positions to which they were named. Indeed, the average age of a group of fifteen men appointed to high-level posts by the viceroy was 36.5. Because of their relative youth at the time of appointment, these bureaucrats would remain in their positions for many years to come, thereby closing off normal channels of advancement to those below them. In essence, this produced a situation in which numerous opportunities for advancement and employment quickly gave way to rather limited ones. Only after 1795 was there any noticeable opening of positions. At that time a group of oficiales primeros, many of whom had waited for promotion for fifteen to twenty years, moved into top-level jobs.

The third category of occupants of high-level bureaucratic positions, those who were blood relatives of a viceroy or intendant, was surprisingly small, a reflection of the extent to which Bourbon reforms had succeeded in controlling the Hapsburg plague of nepotism. During the entire viceregal period, only five individuals can be documented as having received a bureaucratic appointment under the sponsorship of a viceroy-kin, and only two of these were to high-level positions. The most unpopular of these appointments was that of Andrés de Torres, nephew of Viceroy Loreto, named secretario of the Secretaría de Cámara in 1783. Loreto, a closed and cautious man, was by nature opposed to entrusting what he viewed as confidential material to a stranger. Indeed, as the position of secretario had evolved from that of personal secretary of the governor and by definition had to enjoy the confidence of the viceroy, his preference of a pariente was not unusual. But unfortunately for administrative harmony, Torres was a rather lackluster, not to say incompetent, bureaucrat, little interested in his official duties, and prone to leave his work to disgruntled underlings.

Charges of favoritism in career advancement were not new, but as chances for career advancement slowed and the ability to grow rich through government service was also reduced, complaints tended to become more bitter. The case of José María Roo and Luis Herrera Izaguirre is instructive. Roo, the porteño-born son of Cornelio Matías Roo, a bureaucrat who had served as *oficial de contaduría* (clerk in the accounting section) and contador ordenador interino of the Tribunal de Cuentas, had followed his father's footsteps by entering into the royal bureaucracy in 1774 at age twenty-two. Aided no doubt by his father, the younger Roo had slowly climbed the bureaucratic ladder, serving first in the Real Hacienda, then in the Tribunal de Cuentas, and finally in the Montevideo Aduana office. Roo, after twenty-five years of government service, had finally worked himself up to the post of oficial primero in the administration and accounting section of the Aduana when the contador retired. Don José María fully expected to be promoted to this vacant spot, for he himself, his late father, and his brother-in-law, Justo Pastor Lynch, had all served the crown well. Unfortunately, the acting viceroy, Antonio Olaguer Feliú, had an even better candidate for the Aduana post—Luis Herrera Izaguirre.

Herrera, born in Buenos Aires in 1763 (and therefore eleven years younger than Roo), was the son of Antonio Herrera, a local church notary. He entered government service at age nineteen when he was named oficial tercero of Superintendent Fernández's Secretaría. On 4 September 1793, while still employed at the same position, Herrera married Gervacia Basavilbaso, daughter of Francisco Antonio Basavilbaso, escribano mayor de gobernación, and María Aurelia Ros.[62] Basavilbaso was related to one of the major mercantile clans of the family, the Basavilbaso-Azcuenaga family.[63] Furthermore, his niece, Ana de Azcuenaga, had only five years earlier married Antonio Olaguer Feliú, brigadier general of the Royal Army and inspector general of the Viceregal Troops. Luis Herrera's marriage into the Basavilbaso family provided him with a wealth of contacts with which to advance his career.

In May 1797 Antonio Olaguer Feliú was named acting viceroy of the Río de la Plata. The new viceroy lost little time in filling the Montevideo Aduana post, but to Roo's enormous dismay instead of choosing him, the man next in line, the viceroy opted for none other than his wife's first cousin's husband. Herrera who had never before served in any branch of the Aduana was soon confirmed by royal order in his new post.[64] Roo, greatly disappointed, lost no time in petitioning the crown.[65] He appealed to royal clemency, pointing to the "irreparable harm that had been caused to his poor and growing family" and alluding to the reason for Herrera's promotion ("the wife of Herrera is a first cousin of the wife of Señor Olaguer"). He also reminded the king that this action was in direct contradiction to "repeated royal orders stressing that no government employee be deprived of his just promotions." But Herrera's appointment stood. Roo well understood the fate that would now befall him. "I remain submerged in the lesser bureaucrat group for the rest of my days, [with] the only hope that kept me going now dead."

Government officials at all levels paid close attention to their progress in the bureaucracy as compared to that of their peers and were quick to complain when they believed they had been passed over for promotion. These complaints, especially when they involved promotion at the minor ranks, engendered bitter letters to the crown. Most frequently, the fourth or fifth official who had not been promoted charged his superiors with unfair favoritism; his superior usually responded by arguing that other candidates were more competent for the job in question. Occasionally, these disputes also included ad hominem attacks that reflect both intergenerational social mobility and the precarious socioeconomic position of the lesser bureaucrats.

In 1805, for example, Diego José de Sosa y Marqués, a native of Buenos Aires, complained that fellow porteño, Justo Pastor Lynch, contador of the Buenos Aires Aduana, had promoted escribiente Mariano de Lazcano to oficial cuarto, although he, Sosa, had much more experience.[66] Sosa, in fact, had served the crown for nineteen years, first as a meritorio and then as an escribiente. The contador "because of capriciousness, predilection, and partiality" had unjustly ignored Sosa's "right, service, and antiquity," and this was clearly unjust.

Lynch replied to Sosa's charges, which he labeled "false and excessive," by pointing out that Diego (without the use of the honorific "Don") was "notoriously known as being of mulatto origin." In Lynch's eyes his racial inferiority explained the supposed baseness of Sosa's actions. Sosa, in turn, replied questioning Lynch's social origins: "The undersigned admires the contador's boldness, for it is commonly known around here, even by his fellow countrymen, that his parents were of a most despicable social category and that only the grace of good fortune has made them so haughty."

By throwing dirt on each other's social quality, both men revealed the truth, and both gave witness to a degree of social mobility, albeit severely limited, in colonial Buenos Aires. Lynch, the español of humble origins, had successfully come up the bureaucratic ladder, and the mulatto Sosa had been allowed into royal service in spite of the required proof of "purity of blood." But race was a difficult obstacle to overcome. Once admitted to the fellowship of Aduana employees, Sosa had found promotion even more slow than his pure-blooded peers, not surprising given the racial prejudice inherent in Spanish culture and the growing competition for a finite number of government jobs. Nonetheless, Sosa had not hesitated to defend his rights when he perceived that he was the victim of Lynch's favoritism.

Increasingly frustrated with the static nature of their professional situation, bureaucrats of all rank became ever more quick to cry out against any of their colleagues jumping in front of them within the hierarchy. Because their requests for advancement based on merit had so frequently been answered with worthless royal orders, the ambitious also devoted much time to keeping track of positions that were open and identifying those men who had just died or were most likely to retire or to die in the near future. They thereby hoped to gain a preferential place for nomination and promotion in the local agencies. This constant surveying of the field in a desire to advance seems to have informed the conduct of all, from the lowest-ranking clerks to men at the top of the bureaucracy. For example, José Barreda, oficial primero of the Secretaría, wrote to the crown in 1804 asking that he be named contador of the Consulado (newly created), oficial mayor of the Real Renta de Tabaco (the incumbent had just died), or alcaide of the Real Aduana of Montevideo (again the incumbent was recently deceased). Before he could get his letter into the mail, he received news of the death of the contador ordenador of the Tribunal de Cuentas and quickly appended this job to his list. Barreda, who had received a royal order instructing that he be considered for promotion in 1793, was no more successful this time.[67]

Some bureaucrats went as far as suggesting that the crown retire their colleagues; others took advantage of any delay in a peer's normalization of título to obtain the disputed post for themselves.[68] Still others suggested ingenious financial arrangements, such as sharing salaries with kin in order to gain appointment or promotion.[69] Those seeking appointment or promotion could do little to remedy the basic problem—the local bureaucracy had reached its numerical plateau by the 1800s. Thereafter, the crown was both unwilling and financially unable to decree sustained additional growth.

Internecine warfare need not only occur over promotion. More frequently, it was power, although often petty and severely limited, that the bureaucrats did battle for. Antonio de Pinedo Montufar, tesorero of the Reales Cajas, wasted no time in filing a complaint when Antonio Carrasco, the newly appointed contador of the same agency, was invited to attend a meeting of the Junta Superior de Real Hacienda. The viceroy was merely following a precedent that had been established under Carrasco's predecessor, Pedro Medrano, but Pinedo Montufar was quick to point out that he, because of his longer service in the Reales Cajas, deserved to be tapped for this honor.[70]

Disputes over power could occur between agencies or within an agency. Although the clear hierarchy established within each agency should have prevented internal dissension, uncooperative bureaucrats tended to make these incidents more common than the crown would have desired. The director of any agency was clearly to have power over all other officials in his agency, but the director was occasionally forced by intransigent underlings to appeal to the superintendent, viceroy, or Tribunal de Cuentas for support.

Such a case occurred in 1786 when Pedro Dionisio Gálvez, director of the tobacco monopoly since 1783, failed to receive a reply to his request that his contador general, Francisco Urdaneta, account for funds on hand in the Renta belonging to the playing cards monopoly. Gálvez, whose repeated requests to Urdaneta had gone unheeded, finally turned to Superintendent Francisco de Paula Sanz, a man well acquainted with the workings of the Real Renta de Tabaco, who had preceded him as director. Sanz's response was fast and unequivocal; by nine o'clock in the evening he appeared personally in Urdaneta's house demanding that a full accounting of the playing card funds be made immediately. Two-and-a-half hours later, the *escribano del Rey* (king's notary), acting under Sanz's orders, informed Joa-

quín Yoldi, the general treasurer of the Real Renta de Tabaco and Urdaneta's underling, that he was to appear immediately at the Renta headquarters prepared to turn over the key to the main door of the treasury.
Two days later, on 15 January 1785, Sanz, accompanied by José Antonio
Hurtado y Sandoval, contador mayor decano of the Tribunal de Cuentas,
by Pedro Dionisio Gálvez, by Urdaneta, and by Yoldi met to check out
each *talega* (money bag) of the *naipes* (playing card) revenue sent down
from Potosí. Luckily for Urdaneta and Yoldi, a satisfactory accounting was
made: "counting and weighing each money bag, the director made sure
that everyone was in conformity with its accompanying statement . . . and
thus the scrutiny of accounts proceeded, as those accounts that had no
questions associated with them were checked off, and the contents of the
money bags with less than 1,000 pesos were counted."[71]

Urdaneta and Yoldi had been vindicated, but Yoldi was not yet satisfied. Within days he presented a formal complaint to Sanz, charging that
Gálvez had insulted him by publicly demanding the key and an accounting
of the funds. "My sense of honor cried out (as well it should) against the
grievous blow of such an undeserved affront; and seeing all just proportion crushed, I had to defend my honorable conduct in carrying out the
post the king turned over to me. I was forced to find out where this insult
had originated." Yoldi furthermore accused Gálvez of "scandalously dis-
honoring me and casting aspersion on my well-known loyalty." Sanz managed to diffuse Yoldi's anger. Within two years Gálvez was promoted to
contador mayor of the Tribunal de Cuentas of Lima and Urdaneta named
new director of the Buenos Aires Real Renta de Tabaco. Yoldi himself continued to head the Renta's treasury until 1802, although the treasury was
subsumed by the Contaduría by 1790.

In their climb up the bureaucratic ladder, government officials also attempted to guard any attendant perquisites they had earned in earlier
posts. Bureaucrats sent to Buenos Aires frequently tried to transfer previously awarded housing allowances. This was understandable, for housing was both hard to find and expensive in Buenos Aires. Pedro Nolasco
Viguera, newly appointed treasurer of the Aduana, for example, requested
that the government provide him with a 500 peso housing allowance in
1802.[72] Viguera had previously served as administrador of Temporalidades
in Chile and Buenos Aires. When the Temporalidades office was disbanded, Viguera was transferred to the Aduana, a move that was inter-

preted by him as a demotion even though it had no effect on his salary.
Worst for Viguera was the loss of the house that he had enjoyed in Temporalidades. Five hundred pesos, Viguera pointed out, "was the annual
rent for a house in this city." In fact his house, although it was one quarter
of a league away from the Aduana, rented for even more.

Viguera, in his petition for a housing allowance, argued in a novel
fashion that the government should pay his rent because his home served
as an extension of his office. "Treasurers should have their money under
their care stored away in their homes" so as to better protect the funds for
which they are responsible. But housing was also an important perquisite
because it was usually only awarded to the heads of specific agencies and as
such was an indication of special position. Indeed, requests for housing
and for other perks reflected a self-consciousness by bureaucrats of the importance of their agency and their respective role within colonial society.

Jealously guarding their positions and any tokens of power that should
have fallen their way, government officials were seriously concerned with
matters of etiquette, formality, and precedence between individuals and
between agencies. The ministers of the Real Hacienda complained to the
king that the viceroy and other "lesser chief administrators" insulted them
by referring to them in written correspondence as "los Ministros de Real
Hacienda" instead of the more polite "Señores Ministros de Real Hacienda." In response to this complaint the crown issued two royal orders
aimed at correcting the slight. "It is not right that such a style of address be
used for individuals whose distinguished and important services are so
prized by His Majesty and by our laws," observed the king, calling for all
government bureaucrats, regardless of rank, to treat the ministros with
greater respect.[73]

In spite of royal orders clearly stressing that they were to be addressed
as "Señores," the ministros remained ever on guard to protect their honor
and carefully perused all correspondence that arrived on their desks for any
slights. They again complained in 1806 about an improper form of address,
citing Domingo Reynoso, the intendant of Buenos Aires, for failing to use
"the form of address that befits us." Reynoso, who himself had served in
the Reales Cajas for four years prior to his nomination as intendant, was
clearly intending an insult. Furthermore, he failed to include the ministros
in the *Guía de Foresteros*, a directory of government bureaucrats. The ministers, citing the Recopilación de Indias, Reales Ordenes, and learned

treatises to support their case, argued that as accountants and treasurers of military funds, as ministers of the Royal Treasury, and as individuals qualified to attend governmental juntas they deserved proper respect. Complaining that "the Royal Order of 14 May 1791 is not being observed in any way," they requested that the viceroy remedy their situation.[74]

Although these quarrels caused lasting dissension between agencies, the crown hoped local feuds would not affect the performance of its agents. The ideal viceregal bureaucrat was to attend to his job in a competent manner. His duty consisted of producing the reams of reports, accounts, and papers required by the crown and the local bureaucracy. He was neither required nor expected to be innovative nor overly ambitious, although sloth was also to be avoided. Change and reform were to be generated in the royal councils of Spain, not in branches of agencies in the New World. Bureaucratic reform, from major reorganizations such as the creation of the intendancy system to lesser changes such as the introduction of double-entry bookkeeping, came about only after slowly progressing through the metropolitan councils.

More than discouraged, a show of local initiative in inventing and introducing changes could eventually provoke royal wrath. Such was the case of Antonio Carrasco, a bureaucrat who served first as contador interventor and then as contador of the Reales Cajas in Buenos Aires. Carrasco, who had moved into the Exchequer after first serving in the Contaduría de Ejército, became interested in 1799 in the problem of supplying wood for naval construction. He drew up a proposal that called for the use of Real Hacienda funds to underwrite the cutting of wood in the forests of Paraguay and Misiones, a plan that he argued would provide cheaper lumber more rapidly to the shipbuilders in Montevideo. On June 6 the viceroy sent Carrasco's proposal to the crown. Within five months the crown granted Carrasco permission to put his plan into effect with the "greatest degree of scrupulosity." Under terms agreed to by the crown, he was to provide wood to the navy, the artillery and to all other royal workers from lumber cut and paid for by the Real Hacienda. To convince the crown of the feasibility of his plan Carrasco had offered to personally underwrite the expenses of the "first trial"; he would only be reimbursed if the plan proved feasible and beneficial to the treasury.[75] In return the crown ordered all local military officers to help Carrasco in putting his plan to work.

Carrasco was initially successful and heartened by demonstrated savings. He now further proposed that those brigantines to be constructed with the lumber supplied by the Real Hacienda be contracted to private shipbuilders instead of the Montevideo naval station. He also suggested that the crown set up a meat salting plant and a "factory manufacturing pipe staves for meat packing," again financed by the Real Hacienda, to provide meat for the troops. Carrasco's new ideas produced an open breech with the navy in Montevideo. Military officers who had said nothing about the wood-cutting project, now complained that the contador was overstepping his jurisdiction and asked that all his projects be disbanded.

After studying the problem, the crown agreed with the marina. Royal orders were fired off to Buenos Aires and Montevideo, instructing the *comandante de marina* (navy commander) that he need not accept any wood supplied by Carrasco.[76] Carrasco was told in no uncertain terms that he was not to have anything to do with the cutting of lumber and that any future correspondence with Spain was to be made only through his superiors (in this case the viceroy).[77] In addition, another royal order was sent to Carrasco admonishing him for his behavior.

> His Majesty completely disapproves Carrasco's plan, which has caused supreme discontent; His Majesty orders that he be admonished for his ambitious designs. . . . it has caused the king much displeasure to see a minister of the Royal Treasury getting involved in questions that are outside of his jurisdiction, and of which he has no knowledge. The king therefore commands that in the future Carrasco abstain from making suggestions that are offensive to people of the highest character because of his overweening ambition, which is even apparent in his letters.[78]

Frustration with the lack of opportunities for innovation and career advancement eventually resulted in a high degree of alienation among bureaucrats. To this was added the normal inertia that comes from the repetition of boring tasks. Alienation and inertia were demonstrated in several ways but chiefly in a general lessening of interest in the duties assigned and in growing absenteeism. Clerks who had been judged to be "outstanding in aptitude and talent" eventually realized that exceptional effort did little to guarantee either advancement or success. Later reports often record their growing lack of interest as their grades fell first to "superior" and then to "good." As long as one's work was passable, one ran no risk; rather, "outstanding" work itself could make one suspect of being overly ambitious. The same pattern was repeated over and over: young men who performed well in the early years of their employment became frustrated with their lack of progress, and realizing that outstanding service produced no benefits, became "average" workers within six or seven years.

The rate of absenteeism among government bureaucrats was another reflection of disenchantment with government service. Hojas de servicio for employees in any agency are instructive. In 1804 of ten clerks in the accounting office of the tobacco monopoly only two attended work daily.[79] The other eight were absent an average of 100 of a possible 285 workdays (the range of days missed ran from 53 to 197). This high rate of absenteeism affected the speed and efficiency with which clerks performed their tasks and no doubt contributed to the continual cry on the part of agency directors for additional employees. As bureaucrats did not have their salaries docked for days missed, there was little incentive to make a special effort to come to work.

Because their much-desired promotions were so slow in coming as to be barely existent, colonial bureaucrats, especially those of the rank of contador and below, began to besiege the crown with personal requests for gracias. They considered themselves men forced to spend years in what they viewed as isolated posts, waiting endlessly for promotion, and were at first convinced that all they need do was to bring their case and their special merits to the attention of the Spanish crown. A fair number of those in Buenos Aires were able to convince the viceroy that promotion was overdue, and through his offices special petitions were sent to the crown pointing out that an individual, although deserving, had not been promoted for several years.

Initially, these requests, which consisted of letters outlining an individual's merit, hard work and long service, asked for promotion. Periodically, these requests were reviewed by the staff of the Ministry of Finance and lists were made up of those judged ready for promotion. A royal order would then be dispatched to the viceroy, containing the names of four or five individuals who had convinced the crown that they were deserving of advancement. The viceroy was encouraged to "keep these people in mind when suitable vacancies occurred," but little more was done to reward these faithful civil servants. Unfortunately, these orders had little effect, for openings did not present themselves frequently; it was indeed the very absence of openings that had generated the request.

In 1790, for example, such a royal order sent to Viceroy Arredondo requested that Gregorio Canedo, *primer oficial segundo* (second first clerk) of the Buenos Aires Aduana; José Sánchez del Valle, *visitador de tabacos* (tobacco inspector) in Montevideo; Pedro Francisco de Arteaga, oficial tercero of the viceregal secretariat; Lorenzo de Figueroa, subalterno of the Tribunal de Cuentas; and José de Villanova, primer oficial of the Buenos Aires Aduana, all be considered for promotion.[80] Up to that time the four of these men in Buenos Aires had spent an average of thirteen years in the city, and none had been promoted for ten-and-a-half years. Yet no immediate action could be taken. Only in 1794, when Arteaga was advanced to oficial segundo, did any of the group receive advancement.

A royal order did not automatically produce the much desired promotion, nor did it even guarantee that when a position became available the bureaucrat under consideration would always get the job. As bureaucrats came to realize that a successfully answered petition was in itself of little value, they attempted to avail themselves of new strategies in dealing with the crown.

By the 1800s, although the by-now traditional requests for promotion continued to arrive in Spain, many low-ranking bureaucrats had become aware that even if successful they stood slight chance of living long enough to enjoy their promised promotions. Increasingly, they also began to seek an additional gracia, one which would convey some appointment, even the very position they held, on a family member.[81] In effect, the very members of a bureaucracy supposedly based on personal merit (or achievement) were increasingly requesting that the crown transform the bureaucracy into one based on inherited privilege (or ascription).

The idea that personal service could and should be transferred from father to son was of course an old one within the Spanish world. Although the Bourbons tried to supplant this system with one more open to an individual's achievements, lack of movement within the system forced supposedly modern men to fall back on traditional behavior patterns. Men already in the bureaucracy worked to prepare a future for their children; those attempting to enter the service increasingly called on the crown to help them because of the "merits of the service" of their fathers and grandfathers.[82] But the increasing desperation of their requests did not move a crown already overburdened with fiscal problems to respond positively. Repeatedly, the answer given the supplicant was the same: "His Majesty has not agreed to this request."

Still another approach, a more direct and dramatic assault on various Spanish ministries and/or the Council of the Indies, was needed if promotion was to come. Although legally all colonial bureaucrats below the level of viceroy, superintendent, or Audiencia judge were forbidden direct communication with the crown, individuals increasingly sought out agents in Spain who could place a few well-chosen words in influential ears. When this too seemed to produce sparse results, bureaucrats of middle to high rank began to request leaves of absence, often on the grounds of failing health, so that they could personally journey back to the motherland. Although this sometimes proved fruitful, oficiales could spend years in Madrid petitioning for a new appointment while their duties back in Buenos Aires were filled by an interim appointee. Such was the case of Francisco Cabrera, contador mayor of the Tribunal de Cuentas from 1777 to 1796, who returned to Spain in 1796 supposedly because of his "poor health, broken in the desire to serve the king." Cabrera left his son-in-law, Martín Altolaguirre, as his temporary replacement. Although he remained in Spain for eleven years, he was unsuccessful in obtaining a new position. Faced with the prospect of returning to Buenos Aires, Cabrera, age sixty-nine, instead decided to retire from his post.[83]

Although permission to return to Spain was difficult to obtain, the local bureaucrats, desperate for promotion, continued to petition the crown for passports. They were convinced that it was the surest way in which to advance a career. Ramon Miguel de Oromí, for example, born in Málaga of a distinguished family, found himself without a secure bureaucratic post when Viceroy Loreto closed down the Fábrica de la Nueva Labor de Tabaco, which Oromí headed in 1789.[84] Oromí, married to Agustina Lasala, a member of one of the most prominent porteño families, petitioned the crown for return to Spain. Four years later, in 1793, he finally received the necessary passport.[85] He set sail immediately accompanied by his wife and four children. After a four-year stay in the mother country, Oromí was finally successful. On 24 August 1797 Oromí received a royal decree naming him contador mayor supernumerario of the Buenos Aires Tribunal de Cuentas and assuring him of the continuance of his previous salary of 2,000 pesos per year.[86]

Analogous to the desire of the bureaucrat posted in Buenos Aires to return to Spain was the desire of those stationed in the lesser cities of the vicroyalty to make their way to Buenos Aires. Again health was the osten-

sible reason for the requested leave of absence; again the true motivation
was the need to make personal contact with those who had the power to
advance one's career. The frequency of requests because of ill-health and
the true underlying motive of travel did not escape royal attention, and in
1779 the king issued the first of a series of royal orders chastising government officials for abusing Spanish visits.[87] Nevertheless, requests to return
home because of "ill-health" did not stop. As this travel was always undertaken at the individual bureaucrat's expense, only those of relatively high
rank continued to invest (or risk) time and money in this method of advancement, especially as the chances of success grew slimmer.

Nevertheless, some bureaucrats were so desperate to return to the
motherland that they used the pretext of illness of other members of their
family to justify their requests. Antonio Carrasco, accountant of the Royal
Treasury, for example, presented medical evidence as to the poor health of
his wife and daughter in an attempt to leave Buenos Aires.[88] Although the
evidence was convincing, the crown remained firm in its policy of rejecting
these requests lest they produce a groundswell.

Officials could also try to further their careers by coming to the financial aid of the crown in times of need. Bureaucrats making such "donations" hoped that the crown would take special note of their contribution.
The crown, in turn, was eager not only to get those extra funds but also to
commend civil servants who by their generosity could serve as models for
the entire community. In 1794, for example, the crown expressed "much
satisfaction with the royal subjects who to date have paid into the Royal
Treasury the sums that they had donated to help meet the present-day costs
of the war . . . His Majesty wants to express his thanks to those who have
displayed fervor in support of religion and the good of the state, which are
the objects of this war." Specially mentioned was Alexandro de Ariza, the
contador mayor of the Tribunal de Cuentas, who had donated 500 pesos
from his yearly salary of 4,000 pesos.[89] Such donations and royal commen-
dations were of course enshrined in the bureaucrat's service record.

In actual practice in every branch of the bureaucracy, although there
were various other criteria, length of service remained the overriding criteria for promotion. Positions within the bureaucracy were ranked, and the
vast majority of bureaucrats found themselves slowly working their way
from lesser to greater rank in an orderly progression. Only rarely was an
individual allowed to skip a step or be promoted ahead of a higher-ranking

colleague, and when this did occur, the viceroy and chief administrators took time to document fully this unorthodox behavior.

Regardless of the lack of advancement and low pay, government employment was a steady job. All oficiales held their posts by virtue of some type of royal nomination, and even if they incurred the wrath of their superiors, it was virtually impossible to oust an incumbent from his position. While some became disenchanted with the reality of a government clerkship and the static future of the job and returned to Spain, the majority remained at their desks for their whole lives, preferring a steady position with little mobility to no position at all. Because royal appointments were for life, government bureaucrats were not forced to leave their positions because of age or illness.

Not all clerks had come into their positions as young men, and those who achieved a low-level clerkship later in life tended to be more content with remaining in the same job. Those who remained in these positions for years and years were hardly inventive or adventuresome, for it was clearly not in their best interest to challenge the system that employed them. Passivity was also the natural by-product of years of tedious and routine tasks.

After 1790, at the same time as the meritorio system reached its apogee, the government began to name more experienced bureaucrats to supernumerary posts. This was an attempt to placate high-ranking bureaucrats disillusioned with their lack of professional mobility. For men such as Pedro José Ballesteros, contador of the Contaduría de Proprios y Arbitrios the next logical step was the post of contador mayor of the Tribunal de Cuentas. As there was no opening at this level, in 1790 the crown created a supernumerary appointment, guaranteeing that the so-named individual would be first to move into a regular post as soon as it became vacant. By 1797 two additional supernumerary contadores mayores were named. In effect the crown revitalized an institution it had used during the days of sale of office, this time not to improve the fiscal situation of the throne but instead to pacify its bureaucrats.

As has been mentioned earlier, another attempt to appease high-ranking bureaucrats—those bureaucrats stationed outside of Buenos Aires—was the practice of awarding honorary positions in the local bureaucracy. While gaining no increase in salary, the honorary contadores were, nonetheless, to be given all the respect and public deference due their new position. In a society that viewed outward manifestations of rank with great reverence, these honorary posts were welcomed as a sign of career advancement by the bureaucrats of the interior.

In its early years the creation of the Viceroyalty of Río de la Plata created an unprecedented opportunity for rapid advancement for those with prior experience in Lima or some other major administrative center. In essence it introduced a host of newcomers who first complemented and then replaced a local-born bureaucracy.

As the colonial bureaucracy stabilized and entered into a period of slow growth as compared to the dramatic increase that had marked its development from 1770 to 1780, it became more difficult for even the most highly qualified applicants to gain a toe hold in the bureaucracy. Manuel Moreno, a talented young porteño, could only find a bureaucratic position as *oficial tercero* (third clerk) in the Secretaría, a position he occupied after service as meritorio in the Secretaría for six years. The few creoles who had entered the bureaucracy had always to display higher levels of education, but their frustration must have increased in the decade preceding Independence when even education, good birth, and local influence added up to nothing more than a place on the waiting list.

Although the new system of professionalization and promotion was supposed to encourage the rapid advancement of the most-talented and dedicated civil servants, in reality promotion followed a strict one-step progression. No civil servant, regardless of how splendid his performance, ever found himself promoted from sixth clerk to third clerk. Instead, he tediously moved from sixth to fifth and then perhaps to fourth clerk, labouriously making his way in small steps. In addition, once all posts in an agency were filled, that is within one to two years after the creation of that agency, promotion only occurred when someone of a higher rank in the bureaucratic hierarchy was transferred, promoted, or died. The death or departure of a first clerk usually meant that each succeeding clerk was moved up one notch. The last slot in the bureaucracy, fifth or sixth clerk, now vacant would be filled by either a meritorio or a candidate with special influence.

Regardless of the poor opportunities for advancement, the bureaucratic career continued to attract men throughout the viceregal period. In fact the demand for these positions outstripped the supply by about 1790, and government departments increasingly began to appoint more young men to meritorio positions, giving candidates the right to await future vacancies at the lowest clerkship level. The creation of these positions coincides with an increased tendency toward the end of the colonial period for an officeholder to remain in situ regardless of the lack of career mobility. Both of these trends are the result of a limited supply of positions in the face of an ever-increasing demand. As it became increasingly difficult to obtain a bureaucratic position, it became increasingly desirable to occupy one of these jobs.

Entering the bureaucracy with great hopes of promising and lucrative careers in this newly established viceroyalty, most government officials were far from encouraged by the reality of the system. Opportunities for rapid professional advancement quickly disappeared as the personnel of each agency became stabilized. Because of the royal devotion to rank-order promotion, only the death or reappointment of a superior could occasion promotion. Exceptional performance rarely translated into a brilliant bureaucratic career. As a result, lethargy and inertia seemed to have become the norm among the scores of oficiales who labored in local government offices.

Although some individuals had experienced rapid professional mobility during the years before and after the creation of the viceroyalty, as government agencies moved past a period of creation and growth, even gradual career advancement for civil servants became more problematic. Not all bureaucrats experienced the same level of frustration because of this lack of movement—witness the Aduana bureaucracy—but for the majority of those who had entered the bureaucracy as dedicated and ambitious young men and who increasingly found themselves facing middle age with little progress to show for the years spent in royal service, deception increasingly became the rule.

6. Salary, Retirement, and Montepío

ONE OF THE AIMS OF THE BUREAUCRATIC reorganization that accompanied the founding of the platense viceroyalty was the creation of a salaried, disinterested civil bureaucracy that would provide the necessary manpower to carry out reform of government and increase royal revenue. Although paying bureaucratic salaries would add great expense, the profit that this corps of individuals would produce was believed to be a worthwhile investment, for by providing effective and responsive government the crown could better control and defend the area, encouraging necessary reforms, enhancing production, and generating new royal revenues. Salaried bureaucrats, it was hoped, would also be less prone to corruption, a problem that had plagued royal finances and cut deeply into expected revenue.

While the goals of the Bourbons in establishing a salaried bureaucracy are clear, the effective long-term results of this policy are more difficult to judge. What were the economic costs and benefits in creating this salaried bureaucracy? How did the administrative and economic reforms that resulted in the creation of a salaried bureaucracy affect the bureaucrats themselves? By providing government officials with a fixed salary, was corruption lessened, and was a more dedicated corps of civil servants created?

The transformation of the bureaucracy from one dependent on fees to one paid an annual salary affected different groups of bureaucrats in dissimilar ways. For the highest-ranking officials in the Reales Cajas, for example, the reforms clearly decreased their legal incomes. Before the reform of the bureaucracy, the ministros of the Reales Cajas were legally entitled to receive and divide among themselves one-sixth of the value at which embargoed contraband property had been auctioned. These emoluments (*emolumentos*) were in theory a payment to the contador, treasurer, and factor for their work as judges in contraband cases. As two judges sat on each case, each would receive 8.34 percent of the total *comiso* (confiscation) value. Because of incomplete documentation, it is difficult to determine how much each ministro could legally expect to supplement his 1,286 peso salary per year. Martín de Altolaguirre claimed that during a ten-month absence in 1753, he was deprived of an additional income of 315 pesos that had been produced by twenty-six comisos.[1] Although by law a royal official could only receive 200,000 maravedíes (approximately 737 pesos) in commissions,[2] by 1764 the Council of the Indies believed each ministro to be earning at least 2,800 pesos through emolumentos (in addition to their regular salary).[3]

> It would be difficult to find anywhere in America royal officials who earned as much in fees and customs duties as those in the Buenos Aires Division of Confiscated Goods. The prodigious quantity of seizures has grown so great because of the proximity of Côlonia that their commissions provide enough money to be able to live in splendor without even considering their salary. This can be seen by looking at the never-ending remittances of money that are always being sent here to the council, some of 100 pesos and others of even more.

How much additional income was generated illegally through bribes paid to avoid confiscation of contraband is hard to determine. With the capture of Côlonia by the Spanish comisos (seizure of prohibited goods) fell off dramatically. Two years later the ministros were legally deprived of the right to collect any type of emolument. To compensate for this lost income the ministros' salaries were raised from 1,287 to 2,000 pesos. Some salaried officials such as the superintendent continued to receive fee payment for their special services, but salary increasingly became the major legal source of revenue for full-time bureaucrats.[4]

As each agency was created or reconstituted under the platense viceroyalty, a corresponding reglamento was drawn up under the intendant's guiding hand. In 1782 the rules governing the overriding agency, the Superintendency of Buenos Aires, were promulgated.[5] Although positions purchased from the crown (oficios vendibles) were not all suppressed by the Ordenanza de Intendantes, the government clearly was working to strengthen the role of salaried bureaucrats within the major government agencies, while making the highest-ranking Real Hacienda posts attractive to capable men. One of the many aims of the 1782 Ordenanza de Intendantes was to deal a final blow to the older system of government sale of treasury offices. All proprietary Royal Treasury branches were transformed into regular treasuries. The purchased post of *factor oficial real* (royal agent) in the Buenos Aires Treasury was suppressed, and only salaried officials were employed.[6]

To make the reforms more palatable to "traditional" bureaucrats, both the contador and tesorero generales of all principal treasuries were granted use of the *fuero militar* (military exemption from civil justice), as were salaried officials and others employed in the Tesorería y Contaduría Generales de Exército.[7] Furthermore, all bureaucrats employed in any agency collecting government revenues were to enjoy the fuero militar in legal cases, either civil or criminal, arising from their official duties.[8]

In general, the highest-ranking bureaucrats suffered a decline—or at best a leveling-off—in their income. Middle- and low-level bureaucrats probably improved their economic position as a result of the creation of salaried office. Although few in number before the establishment of the viceroyalty, clerks had previously been paid out of the pocket of the men for whom they worked. Their salaries had therefore depended to a greater or lesser degree on the whims or generosity of the office purchasers and perhaps to some degree on supply and demand. With the creation of a salaried bureaucracy, these people were now guaranteed a base salary that was more or less standardized. At the same time as clerk salaries rose with the initial professionalization of the bureaucracy, this standardization and the fact that any salary scale changes would increasingly be dictated by Madrid worked to neutralize the effect of local conditions on legal bureaucratic earnings.

Three rubrics included in the Royal Treasury extracts of yearly accounts *(sumarios de cartas cuentas)* allow us to reconstruct global salary outlays for the entire viceroyalty. The first of these rubrics, *sueldos de ministros políticos y de justicia*, consisted of salary paid to oidores, fiscales, and escribanos in the Real Audiencia plus other assorted royal officials. The second account, *sueldos de real hacienda*, consisted of employee salaries of the Reales Cajas and the Tribunal de Cuentas. The third rubric, *sueldos y gastos varios atrasados*, included all government salaries being paid in arrears. Unfortunately, these accounts do not reflect all salary expenditures. The viceroy was paid under another account. Moreover, Bourbon bookkeeping often allowed salary payments to be charged to unrelated accounts. In 1779,

Table 6.1   Yearly Expenditure on Bureaucratic Salaries, Viceroyalty of Río de la Plata, 1776–1809

Year	Salaries	Atrasados	Total
1776	45,449	–	45,449
1777	29,688	–	29,688
1778	136,588	–	136,588
1779	128,666	–	128,666
1780	108,274	–	108,274
1781	88,592	–	88,592
1782	–	–	–
1783	113,281	–	113,281
1784	135,551	13,764	149,315
1785	170,873	70,014	240,887
1786	148,076	44,630	192,706
1787	153,986	186,179	340,165
1788	159,212	59,266	218,478
1789	126,408	7,903	134,311
1790	195,737	49,448	245,185
1791	141,971	37,616	179,587
1792	98,386	18,948	117,334
1793	–	–	–
1794	142,265	128,645	270,910
1795	647,734	21,046	668,780
1796	147,376	34,476	181,852
1797	123,709	2,657	126,366
1798	120,138	310	120,448
1799	143,691	5,568	149,259
1800	140,191	25,893	166,084
1801	156,159	5,209	161,368
1802	194,133	76,735	270,868
1803	95,878	–	95,878
1804	(100,000)*	–	100,000
1805	(100,000)*	–	100,000
1806	–	–	–
1807	186,098	–	186,098
1808	38,232	–	38,232
1809	194,713	–	194,713

*This figure represents approximately 2.6 percent of the total yearly expenditures. As such it is a low estimate of government salary outlay.

Source: Klein and Te Paske, *The Royal Treasuries of the Spanish Empire in America*, vol 3: *Chile and the Río de la Plata* (Buenos Aires, 1776–1809).

for example, of the 3,000 pesos paid to six dependientes in the Buenos Aires treasury, 650 pesos (or 22 percent) were taken from funds in the *ramo municipal de guerra* (municipal war account) (350 pesos) and the *fondos de Temporalidades* (ex-Jesuit property funds) (300 pesos) instead of the treasury salary account.[9] This practice continued throughout the viceregal period. In 1799, when a bureaucratic reshuffling added 1,390 pesos in salaries paid to oficiales in Reales Cajas, a royal order specified "so that the Royal Treasury is not burdened by the increase in these new salaries . . . they are to be charged against the profits of the *ramo municipal de guerra* and of *sisa* (tax on internal trade)."[10] In this case, by shifting accounts, 16 percent of the total monies paid to clerks were not reflected in the salary account. Furthermore, salaries of persons employed in certain government agencies such as the Real Aduana, the Real Renta de Tabaco, and the Temporalidades were never included in *sueldo* (salary) accounts. On the other hand, payments made under the third rubric, *sueldos y gastos varios atrasados*, included several other expenses in addition to past-due salary.[11] Expenditures made under these three headings do serve, therefore, as a rough (albeit underestimated) guide to the growth of total expenditures spent on staffing a bureaucracy.

Tables 6.1 and 6.2 and figure 6.1 present yearly information from the sueldo accounts included in the Buenos Aires *cartas cuentas* (annual accounts) from 1776 to 1809.[12] Because of the methods with which accounts were kept and because of delays in payments to bureaucrats caused by war,

Table 6.2   Salary Expenditures by Five-Year Intervals

Years	Salaries (including atrasados [payment in arrears])	Average per year
1776–1780	448,665	89,733
1781–1785	592,075	118,415
1786–1790	1,130,845	226,169
1791–1795	1,236,611	247,322
1796–1800	744,009	148,802
1801–1805	728,114**	145,623
1806–1809*	419,043	104,761

*This is a four-year interval.
**Includes approximate figures for 1804 and 1805.

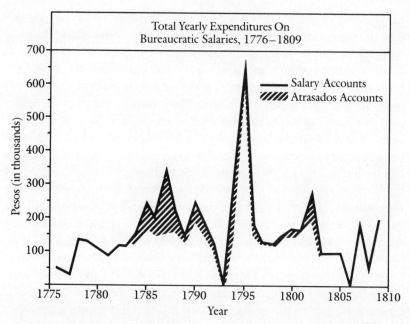

Figure 6.1   Total Yearly Expenditures on Bureaucratic Salaries, 1776–1809

emergencies, natural disasters, or incompetence, yearly totals from the cartas cuentas display rather wild fluctuations. In 1781, for example, the Tupac Amaru rebellion in Upper Peru seriously upset the payment schedule for government bureaucrats, forcing emergency measures that reallocated funds earmarked for salaries to defense.[13] In 1793 European war disrupted payment of local bureaucrats when all local treasuries were requested to return funds to Spain as a wartime measure. Again in 1806 war, this time the English invasion of Buenos Aires, interrupted regular payment of government salaries.[14]

These disruptions caused psychological and economic hardship on the bureaucrats and possibly helped to slowly undermine the bureaucratic esprit de corps. As soon as possible, the local treasury attempted to repay bureaucrats, but often this took several years. In 1795, for example, the yearly total spent by the Royal Treasury under all salary headings jumped to 647,734 pesos. At least part of that expenditure was used in the payment of back salaries due from 1791 to 1794, years in which war with the French disrupted the functioning of the Spanish treasury.

In an attempt to better undersand the long-term movement of total salaries, without the dramatic effect of these fluctuations, figure 6.2 presents salary information calculated as seven-year moving averages. Both this figure and table 6.2 show that, in general, during the years between the founding of the Viceroyalty of Río de la Plata and 1790 a gradual upswing in total salary expenditures took place. The first half of the 1790s marks the high point in government outlays for bureaucratic salaries, but from the end of this decade to the time of Independence there is a gradual decrease in yearly disbursements.

This steady decline in total salary expenditures reflected the worsening economic situation that faced the Spanish government from the mid-1790s on. Potosí revenue began to fall off just as the Spanish government's demand for currency to finance its European wars increased. Bureaucrats in the Río de la Plata were increasingly called upon to produce greater revenues, either by improving the way in which monies were paid into the royal accounts or by tapping new sources of revenue. This tightening of collection produced some startling revenue *increases*—*diezmo* (tithe)

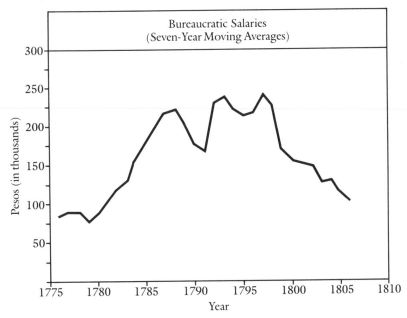

Figure 6.2   Bureaucratic Salaries (Seven-year Moving Averages, 1775–1810)

collection increased from 70,000 pesos in 1796–1800 to 206,000 in 1801–5; Aduana revenues jumped from 1,181,383 pesos to 2,425,540 pesos during the same period, only in part because of increased trade.[15]

The crown's fiscal plan called for increasing revenues at the same time as salary expenditures were reduced. The ratio of salaries to revenues would thereby be improved as each bureaucrat would generate greater net income. Unfortunately, this goal was never reached. Government salaries consumed approximately 17 percent of total income during the 1776–90 period, rising slightly to 19 percent after 1791. These ratios are generally comparable to those cited by von Humboldt in his review of Mexican finances and, like those numbers cited by von Humboldt, are indicative of a fairly inefficient administration.[16] Regardless of how much the crown sought to reduce expenditures on salary and improve collection of revenues, the Viceroyalty of Río de la Plata was never an efficient or major revenue-producing unit of the Spanish empire.[17]

The crown's search for revenues also extended to its own bureaucrats, where it took the form of savings or taxes on salaries. As early as 1787 all government officials in the New World were forbidden to raise salaries without the expressed consent of the king.[18] The same year supplementary salary in the form of a *gratificación* (expense allowance) or *ayuda de costas* (financial assistance) was forbidden to all members of the Real Hacienda staff; the crown went so far as to revoke two special allowances earlier granted to the contador of the Real Hacienda and the contador mayor of the Tribunal de Cuentas.[19] The crown also requested a list of all bureaucrats or government officials enjoying two salaries with the expressed intention of ending this practice in the New World (it had already been declared illegal in Spain).[20] Last, the crown further suggested that interim appointments only be made when there was to be a long delay before the *propietario*'s (officeholder's) arrival, thus saving the crown some half-salaries.[21] New directives to local agencies also sought to control the growth of positions in each agency while lowering the salaries of those bureaucrats who continued to be employed whenever possible. As part of an empirewide plan to reduce Audiencia expenses, the salary of the regent of the Buenos Aires Audiencia was cut from 6,000 to 5,250 pesos, while all other judges found their 4,000 to 5,000 pesos salaries fixed at 3,500 pesos.[22] The move to economize through staff reduction met with only partial success because of the legal difficulty in dislodging a bureaucrat who held his post by virtue of a título and because additional bureaucrats were needed to enforce stricter collection of revenues. The growth of bureaucratic salaries was somewhat alleviated, however, by resorting to two old formulas—the use of unpaid trainees (meritorios) as clerks and scribes and the sale of some offices.

Meritorios had always been employed in government agencies, but increasingly after 1795 government agencies allowed their numbers to grow. Instead of one or two meritorios, four or five would now be found in the Tribunal de Cuentas, Aduana, or Real Hacienda. The average length of time spent as a meritorio also increased from one year to three. More young men were therefore providing free labor for a longer period of time.

The crown also quickened the pace at which it created and auctioned off a series of posts, such as canciller, recepter de penas of the Buenos Aires audiencia and *alcalde provincial* (provincial magistrate).[23] The ability of these agencies to generate income was thereby increased, while royal income from the oficios vendibles account grew. For salaried bureaucrats, however, the increased number of positions at auction produced fear rather than joy, for few greeted the growth of a system they could little afford to buy into. Still another expediency adopted to contain salary outlays was the reorganization or disbanding of minor agencies viewed as nonproductive. In 1801, for example, the Contaduría de Propios y Arbitrios, an agency created to monitor Cabildo accounts, was reabsorbed by the Tribunal de Cuentas.

These cost-cutting strategies did not solve the problem of adding staff while keeping total salary expenditures down. The crown was especially loathe to increase the number of high-ranking bureaucrats employed by any agency, for this group was naturally the highest-paid. Instead, the government resorted to still another series of expedients aimed at increasing manpower without increasing salaries. In the Tribunal de Cuentas the crown began to appoint contadores mayores as supernumerarios. Those named contador mayor supernumerario were civil servants from other branches of government on loan to the Tribunal to help overcome the growing backlog of unfinished accounts. The crown profited from naming supernumerarios instead of expanding the number of regular appointments because the supernumerarios continued to earn the same salary of their old positions, salaries that were uniformly lower than those of line contadores mayores. When through death, reappointment, or retirement line positions became available, contadores mayores supernumerarios had first rights to these regular appointments. Much the same idea was involved in naming contadores ordenadores *habilitados* (especially empowered) to serve as contadores mayores, another strategy used by the crown in the final decades before Independence. Unlike the supernumerarios, habilitados did not have legal claim on contador mayor positions when they came open, although being habilitado conferred a degree of power and prestige to contador ordenador. Again habilitados continued to draw the salary of their official position, or their position "de número," thus saving the crown money. These attempts at shifting manpower between agencies did not solve the basic problem, for some agency was always left even shorter of people to accomplish the never-ending business of government.

Because both the administrative and the commercial reorganizations of the Río de la Plata occurred in such close chronological proximity, it is difficult to disaggregate the effect of the two reforms in the local economy. The creation of Buenos Aires as the seat of a new viceroyalty served geographically to redistribute royal income from Potosí to Buenos Aires, thus supporting the military and bureaucratic growth of the litoral up to the beginning of the nineteenth century.[24] Moreover, the viceregal government played an important role, both directly and indirectly, in the local economy. Most dramatic was the effect of salaries paid to local bureaucrats, for much of this money found its way into the Buenos Aires economy through sums paid for housing, clothing, food, and slaves. The large yearly expenditures on salaries fueled the local economy by creating an increased demand for primary and luxury goods.

The single largest expense of the royal government in the Viceroyalty of Río de la Plata was the maintenance of its own civil, religious, and military bureaucracy.[25] Military outlays were paramount, but the salaries of political, judicial, and Real Hacienda employees throughout the viceroyalty accounted for an average of 5 to 6 percent of total yearly expenditures. Approximately 40 percent of these salaries were paid to officials stationed in the city of Buenos Aires.

Of the ten branches and agencies of royal government with offices in Buenos Aires, the most expensive to administer in terms of total salaries was the viceroy and his office staff (23 percent). The viceroy's salary alone came to over 19 percent of the total salary expenditures. Next were the Real Audiencia and the Tribunal de Cuentas. According to a list of expenditures on salaries drawn up at the beginning of the nineteenth century, of a total of 206,585 pesos spent in Buenos Aires bureaucracy for salaries, these three government branches together accounted for over 60 percent of expenses. The Aduana was the next most costly agency, claiming 13 percent of the total salaries, but it, like the Reales Cajas (9.5 percent) and the Dirección General de Tabaco (9 percent), also produced revenue.[26]

Good salary data for the Real Renta de Tabaco demonstrate patterns found in all branches of the Buenos Aires bureaucracy. (See table 6.3.) Indeed, the tobacco agency stands as a surrogate for viceregal bureaucracy in both the level of salaries and numbers of employees found in white-collar jobs. The data, which traces salaries over a nineteen-year period, shows that only five individuals earned salaries above 100 pesos per month. The director general's salary was 3,000 pesos per year, while the second highest paid individual, the contador, earned 2,500 pesos. These salaries were comparable to those paid to the administrador and contador of the Aduana, the chief secretary of the Secretaría, and the contador and treasurer of the Real Hacienda. While these few individuals were well paid by the standards of the time, most salaries below the rank of oficial mayor were not high. Ordinary clerks earned from 300 to 800 pesos per year, with the latter considered to be an exceptionally good salary.

In addition to the generally low salaries of those fortunate enough to be earning wages (meritorios not included), government salaries displayed overall stability throughout the colonial period. Only five of the eleven positions created in 1778 had been upgraded in salary by 1809. In addition, two employees, the tesorero and the contador, had been granted a raise in the form of a supplemental housing allowance of 360 pesos per year in 1785, but this allowance was later rescinded. The largest raise granted was that of 350 pesos to the *fiel* (inspector) of the almacenes generales. Two other individuals, the oficial segundo of Contaduría General and the oficial de libros of Tesorería General, also received salary increases by 1797, but it should be noted that when these individuals were first promoted to their new posts, the salary granted them was lower than that granted the previous incumbent. The salary attached to any position was not fixed; rather, the new incumbent and the crown attempted to bargain within a general salary range, with the crown in a generally stronger position. Employees did have the option of petitioning the crown for a raise on the grounds of extreme financial hardship, but the crown, anxious to export surplus revenues to Spain, was loathe to grant these requests.

While a few salaries were increased, other salaries fell, such as the sal-

Table 6.3   Salaries of Tobacco Monopoly Employees

Position	1778[1]	1786[2]	1797[3]	1809[4]
Dirección General				
Director General	3,000	3,000	3,000	3,000
Oficial Amanuense	600	600	600	600
Escribano		200	200	200
Portero		250	250	250
Asesor				400
Contaduría General				
Contador	2,500	2,500*	2,500	(2,500)
Oficial mayor	1,400	1,400	1,400	1,400
Oficial 2o	700	800[a]	800	800
Oficial 2o 2o			800	
Oficial 3o	500	500	500	600
Oficial 4o			400	400
Oficial 5o			400	400
Escribiente 1o		400	250	250
Escribiente 2o		400		
Oficial entretenido		250		
Oficial entretenido		—		
Comisionado para arreglar papeles			800	
Tesorería General				
Tesorero	2,200	2,200*	2,000	2,200
Oficial de libro	650	800[b]	800	800
Oficial 2o		500	500	500
Administración General				
Administrador	1,700	1,700	1,700	1,700
Oficial Interventor	650	800[c]	800	800
Visitador	500	350		
Oficial 1o		300	350	350
Oficial 2o			300	300
Almacenes Generales				
Fiel	650	1,000[d]	1,000	1,000
Mozo de confianza			192	192
Mozo de confianza			42	144
Fábricas de cigarros				
Sobrestante		400	400	400

Table 6.3   Salaries of Tobacco Monopoly Employees (*continued*)

Position	1778[1]	1786[2]	1797[3]	1809[4]
Interventor		300	300	300
Fabricante de polvillo		480	240	240
Ayudante 1*o*		120		
Ayudante 2*o*		120		
Mozo de mulas		144		
Portero			180	180
Peon			4@60	
			(240)	
Tercena da la Administra-				
cion General				
1*o* tercenista		400	400	
2*o* tercenista		300	300	
Resguardo de la Capital				
Visitador		600	600	
Teniente de visitador		10@250	14@250	
		(2,500)	(3,500)	
Cabo 2*o*			360	
Ronda Volante				
Visitador		500	600	
Teniente Visitador			500	
Cabo 1*o*		360	380	
Cabo 2*o*		300	380	
Dependientes		2@250	15@250	
		(500)	(3,750)	
Marineros			4@144	
			(576)	
Reconocedor de Tabacos		3@25	2@25	2@25
Tabaco regular		(75)	(50)	(50)
Tabaco negro		20	20	20
Peones				
1*o*		96		
2*o*		72		
Viudedad		257.4[c]		
Nuevas Labores				
Director			2,000	
Total	15,050	27,464.4	35,590	20,576

Table 6.3　Salaries of Tobacco Monopoly Employees (*continued*)

*In addition to this salary a yearly housing allowance of 360 pesos was provided.
ª Salary raised from 600 to 800 pesos in 1785.
ᵇ Salary raised from 500 to 800 pesos in 1783.
ᶜ Raise granted in 1781.
ᵈ Raise granted in 1782.
ᵉ This expense is a widow's pension.
( ) Post temporarily vacant.
Sources:
1 AGI, Audiencia de Buenos Aires, legajo 417.
2, 3 AGNA, Dirección General de Tabacos y Naipes, Empleados, 1785–1812, IX-19-s/a-4.
4 AGNA, División General de Tabacos y Naipes, Lista de Sueldos, 1778–1809, IX-46-4-6.

ary of the visitador of the Administración General. One salary, that of the *fabricante de polvillo* (snuff maker) in the cigar factory, was reduced by half when the job changed hands, perhaps because the person who worked at this lower salary was a woman, Doña Dominga Baldovinos, employed as *maestra* (master craftswoman) from 1797 to 1809.

Data contained in table 6.3 show a general tendency to increase the numbers of low-level bureaucrats employed by the tobacco agency, a trend similar to that experienced by other agencies. In 1778 twelve bureaucrats held white-collar jobs in the agency; by 1786 the number had grown to eighteen; and by 1797 twenty men were so employed. But because growth occurred at the lowest levels of the bureaucracy, the net result was that the average salary paid to the white-collar employees of the Real Renta de Tabaco tended to decline. For the twelve individuals in this category in 1778 the average salary was 1,254 pesos; in 1797 the average for twenty employees was 985 pesos. Comparable averages for other colonial agencies displayed the same general trends.

Nonetheless, government expenditures on Real Renta de Tabaco salaries, like government expenditures on all bureaucratic salaries, increased greatly during the first part of the viceregal period. This increase, which in the case of the Renta was 136 percent over nineteen years, reflected not so much an increase in individual salaries as a general tendency to add new line positions to subagencies and to create new government divisions. Overall, salary expenditures were somewhat higher in the Renta because of the creation of a cigar factory, a *resguardo* (customs service), a *rondo volante* (patrol), and an experimental factory (*fábrica de nuevas labores*), expenditures that it was hoped would increase the Renta's product, sales, and profit. Nevertheless, those employed in purely bureaucratic departments within the Renta also grew from twelve to twenty. Most of this administrative growth took place before 1786 and was not unlike that being experienced by all branches of royal government in Buenos Aires at that time.

Although the production branches of the Real Renta de Tabaco continued to add new employees after 1786, some degree of economy was finally introduced into the Renta during the final years of the viceroyalty. The decrease in total expenditures reflected in the 1809 figures is the result of the disbanding of an independent tobacco resguardo and ronda volante (a unified resguardo combining the duties of the Renta and Aduana services had been created in 1802) and the closing of the experimental fábrica de nuevas labores. Financial pressures had forced the crown to restructure or abandon several experiments, but the administrative branches remained intact.

A similar range and variation in salaries for a specific post can be seen in other agencies. In the Tribunal de Cuentas salaries theoretically ranged from 250 pesos per year for an archivero to 4,000 pesos per year for a contador mayor. In reality the crown frequently made appointments at a lesser salary. In 1785, for example, while all three contadores ordenadores received the same salary, 1,620 pesos, only one of the contadores mayores, the second in command, was paid 4,000 pesos. The other two received approximately 10 percent less.[27]

The crown's tendency to keep bureaucratic salaries low and to resist salary increases was especially troublesome in the face of the rising cost of living experienced by those residing in Buenos Aires. This inflation, which began in the 1770s and continued unabated throughout the late colonial period, was probably the result of the city's dramatic population growth. This growing population, which increased at an average rate of 2.5 percent per year, had swollen consumer demand, allowing the relatively few artisan producers in the city to raise prices. By 1787 Buenos Aires, which only fourteen years earlier had surprised visitors because of its low cost of living, was dubbed "the most expensive, dearest city in the kingdom."[28] By the turn of the century the Audiencia commented that "the pace at which this city has grown, the increase in luxury consumption, and the incredible jump in the prices of basic foodstuffs, make it impossible to compare life here with the advantages of twelve years ago."[29] Furthermore, "artisan production such as shoes, clothing, carpentry, and similar goods are higher here than in any other city of the kingdom."

Bureaucrats complained constantly about Buenos Aires' inflation, and agency heads bombarded the crown with petitions to increase salaries. In some cases they met with success. Contadores ordenadores in the Tribunal de Cuentas, for example, experienced a 50 percent increase in their average salary between 1785 and 1809. The largest salary increase granted to several Tribunal's employees, a raise averaging 55 percent, was aborted by the Napoleonic Wars and events following the Cabildo Abierto.[30]

Regardless of the experienced and promised increases, bureaucratic salaries in the Tribunal de Cuentas, as in all other agencies, were generally low. Nevertheless, the crown, in its perpetual search for funds, was not adverse to further depressing salaries by employing the mechanism of interim appointment. Appointment as an interino normally entitled the employee to only half the regular salary associated with that position, although the interino had the same responsibilities and duties as a regular appointee. Nonetheless, several individuals, hoping to use the possible leverage of an interim appointment when a regular appointment was finally made, held these appointments for periods ranging up to eight years.[31]

The same general pattern can be seen in the Aduana. In 1778, when the Aduana was established, the pay scale enacted provided salaries ranging from 2,500 pesos per year for the administrador to 300 pesos for the lesser oficiales de contaduría. The chief customs inspector was to be paid only 1,500 pesos. By 1781 Intendant Fernández requested that because of the fine job being done by the local Aduana, seven lesser-ranking employees be rewarded with a raise in salary. Although the Aduana had forwarded 224,495 pesos in liquid capital to the Royal Treasury between September 1778 and December 1779, José de Gálvez turned down Fernández's suggestion pleading that wartime demands on the Royal Treasury made any salary raises impossible at the time.[32] Two years later Aduana administrator Ximénez de Mesa proposed that the Aduana's salaries be increased because of the high cost of living in Buenos Aires.[33] His request was supported by Superintendent Sanz who forwarded it to Spain, but because of its need to control expenses, the crown rejected any increases for the Buenos Aires customs employees.

The case of Aduana salaries points out a fundamental inconsistency in the crown's policy. While committed to providing efficient bureaucrats by paying decent salaries, the crown consistently refused to raise these salaries to correspond with the local high cost of living. The low salary scale coupled with the long years needed to progress to a higher rank and a correspondingly better pay produced economic hardship for lower-level bureaucrats. Inadequate salaries forced government bureaucrats to turn first to their agencies and then to merchants and other providers of liquid capital for loans. Internal accounting records show that after 1783 royal bureaucrats increasingly sought and received viceregal permission to be granted "advances against future salaries."[34] These interest-free loans ranged from 400 to 3,000 pesos and were repaid by deducting one-third of the employee's monthly salary until the principal had been recouped. As the amount of the loan did not necessarily correspond with the salary of an individual, minor clerks who received large loans could spend six to seven years repaying the sum. But in spite of the increased frequency of loans to employees, all agencies were careful to never extend more than one loan at a time to any individual. As a result, those who had exhausted their internal credit were forced to seek loans at interest rates of three to six percent from private individuals.

While salaries were low and failed to respond to the increasing cost of living during the viceregal period, additional complications were introduced into the picture when a bureaucrat served in an interim position for a long period of time. Thus, during the thirteen years (1784–97) that Juan José Ballesteros served as contador interino of the Contaduría de Propios y Arbitrios, he received only 1,000 instead of 2,000 pesos.[35] But when interim positions were filled by bureaucrats who had other positions, the question of which of the two salaries the individual was to draw inevitably was raised. Until 1796 there seems to have been no hard-and-fast rule, except that the Reales Cajas and Tribunal de Cuentas usually advised the king to pay the lower of the two salaries in the interests of economy, a suggestion usually accepted with alacrity.[36] Nevertheless, each determination was made separately, taking at least a year to decide. Further complications could also be introduced into the picture when the medium of payment of the two salaries was different, for the question became not only that of which salary but at which exchange rate.

Each salary case could be complex and its outcome surprising. Consider the salary question raised by José Ortiz, one of the few bureaucrats to belong to the Real y Distinguida Orden de Carlos III. At the end of seven years' service as the representative of the Real Hacienda on the First Boundary Commission, Ortiz was awarded an appointment as comisario de guerra of the Royal Army. The new position carried with it a salary of 150 *escudos de vellon* per month, or 18,000 *reales de vellon* per year. Before he could draw his first salary, Ortiz was also named interim secretary of the viceroyalty, "under the same terms and with the same privileges as the secretary," a job which he began in September 1792.[37] After fifteen months in office without drawing a salary, Ortiz appealed to the ministers of the local Real Hacienda to decide quickly which salary was forthcoming. He was growing short of funds so urgently needed for "respectable sustenance."[38]

Within a month the Real Hacienda ministros met, but instead of deciding Ortiz's salary, they outlined three different options and passed their recommendation on to the Tribunal de Cuentas. The ministros rejected Ortiz's claim that he was entitled to the full salary of the secretario (2,600 pesos per year), pointedly referring to Ortiz as "the Señor Commissario de Guerra." Their first suggestion in this case, which was "so questionable . . . that any decision is full of risk," was that Ortiz be paid the usual interim half-salary of 1,300 pesos. A second possibility was to change the escudo salary into pesos, allowing a one-for-one exchange rate (as infantry officers' salaries were discounted); this would provide Ortiz with a salary of 1,800 pesos per year. Thirdly, Ortiz's military salary could be discounted at the exchange rate of 13 reales 2 maravedíes of vellon for each American peso, the official exchange rate established by the Royal Order of 6 August 1776. This solution, the least favorable to Ortiz, would generate a salary of 1,195 pesos 2-1/2 reales.

The ministros did not favor any one of these choices. Instead, they forwarded their deliberations to the Tribunal de Cuentas, which in turn stressed that Ortiz was interim secretary and supported the first solution. They, in turn, passed their recommendations on to the Audiencia where the fiscal de lo civil, José Marqués de la Plata, added his recommendation. He agreed with the tribunal, stressing that because Ortiz was serving as interim secretary of the viceroyalty "there seems to be no other salary that makes sense than half of the amount that this position usually receives." In addition, he pointed out that the Royal Exchequer was already burdened with continued payment of a salary to Juan Andrés de Arroyo, the ex-secretario of the Superintendency, who had lost his position in the recent reorganization of the Secretaría. On 8 April 1794 the Audiencia decreed payment of a 1,300 pesos salary to Ortiz. Nevertheless, although all local bureaucrats had worked hard to save money for the treasury, within six months a royal order overruled the frugal oficiales. The king decreed that Ortiz was to be paid the full salary of 2,600 pesos annually for as long as he held the position of secretary, disregarding all precedents governing interim salaries. Until March 1795, when he stepped aside to allow the proprietario, Manuel Gallego, to take on the secretario job, José Ortiz therefore earned a salary that contravened the decision of the local Reales Cajas, Tribunal de Cuentas, and Audiencia. In his case, the crown had been generous.

Work hours, like salaries, varied from agency to agency. Some agencies were notorious for overworking their staff. Employees of the Real Hacienda were expected to put in a five-hour day; those employed in the Secretaría de Cámara worked a seven-hour day. Periodically, the need to ready the viceroy's correspondence for departing ships added to the pressing load of secretariat work and caused employees of the Secretaría to work overtime. Pedro Francisco Arteaga, a Secretaría oficial, described the work routine in his agency as follows: "Other offices have their fixed hours, their work days, their slack period, but the Secretaría has neither seconds nor hours nor even the most holy days without work."[39]

Paradoxically, even before 1795 growing outlays for bureaucratic salaries did not translate into improved salaries for individual bureaucrats. From the beginning of the viceroyalty the effect of the crown's desire to limit the costs of the enlarged viceregal bureaucracy was strict adherence to policy that only granted salary increases to bureaucrats under conditions of extreme duress. Although the number of bureaucratic posts grew rapidly from 1776 to 1785 and then again in the early 1790s, once a position had been endowed with a certain salary, there was little tendency for that salary to be increased. This is not to say that there was no upward movement in salaries. Rather it was limited and tended to be confined to the earlier years immediately following the creation of an agency. It is almost axiomatic that if a salary increase was not achieved within five years of the creation of a position, it would not be achieved for twenty-five years. The net result of the growth of government spending on the bureaucracy was the creation of an ever-increasing corps of poorly paid civil servants.

Fiscal exigencies resulted in constant attempts, usually successful, on the part of all chief administrators of agencies to keep those salaries that they controlled as low as possible while still maintaining a work force. In Spain government ministers exerted these pressures on the salaries of the high-ranking bureaucrats; in Buenos Aires these bureaucrats themselves exerted the same pressure on their underlings. Even when forced to create new bureaucratic openings because of mounting paperwork, the rule of thumb was to do it as inexpensively as possible.

Such was the case in the negotiations leading to the establishment of a position as relator of the Junta Provincial de Temporalidades. In 1778 the four-man junta, citing "the grave work load that . . . [the junta] has not been able to reduce over so many years" and specifically mentioning "two hundred arduous and difficult expedientes that they now find themselves burdened with," asked Viceroy Cevallos to create a relator post. The viceroy, obviously convinced that the junta's request was both urgent and legitimate and that the escribano who was trying to fill both roles on an ad hoc basis could not provide the needed legal expertise, acceded to the junta's request and instructed them to present the names of three qualified lawyers as nominees. No definite salary was mentioned in the viceroy's reply to the junta.

Two weeks after receiving viceregal approval, the junta submitted its list of candidates and suggested that the salary assigned to the post be 600 pesos per year plus the "fees charged for those cases that concern private parties." The very next day Viceroy Cevallos named the junta's top candidate but assigned him a salary of only 500 pesos. Although more than willing to allow the new relator to augment his salary by charging litigants for his services, the viceroy stressed in the terms of the appointment that "in [drawing up] all those legal abstracts that are part of his official duties he is forbidden to charge the government any extra duty or cost." Thus Cevallos made sure that the relator could not charge the junta for any hidden costs.[40]

Succeeding viceroys, like Cevallos, would work to keep government salaries as low as possible, but what effect did these fiscal policies have on the bureaucrats stationed in Buenos Aires? To understand the economic position of the local bureaucrats over time, a weighted index of bureaucratic salaries based on twenty-five representative salaries was constructed for the years 1773–1810. (See table 6.4.) Weights were distributed in a manner that reflected the approximate number of bureaucrats at different salary levels, and an index was constructed using 1776 as the base year.

Table 6.4   Weighted Index of Bureaucratic Wages (1776 = 100)

Year	Bureaucratic Wage	Year	Bureaucratic Wage
1773	78.98	1792	100.01
1774	78.98	1793	100.01
1775	91.38	1794	100.01
1776	100.00	1795	99.69
1777	100.00	1796	99.69
1778	88.70	1797	99.55
1779	90.70	1798	97.38
1780	91.35	1799	96.96
1781	91.35	1800	94.71
1782	91.35	1801	94.71
1783	94.11	1802	95.80
1784	94.11	1803	95.80
1785	97.37	1804	95.80
1786	99.18	1805	95.80
1787	101.36	1806	98.13
1788	101.36	1807	98.13
1789	101.36	1808	98.13
1790	100.01	1809	98.40
1791	100.01	1810	98.40

Note: The following weights were assigned for the bureaucrat index: high-ranking administrators (1), medium-level administrators (2), oficiales and clerks (7). This is approximately the proportion of bureaucrats found in each department of all viceregal agencies (see table 3.3).

Several interesting patterns become apparent from reviewing this weighted index of wages. The first is the influence of the founding of the viceroyalty and the new bureaucratic positions thus created on the salary of those positions. At the time that the viceroyalty was founded, there is a suggestion that a growing bureaucracy's need for skilled men outstripped the local supply, thereby forcing a raise in wages to entice talented men to Buenos Aires. Bureaucratic salaries declined soon after, an indication of the rapidity with which both Spanish- and native-born young men flocked to Buenos Aires to take advantage of the newly created employment opportunities, thereby creating a temporary glut. By the mid-1780s salaries once again began to move upward, in part a reflection of the gradual ad-

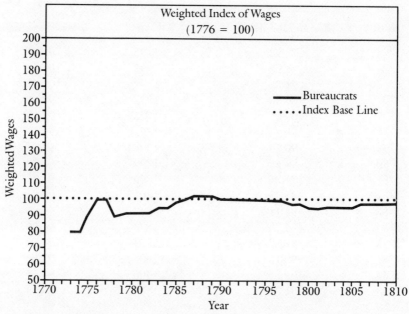

Figure 6.3   Weighted Index of Wages, 1773–1810 (1776 = 100)

justment of supply and demand, in part the result of growing pressure from agency heads to raise the lowest clerical salaries so that holders of these offices could survive. This general tendency to slightly higher bureaucratic salaries was reversed by the middle of the 1790s when the effects of prolonged European conflict caused the Spanish government to begin a series of emergency fiscal measures that included lower salaries for those entering new posts. Not included in this calculation are the voluntary and involuntary donations that even further reduced bureaucratic earnings. Although salary levels began to climb slowly after 1802, the year that Spain signed the Amiens peace treaty with the British, only after the second defeat of the English invaders of Buenos Aires in 1806 did a marked rebound occur. Nonetheless, by 1810 bureaucratic salaries were still below the levels of the 1776 period.

Although wage levels were not static, figure 6.3, showing the weighted index of wages for bureaucrats, suggests that the range over which bureaucratic salaries tended to move was rather limited. In addition, movement up or down tended to be accomplished through small increments rather than through dramatic jumps. In general, wages (or profits) paid to other groups such as artisans, merchants, or landowners could respond more directly to the market forces of supply and demand. Bureaucrats on the other hand were insulated from quick wage swings, for modifying their wages in any direction involved slow bureaucratic procedures.

A bureaucratic career provided more than prestige. It also gave those lucky enough to obtain office a wage insurance, a guaranteed yearly income that even the most prosperous merchant could not depend on. But bureaucrats paid for security and prestige in the form of stagnant wages.

What was the effect of the generally flat average bureaucrat salary in the face of Buenos Aires' inflated cost of living? Although historians have yet to study fully the movement of prices during the period, a commodity index based on the prices for basic foodstuffs has been devised.[41] Rising prices for basic necessities marked much of the colonial period. As can be seen in figure 6.4, probably only in one period, the years between 1788 and 1794, did a decline in commodity prices allow bureaucrats to experience a significant rise in their purchasing power. By 1810 Buenos Aires bureau-

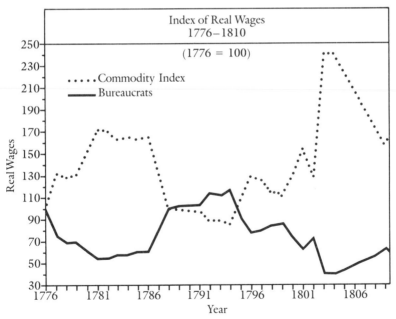

Figure 6.4   Index of Real Wages, 1776–1810 (1776 = 100)

crats probably found their purchasing power almost halved. Because bu-reaucratic salaries remained stable in the face of dramatic price increases, the result of a fiscal policy of austerity in the face of rising costs in basic necessities was the gradual impoverishment of royal civil servants.

High- and medium-ranking bureaucrats earned salaries generally comparable to prosperous retail merchants. Low-level bureaucrats, clerks, escribanos, and porteros earned salaries within the same range as those paid to master craftsmen and journeymen. After 1806, when labor experi-enced rapid upward movement in wages, journeymen and semiskilled la-borers came to outstrip government oficiales in average annual salary.[42] Al-though government service provided greater prestige and more secure employment, a growing awareness of their faltering economic position, a position that a beleaguered crown could do little to alleviate, disheartened local bureaucrats. In addition, because of their social position, the former incurred a variety of expenses in order to maintain their position as *gente decente* (well-born Spaniards). It did not escape the attention of govern-ment clerks, many of whom were from rather humble backgrounds or were the younger sons of minor branches of illustrious families, that their economic position vis-à-vis the porteño artisans was none too secure.

In addition, most bureaucrats were adversely affected by the price of housing in Buenos Aires, a commodity that was in short supply during the whole viceregal period. The influx of bureaucrats exacerbated the already acute housing shortage caused by the city's population growth. Here again low-level bureaucrats suffered vis-à-vis skilled artisans, for while the latter could live in relatively inexpensive *quintas* (villas) and houses in less desir-able sections of the city, government officials, in housing as well as dress, had to maintain proper standards. Middle- and lower-level bureaucrats often rented rooms and *esquinas* (corner apartments) in the central zones of the city. It was not uncommon for several young men serving clerkships to share quarters, thus reducing costs. Nevertheless, on low salaries of 300 to 500 pesos per year, even a modest rental must have represented a rather formidable expense. Again inflation only worsened the situation for low-level bureaucrats on a fixed income. Small apartments that had rented for 3 to 8 pesos per month in 1783 were only available for 32 pesos per month by 1799.[43] Low-ranking bureaucrats found the purchase of food, clothing, and housing of an acceptable standard to be an ever-increasing burden on their meager salaries.

While higher-level bureaucrats could afford to rent suitable quarters or even purchase their own residences, property values on large houses also reflected this growing demand for housing, and rents for dwellings befitting the bureaucratic leaders of the viceroyalty were especially inflated. Although rents rose dramatically, demand was still far greater than supply. Middle- and high-ranking bureaucrats, men with families whose social pretensions required larger and more luxurious housing and a servant or two, frequently complained of the high cost of living in Buenos Aires. As early as 1781 bureaucrats and their widows were pointing out to the crown that "a few years ago it was not as expensive, as it is now, to maintain a family here in Buenos Aires."[44]

Outrageously high rents were constantly reported by newly arriving heads of agencies; high rent was a factor used to justify continual requests to raise government salaries. As early as 1779 the administrator of the Aduana, Ximénez de Mesa, after having been in the city for less than a year, reported that "rents have gone up so dramatically that salaries can no longer suffer housing."[45] Almost forty years later the dearness of life in Buenos Aires, including the high price of housing, was still eliciting comment. By 1808 Viceroy Liniers reported to the crown that "Buenos Aires, which used to be the most abundant and comfortable city in America, is today the most expensive of all for all things even those that are most basic. High prices are reflected in the cost of goods necessary for survival, in the ever-mounting value of housing, and in the price of all cloth goods for clothing."[46] Indeed while rents for rooms varied according to size, comfort, and location, a good house befitting the rank of a high-level bureaucrat rented for at least 50 to 60 pesos per month (600 to 720 pesos per year).

A few particularly fortunate bureaucrats enjoyed the perquisite of government housing. Among these were the chief officers of the Real Renta de Tabaco, the Aduana, and the cigarette factory. These individuals, instead of renting private quarters, were usually furnished with rooms within the agency; when this was not feasible, an extra allowance was granted.[47] While the director of the Real Renta de Tabaco lived in a series of rooms contained within the Casa de Dirección, the contador and the tesorero both had their respective rents of 360 pesos per year paid by the tobacco monopoly.[48] But government housing was the exception, not the rule.

The problem of housing was especially acute for those bureaucrats, usually at the higher levels of government organization, who had come from Spain with wives and children. Not only did they need relatively large living quarters, but they had no friends or relatives to help them in their search for housing. In desperation some officials even attempted to evict people forcibly from the quarters that they wished to rent. Nicolás Torrado, contador of the Aduana, found housing so tight that, shortly after arriving in the city in 1779, he petitioned the local courts to force merchant José de Lezica to remove members of his family from a house that he owned in order to rent it to Torrado.[49] Needless to say, proceedings such as these did little to endear the newly arrived bureaucrats to the local elite. On the other hand, bureaucrats increasingly perceived all local property owners as greedy and suspected them of price-gouging.

Cost of living indexes and housing outlays do not take into account other expenses that served to reduce bureaucrats' incomes. All bureaucrats received their salaries at the end of the calendar month after having completed work for that month. Those bureaucrats who received their appointments in Spain or who were transferred to Buenos Aires from a branch of the bureaucracy outside of the capital city incurred expenses in moving and relocating during a time when no income was forthcoming. Some bureaucrats, especially those from more prosperous families or those who had managed to put aside savings in prior government service, were able to effect these transfers using their own funds. The majority, however, turned either to royal funds or to individual coffers to borrow money for their *habilitación* (preparation). For example, four of the nine tobacco monopoly officials appointed in 1777 and 1778 arrived in Buenos Aires owing "money for their habilitación" that had been loaned to them by the *depositario de Indias* (depository of funds from the Indies) of Cádiz. These loans ranged from 100 pesos provided to Antonio Cárdenas, the oficial tercero of the Real Renta de Tabaco's contaduría section, whose salary was to be 500 pesos per year, to 2,300 pesos provided to the contador general, Francisco Urdaneta, against his yearly salary of 2,500 pesos.[50] Sums lent from government funds under the rubric of habilitación could be as little as 20 or as much as 95 percent of a bureaucrat's first year's salary.[51] Although payments were distributed over three years, the net effect of repaying this loan was to lower the real annual wage for at least half of the high-ranking bureaucrats.

Another expense faced by high-ranking bureaucrats resident in Spain before they set sail for Buenos Aires was the cost of travel to Madrid to take the oath of office. For those residing in the south of Spain at the time of their appointment, this trip to Madrid not only increased expenses but delayed departure to their new post. Several men stationed in Córdoba, Granada, or Seville therefore petitioned the crown for permission to take their oaths in Seville before setting sail. By the late eighteenth century, this permission seems to have been granted routinely after the bureaucrat made a donation of 50 pesos to the *colegio seminario* (seminary school) of San Telmo in Seville.[52]

Almost all bureaucrats were also liable to pay a tax to the crown. For those who were salaried government employees, this tax, the media anata, consisted of half a year's pay. The tax was imposed on all posts within the government bureaucracy, from viceroy and intendant to clerk and portero, and included interim and honorary appointments. The only universal exemption to media anata was that which the first holder of a new position enjoyed. In the case of Buenos Aires, this exemption served as an indirect salary supplement for those lucky enough to receive appointment as new agencies were being created. For those who replaced the original appointees, however, this tax imposed a harsh burden.

In addition to the media anata tax itself, government employees were required to pay an additional 18 percent above their half salary, a charge that theoretically covered costs incurred in forwarding the funds to Spain. The media anata, which therefore totaled 59 percent of an employee's first year salary, was especially onerous since the very same individual who was liable to pay this tax had also just incurred expenses in moving to Buenos Aires and locating housing. Some relief was provided by a government policy that allowed the media anata to be paid in four yearly installments during the first four years of office, but this facility seems to have only been extended to those whose salaries were in the range of 3,000 pesos or above. Once an individual was in the bureaucracy, subsequent media anata was only assessed on salary raises, rather than on the entire new salary. The major onus of the tax therefore fell on those entering government service.

Military salaries were also specifically exempted from the media anata. As a result, those bureaucrats who had posts that included both civilian and military duties (i.e., the viceroy, the intendant) only paid media anata on that part of their salaries judged to correspond to their civil duties. Another such position that combined civilian and military functions was the joint position of *asesor del virreinato* (legal adviser of the viceroyalty) and auditor de guerra. The asesor-auditor's salary in 1778 was 4,000 pesos, but the media anata only totaled 500 pesos as only 1,000 pesos of this salary corresponded to the civilian post.[53]

Those bureaucrats liable for payment of media anata often managed to procrastinate several years before settling accounts. While the crown was somewhat lax in enforcing quick payment during the early years of the viceroyalty, after 1795 the search for funds extended to more efficient collection of this tax too. Between 1790–1800 and 1801–5 the total revenues collected in this account increased sevenfold.[54] While some of this increase was due to an increase in the number of positions no longer exempt from the tax, most was the result of stringent treatment of colonial bureaucrats. Bureaucrats, who were "turning the screws" on the local populace in the collection of taxes, were in turn having the "screws" turned on them.

Media anata was an unpopular internal tax but one that government employees were ultimately willing to pay to hold their positions. Nevertheless, with growing pressure on their fixed salaries, government workers hesitantly began to point out inequities in the media anata. In 1806, for example, an anonymous complaint was sent to the minister of the Indies signed by "an employee in His Majesty's service." The letter pointed out that since the time of Viceroy Loreto, because of the error by the fiscal of the Real Audiencia in interpreting regulations, all viceroys of the Río de la Plata had mistakenly paid only one-fourth of their salary in media anata. The writer asked that this inequity be redressed.[55]

Increasing economic pressure, brought on by virtually incessant warfare in both Europe and America, forced the Spanish crown to seek still additional revenues from its subjects. Beginning in 1794 and continuing through the first decade of the 1800s, one or another type of voluntary or involuntary donation to the crown was instituted in the platense viceroyalty. The most lucrative donativo collected in the area was the so-called *donativo voluntario* (voluntary donation), also referred to as the *donativo para la guerra* (donation for the war). Between 1794 and 1808 a total of 1,024,543 pesos was collected under this rubric.[56] By no means did all of this money come from government bureaucrats, but at least some local crown servants, caught up in the patriotic fervor of the moment or seizing the opportunity to impress the viceroy and other authorities with their devotion to the cause, did come forth with sizable contributions. In 1801, for example, Miguel García de Tagle, serving as alguacil mayor of the Real Audiencia, volunteered 3 percent of his income to the crown "for the duration of this war."[57]

In addition, beginning in 1794 and continuing through 1797, all salaried government employees earning more than 600 pesos per year were required to make a contribution of 4 percent of their salary to the crown, again to be used for the defense of the Spanish empire.[58] Although no doubt fired with the same fervor as those citizens who were not on the government payroll, there is some indication that this contribution was slow in being collected. Bureaucrats who were underpaid, suffering from inflation, and subject to the payment of the media anata and/or montepío contributions probably had little desire to further reduce their expendable incomes. As late as 1802 money was still dribbling into the 4 percent account. The total collected for the crown through this involuntary tax was 15,398 pesos.[59]

Although victims of a general upward trend of prices and the failure of their salaries to maintain an adequate and decent standard of living, as late as 1809 the bureaucrats of the city again supported the Spanish government by responding to a request for emergency funds. The donativo *patriotico* enacted in 1809 was still another in a long series of donativos, but seventy-seven bureaucrats resident in Buenos Aires contributed a total of 11,554 pesos to aid the economically failing imperial government.[60] Contributions ranged from 1,753 pesos (donated by the ex-viceroy, Marqués de Sobremonte) to four pesos (several donations by minor clerks in the Aduana and tobacco agencies). The average bureaucratic contribution of 150 pesos was far above the average private contribution of 52 pesos. In addition, although government bureaucrats comprised only 5.8 percent of those who made donations, they donated 16.8 percent of all funds collected.

Bureaucrats did have job security, the almost certain knowledge that they would be employed for their entire lives. Indeed, the idea of retirement did not exist in the eighteenth century. Occasionally, a bureaucrat could receive a leave of absence with pay because of sickness or a leave without pay for another pressing reason, but there was no formal retirement system within the colonial bureaucracy. Government bureaucrats who held a título (formal royal title) held their position until death. Retirement was rare and was not seen as a right that a civil servant earned when he reached a certain age. This attitude, and the lack of any mechanism to provide funds for those who had left government service because of advancing age, was responsible for frequent complaints about decrepit employees, increasing absences from work because of sickness or poor health, and a general decrease in government efficiency. Government bureaucrats literally died at their desks because there was no mechanism that allowed them to retire from civil service.

Nevertheless, men who were old, aching, and infirm could and did petition the crown for special permission to retire with pay. It is hard to determine what percentage of these requests were granted, but each case seems to have been unique in the terms conceded by the crown. Sebastián Velasco, senior oidor of the audiencia of Buenos Aires, for example, requested retirement when he reached the age of seventy-nine, citing his "advanced age and broken health." The crown granted Velasco's request in 1804, paying him two-thirds of his regular salary. The other third became the salary assigned to Velasco's son Manuel, oidor-elect of Manila. In effect, this solution forced the younger Velasco to subsidize his father's retirement.[61]

Although a universal retirement system was never instituted, one major reform in that direction affected a small group of bureaucrats. This was the decision made in 1803, as a result of the de la Vega visita, to include all treasury employees under a uniform retirement code, allowing those who had served the crown well for a minimum of twelve years to retire because of extreme ill health.[62] For the first time funds for widows and orphans (montepío monies) were made available not only to the survivors of deceased government bureaucrats, but also to old bureaucrats who could use these pensions to retire. According to the 1803 cédula, those who could no longer "perform their duties" because of "ailing old age" could draw pension determined by their length of government service. Those who had served the crown for thirty years or more were entitled to retire at full salary of their last post; those who had served for twenty to twenty-nine years would be awarded two-thirds of their salary, and those who had worked from twelve to nineteen years would receive half. This new legislation was clearly aimed at making retirement from government service more attractive, thereby remedying the perpetual problem of old, sick employees who failed to meet their bureaucratic obligations but nonetheless held on to their posts until death. At the same time the crown was careful to establish minimum length of service before any pension could be drawn; the only employees who could claim a pension after fewer than twelve years of service were those who could prove they had been disabled in the service of the crown.

The reform was never applied to other branches of government, nor did it have a marked affect on the numbers of treasury employees who chose to avail themselves of the new provisions. Perhaps most of those eligible believed that they would lose both influence and (except for those employed more than thirty years) salary. Only Mariano Aoiz, third oficial of the Secretaría seems to have taken advantage of the new regulations, retiring at two-thirds salary from the bureaucracy.[63] Failure of bureaucrats to retire, even with more generous possibilities, meant that no increase in the number of openings in the viceregal bureaucracy occurred in the years immediately preceding Independence. It nevertheless signaled future post-Independence bureaucratic reform.

Perhaps of more concern than retirement benefits or the lack of them for married bureaucrats was the government's policy of pensions paid to widows and surviving minor children through the montepío system. Coverage was far from uniform although over the viceregal period it was gradually extended. Initially, no government bureaucrats except those who were also military officers qualified for inclusion in the montepío, thus none contributed to a pension fund and none were able to insure that their widows would enjoy a degree of financial security. Individual widows could and did petition the government for support, usually claiming meritorious service on the part of their late husband (including loss of life while serving the crown) or extreme penury. They met with varying degrees of success, as each case was decided on its merits by the Council of the Indies. Growing dissatisfaction with this system on the part of high-ranking local bureaucrats throughout the empire eventually led to limited reform. In the case of Buenos Aires the reform first resulted in the creation of a montepío for important government bureaucrats. Membership in the Montepío de Ministros de Justicia y Real Hacienda was in fact one of the most important perquisites given to a limited number of officials.

Montepíos, an eighteenth century institution that had begun in Spain and had gradually been extended to the New World, had as their goal the provision of pension funds for widows, children, and widowed mothers of those who had served the crown well.[64] The original montepío set up in 1761 was limited to army officers of the rank of captain or above, but within ten to fifteen years other montepíos were created under government auspices to provide survivor benefits for naval officers, government ministers, army surgeons, and army engineers.[65] In general, these later montepíos were modeled along the same lines as the military one. Membership in these groups was limited to high-ranking bureaucrats in the institutions involved and was not voluntary.[66] Those included under the umbrella of a montepío were required to pay an initial fee and then to continue contributing a portion of each month's salary into the fund. Widows and minor children of those who had been members of a montepío would, after presenting the necessary documentation attesting to their legitimate status as heirs of the deceased, receive monthly stipends from the fund.[67] The major difference between the military montepío and that which protected government bureaucrats was that the former was administered from centralized offices in Spain while the latter enjoyed a high degree of local administrative autonomy. While the autonomy of montepíos de ministros throughout America made it easier for widows and orphans to apply for pensions, it greatly complicated the process of transferring pension funds for those bureaucrats who had come from other jurisdictions. Furthermore, local montepíos gave differing interpretations as to who was eligible for membership. Indeed, a bureaucrat could find himself included in the montepío in one area of the New World but excluded in another.

The Buenos Aires montepío de ministros began in 1768 as a branch of the same institution in Lima. From 1768 until 1778 all montepío funds collected in Buenos Aires were remitted to the montepío in Lima; from 1779 on the local office of the montepío had the power to collect and disperse funds, although it was not until 1785 that an autonomous montepío received royal approbation and a governing junta de montepío began to function. This junta, charged with administering the local montepío, was composed of a five-man board (a director chosen by the viceroy from among the Audiencia judges for a four-year term and four other high-ranking officials from the Audiencia, the Tribunal de Cuentas, the Real Hacienda, and the Real Renta de Tabaco named by the viceroy to two-year terms). In addition, the junta employed a staff of two to four people who attended to the daily administration of the pension fund. Staff members were also appointed by the viceroy at the suggestion of the montepío board members. Because of special perquisites granted to the montepío staff after 1790, these positions were viewed as plum appointments and always were awarded to experienced bureaucrats who had impressed their superiors. In 1790, for example, the treasurer of the montepío was Antonio Pablo Marín, a man who had served the Real Renta de Tabaco since its creation in 1778 as the oficial mayor of the accounting section.

From its creation in 1768 to the end of the viceregal period, the number of bureaucrats included under the protection of the montepío grew. This was the result, in part, of growing numbers of high-ranking bureaucrats within the Viceroyalty of the Río de la Plata and, in part, the gradual extension of the montepío to new groups within the bureaucracy. The royal order that extended the montepío de ministros to the New World specified that this institution was to cover Audiencia ministers, ministers of the Tribunal de Cuentas, and ministers of Real Hacienda, but in the case of Buenos Aires the only bureaucrats included in these categories and present in the city from 1768 to 1778 were treasury officials. The creation of the platense viceroyalty, the consequent growth of the bureaucracy through the area, and the creation of an Audiencia in Buenos Aires greatly enlarged the number of men required to join the montepío. By 1785 those in Buenos Aires covered by the montepío now included the regent, oidores, and fiscal of the Real Audiencia; the contadores mayores, contador de retasas, and contadores ordenadores of the Tribunal de Cuentas; the ministros of the Real Hacienda; the contador de proprios y arbitrios; and the asesor of the viceroyalty. In addition, members of the Real Audiencia of La Plata and ministros of the Real Hacienda in Montevideo, Santa Fé, Asunción, Córdoba, Salta, Oruro, La Paz, Carabaya, Carangas, Chucuito, and Cochabamba were also members of the fund. Both the ministros of the Real Hacienda in Potosí and the contador and treasurer of the Casa de Moneda were included in the montepío.[68] In 1786 the two fiscal agents employed by the Buenos Aires Audiencia were also brought into the organization.[69]

Searching for additional revenue, the crown continued to enlarge the montepío membership list, an expedient that produced a short-term rise in capital as new members began to pay into the fund. By 1787 montepío membership was extended to the director, contador, and treasurer of the Real Renta de Tabaco. In 1790 staff members of the montepío itself were included in its coverage as were the administrador, contador, and vista of the Real Aduana. Five years later the administrador, contador, and tesorero of the Real Banco de San Carlos in Potosí were made members, and in 1797 the administrador, contador, and oficial primero of the Administración de Correos in Buenos Aires were given the option to join the fund.[70] All did. In 1801 the local junta de montepíos suggested that the administrador of Temporalidades and the *tenientes letrados* (assistant counselors) of the viceroyalty be included in the montepío.[71] Two years later participation in the montepío was extended to "employees of the administration of Real Hacienda who have served well and faithfully."[72]

Although viceroys and intendants never joined the montepío de ministros (as military officers they were covered by the more prestigious and better paying military montepío), the fund, which covered fifty-one high-ranking bureaucrats in 1785, had been extended to ninety-four by 1801. Nevertheless, with the singular exception of the montepío staff members, this protection was only accorded to the bureaucratic elite of the city. The vast majority of government bureaucrats, even those who had served the crown for thirty to forty years, were never provided any survivors' benefits. Not all agencies were included in the montepío, and employees below the rank of minister were also generally not covered. Thus, survivors of those who had worked in the Secretaría still had to petition the government for special pensions after the death of their husbands.[73]

The montepío de ministros was never intended to be a free service provided by the crown. Instead, from its very inception the Buenos Aires montepío, like all others, was conceived of as a mutual fund into which all members made the requisite contributions. In the case of bureaucrats covered by the Buenos Aires montepío, the following costs were to be paid by fund members: upon joining the montepío all members were to pay one-and-one-half-months' salary as their initial contribution; once covered by the montepío regular yearly payments of 8 maravedíes for every peso earned were to be made to the fund. In addition, whenever a bureaucrat received a salary increase, one payment covering the difference between his old salary and his new one was due the montepío. Lastly, at the time of death the Royal Treasury added its contribution, taken from the *vacantes mayores* (vacant bishoprics) fund and equal to the last two-months' salary of the deceased bureaucrat.

Survivors' benefits for those lucky enough to be covered by the montepío were structured so as to provide economic protection for a bureaucrat's widow and minor children. The underlying concept was one of maintaining at least a modicum of the economic and social position that the high-ranking civil servants had enjoyed, for it would indeed be a disgrace if the widows, sons, and daughters of men who had headed the Spanish bureaucracy were reduced to penury after the bureaucrats' death. In the case of Buenos Aires the yearly pension was one-fourth of the last salary earned by the deceased, although only the base salary (excluding salary supplements or any special commission) was used for this calculation. As salaries of montepío members ranged from 1,000 to almost 10,000 pesos, actual pensions awarded varied from as low as 300 pesos per year to pensions almost ten times as large. Although the montepío provided a minimum monthly subsidy for those widows receiving the lower benefits, maintaining an adequate life style was very difficult indeed.

In order to maintain her survivor's pension, the widow of a bureaucrat had to conserve her civil status. Remarriage or the taking of religious vows automatically disqualified a widow from continuing to receive payment. The number of surviving children did not influence the size of the benefits. Furthermore, all children continued to collect pensions after the death of both parents. Male children were pension recipients until the age of twenty-five, the colonial age of majority. Female children were covered until they married. All recipients of the montepío pensions could only receive payment while living within the dominions of the king of Spain, although they need not continue to live in Buenos Aires.

In theory, all montepíos were to be economically self-sufficient. Only bureaucrats who paid into the montepío were entitled to its benefits. The fund was not to be a drain on royal finances; indeed, quite the contrary, it was to provide an additional source of capital for the crown in the short run. In addition, it was hoped that local costs of administering the montepío could be kept low. The principal members of the local montepío board were high-ranking bureaucrats, men themselves protected by the fund. In addition, the montepío was to borrow seasoned clerks from other agencies to handle the daily chores of secretary-accountant and treasurer.

Unfortunately, the schedules of contributions and benefits were drawn up by bureaucrats who had little understanding of actuarial tables. Those who designed the montepío failed to realize that the large difference in age at time of marriage between men and women meant that women would generally outlive their husbands by several years. The social conventions that called for an established (i.e., older) man to marry a young, nubile woman choked the montepío rolls with young widows and younger children, all drawing government pensions that eventually outstripped their husbands' contributions. In 1789 the crown, realizing this weakness in the montepío structure, decreed that the widow and children of any bureaucrat who had married after age sixty could not collect a pension.[74] But few bureaucrats had married so late in life, and this limitation failed to remedy the economic weakness of the montepío.

In the case of the Buenos Aires montepío the institution's internal finances were further complicated by the delay in collecting initial membership payments and by the reluctance of Lima to turn over funds from the *ramo* (branch) de vacantes mayores, which were to supplement the montepío. In 1785, as part of a campaign to have some vacantes mayores funds transferred to its accounts,[75] the montepío drew up a *relación* (account) demonstrating an annual income of 5,979 pesos. Against this income the montepío had expenses totaling 8,451 pesos (7,401 pesos in pensions and 1,050 in staff salaries).[76] The next year montepío income rose to 6,472 pesos, but expenditures also rose to 9,055 pesos (8,005 pesos in pensions and again 1,050 pesos in staff salaries).[77] The montepío was thus operating at an annual deficit of approximately 2,500 pesos per year.

The Buenos Aires montepío was eventually successful in collecting an annual award of 1,500 pesos from the vacantes mayores, although this was only half of the amount originally assigned to it by the Lima montepío. Moreover, economic problems caused by a basic misunderstanding of the capital reserve needed in the survivors' fund continued to be a major problem. These financial difficulties were not unique to the Buenos Aires montepío but rather plagued all Spanish and American institutions. In 1787 the crown decided to act, issuing a royal order that instituted a series of rate-structure reforms in all American montepíos. Incoming montepío members, and those who had received a salary raise, were now required to pay an initial two months' salary into the fund. Monthly contributions were increased from eight to twelve maravedíes per peso of salary. In addition, the contribution to the fund from vacantes mayores was increased from two to three months' salary. Nevertheless, a review of the cartas cuentas of the Royal Treasury shows that rarely did the Buenos Aires montepíos income exceed its expenses. The result of this chronic shortage of funds was delayed payment of pensions to the widows and orphans who were so dependent on these monies. Those widows and children who had returned to Spain found it exceptionally difficult to collect funds coming from the Buenos Aires montepío with any regularity.

One more attempt was made to improve montepío assets in 1808 when Viceroy Liniers, following a request from the montepío junta, asked the crown for permission to once again increase both initial membership fees and the crown contribution coming from vacantes mayores. In essence, Liniers was attempting to institute reforms similar to those put into effect in Mexico more than twenty years earlier. Liniers's request was rejected by a Spanish government hard-pressed for funds to continue campaigns against Napoleon. Instead, the authorities, in a reply that arrived well after the city of Buenos Aires had effectively ended its ties with the Spanish world, suggested an increase in monthly contributions coupled with a reduction in pensions paid to survivors.[78]

The revolutionary government that took power in May 1810, motivated in part by the need to maintain a corps of trained bureaucrats loyal to the revolution, soon realized that it was in their interest to continue the montepío. By October 1810 the revolutionary government extended membership in the montepío to an additional group of government bureaucrats, those employed in the Secretaría de Gobierno y Superintendencia.[79] Three years later the General Constituent Assembly reconfirmed the rights of widows and orphans of bureaucrats who had served the viceregal government to draw pensions from the montepío, although widows of those civil servants judged to be traitors to the revolutionary government were struck from the montepío roles.[80]

As seen earlier, the reality of the new bureaucracy changed little from that of the pre-viceregal one. Opportunities for rapid professional advancement, although available for a few who were already on the scene, quickly disappeared as the personnel of each agency became stabilized. Because of the royal devotion to rank-order promotion, only the death or reappointment of a superior could occasion promotion. Exceptional performance rarely translated into a brilliant bureaucratic career. As a result, lethargy and inertia seemed to have become the norm among the scores of oficiales who labored in local government offices.

Added to the professional disillusionment that was experienced by many civil servants, economic stagnation, made even more acute when compared to the gains made by local artisan groups, also disheartened the bureaucrats. While an Audiencia judge, secure in his social position and earning an annual salary of 4,000 pesos, had little to fear from a skilled artisan, the same was not true of a fifth oficial in the Royal Treasury. Low-ranking clerks had spent several years as unpaid meritorios in order to qualify for their jobs. Proud of their positions among the gente decente, these clerks, whether creole or Spanish-born, nonetheless had visible proof that at least some artisans could live, eat, and even marry better than they. While a chronic labor shortage forced up artisan wages in Buenos Aires, an oversupply of eager, educated young men, coupled with royal insolvency, kept bureaucratic wages stable. Moreover, bureaucrats were faced with ever-increasing expenses in the form of internal taxes, "voluntary" contributions, and the rising cost of living. The result of a royal policy of salary austerity in the face of these costs was the gradual impoverishment of the royal civil servants.

While government employment was a never-ceasing goal of both Spaniards and local young men, only the highest-ranking administrators in each agency received attractive wages and valuable perquisites. At a time of growing inflation and rising rents, the Spanish bureaucracy failed to increase its employees' wages. The crown, faced with a constant demand for the creation of additional positions and the resultant growth in the total expenditure on bureaucratic salaries, was hardly sympathetic to any request for raises. As a result, outstanding performance only rarely received a financial reward. Bureaucrats had only two ways to increase their personal revenues: waiting for promotion to a more important job that usually brought a higher salary and indulging in corruption. Clearly, the choice of one option did not obviate the possibility of the other.

7. Local Ties, Marriage, and Family

TO GOVERN AMERICA THE SPANISH CROWN had always strived, in theory if not in practice, to create a disinterested bureaucracy, a corps of civil servants unencumbered by personal and familial ties to local groups. From the earliest days of Spanish colonization of the New World, the crown had attempted to provide its colonies with royal officials who were "incorruptible." This was especially important in the realm of justice, an essential role of the crown. One of the ways envisioned to maintain a disinterested bureaucracy was to prohibit marriage with local women. As a result, Hapsburg legislation decreed that no Audiencia oidor, nor any of his children, could marry a native of the same Audiencia district. Indeed, a magistrate could only marry a criolla from another area after special royal permission had been secured.[1] Regardless of legislation, in the Audiencias of Mexico, Lima, Santiago de Chile, and Santa Fé de Bogotá, criollos and Spaniards married to local women came to dominate the halls of justice and the fiscal administration of the colony. The Bourbon reforms, especially the policies of the third Bourbon king, Charles III, signaled a reaction against this growth of local influence; one of the cardinal objectives of Charles's program was to reconquer America from the hands of the creoles.[2]

In addition to legislation aimed at creating a unified civil service for Spain and the colonies—legislation that indirectly limited local creole participation—on 9 August 1779 a royal order was promulgated that expressed Charles III's intention to enforce preexisting marriage legislation to the letter.[3] This royal order, directed to all viceroys, presidents, and Audiencias in America, reiterated earlier laws requiring royal permission for Audiencia judges to marry and added an important new group of officials to be covered by these prohibitions, those employed by the Real Hacienda. Included in the category of bureaucrats now needing special royal permission to marry were the contador mayor of the Tribunal de Cuentas, the director general of the Real Renta de Tabaco, all Royal Exchequer officials, the *contador de tributos* (accountant of Indian tribute), the administrator of the Real Renta de Tabaco or whomever directed the local Reales Cajas, and whomever was in charge of checking royal accounts, including contadores interventores, and all oficiales subalternos.

Charles III's programs worked to lessen creole control in the Audiencia and by extension in royal government, but much of his legislation was either ignored or greatly amended by his successors.[4] A rapid return to earlier policies is most evident in edicts concerning the marriage of government officials. In 1789 a royal order gave viceroys explicit authority to issue special marriage licenses to contadores, oficiales reales, and other employees of the Real Hacienda as long as both partners were of "the same rank, background, and corresponding condition."[5] Two years later another royal order exempted Hacienda bureaucrats below the rank of contador interventor from obtaining royal permission "as long as the circumstances of the bride are not inferior to those of the groom."[6]

The crown, nevertheless, remained firm in its desire to control the marriage of high-ranking fiscal and judicial bureaucrats, especially when their partners were locally born women. On 24 March 1791, just four days after the above mentioned royal order exempted lower-level bureaucrats from royal approval, another royal order reiterated the general prohibition against high-ranking officials marrying those born in the same district where the official was employed. This royal order further hinted that exemptions would be sharply curtailed.[7] The warning about bureaucratic marriages to criollos was a result of "the continuous repeated instances in which different employees in the ministerios of those dominions have requested royal permission to marry determined people, natives of their respective districts."[8] Nevertheless, neither before nor after this 1791 royal order was any request to marry a local woman denied a prospective groom. The Spanish crown showed itself only two willing to disregard its own policies, granting permission to all those who petitioned the crown.

By 1798 the continued demand for special permission to marry local women and the exigencies of war forced the crown to once again modify its policy. A *communicación real* (royal communiqué) of 21 July informed the viceroy that while the crown was at war, and communication with the metropolis was sporadic, the viceroy had full power to issue licenses to marry to any officials within his jurisdiction who would suffer greatly because of a prolonged delay.[9] The viceroy was only required to send all supporting documents to Spain after the licenses had been granted.

The desire to control the marriage of government bureaucrats was of course tied to the realization that family created close and often undesirable obligations in colonial society. The crown believed that the creation of these powerful bonds always worked against royal interest. In addition to regulations concerning marriage to creoles, the crown was also intent upon preventing marriage between high-ranking treasury officials and the daughters, sisters, or related female kinfolk to the fourth degree of their peers. Two laws stressing these prohibitions were incorporated into the Leyes de Indias.[10] Furthermore, even a promise of marriage between Real Hacienda officials and these women, "be it verbally . . . or written or made in the hope that we will grant a special license to marry" was to be viewed as tantamount to disobeying the royal will.[11] The punishment for disobeying this prohibition was loss of office.

In theory government bureaucrats were not only to avoid marrying women kin of fellow bureaucrats, they were also to have no other kindred ties with each other. According to a royal cédula issued in 1775 and reissued in 1785 and 1799, no two members of the same family were to be employed in the same agency.[12] This prohibition covered a myriad of familial relations including father/son, father-in-law/son-in-law, brothers, and uncle/nephew.

The major weakness in all legislation directed at controlling the marriage of government officials was that it was highly unrealistic. The law forbade marriage to those two groups of women with whom an unmarried bureaucrat was most likely to have social contact—local residents and the daughters of fellow workers. Fortunately for the royal servants in Buenos Aires, all legislation also provided exemptions through "special royal license." Special exemptions, of course, made it all the more difficult to control the fundamental problem, the fact that marriage to local women or among government officials "could result in improper behavior and impede the good exercise of their profession."

Even had it been willing to enforce its own legislation on marriage, the crown could not easily dismiss or replace officials who had worked in government offices before the founding of the viceroyalty. Instead, bureaucrats already in Buenos Aires before 1776 were maintained in managerial positions while staff was also augmented at all levels. As a result of this policy, based on the perceived need to provide continuity and as a result of the lack of a policy that encouraged the retirement of older bureaucrats, men who came to head "new" agencies were products of an older mentality. While Charles III was trying to lessen bureaucratic ties to the local elite, many of those heading the agencies of Buenos Aires were men who at an earlier date had carefully established just those ties. These government bureaucrats held power for the first twenty years after the establishment of the viceroyalty. While more professional than their early eighteenth-century counterparts (they did not openly engage in business, nor did they hold local offices as men such as Manuel Mena and Juan Antonio Jijano had done before midcentury), they nevertheless were far from disinterested bureaucrats without local ties, coldly pursuing policies only advantageous to the crown.

Perhaps the best example of this "transitional" type of bureaucrat was Pedro Medrano. Medrano, born in Nabarrete, Calahorra, in 1734, was the son of Don Pedro Medrano Corral and Doña María de la Plaza. His father, although neither wealthy nor socially prominent, had at one time served as Alcalde de la Santa Hermandad in his native village. In 1746 young Pedro, in search of a future, traveled to Madrid to obtain some minor post in the American bureaucracy. Although it is not clear whether he met with immediate success, he decided to continue on to Cádiz and from there to the New World. After presenting the necessary *informaciones de legitimidad* (proofs of legitimacy) and *limpieza de sangre e Hidalguía* (purity of blood and nobility), the young man made his way to Buenos Aires.[13]

Details of the next ten years of his life are unknown, but by 1756 Medrano, age twenty-two, was employed in Buenos Aires as secretary to Governor Pedro de Cevallos. On 29 July of that year Medrano married Michaela Montañer, daughter of Bartolomé Montañer (a merchant, sometime treasury official, and *cabildo regidor*) and Margarita de Oliva y Tofre. Seven years later, on 8 May 1763, Cevallos named Medrano *ministro tesorero* (chief treasurer) of the Reales Cajas.[14] Medrano was by then a childless widower. In 1764, at age thirty, he married again, this time to Victoriana Cabrera, age eighteen, a native of Buenos Aires and daughter of Francisco Cabrera, an important local merchant and militia officer, and Antonia de Saavedra.[15] Not only did the groom receive the lavish dowry of 25,428 pesos 4 reales (of which 15,601 pesos were in cash) from the bride's parents (the dowry was of course awarded to their daughter but turned over to their new son-in-law), but he had also become a member of one of the city's most distinguished families.[16] The bride's mother, Antonia de Saavedra, traced her lineage to the sixteenth-century founders of the city. She belonged to a family "that has been honored by all the local inhabitants, as much because it is an illustrious family, as because individual members have held positions of importance, for innumerable years, in the Cabildo, the military, and the Church[,and] . . . some members of the family have been named to the Holy Tribunal of the Inquisition."[17] In addition, his new father-in-law, Cabrera, as a leading merchant of the city, had served on the local Cabildo, as had several maternal relatives of his wife.

No doubt Medrano had made an important marriage. While his wife began to busy herself with bearing children (thirteen within the next twenty years), he continued to work in the Reales Cajas. Unfortunately, Medrano and his fellow ministros in the Reales Cajas soon found themselves faced with a hostile governor in the person of Francisco Bucareli. Shortly after arriving in Buenos Aires in 1766, Bucareli became suspicious of the manner in which the three high-ranking officials of the Reales Cajas were conducting business. One of the specific charges brought against Medrano was that he had hidden a royal cédula that ordered the estate of his late father-in-law, Bartolomé Montañer, to make a substantial repayment to the treasury. Bucareli suspended all three men, and when Medrano hinted that he would challenge the governor's action, Bucareli began additional proceedings against Medrano for *fanatismo*. However, with Bucareli's departure in 1770 Medrano was able to return to his post in the Reales Cajas. Six years later he received orders assigning him to the position of contador of the Reales Cajas in Santiago.[18] Before leaving Buenos Aires he was also charged with conducting the residencia of his old mentor, Governor Pedro de Cevallos. A new royal order soon cancelled the Chilean appointment, and Medrano was told to remain in Buenos Aires.[19] Probably, Pedro de Cevallos, preparing to return to Buenos Aires as the first viceroy of the newly created platense viceroyalty, was instrumental in this change. Cevallos went even further, submitting a proposal to create a Tribunal de Cuentas in Buenos Aires and suggesting that Pedro Medrano be named as its first contador mayor. Although his candidacy was rejected by the crown, Medrano had clearly returned to a position of favor within the royal bureaucracy.[20]

In 1778 Pedro Medrano, tesorero of the Reales Cajas of Buenos Aires, lived with his wife, seven sons, and one daughter in the center of the city. In addition to a sizable family, he employed a staff of twenty-six servants (sixteen men and ten women), all of whom are listed as free mulattoes or blacks. Probably many of the men listed as residing in the family's house were actually employed in the quinta located three leagues to the north.[21] Nonetheless, the large number of servants attests to the relatively opulent life-style that Medrano and his family were able to enjoy, due no doubt in part to Victoriana Cabrera's significant dowry.

Although he enjoyed favor with Cevallos, Medrano failed to win quick promotion from the post of tesorero of the Reales Cajas. Only in 1786, after receiving repeated requests for retirement from the contador Martín José de Altolaguirre, did the crown propose that he and Altolaguirre switch posts.[22] For the next nine years Medrano therefore served as contador of the Real Hacienda. He also profited from the special assignments that allowed royal officials to earn extra funds; in 1781 Viceroy Vértiz suggested that Intendant Fernández name Medrano to a commission that was being formed to grant indemnifications resulting from the Rio Grande campaign. According to Vértiz "the treasurer Don Pedro Medrano, because of his experience and because he has served as the secretary since the beginning of this entire matter, has great knowledge of everything that has happened."[23] Although now occupying the most important post in the Reales Cajas, Medrano continued to yearn for promotion to contador mayor of the Tribunal de Cuentas. In 1792 he again requested this transfer and was again turned down.[24] Instead, the crown instructed the viceroy to placate Medrano by placing his sons in a Real Hacienda position "as soon as there is a vacancy."

Of the eleven surviving Medrano children, two sons, Martín José and Manuel, did in fact enter the royal bureaucracy, beginning as meritorios. Manuel eventually rose to contador ordenador interino of the Tribunal de Cuentas. (After Independence, Manuel received a regular appointment as *primer* (first) contador ordenador.) Martín José, the oldest child, had a far more problematic bureaucratic career. His marriage to María Pascuala Iraola, a woman of lower-class origin, was opposed by his father and did little to help him.[25] He never rose above the rank of escribiente and eventually left the bureaucracy for the military. Francisca Paula Medrano, the contador's oldest daughter, made a far more advantageous match. In 1785 she was wed to José María Romero Nuñez, son of merchant and government contractor Tomás Romero, an arrangement no doubt mutually advantageous to both Medrano and Romero.[26] In 1798, three years after Pedro Medrano's death, José María Romero was named tesorero supernumerario of the Reales Cajas. Still another Medrano son, Mariano, became a priest. Eusebio José, Julián, and Juan Nepomuceno followed military careers. The former was sent to Spain in 1789 at age fourteen to join the navy. The latter two joined the army and were both killed during the English invasions of Buenos Aires.

Because of the strong local ties that his wife provided, Pedro Medrano identified with Buenos Aires. The fact that he thought of himself as a permanent resident instead of a temporary transient is shown in his purchase of urban and semirural property. Shortly after his first marriage Medrano purchased the house that he and his family later inhabited in the city; he also owned a lot in the *barrio* (neighborhood) of Monserrat. In 1785 he successfully petitioned the city for permission to construct rental units on this property.[27] Medrano also owned a *quinta y chacara* (villa and farm) "along the river . . . in the vicinity of San Isidro," a property purchased in 1773 for 3,210 pesos.[28]

In spite of attempts to limit their choice of brides, the majority of the local bureaucrats did marry. The actual marital experience of the bureaucrats of Buenos Aires is contained in table 7.1. In every agency the percentage of low-ranking bureaucrats marrying is far smaller than for high-ranking ones. Indeed, in no government agency were more than 50 percent of the oficiales married, while frequently all administradores or ministros were married. The close correlation between bureaucratic rank and marital state suggests that for many economic constraints weighed at least as heavily as any necessary royal permission.

Only after long years of service, when one had achieved the rank of oficial mayor or higher, did the average Spanish bureaucrat have the economic security needed to support a wife and children. A man earning a salary of 300 to 800 pesos was usually not a desirable marriage partner for the elite women of the city. The young oficiales awaited promotion before they could aspire to the hand of a socially acceptable young woman; if pro-

Table 7.1 Marriage of Porteño Bureaucrats

Agency and rank	N	Married	Unmarried	Percentage married
Viceroy	11	10	1	91
Intendant	3	1	2	33
Real Hacienda				
ministro	3	3	—	100
contador	2	2	—	100
oficial	24	10	14	42
Secretariat				
secratario	5	4	1	80
oficial	13	3	10	23
asesor	12	10	2	83
Tribunal de Cuentas				
contador mayor	7	7	—	100
contador ordenador	12	10	2	83
oficial	19	8	11	42
Aduana				
administrador	2	2	—	100
contador	5	4	1	80
oficial	18	9	9	50
Tabacos				
administrador	3	3	—	100
contador	9	7	2	78
oficial	31	13	18	42
Total	179	106	73	59

motion failed to come after several years, they sometimes settled for a less desirable spouse or remained single throughout their life. For those bureaucrats born in Buenos Aires the pattern was somewhat different, for they could fall back on parents and kin to support a marriage. Considering only those lower-ranking oficiales who married, almost half had been born in Buenos Aires or nearby areas.

So prevalent was marriage among the porteño-born bureaucrats that even a few meritorios married, some to local women from fairly prominent families. This choice of marriage partner is in part a reflection of the fact that these meritorios were sons of the local elite, young men whose fathers could help support a family while they accumulated the training and merit that it was hoped would place them in a bureaucratic career. For this small group the asset of being the son of an important merchant or bureaucrat outweighed the liability of not earning a salary.

There was also a relationship between the rank of a bureaucrat at the time of marriage and the socioeconomic origin of his bride. (See table 7.2.) Men who married as oficiales displayed a strikingly different pattern from those who married after they had achieved higher rank. The majority of these oficiales were Spaniards who had come to Buenos Aires in search of a living. With limited influence and connections but some prior government experience, they had managed to secure low-level positions, but these positions provided neither lucrative incomes nor great prestige. Relative outsiders of limited attraction as marriage partners, oficiales could not aspire to marry the most socially prestigious young porteño maidens. Instead, they had to settle for women from "humble but honest backgrounds," daughters of *quinteros* (farm owners), retail merchants, bakers, *pulperos* (grocers), and craftsmen, the middle groups of Hispanic society. Paradoxically, marriage to these women sealed them into low-level positions, for their brides lacked the social, political, or economic influence to further their careers. These men often found their limited chances for advancement in the bureaucracy even more restricted by the fact that marriage had not tied them to a prestigious *parentela* (kinship group). The few oficiales who were already married at the time they were promoted to

Table 7.2   Socioprofessional Origin of Bride's Family

Rank of bureaucrat	Bureaucrat N	Merchant N	Retailer or minor landowner N	Total
High (administrador)	7	2	—	9
Middle (contador)	8	3	4	15
Low (oficial)	6	2	22	30
Total	12(39%)	7(13%)	26(48%)	54

middle-level positions were promoted because of their own personal merits and long service, not because of connections. Nevertheless, it should be stressed that as a group the oficiales married local women, thereby tying their fortunes to the inhabitants of Buenos Aires.

While it was not uncommon for porteño-born bureaucrats to marry while they were still serving an unpaid apprenticeship, for the Spanish born marriage was tied to achieving at least a regular bureaucratic appointment. For example, Lorenzo Fuentes, born in the Villa de Balgañón, La Rioja, Burgos, began work in the Buenos Aires viceregal Secretaría as a meritorio in 1783. He finally received a permanent position, oficial tercero, in the Secretaría in April 1794.[29] In January 1795 Fuentes, who was at last earning a fixed salary, married Juana Arguibel, daughter of a local hide dealer.[30]

Those who waited until they achieved the middle-level rank of contador before marrying were usually able to wed more prominent local women. The social and economic distance between oficial and contador was considerable, and contadores were able to secure daughters of middle-level merchants, local bureaucrats, and military officers as their brides. Almost all of the highest-ranking bureaucrats, (contadores mayores, ministros, administradores, or secretarios) were already married by the time they took office, but those who had been promoted to this position from posts in the American bureaucracy tended to display the same marriage patterns as the contadores.

As can be seen in table 7.3, for a group of 101 bureaucrats for whom information is complete, the geographical origin of the groom usually differed from that of the bride. Bureaucrats at all levels were predominately Spanish-born, so it is no surprise that among those marrying at every rank but the lowest the same predominance of Spanish-born men is also found. Brides, on the other hand, were overwhelmingly from Buenos Aires, although there is a negative correlation between Buenos Aires birth and marriage to a man of high professional rank. In general, the higher the rank of a married bureaucrat, the greater the chance that both he and his wife had been born in Spain.

On the whole, royal desire to curb marriage to creole women was a dismal failure. In the Tribunal de Cuentas, for example, of the thirty-seven bureaucrats who married, 86 percent married women born in the New World (81 percent married women from Buenos Aires) after first obtaining

Table 7.3   Geographical Origin of Bride and Groom by Rank of Groom in
Buenos Aires Bureaucracy (101 Couples)

	Origin of groom			*Origin of bride*		
	Spain	*Buenos Aires*	*Other America*	*Spain*	*Buenos Aires*	*Other America*
High-level bureaucrat	20	2	3	8	13	3
Middle-level bureaucrat	19	7	5	9	24	3
Low-level bureaucrat	22	23	—	2	35	4
Total	61 (60%)	32(32%)	8(8%)	19(19%)	72(71%)	10(10%)

royal permission. The desire to set up a home and family when it could be
afforded and the belief that marriage to the daughter of a local bureaucrat
or merchant, if possible, would further one's career were potent factors
among Tribunal employees. In addition, when faced with marriage requests from bureaucrats, the crown generally gave its consent.

Marriage patterns of the highest-ranking bureaucrats demonstrate the
existence of a small group of powerful interrelated civil servants who were
tied together, much in the same fashion as the wholesale merchants of the
city, through marriages to porteña sisters. In addition, as can be seen in
table 7.2, the most successful bureaucrats chose the daughters of other bureaucrats as spouses. Over time the crown was increasingly able to prevent
its agents from allying with the local aristocracy. At the same time Buenos
Aires merchants, the most powerful local elite group, came to prefer marrying their daughters to other merchants. But the crown could not stop
the creation of a bureaucratic elite in which members were tied to each
other through marriage. Indeed, the major change in marital patterns of
bureaucrats who married while in Buenos Aires was in the choice of bride;
while government officials had married the daughters of merchants and
other local leaders before the creation of the viceroyalty, after 1776 they increasingly came to choose their wives from among the daughters and sisters of fellow bureaucrats.

To the degree that professionalization of the bureaucracy increasingly made purchase of position impossible, kinship ties to a man at the top of the local agency bureaucracy, or at least at the higher rungs in the bureaucratic ladder, became even more desirable. Those bureaucrats with position and the economic ability to maintain a family overwhelmingly chose the daughters of their colleagues. Marriage to the daughter of a government bureaucrat became the preferred match for an ambitious young man making his way through the middle levels of a career.

The choice was of course mutual—not only did a striving bureaucrat choose another bureaucrat's daughter as his prospective wife, but the second bureaucrat also accepted the former as his son-in-law. After 1776 relatively few bureaucrats married into other sectors of local society, and this was especially true of those who had been born outside of Buenos Aires. Again this pattern evolved through mutual agreement. In most cases an oficial tercero had little to offer a prosperous merchant or military officer as a marriage partner for his daughter. As a result the Buenos Aires bureaucracy was increasingly isolated from the local populace, although never as completely as the king would have wished.

Only one agency's employees displayed a markedly different marriage pattern in their choice of partners—the Aduana bureaucrats. Among those Aduana employees who married in Buenos Aires, almost to a man they were wed to the daughters of men involved in commerce. Clearly, merchants did not encourage their daughters to marry Aduana officials because of their social status or their official salaries, for those employed in the Aduana were, in social position and pay, well below employees of agencies such as the Tribunal de Cuentas or the Real Hacienda. Nevertheless, Aduana officials probably enjoyed more opportunities to supplement their incomes through extralegal payment for their services. Moreover, from the point of view of a merchant it was advantageous to marry one's daughter to an Aduana employee and thus gain preferential treatment. The degree to which merchant fathers-in-law in league with their Aduana-employed sons-in-law engaged in outright fraud is of course impossible to document, but having a close relative in the Aduana could always help expedite shipping and receiving goods. It should be stressed that the most important merchants did not marry their daughters to Aduana employees, for the lack of prestige and fortune was too great for these most exalted socioeconomic leaders. The most powerful Buenos Aires merchants chose their sons-in-law from among the ranks of promising Spanish merchants. But for the less prestigious groups of merchants who were anxious to work their way into commercial prosperity and desirous of any bureaucratic connections that could give them an edge, as well as for the more adventuresome merchants whose unorthodox dealing depended on bureaucratic connections and often bordered on the illicit, Aduana bureaucrats were most attractive family additions. This was especially true for those merchants engaged in the hide trade. Families such as Arguibel, Belgrano, and Lazcano looked at an Aduana employed son-in-law as good commercial insurance.

In addition to establishing familial relationship through marriage with high-ranking Aduana employees, hide merchants frequently sought overlapping kinship relations with the same individuals. For those merchants who chose not to marry their daughters to Aduana officials (or who were unable to effect this alliance because of the limited number of Aduana employees) and for those Aduana employees who were already married before they arrived in Buenos Aires, ritual kinship ties served as alternative mechanisms in linking bureaucrats with merchants. More than any other group of government bureaucrats, the Aduana officials can be found repeatedly as *compadres de casamiento* (marriage sponsors) or *compadres de bautismo* (baptismal godfathers) in life-cycle events of middle-ranking merchants. In addition, merchants seemed especially eager to establish economic relations with Aduana employees and were frequently found lending money to these bureaucrats or serving as bondsmen.

Of all the merchants who worked hard to maintain close contacts with Aduana employees, the Belgrano family is perhaps the most famous. Domingo Belgrano Pérez, the founder of the family, was a moderately successful hide merchant who served as the secret partner of the Aduana administrador, Francisco Ximénez de Mesa, for several years. Because government officials were forbidden to engage in commerce, Belgrano lent his name to several transactions undertaken by Ximénez and also invested funds in Ximénez's nefarious dealings. With the discovery of Ximénez's fraud, Belgrano was placed under arrest and all his goods were embargoed. Nevertheless, his family continued to have strong connections in the Aduana. His son-in-law was José María Calderón de la Barca, vista segundo, who although accused of introducing a shipment of contraband among his personal goods at the time he arrived from Spain to take up the post, was nevertheless "purified" of the charge by royal order and allowed to maintain the position.[31] His son Joaquín Belgrano González served as escribiente in the contaduría section of the Aduana from 1790 to 1804. Both men no doubt proved useful to other members of the Belgrano family who continued in commerce.

The crown was even unable to prevent four men who eventually became viceroys from marrying local women.[32] These men were Antonio Olaguer Feliú, who as inspector general of the viceregal troops married Ana de Azcuenaga in 1788;[33] Joaquín del Pino, who married Rafaela Francisca de Vera Muxica in 1783 while serving as governor of Montevideo; Fernando Rafael de Sobremonte, who married Juana María de Larrazabal y Avellaneda in 1782 while serving as intendant of Córdoba; and Santiago de Liniers, whose second wife was María Martina de Sarratea y Altolaguirre. All of these marriages took place while the grooms were high-ranking officers in either the civil or the military bureaucracy and all were to young women from prominent and wealthy families. All the marriages also created close kinship ties with men important in the mercantile world of the port city. Olaguer Feliú, for example, married into the powerful Basavilbaso-Azcuenaga-Santa Coloma clan, while del Pino became the brother-in-law *(concuñado)* of the important merchant Juan José de Lezica. In addition, at least two brides were connected to families with strong military connections—the Vera Muxica family of Santa Fé and the Larrazabal clan of Córdoba. In choosing local brides, these four future viceroys clearly chose well.

While the crown was willing to grant special marriage licenses to most bureaucrats allowing them to marry local women, royal policy was very different vis-à-vis the Audiencia judges. Oidores were men usually well past middle age, who had entered the high courts after serving as lawyers, asesores, and fiscales in Spain or in other parts of America. Almost all were already married at the time of their arrival in Buenos Aires. Two judges—Tomás Ignacio Palomeque and Joaquín Bernardo Campuzano—married criollas while serving in Buenos Aires, but both were immediately transferred to other courts.[34] The Palomeque and Campuzano cases demonstrate that at least in the arena of justice, the crown was serious in obeying its own dictates concerning an uninvolved bureaucracy.

Although oidores did not usually marry prominent porteñas, lesser-ranking members of the Audiencia—canciller, relator, escribano, alguacil mayor, and receptor, many of whom purchased their posts from the crown during the viceregal period—were always closely allied to local power-ful families. Both Spaniards and porteños in these positions tended to marry local women, establishing close personal ties in the city with mer-chants, military men, and important landowners. Furthermore, unlike the standing judges of the Audiencia who were subject to transfer to other ju-risdictions, this cadre of bureaucrats established permanent residence in Buenos Aires.

Those bureaucrats who did marry conformed to the societal norm for marriage of people of Spanish descent, that is they tended to choose women several years their junior as marriage partners. (See table 7.4.) The reason for the age disparity between husband and wife was in part eco-nomic; few men could afford the costs involved in supporting a wife and children until they were past the age of thirty. The fact that so many bu-reaucrats waited until they reached the rank of contador or better before marrying and the generally slow promotion patterns found within all gov-ernment agencies produced an average age at first marriage for men of 34.27 years. The average age for their wives was 21.05.[35] Here cultural pref-erences for young, virginal women played an important role. No man in his thirties would seek a woman of the same age, both because her vir-ginity and innocence would be suspect and because her promise of fertility would be greatly reduced. There was also an interesting correlation be-tween the position of the husband within the bureaucracy and the age dif-ferential between husband and wife. In general, the higher the bureaucratic rank of the husband at the time of marriage, the greater the age gap be-tween him and his spouse. Whether or not this was the first or second mar-riage for the man, as an important and relatively well-paid bureaucrat, he

Table 7.4   Age of Bureaucrats and Spouses Married While in Office, 1769–1810

Rank at time of marriage	Age			
	Male		Female	
	Mean	sd	Mean	sd
High-level bureaucrats	37.75	11.74	17.2	3.7
Middle-level bureaucrats	35.33	5.94	21.75	4.46
Low-level bureaucrats	31.13	8.29	22.9	9.2
Total	34.27	5.85	21.05	6.74

could now afford to purchase a young wife. Those who held lesser positions in the bureaucracy had to content themselves with women who were older at the time of marriage. Because they were limited in their choices, in some cases low-ranking bureaucrats had to settle for Spanish women who were well on their way to spinsterhood by the standards of the day.

Occasionally, bureaucrats did marry older women, but this was rare and usually involved the remarriage of a widow. In these cases it can only be assumed that the widow's social or economic position was more attractive than her lack of bridal innocence. Pedro Martínez de Velasco, for example, a young man who had immigrated from Spain to Buenos Aires in hopes of establishing himself in a bureaucratic career, married María Ventura Morales, the widow of Francisco López Garcia, a relatively prosperous hide dealer, although María Ventura was sixteen years older than he and the mother of six children.[36] Their marriage probably enhanced Pedro's economic and social position, for by 1785 at age twenty-five he had purchased an escribania and was also serving as the oficial mayor of the Intendancy Secretaría.[37]

Those bureaucrats fortunate enough to marry prominent women often benefited from both the social connections and economic aid that their wives could provide. The case of Antonio Pinedo Montufar is illustrative, for when Pinedo suffered such economic reverses because of the 1782 Indian uprising in La Paz that he decided to travel to the court to plead for special consideration in bureaucratic advancement, his wife's family could afford to indirectly supplement the undertaking by providing funds for her upkeep in Buenos Aires. "I hereby declare that during my absence in Spain (where I went to request and obtained the post of minister of the Royal Exchequer) . . . Doña Barthola de Arce, the mother of my wife Doña Rafaela, provided her with 900 pesos for her food. Because of my difficult financial situation I could not leave her any money for her expenses."[38]

Even for prominent bureaucrats the course of courtship did not always run smoothly. Manuel José de la Valle, contador of the Buenos Aires tobacco monopoly, for example, found himself faced with parental opposition in his desire to wed Mercedes González. Manuel, a thirty-seven-year-old lawyer, not only held a relatively important position in the local bureaucracy, he also had impressive family credentials. His father, Símon de la Valle, was a retired ministro in the Reales Cajas de Trujillo and a member of the prestigious Order of Calatrava. Yet when Manuel tried to woo Mercedes, a young lady who was already twenty years old, her father, retired military captain Juan González Bordallo, objected most strenuously.[39] González Bordallo used physical and mental coercion to convince his daughter to reject de la Valle and then sent her off to the home of merchant Agustín Erezcano and his wife in an attempt to convince her to marry another candidate. At this point de la Valle successfully petitioned the court to remove Doña Mercedes from her father's care, claiming that González Bordallo was violating "the freedom which all children had in their choice of civil state." Mercedes was fetched in the carriage of Ramón Oromi, director general of Nuevas Labores in the Real Renta de Tabaco, and placed under the care of Manuel Lezica and his wife. While the young lady waited, free from parental influence, de la Valle requested that her father show cause for rejecting his marriage suit. González Bordallo's opposition gradually dissipated and he agreed to the marriage.[40] Two years later, the retired military man gave power of attorney to draw up his will to his wife and son-in-law, an action that suggests that he had come to accept a marriage he had once opposed.[41]

The path to marriage was not always smooth for bureaucrats or for their children. Bureaucrats, especially those in top-level positions within the local bureaucracy, were, like most Spaniards of their social class, ever on guard to prevent a dishonorable marriage involving their children. Such a case was that involving Pedro Medrano, treasurer of the Royal Exchequer, and his son Martín José. Martín, who had entered the Tribunal de Cuentas as a meritorio in 1786 and had slowly advanced to oficial subalterno, was twenty-nine years old when he gave a written pledge of marriage to Maria Pascuala Iraola, age twenty-five. Since neither of the contracting parties were legal minors, parental permission was not required for marriage, but Martín's father nonetheless moved to stop the union on the grounds of racial inequality of the future bride's family.[42] Medrano had worked hard at furthering his own career in the Royal Treasury and at placing his sons in entry-level positions in the local bureaucracy. To see this social position threatened by one son's marriage to an "older" woman, daughter of a poor Basque immigrant and granddaughter of a known bullfighter (*torero público*), was unacceptable. For three years Medrano successfully delayed the marriage, until María Pascuala, fearful that the marriage would never be performed, began legal action against her betrothed's father.[43] In spite of the elder Medrano's opposition, the court ordered the marriage to take place, for although the bureaucrat had proven María Pasquala's humble origins, her racial purity was beyond reproach. Her husband was dismissed from his Tribunal positions but was later successful in obtaining a royal order ordering his reinstatement. Moved to a low-level position in the Real Renta de Tabaco, Medrano eventually resigned from the bureaucracy.[44]

Difficulties were even greater when the marriage involved minors. According to a Real Prágmatica of 23 March 1776, all those marrying below the age of twenty-five needed the consent of their parents or guardians.[45] When this permission was not forthcoming, at least a few minors brought legal suit against the dissenting adults. Julián Gregorio Espinosa, son of the late Julián Gregorio Espinosa and María Florencia Belgrano Pérez and grandson of Domingo Belgrano Pérez, sued his grandfather successfully because the latter failed to give the young man (age seventeen-and-a-half) permission to wed María Candelaria Somellera, daughter of Andrés de Somellera, contador ordenador of the Tribunal de Cuentas.[46] Young Espinosa had given a verbal promise to marry Candelaria and then, to further demonstrate his honorable intentions, had signed a letter agreeing to a future marriage. Clearly, the prospective bride's father supported the union, for although Julián was young and inexperienced, he belonged to a moderately important mercantile family. With paper in hand, Somellera approached Belgrano Pérez requesting a formal meeting "to talk about the marriage." When Belgrano failed to answer within three days, a note "demanding a reply" followed. Belgrano's intransigence was caused by concern over the young man's age, the lack of economic prominence of the Somellera family, and the fact that Somellera had no connection to the Aduana. Judging the bureaucrat and his wife to be among "the most noble people living in this city," the court found that Belgrano had no legal grounds on which to deny the marriage and ordered him to consent.

Occasionally, bureaucrats who came to Buenos Aires tried to forget about their wives and children back in Spain. This footloose attitude was discouraged by the crown, which generally encouraged wives left in Spain to come out to the Indies and live with their husbands. When this failed, the crown sometimes forced bureaucrats to resign and return to Spain, especially if these bureaucrats did not hold an official título. In 1786, for example, Juan de Ariza, employed as the teniente de visitador of the Real Renta de Tabaco in Buenos Aires, was ordered to leave his employment and reunite himself with his wife in Spain.[47]

Not all marriages of bureaucrats were public knowledge. One of the most bizarre secret marriages involved Manuel Gallego, secretario of the unified Secretarías from 1790 to his death in 1808, and Doña Ana Josefa Andonaegui. Ana Josefa, the granddaughter of the late governor of Buenos Aires, General José de Andonaegui (1745–56), secretly married this important civil servant sometime during his tenure in Buenos Aires. The couple never publicly lived together, and word of the marriage only became known after Gallego's sealed will was opened after his death. The reason given by Gallego for keeping his marriage secret was "because various political considerations related to the duties incumbent in my job, pushed me toward suggesting the conditions to which she agreed, that of hiding our marriage while I kept my position in this city."[48] He took pains to point out that the secrecy of the marriage should not be interpreted as a negative estimation of the rank and lineage of his wife.

Although "no dowry was drawn up, and my wife's property has been kept completely separate from mine," Gallego did turn over money to his wife both at the time of marriage and after. She first received "one hundred ounces of gold and some other small amounts of money, which could total 2,000 pesos and were given to her as a prenuptial donation to free her from pressing obligations." During the marriage Gallego covered other expenses, possibly providing for all of Ana Josefa's outlays. In his will he specifically made mention of "the expenditures that I have had to make for the support of my said wife." Furthermore, Gallego claimed that because there had been no increase in his total estate since his marriage, his childless widow was to receive only 2,000 pesos in the form of a special legacy. Whether the strain of keeping her marriage secret, the public shame at being discovered, or the death of her husband influenced her mental state is hard to determine, but by 1811 Ana Josefa Andonaegui was declared legally insane, and her sister, María Mercedes, widow of merchant Joaquín de Arana, was named her legal guardian.[49]

Once married, life-long harmony was not always insured. At least one local government official, Francisco de Valdepares, contador ordenador of the Tribunal de Cuentas from 1807 to 1812, found it increasingly difficult to control his rebellious wife, María de la Encarnación de Andonaegui. Encarnación, porteño-born daughter of José de Andonaegui (hijo) and María Catalina Herrera and sister of the aforementioned Ana Josefa Andonaegui, had come into marriage with a fair amount of property, including quintas close to the capital city. Within a few years, she became disenchanted with her personal situation and, under advice from her doctor, having secured her husband's permission, she retired to one of her country homes to live. The couple seemed to have found an amicable solution in this mutual unofficial separation, until Encarnación began to suspect her husband was secretly disposing of some property and deliberately allowing other property to fall into disrepair. From the quinta she began legal proceedings against him, while he demanded that she return to his home in the city and accused her of scandalous behavior.[50] Encarnación returned to Buenos Aires in 1812, but instead of joining her husband, she moved into the home of the José Pueyrredon family and demanded that her husband provide 50 pesos a month for her support. Her request became a moot issue when Valdepares was arrested and executed for complicity in the Alzaga-Tellechea treason.

Because they felt compelled to live in a style befitting Spaniards of their class and position, although they earned salaries that can only be described as meager, the lower-ranking bureaucrats, especially those who married and had children, were constantly at the brink of penury. Maintaining a wife and children on a salary of 400–500 pesos a year clearly imposed great hardship on these men. Although one must distinguish between rhetoric and reality in reading petitions for promotion or salary increase, the frequency with which personal economic problems are mentioned suggests that this was more than histrionic behavior. The petition of Manuel Moreno Argumosa to double his yearly salary of 400 pesos is most typical. "Because of the merit that I have earned in sixteen years of service . . . I request that my salary be raised to 800 pesos . . . or failing this that I be placed in another position whose salary is sufficient to provide for my survival and that of my family, which the 400 pesos I now receive cannot do. . . ."[51]

The responsibility of marriage and family weighed most heavily on the lowest level of bureaucrats, the oficiales. Not only were they required to support a family on inadequate salaries, but any career-related absences, usually undertaken in the hope of professional advancement, were all the more onerous. Underlining the hardship that had been caused his family, Fermin Sotes, employed as a plumista in the Real Renta de Tabaco, described the tribulations that his family had suffered. "I have been away from my family for almost five years, and they are without the necessary help to survive. . . . [M]y wife has been separated from her husband and my children from their father because I do not have enough aid nor stability in my employment."[52] It fell to the wives of these bureaucrats to hold their families together in spite of economic straits.

Even more pitiful was the economic situation that confronted the widows of bureaucrats. For example, Nicolas Torrado, one of the contadores of the Aduana sent to Buenos Aires in 1788, died within four years, leaving a widow, three young children, an estate worth 577 pesos 5 reales, and debts of over 8,000 pesos.[53] Manuel de Ortega y Espinosa, the asesor general of the newly created viceroyalty, died within a year of his arrival in Buenos Aires, leaving his widow and son stranded in the capital and deeply in debt.[54] Not only had Ortega borrowed 2,000 pesos in Cádiz from the Royal Treasury to cover his *habilitación y transporte*, he had also borrowed another 3,000 pesos from Cádiz merchants and at least 2,000 more from their Buenos Aires counterparts to pay for *subsistencia* and rent. At the time of his death in 1780 his widow found that her husband's total estate was worth only 246 pesos, an amount clearly insufficient to cover his outstanding debts and his unpaid media anata. Furthermore, as a recent arrival from Spain, Doña Rosalia Salgado lacked friends and kinfolk who could have helped her survive. The Ortega and Torrado cases are similar in more than the pathetic situations in which their widows were left. Both men had gambled in coming to Buenos Aires, incurring debts in order to advance their careers, and neither had survived long enough to recoup what they believed would be a profitable investment. Instead, they bequeathed to their wives and children a precarious economic and social position.

Further complicating the situation were the manifold problems of inheritance faced by the surviving widows and children of bureaucrats. Heirs often found themselves involved in long and often fruitless attempts to collect outstanding salaries. María de la Concepción Cabrera, daughter of Francisco de Cabrera, the late contador mayor of the Tribunal de Cuentas, had still not collected her inheritance of approximately 8,000 pesos in outstanding salary six years after the death of her father.[55] Clearly, the crown, beset by other financial problems of a far greater magnitude, was in no hurry to settle such accounts. For those female heirs already married at the time of their fathers' death, this delay was an inconvenience, but for unmarried daughters dependent on their inheritance to attract an acceptable husband or for widows planning to support themselves on their inheritances, the crown's tardiness could produce great hardships.

Regardless of royal attempts to limit the creation of powerful local bureaucratic dynasties, such clans did emerge in Buenos Aires, often built on families that had been prominent in the bureaucracy before the founding of the viceroyalty. Their ability to hold on and indeed to enhance their power, even in the face of the crown's expressed desire to create a bureaucracy free of local connections and influence, attest to their tenacity and the crown's schizophrenic policy. For while the Spanish crown declaimed that local ties were to be avoided, established legislation requiring special royal permission before marriage to a local woman, and invoked regulations that sought to prevent two members of the same family from working in the same agency, the same crown was more than willing to ignore its own dictates and grant special permission to those who sought it.

The most powerful bureaucratic clan in viceregal Buenos Aires was that of the Pinedo family, a group with strong local ties. The Pinedo clan had begun when Juan de Baéz Alpoin, a powerful merchant, smuggler, and bureaucrat of the early eighteenth century, married his daughter, Juana, to Diego Sorarte, a treasury official who purchased the post of contador in 1728. Another daughter, María Baéz, married Alonso Arce y Arcos, son of Coronel Alonso de Arce, who had served briefly as governor of Buenos Aires in 1714 and treasurer of Reales Cajas from 1726 to 1767. After Arce's first wife died, he married Petronila Sorarte, his niece and daughter of Diego. The relationship that thus emerged in the Reales Cajas was that the contador and the treasurer—Sorarte and Arce—were first tied together as brothers-in-law and later as father and son-in-law.

Alonso Arce y Arcos and Petronila Sorarte produced three surviving children, but it is their first daughter, María Bartola, who joined their family to that of the Pinedos by marrying Agustín de Pinedo in 1743. Pinedo, a military man with bureaucratic experience, went on to serve as governor of Paraguay from 1772 to 1778. (María Bartola's sister Tomasa Arce also continued in the family tradition when she chose as her third husband Blas Gascón, the contador of the Reales Cajas in Oruro). At least seven children were born to this couple, but in the family tradition—indeed a tradition common to upper-class merchants and other bureaucrats—it was through the marriage of daughters that bureaucratic ties were forged. Ana Pinedo, the oldest surviving daughter, married Juan Andrés de Arroyo in 1772 while he was serving as private secretary to Governor Bucareli. He later went on to a long career as the secretario of the Superintendency (1778–90) and contador mayor of the Tribunal de Cuentas (1796–1807). Andrés de

Arroyo was also honored with membership in the Order of Carlos III (caballero de Santiago, 1795). In 1796 his daughter Ana was wed to Juan María Almagro de la Torre, a lawyer who served as asesor general and auditor de guerra of the viceroyalty until 1810.[56]

Rafaela Pinedo, the second surviving Pinedo-Arce daughter, married Antonio Pinedo Montufar, a first cousin who had begun his bureaucratic career as corregidor of La Paz (1747–51) and then moved on to a post as treasurer of the Reales Cajas of Carabaya. Antonio, a widower with one child, was still living in Alto Perú at the time of the proxy marriage in 1780 and only returned to Buenos Aires in 1786. In addition to his membership in the Order of Santiago, Pinedo's kinship ties no doubt helped him to quickly gain appointment as treasurer of the Reales Cajas (army accounts). Seven years after his death in 1802, his widow remarried, choosing José Mendinueta, a minor official in the Reales Cajas (oficial segundo) who had served as second executor of her husband's estate.[57]

The last surviving daughter of the Pinedo-Arce marriage followed the lead of her two sisters by marrying Juan Isidro Casamayor, secretario of the viceroyalty (1777–78), who continued his career first in New Granada and then in Spain. Through a pattern of female marriage, seven important bureaucrats (and at least two minor ones) had been part of the clan over a ninety-year period. Indeed, through their marriage to sisters in 1790 the first secretary of the Intendancy and the treasurer of the Reales Cajas were brothers-in-law.

The case of the Altolaguirre family is another example that illustrates the continued strength of local ties and intragenerational continuity among bureaucrats in the face of the changes that professionalization ostensibly brought about. The founder of the family in the Río de la Plata was Martín de Altolaguirre, son of Juan de Altolaguirre and Catalina de Garmendia, natives of Villa de Alviztru, Guipúzcoa. Although his parents were medium-sized landowners (Altolaguirre's will states "I inherited my family's traditional home, called Urquiri Garaicoa, with its cultivated fields, forested areas, which could be used to build boats or to produce charcoal, and other implements"[58]), Martín de Altolaguirre, pushed by economic necessity or by wanderlust, left the Basque region for Buenos Aires sometime before 1730. In that year, at age twenty-two, he married the porteña María de Pando y Patiño, daughter of a local military captain and one year his junior. For the next twenty years, while his bride bore him numerous children, eight of whom survived to adulthood, Martín engaged in local commerce, occasionally speculating in urban and semirural properties. He eventually decided to combine an official career with commerce, and in 1751, after having served as a member of the first Spanish-Portuguese boundary commission, he purchased the post of factor of the Real Hacienda in Buenos Aires. At the time of this transaction, Francisco de Solo-aga, a local merchant, served as fiador for Altolaguirre.

Altolaguirre served as factor for the next sixteen years, no doubt earning a substantial living from his government post. Although he no longer participated openly in commercial transactions, he increasingly lent money directly and indirectly to merchants to finance purchase of goods.[59] In addition, Altolaguirre stepped up his investment in real estate, buying several pieces of urban property, which he rented out as stores and apartments. Another important asset that he acquired while serving as factor of the Real Hacienda was his quinta, located near the Santa Recolección on the road to Las Conchas. At the time he drew up his will, in 1781, Altolaguirre could state, perhaps a bit too optimistically, that "because it consists of such sound investments in real property and movable goods, my estate will not lose value between now and the time the estate is probated."

Although he retired from the Real Hacienda in 1767, turning his post over to one of his sons (he had purchased his job with the right to name his successor), Martín de Altolaguirre continued to live in Buenos Aires until his death in 1782. In 1778 he, his wife, and three of their sons inhabited a large house in the center of the city.[60] The opulence of the Altolaguirre family life is reflected in the fact that fifteen adult slaves were present in the family's household. Another eleven slaves and five peons were employed in the family quinta, which was both a place of recreation and a farm producing foodstuffs for the local market.

As mentioned earlier, Altolaguirre had eight surviving children, seven sons and one daughter. The girl, Tomasa, married Martín Sarratea, a local merchant, in 1767 when she was fifteen years old. Her younger brother Francisco joined the Franciscan Order. The six other sons all chose bureaucratic (or military-bureaucratic) careers. Bernardino, the oldest was employed by the Real Casa de Moneda in Santiago; Juan Baptista sought a military career, serving as *comandante de la frontera sur* (military commander of the southern frontier) in Córdoba and later as *gobernador* (governor) of Chiquitos and of Santa Cruz. Jacinto, the youngest child, also followed a military career, serving first in the Spanish Infantry and later transferring to the Real Armada. He made rapid progress within naval ranks and six years after being named *alférez de fragata* (naval ensign) in 1774 was promoted to *teniente de fragata* (naval lieutenant) and named gobernador de Malvinas at age twenty-seven (1781–83). His career was cut short in 1787 when he died suddenly in Madrid, where he had gone because of problems associated with his father's estate.[61]

Altolaguirre's three middle sons—Martín José, Pedro, and León—not only entered the royal bureaucracy but were able, eventually, to rise to positions of relative importance in Buenos Aires. Martín José followed his father into the Real Hacienda, serving as factor oficial (1767–75), contador (1775–85), and tesorero (1785–87) of the Buenos Aires Reales Cajas. In 1787 forty-five-year-old Martín José married seventeen-year-old María Concepción Cabrera, Spanish-born daughter of Francisco Cabrera, contador mayor of the Tribunal de Cuentas (1777–96). Although his parentesco with Cabrera prevented him from holding permanent office in the Tribunal, Martín José was acting contador mayor of this august institution in 1796.

Pedro de Altolaguirre, another son who chose a bureaucratic career, worked for many years in the Administración General of the Real Renta de Tabaco. In 1787 Pedro was promoted to the post of treasurer of the Real Casa de Moneda in Potosí, where he served until his death in 1799. Lastly, León de Altolaguirre also entered the local bureaucracy through the Real Renta de Tabaco, working as oficial segundo in the Contaduría General from 1780 to 1790. León was promoted to *comandante general* (commander) of the coast guard in 1801 and director of the Real Renta de Tabaco in 1809.[62]

While occupying some of the most important bureaucratic posts in the colony, such select groups were, nevertheless, small in number. The majority of married bureaucrats, although wed to local women, were not part of this elite clique. It should also be remembered that the total number of bureaucrats marrying local women was relatively low. The opportunity to ally oneself to other Buenos Aires families through both real and affective kinship was limited. The bureaucrat who did not marry a porteña, had neither her family nor compadres de casamiento as his natural kin group. Moreover, the large numbers of bureaucrats who never married and who therefore did not sire legitimate children also limited the opportunity to form additional kin bonds with compadres de bautismo. Conversely, unmarried bureaucrats were rarely chosen by others to serve as godparents, a reflection of their isolation in local society.

The situation was of course different for those bureaucrats who married local women. Among the top-ranking bureaucrats the compadres de casamiento usually were chosen from two different groups—fellow bureaucrats, preferably of a higher rank, who it was hoped would look favorably on the groom's professional progress, and blood relatives of the bride. When Don Manuel Amaya, administrador general of the Real Renta de Tabaco, wed the porteña Valentina Zenzano in 1780, for example, the couple's compadres included Manuel Fernández, intendant of Buenos Aires; Francisco Ximénez de Mesa, administrador of the Aduana; Rufino Cárdenas, contador of the Real Renta de Tabaco; and the bride's sister Juana Zenzano.[63] Lesser-ranking bureaucrats usually chose only blood relatives, possibly fearing even to approach their superiors with the request that they serve as compadres. Matías Bernal, oficial primero of the Real Hacienda, turned repeatedly to his wife's family for both compadres de casamiento and compadres de baptismo for their five children.[64] Likewise, Luis Herrera, porteño-born third oficial in the Secretaría (superintendency section), turned to his wife's parents as compadres de casamiento in 1793.[65] Although his father-in-law, Francisco Antonio Basavilbaso, was the chief notary of the viceroyalty and eventually aided Herrera's career, he probably asserted little direct influence over the bureaucrat's advancement until 1799.

Although many bureaucrats did not marry, it can be assumed that at least some officials engaged in liaisons with local women. These ties occurred at all levels of the bureaucracy and were usually formed with women from lower social groups, women who could exert no social pressure leading to marriage but could only gain from their liaisons with men perceived of as having power.

The most important bureaucrat known to have had a local woman as his mistress was Pedro Antonio de Cevallos, first viceroy of the Río de la Plata. Although Cevallos only spent eight months as viceroy, this was sufficient time to begin a liaison with María Luisa Pintos Ortega, a local single woman.[66] When the bachelor viceroy left Buenos Aires in June 1778 to return to Spain, he was probably not aware of María Luisa's "condition," but eight months later on 15 February 1779 the young woman gave birth to a

son, baptized, in honor of his father, Pedro Antonio.[67] Unbeknownst to
the new mother, her lover was already dead. Cevallos had died en route to
Madrid in December 1778, leaving a will that mentioned neither mother
nor child.[58] Although the boy was publicly accepted as being the "mani-
festly known natural child" of the ex-viceroy, and as such was baptized in
the Buenos Aires cathedral by the catedrático de prima of the Real Colegio
de San Carlos, later attempts to be recognized as Cevallos's legal heir were
rejected by the crown.

Romantic liaisons were often formed by officials, both married and
unmarried, who were transferred to interior posts for long periods of
time. Married officials tended not to bring their wives and children with
them when sent to serve in the interior, in part because they hoped that
these appointments would be of short duration, in part because they realized that conditions in the cities of the interior were harder and less healthy
than those in Buenos Aires. But often temporary absences were prolonged,
and appointments that were only to last for two years actually lasted for
five or six. These absences, of course, functioned as an effective birth control mechanism, at least for the wife who had been left behind in Buenos
Aires, for the legitimate wife of any government official was expected to act
decorously while she awaited the return of her husband.

The same type of conduct was not required of her husband, who
could enter into romantic affairs with local women as long as some sem-
blance of propriety was maintained. Propriety meant that there was to be
no public display of extramarital liaisons, no scandal to tarnish either personal reputations or the dignity of the crown. As a result, proof of few of
these unions has survived. One of the more interesting cases, however, for
which some documentation has been preserved, was that of José Manuel
Bustillo de Cevallos. Bustillo, a native of Vargas de Toranzo, Santander,
Spain, was related to the Escaladas, an important Buenos Aires merchant
family. He arrived in Buenos Aires in 1776, accompanying his cousin, José
Antonio de Escalada, who was returning from Spain where he had been
involved in matters pertaining to his late father's estate. Bustillo quickly
found employment in the Contaduría de Cuentas and by 1778 was the
oficial mayor of that agency. (The influence of the Escalada family no
doubt played an important role in Bustillo's placement; the family had always been especially close to Pedro de Cevallos, the viceroy, and was probably distantly related to his family.) In the same year, Bustillo married Juana

María Ibáñez Basavilbaso, twenty-year-old daughter of Pascual Ibáñez de Echeverri, the *sargento mayor* (sargeant major) of the Buenos Aires military garrison and Gabriela de Basavilbaso y Urtubia. Juana, through her mother, was the granddaughter of Domingo de Basavilbaso, another important local merchant and friend of the Escalada clan.

Four years later, Bustillo de Cevallos was sent to Oruro as *ministro contador* (chief accountant) of the Reales Cajas. His wife and two children remained in Buenos Aires. Within months Bustillo began a liaison in Cochabamba with Doña Manuela Camacho y Pinto, daughter of the late *maestre de campo*, Don Sebastián Martínez Camacho, and Rafaela Pinto. How public their relationship was at first is difficult to determine. By 1785 Manuela was confined to the local Monastery of Santa Clara, accused of having beaten Michaela Escalera for stealing her garter and of being Bustillo's mistress.[69] The next year criminal proceedings were brought against Bustillo for concubinage, although he temporarily continued to exercise his job in the Oruro cajas.[70] Found guilty as charged, he was suspended from the job in 1789 but was reinstated by 1796 as ministro tesorero of Oruro.

Three aspects of the episode are worthy of note. First is the passion expressed by the lovers, especially by Manuela, the well-born provincial girl. A letter that she attempted to smuggle out of the convent to Bustillo survives in the court testimony; it is startling for the intensity of emotions expressed and the strength of this young woman when faced with adversity. Manuela, confined before her lover had been formally apprehended, wrote

> My most beloved friend of my soul, delight of my sorrow, I received your letter this morning, my love, brought by José Manuel, in which you speak of your health and the hardship that you are suffering. Don't be silly. Don't allow yourself to die or to come to grief over such trifling difficulties. I, who am a woman, could do that, but I haven't and I'm as fresh as a lettuce because it's nothing to me, so great is the love I have for you. I have no other desire but to love you more and more and that you be true to me. So, my love, don't become despondent or worry. They're not going to take me to be tortured and even if they do, they can't accuse me of murdering anyone or of falsifying money, but only that I love you. Yes I love you and I'm true to you and you must have courage and be strong in your love for me and do more to endure all this as I'm doing. And have patience because the

day will come, my love, when everything will be better. . . . I don't trust Losada or Maldonado or little Diego because they are all in league with each other, and you shouldn't trust anyone either because the friend who seems to be most loyal is your enemy. . . . And so I commend you to God, my joy, my heart, my soul, my consolation, and my most beloved master. I commend you to God with whom I remain. I ask that you be guarded many years so that you can comfort me and that we be given the delight that we want as soon as possible. Your true lover wants to be with you and to kiss you. Manuela Camacho loves Manuel Bustillo until death. . . . Goodbye my love.[71]

Second, the complicity of one of the nuns, Sor Teresa de Jesús y Arrasola, and her sympathy for the lovers is most interesting. In a letter to Bustillo she assured him, "don't worry at all about Manuela for I'm taking good care of her," and spoke of her successful efforts to have Manuela's things brought to the convent. "Please, sir, don't grieve, for everything will work out well," she added, mentioning secret support for the couple from the abbess and other authorities of the convent.[72] Lastly, Bustillo seems to have enjoyed the continued public loyalty of his legal wife, Juana María Ibáñez. Although her husband had been involved in a personal scandal, she continued to refer to him as her husband, although she never joined him in Alto Perú.

Those bureaucrats who did marry and have children often found that financial constraints affected the education they were able to give their male offspring. For those who found it difficult to afford the yearly tuition of 100 pesos per year at the local Colegio de San Carlos, only some years of "primary letters" was possible. It was hoped that sons being trained to follow in their father's profession would find on-the-job training shortly after the completion of this basic education. Those preparing for the priesthood or for a career in the law, usually the sons of the most important bureaucrats, joined the sons of the city's merchants in attending the university in Charcas, Córdoba, or Chile, but the expense of sending offspring to these universities often proved too great. Antonio de la Peña y Vilanova, son of Juan Nepomuceno de la Peña, lawyer and relator of the Junta Superior de Real Hacienda, and grandson of Juan de Vilanova, vista primero of the Aduana, attempted to follow in his father's footsteps by studying law. Within the year he was forced to abandon his studies because they were too costly and would impose a lengthy financial hardship on his family. Back in Buenos Aires, Antonio entered the local bureaucracy as oficial quarto of the hacienda section of the viceregal Secretaría.

Bureaucrats rarely sent their children back to Spain for education, for although they realized that time spent studying in the mother country could help forge important personal contacts, few could afford the costs involved. Those very few sent to Spain for advanced training were the exception rather than the rule.[73]

Once his son had received some education, the bureaucrat was faced with the problem of placing him in a respectable position. Many sought to enroll their children on the government payroll, either as fellow bureaucrats or as military officers. But even for high-ranking bureaucrats with some local influence, the lack of openings within the bureaucracy and the distance from Spain and the court made it increasingly difficult to place their sons well. By 1802 the situation had become so bleak for the sons of high-ranking bureaucrats that Pedro José Ballesteros, contador mayor of the Tribunal de Cuentas, could write to the crown asking that his family be allowed to return to Spain because "I want to give my five sons a decent position in life, which they have no chance of having here, and I want to leave them, in case of my death, among their own people with some hope of a promising future."[74] In fact, the sons of bureaucrats who succeeded in entering government civil service were almost without exception even less successful than their fathers in pursuing a career.[75] These men, creole by birth or by upbringing, found it difficult to progress in a system that was profoundly suspicious of those born in America.[76] Especially difficult was the situation of those sons of bureaucrats who had been orphaned before they received appointment. In spite of repeated pleas and descriptions of their miserable economic situations, they rarely received effective solace.

One law that the later Bourbon kings increasingly enforced in all agencies of the royal bureaucracy of Buenos Aires was that of prohibiting parientes from permanent employment in the same office. A bureaucrat might help his son to find a meritorio slot in his office, but he had to use contacts in other agencies for more permanent placement. Parentesco by birth or marriage could therefore both help and hinder a young man's career. Even a successful bureaucrat could be stymied because of his kindred relationships. For example, Martin José Altolaguirre's marriage to María de la Concepción Cabrera, daughter of contador mayor Francisco Cabrera, helped Altolaguirre receive appointment to the Tribunal de Cuentas when Cabrera was granted leave and returned to Spain. Nevertheless, Altolaguirre, although named interim contador mayor, was pointedly denied permanent status as contador mayor supernumerario because of his relationship with Cabrera.[77]

If used with care, marriage to the daughter of an important Buenos Aires-based bureaucrat could aid a young bureaucrat in advancing his career, but other networks were also available for those who had previously served in other cities within the Spanish colonial world. This network, composed of friends and acquaintances, could help a newcomer quickly establish his social position and status. These personal connections were helpful both to newly arrived officials and to the children of the imperial bureaucrats. Manuel José de la Valle, for example, tobacco official and the son of a Reales Cajas bureaucrat stationed in Trujillo, Peru, had little trouble finding men who knew his father and could attest to his good name. Family acquaintance with men such as José Antonio de Hurtado, contador mayor decano of the Tribunal de Cuentas (a friend of Manuel's father); Diego de Santa Cruz, contador ordenador of the Tribunal de Cuentas (a friend of Manuel's brother José Antonio, the count of Premio Real); and Félix Sánchez de Celis, contador de retasas of the Tribunal de Cuentas (a schoolmate of the same brother) no doubt made acclimation to the world of the local bureaucracy all the easier for the newly arrived contador de tabacos.[78]

Bureaucrats, perennially short of funds, were linked to merchants and other local people by outstanding debts. José Bonifacio Zamudio, the porteño-born son of Juan Gregorio Zamudio, a retail merchant and protector de indios, and Ana María Merlo, was employed as oficial escribiente in the accounting section of the Aduana from 1784 until his death in 1791. Although earning only 300 pesos per year, José was already married to his first cousin Francisca Zamudio, daughter of Ambrosio Zamudio, a retailer and rancher, and María Francisco Diaz, at the time he entered government service. Neither José nor his bride had entered marriage with large assets; José in fact had brought nothing of monetary value into the marriage, while Francisca had a small dowry of 600 pesos. This money had been used to purchase a *sitio* (site) on which the newlyweds had built a house; the house itself was constructed with a 1,200 pesos loan that Zamudio had received from the Catalina Convent.[79] When José died suddenly at the age of thirty-three, he owed a total of 2,954 pesos 5-1/5 reales. In addition to the 1,200 still owing the nuns (he had paid interest on the loan but had yet to service the principal), amounts ranging from 18 to 217 pesos were owed to a medical doctor, a *confitero* (confectioner), and various merchants in the city.

Debt was not limited to the lower-ranking government bureaucrats. Juan Francisco de Vilanova, who as vista of the Aduana from 1778 to 1810 earned 1,500 pesos per year, was deeply in debt even before he arrived in Buenos Aires. (He and his son had borrowed 2,596 pesos from Antonio Sánchez de Taivo, the marqués de Carballo, a Cádiz merchant, 3,376 pesos from Geronimo Traberso, another Cádiz merchant, and other sums from Joaquín Múñoz y Pérez, a Valencian merchant.) [80] Once in the city expenses incurred in housing and other day-to-day necessities increased his indebtedness even more. By 1793 Vilanova publicly acknowledged that he owed a total of 8,433 pesos.[81] While deductions were taken out of his salary to satisfy his creditors, Vilanova was forced to borrow to meet everyday expenses. At the time of his death in 1812 Vilanova owed money to thirteen wholesale and retail merchants, the medical doctor who had treated him for several years, a lawyer, a tavern owner, a chocolate vendor, a grocer, and his landlord, among others.[82]

Not all debts were incurred because of careless management of personal assets. Antonio Pinedo Montufar, treasurer of the Reales Cajas, suffered great loss of property and assets because of the Indian uprising in La Paz. So deeply in debt was Pinedo that he was forced to consent to a list of his creditors being drawn up and to one-third of his salary being deducted for the last nine years of his stay in Buenos Aires.[83]

Although not always linked through marriage, ritual kinship, or even outstanding debts to the mercantile elite of the city, bureaucrats, especially those holding high rank, did turn to merchants in times of distress or when confidence and competence were needed. Frequently, leading bureaucrats requested that merchants be named executors of their estates, a clear demonstration of friendship and trust. Juan Francisco Navarro, contador of the Tribunal de Cuentas, turned to Vicente de Azcuenaga and José Lezica, two local merchants, on his death bed, asking them to draw up his will.[84] Only friendship bound them together.

Although identifying themselves with the elite of Spanish society, most bureaucrats took a surprisingly limited role in the religious life of the city. A very small number of government officials participated in the city's third orders, institutions that were among the most prestigious socio-religious groups in Buenos Aires. Only two high-ranking bureaucrats who served during the viceregal period—Lucas Múñoz y Cubero, the regent of the Real Audiencia, and Manuel Gallego, viceregal secretary—joined the Third Order of San Francisco after 1776.[85] A handful of other bureaucrats—Pedro Medrano and José Manuel Bustillo de Cevallos of the Reales Cajas, Melchor Albin, oficial primero of the Correo, and governors Andoneagui and Ortiz de Rosas—had joined the organization before the professionalization of the Buenos Aires bureaucracy, that is, before the establishment of the Viceroyalty of the Río de la Plata. All of these men had strong local ties and were married to local women and related to prominent local families. While merchants and lawyers continued to flock to the third orders during the viceregal period, bureaucrats, either because they failed to establish close personal ties with the local elite or because the majority could not afford the time and expense involved, no longer comprised an important segment of these orders.

The same generally low level of participation can be seen in the membership of the Hermandad de la Caridad, a most prestigious male religious organization, although here bureaucrat participation was somewhat higher. Among those bureaucrats belonging to the Hermandad in 1790, the highest-ranking officials in the Secretaría, Tribunal de Cuentas, and Aduana figure prominently.[86] Members included Alexandro Ariza, Francisco Cabrera, and José Antonio Hurtado, all contadores mayores of the Tribunal de Cuentas; Juan Andrés de Arroyo, contador mayor supernumerario of the same agency; Juan Núñez, administrador of Aduana; Andrés de Torres, viceregal secretary; and Francisco Ximénez de Mesa, ex-administrator of the Aduana. Some lesser-ranking bureaucrats were also present, but as in the case of the third orders, these were uniformly porteño-born men tied to the city's most prestigious families or men with strong local connections. While few bureaucrats took leading roles in the Hermandad's governance, at least two, Francisco Cabrera and Martín José Altolaguirre, served terms as *hermano mayor* (chief officer) of the brotherhood.

Their limited interest in local religious life can also be seen in the surprisingly small number of *capellanías* (chantries) that the bureaucrats founded. The reasons for this lack of interest in religious foundations, which both enriched the spiritual life of the city and provided much needed income for priests and prospective clergymen, are many. Bureaucrats did not believe that they would be spending their entire professional life in Buenos Aires and therefore had little interest in endowing masses for their deceased family members or for themselves in the city. They also owned little urban real estate, the preferred type of property used to provide capital for paying for masses. Furthermore, given their generally low salaries coupled with high expenses, few bureaucrats could afford to invest sums of 6,000 to 10,000 pesos needed to produce a decent chaplaincy income.[87] This lack of interest in endowing local capellanías was in marked contrast to older bureaucratic families, those who had served the crown at the beginning of the eighteenth century, were closely linked to the local elite, and viewed their lives, both temporal and spiritual, within the arena of the port city.[88]

While only marginally interested in the religious life of the city, Buenos Aires bureaucrats, both those linked to the city and those who dreamed of more exciting appointments, all avidly sought membership in the honorific Spanish-based orders. Because of their relative isolation from the court in Spain, the true center of colonial power, few bureaucrats serving in Buenos Aires were actually rewarded with membership in one of the prestigious military or civil orders. Although several bureaucrats presented vaguely worded petitions to the crown asking that they be given "special honors," only eleven men stationed in the port city had both the professional record and necessary influence to seek order membership. Nine of these men petitioned for membership into the newly created civil Order of Charles III, and at least five were accepted. Even fewer bureaucrats were successful candidates for the military orders. Only one candidate entered the Order of Santiago, and another was accepted by the Order of Alcantara. All aspirants for membership in the orders were heads of government agencies with long records of government service at the time they began to entertain thoughts of being rewarded with these special honors. At least in the Order of Charles III there seems to have been no discrimination against creoles. The two native-born men who successfully entered (of the total five) were if anything less important in the local bureaucracy than their Spanish-born peers.[89]

Whether or not they achieved membership in a royal order, bureaucrats of all levels continued to search for visible symbols of the importance of their positions. One of the most eagerly sought after symbols was a military uniform, desirable both because of the honor associated with being an official in His Majesty's army and because of the clear and easy identification that the clothing afforded. A more practical benefit of wearing a uniform was that it saved money on dress. Although it is impossible to separate and weigh these motivations, it is clear that government officials of high rank in the colony avidly sought the honor of wearing military dress. By 1794 the administrador and the contador of the Aduana were both allowed to wear a military uniform.[90] Although this might have served as an easy way in which to placate civil servants, the crown zealously guarded this honor too, awarding it only in selected cases. When, for example, Juan Calderón de la Barca and Juan de Vilanova, vistas of the Aduana, requested permission to wear military uniform, they were roundly refused.[91]

The Bourbon aim of producing a disinterested bureaucracy never achieved the success that the crown so ardently desired, in part because the crown itself was inconsistent in carrying out its own marriage policies. As a result, a certain subgroup of bureaucrats, those who were single at the time of their posting to Buenos Aires and who also earned good salaries, did marry porteñas. Indeed, in virtually every agency from the viceroy down at least one high-ranking bureaucrat was tied through marriage to the local elite.

At the same time the crown's marriage policy vis-à-vis the lower-ranking bureaucrats was somewhat more successful, not because of more stringent rules, but because of economic constraints. The Spanish-born member of the rank-and-file bureaucracy more often than not failed to marry, to establish any sort of local ties, or to identify with the city in which he spent much of his adult life. He could not afford a wife and family. Although local-born bureaucrats did marry, turning to family and kin to help defray the expenses of maintaining a household and family, they found themselves even more constrained by the disparity between their salary and their prestige. Neither component of the rank-and-file bureaucracy was particularly happy with their economic and social position, and neither could afford to live in affluence or to participate in the religious institutions that made up a great part of the everyday social life of the elite. Searching for other forms of recognition, bureaucrats in general looked to recognition from the crown, be it in the form of promotion, membership in a royal order, or the privilege of wearing a military uniform. Here too they frequently met with frustration.

Government attempts to control the formation of close ties with the local elite was of course posited on the firm belief that civil servants who had no local ties would be purer, more eager to serve all members of the public, and less prone to local corruption. While on the whole the crown succeeded in isolating bureaucrats from the local population, it did not necessarily follow that better, less corrupt government would follow. The next chapter examines the issue of corruption and the degree to which the late colonial bureaucrats of Buenos Aires met the royal ideal of selflessness.

8. Corruption, Scandal, and Political Reaction

THE BOURBONS HOPED TO PROVIDE virtuous bureaucrats, men who would put the interests of the crown above their own. Ideally, all bureaucrats were to be uncorruptible, regardless of what branch of royal government they served. Those employed in government agencies charged with collecting and dispersing royal funds were naturally to be honest. Good civil servants should not steal from royal accounts. Others charged with dispensing justice or directing communication with the crown should be free of corruption and favoritism, treating individuals and cases according to their merits. Moreover, a good bureaucrat should not show favoritism, for all civil servants should have the administration of their duties, rather than their personal likes and dislikes, at heart. This was the ideal, but what was the reality?

To insure honesty among bureaucrats the Spanish government required all those holding high-ranking positions in the Real Hacienda or those bureaucrats dealing with large sums of money (contadores mayores, tesoreros) to present a *fianza* (bond) before taking office. In Buenos Aires bureaucrats had traditionally turned to local merchants to raise this bond, as merchants were the only people with easy access to liquid capital. No doubt prosperous merchants were only too glad to serve as bondsmen, for in much the same way that providing money to purchase positions created ties that could later be exploited, so did providing fianzas. While no direct proof of wrongdoing exists, the list of bureaucrats and their fiadores makes interesting reading. Francisco de Paula Sanz, first superintendent of Buenos Aires and later intendant of Potosí, was insured by Tomás Antonio

Romero, one of the more imaginative late colonial merchants. Romero also figured among a list of merchants who provided the fianza for the corrupt Ximénez de Mesa. Only a little imagination is needed to see how Romero, engaged in a wide range of legal and extralegal commercial activities, would have used connections with the intendant of a major silver-producing area and the chief of local customs to his advantage.

In essence, a system in which a merchant or group of merchants pledged themselves to reimburse the crown in case of embezzlement or other malfeasance could only result in eventual loss of the royal fisc. This dependence of the bureaucrats on the merchants, a dependence that often led to later favors, was in direct opposition to the new spirit of professionalization. Although the charters setting up agencies such as the Real Renta de Tabaco continued to call for the posting of these bonds, the reform-minded bureaucrats argued, quite correctly, that requiring bonds led to collusion. In at least one case, that of bonds required of the administrator and treasurer of the Real Renta de Tabaco, the agency director was able to convince the crown to forgo this requirement because of the possibility of future merchant influence. The crown realized the danger of merchant meddling; "in view . . . of the local circumstances . . . the aforementioned bonds are not required of the administrator and treasurer, so that these ministers will have no motive to be grateful to the merchants of that capital city who are the only ones who are able to supply the funds and would perhaps demand interest or recompense for the sums that they have insured."[1] But the crown stopped short of lifting all bonds, refusing to agree with the intendant that all administrators also be exempted. In this case the crown's response was fortuitous, for one of the administrators was Francisco Ximénez de Mesa, a man who would later swindle hundreds of thousands of pesos from the Aduana accounts.[2]

Bureaucrats, especially those with important posts, also needed ready cash to install themselves and their families in Buenos Aires and to undertake a life-style commensurate with their high status. Again, as in the case of fianzas, they turned to merchants. Among those bureaucrats who at one time or another received cash loans from the aforementioned Tomás Antonio Romero were Pedro Medrano, treasurer of the Real Hacienda (1782); José Ortiz, official mayor of the Secretaría (c. 1785); Antonio de Pinedo, treasurer of the Real Hacienda (1791); Pedro José Ballesteros, contador mayor of the Tribunal de Cuentas; and Manuel Gallego, viceregal secretary.[3]

Collusion with merchants was an on-going problem, but the extent to which government bureaucrats participated in widespread corruption to augment their salaries is difficult to determine. A handful of cases of individuals prosecuted for embezzlement provide limited direct evidence. More widespread are charges and countercharges of bribery, indecent behavior, and illegal business investment that were never documented. Nevertheless, these charges merit serious attention because they were frequent and because they concerned important individuals. At the very least they indicate a widespread distrust of bureaucrats.

Because of the nature of Spanish colonial trade policies, the lure of Potosí silver, and human nature, government officials in Buenos Aires had always been deeply involved in the contraband trade that was a feature of the city's economic life. Reports from the seventeenth and early eighteenth centuries leave little doubt that bureaucrats from the governor on down were either active participants in illicit commerce or bystanders, willing to conveniently ignore the trade for a price.[4] As late as the 1760s and 1770s it is likely that the governor and the few Real Hacienda officials stationed in the city augmented their regular salary and commissions through illegal dealings. Viceroy Cevallos, in a secret letter to the crown, left little doubt that his predecessor Governor Bucareli had been deeply involved in contraband, corruption, and theft.[5] Bureaucratic collusion, although not always documented, was considered acceptable conduct.

Beginning with Viceroy Cevallos, the chief official's direct participation in illegal commerce, corruption, and graft seems to have become far less prevalent. Written reports reaching the crown and residencia testimony are silent about direct involvement of the viceroy himself in any nefarious dealings. Instead, the viceroys resorted to less dangerous forms of self-enrichment. One favorite ploy, used not only by the Buenos Aires viceroys, but by all viceroys sent to America, was that of importing large quantities of goods for sale under the guise of supplying their families and retinues with personal clothing.[6] Before embarking for the Río de la Plata, Viceroy Pedro Melo de Portugal, for example, requested, "just like has been done with other viceroys," that he be allowed to transport 20,000 pesos of "linen goods and other clothing" free of duties. The crown's reply to Melo's request makes it clear that the king was well aware that viceroys and other high-ranking bureaucrats had abused this privilege. But although the crown now clearly made its wish known—that viceroys and other officials should pay duties on all goods except those they could prove were expressly imported for their personal use—it is doubtful that this abuse was ever stopped. Nevertheless, because many viceroys were already in America at the time they were named, it was not among the viceroys or any members of their household that the most notorious cases of corruption and abuse of office occurred.

One group of bureaucrats in an exceptionally advantageous position to augment their official salaries were the Aduana employees. Aduana corruption consisted of two major abuses: overlooking (for a price) discrepancies in merchandise being imported by the wholesale merchants of the city and engaging in the importation and sale of merchandise oneself. Indirect evidence indicates that although most Aduana employees engaged in both these activities, as long as abuses were kept within bounds and hidden from public view, they could be tolerated. Unfortunately, this was not always the case.

The scandal that was to rock the bureaucratic and commercial worlds of Buenos Aires centered around the Aduana and its administrador, Francisco Ximénez de Mesa. Ximénez de Mesa was not one of the more popular figures in the viceregal bureaucracy. The first intendant of Buenos Aires, Manuel Fernández, a man who had worked with Ximénez in setting up the Aduana, distrusted him and suspected that he was involved in shady dealings from the beginning. Nicolás Torrado, his first contador, was hardly an admirer and accused Ximénez of gross incompetence in administrative matters. It should be added that Torrado, a man who had served several years as oficial segundo of the chief naval accounting office in Spain, very much resented the fact that Ximénez, whose only prior government service consisted of seven years service as alcalde of Tabasco in New Spain, had been named to the top Aduana position. Nonetheless, by 1785 both of these adversaries had been removed from the scene, and Ximénez de Mesa had every right to believe that he was safe from further criticism. Moreover, he enjoyed the protection of his superior, Superintendent Francisco de Paula Sanz. Events were soon to prove him wrong.

Ximénez's problems began in 1788 when incriminating papers were accidently discovered in the probate estate of the late Francisco Medina, merchant and owner of the first *saladero* (meat-salting plant) in the Banda Oriental. These documents suggested that Ximénez de Mesa, in conjunction with Francisco de Ortega, Montevideo coast guard commander, was involved in illegal trade. Joaquín del Pino, governor of Montevideo and long-time enemy of Ortega, immediately began an investigation, subpoenaing letters from Ximénez to Ortega that alluded to on-going commercial transactions.[7] The case was quickly transferred to Buenos Aires where Viceroy Loreto demanded that Ximénez present an accounting of Aduana funds on hand. Instead of the 130,000 pesos that should have been in the Aduana cashbox, the viceroy found only 49 pesos.[8] This turned out to be only the tip of the proverbial iceberg.

An investigation soon showed that Ximénez was not only involved in importing goods from Spain, he was also the silent partner of merchant Domingo Belgrano Pérez. In conjunction with Belgrano the Aduana administrador had been shipping hides and flour from Buenos Aires, importing textiles and other goods from Europe, and participating in trade with merchants in Paraguay, Uruguay, Potosí, Peru, Córdoba, Salta, La Plata (Chuquisaca), and La Paz. In addition, he was lending money to bureaucrats throughout the American empire, including men as prominent as Valle Postigo, future asesor of the viceroyalty of Peru. Moreover, Ximénez de Mesa was using royal funds to enrich himself and his associates through these transactions.

An immediate review of all dealings involving Ximénez, Ortega, and Belgrano Pérez was ordered by the viceroy in an attempt to unravel the complicated financial machinations of the group. Within a year 114 different autos relating to Ximénez were begun. In addition to his major partners, the Aduana chief implicated two low-ranking Aduana oficiales whom he had used as fronts for some of his dealings. He also came perilously close to involving at least two hide merchants, Francisco Casimiro de Nechochea and Tomás Antonio Romero, in his fall. Ximénez de Mesa's business dealings ranged from contraband tobacco to investments in ships to distribution of goods to the Indian towns of Misiones and Corrientes. The reason for Ximénez's long delay in preparing accounts to be audited by the Tribunal de Cuentas became painfully clear. The man who claimed he had no experience in preparing complex accounts had stolen 251,939 pesos from the royal coffers.[9]

One of the more interesting aspects of the Ximénez de Mesa conspiracy was the way in which he and Belgrano Pérez profited through the payment of militia men in *géneros* (cloth) and other goods.[10] According to testimony presented by Ignacio Sánchez, "creole from the city of Corrientes and captain of a reformed militia company," his company, after successfully attempting to collect its salary for eight years, had sent him in 1785 to Buenos Aires to deal directly with authorities. Once in the city Sánchez got in touch with Belgrano Pérez, who promised to help the rather rude backcountryman. Within the year the merchant, using his bureaucratic connections, had payment authorized by the Junta Superior de Hacienda in the form of a *libranza* (bill of exchange) for pesos drawn against the Real Aduana. But unbeknownst to Hacienda authorities, Belgrano Pérez had drawn up a prior agreement with Sánchez in which the latter agreed, if Belgrano was successful in collecting the funds from the government, to accept goods rather than cash from the merchant. Instead of cash, Sánchez returned to Correientes with linen, cambric, striped calico, cotton velvet, ribbons, knives, iron spoons, handsaws, and sewing needles, which were distributed to the long-awaiting soldiers. Both Belgrano and Ximénez de Mesa profited handsomely, for they had managed to get rid of surplus goods at premium prices.

The degree to which lower-ranking Aduana members were involved in trade can only be surmised, for formal charges were never brought against other Aduana employees.[11] Nonetheless, Juan Francisco Vilanova, vista of the Aduana, and his son José imported goods worth 88,698 reales de plata (approximately 11,087 pesos), which they resold to local merchants on at least one occasion.[12] Both men were also very friendly with José González Bolaños and Antonio de las Cagigas, two merchants frequently suspected of illegal transactions.

Bureaucratic corruption did not stop with the Aduana employees. Lesser-ranking bureaucrats in other agencies were also involved in defrauding the royal coffers, more often through embezzlemment than through contraband. For example, Félix Gallardo, a third official in the Reales Cajas, working in conjunction with Roque Carrión, successfully stole approximately 100,000 pesos from the royal treasury by falsifying payment orders for expenses supposedly incurred by the Limits Commission. Only in 1798 when the Tribunal de Cuentas finally checked the records of expenses submitted by the commission against the payment records of the Buenos Aires cajas was the embezzlement discovered, but by then Gallardo, aware of the investigation, had successfully fled the region.[13]

The next major viceregal scandal was never made public, but it was more far-reaching than the Gallardo-Carrión embezzlement, implicating numbers of important bureaucrats. It also reflected the way in which royal policy could be undermined by uncooperative officials and demonstrated the failure of crown policy to restrict the development of strong local ties among these bureaucrats. Indeed, this scandal indicated the degree of co-operation that continued to exist between a group of high-ranking bureaucrats and a segment of the local merchant community.

Since this case of bureaucratic corruption was directly tied to official trade policies and to the growing influence of merchants who prospered from changes in these policies, it is important to review the commercial situation in the Río de la Plata area during the 1790s. In 1778 the crown had instituted a policy of so-called free trade that enabled Buenos Aires to trade with other regions of the Spanish realm. This policy, it was hoped, would end the 150 years of endemic smuggling that had developed in response to an artificially imposed Panama-Lima trade route. But free trade never had a chance to be tested in the Río de la Plata, for within five years of its enactment the crown, effectively isolated from its colonies by a British blockade, was forced to allow neutral ships to export Argentine goods. After a brief respite from 1789 to 1791 a series of emergency laws allowed the Río de la Plata area to trade with Portuguese, English, and Anglo-American suppliers, while exporting local products, silver and hides, and re-exporting slaves. The culmination of this emergency policy was the Royal Order of 18 November 1797, which opened colonial trade to all neutral powers.[14]

While this policy clearly aided a group of local merchants intent on exporting silver and hides for the goods of England, France, Germany, and the United States and the bodies of Africa, merchants tied to the more traditional Cádiz-Buenos Aires axis and the crown itself were not happy with the new policy. Liberalization had been adopted as an emergency measure, and as soon as the crown believed the emergency to be past, it promulgated a new royal cédula abolishing trade with neutrals.[15] But the group of merchants who had grown rich under the new laws, in the main exporters of hides and importers of slaves, were loathe to accept a return to the status quo antes. Both in the Consulado and through personal contacts with government officials, they began a determined campaign to thwart the implementation of the 1799 cédula.[16] So effective were these merchants in opposing the new law that Viceroy Avilés suspected the existence of an organized gang that was working to subvert crown policy. Furthermore, the crown had been alerted by an anonymous letter that accused certain civil servants of such a degree of corruption that the inhabitants of Buenos Aires would soon be forced to rise up against the king.[17] Before he could respond to a Royal Order of June 1800 requesting more information, Avilés was transferred to Lima as the new viceroy of Peru, but his successor in Buenos Aires was determined to continue the investigation.

Joaquín del Pino, the new viceroy, had strong personal reasons for wanting to uncover any collusion between merchants and bureaucrats that delayed a return to traditional free trade. In addition to the expected dedication to justice, to carrying out the king's orders, and to weeding out corruption, del Pino was linked through his marriage to Rafaela Francisca Vera to an important group of traditional merchants, the Lezica group. (Juan José de Lezica, the spokesman for the clan, was married to Rafaela Vera's sister, Petrona.)

Shortly after taking office in May 1801, del Pino received a previously commissioned secret report outlining widespread collusion between hide merchants, slavers, and high-ranking government officials. This report and additional investigations undertaken by the viceroy form the basis of a secret letter that del Pino sent to Manuel Godoy, the first secretary of state.[18] Like Avilés, del Pino was convinced that "many of the individuals employed in public administration" were members of a "gang" tied to those merchants most involved in "smuggling and clandestine trade." Several high-ranking bureaucrats were believed to be in the pay of either Tomás Antonio Romero and his partner, Pedro Andrés García; Anselmo Saenz Valiente, and his partner Francisco del Sar; or Ventura Miguel Marcó. All these merchants had continued in neutral trade despite the Royal Order of 20 April 1799, which declared this trade once again to be illegal.

Both Viceroy Avilés and his successor, Viceroy del Pino, believed Romero, the most daring and inventive merchant in Buenos Aires during the viceregal period, to be the mastermind of the entire operation. Romero, a native of Moguer, had come to Buenos Aires from Potosí in 1780. He successfully combined mercantile expertise, political connections, and commercial imagination with a sharp eye for new and profitable investments. In addition to winning a series of government contracts, including being the supplier of salted meat for the army and transporter of mercury and silver coin for the government, Romero had led the fight for neutralization of trade in Buenos Aires. More than just a merchant, Romero had invested some of his vast profits in ships, ranch lands, and saladeros, attempting to exercise vertical domination over the production and export of hides and other cattle products from the Río de la Plata area. A powerful man who held several positions of prominence in local society, including that of hermano mayor of the Brotherhood of Charity, Romero had also been the most vocal supporter of legislation declaring hides to be exportable *frutos del Pais* (local commodities). He also emerged as the most important slave trader in the area. Until 1801 Romero had met with little but success, but in that year a relatively minor incident, the capture of a ship engaged in smuggling, signaled a dramatic turn in his good fortune.[19]

The incident that led to the denouement of Romero occurred two months before Viceroy del Pino took office. On March 1801 a frigate named "La Mariana" arrived in the Río de la Plata area loaded with a cargo of 556 boxes of merchandise. The ship was apprehended while surreptitiously unloading cargo along the coast by the commander of the coast guard, the creole León Altolaguirre. Upon his arrival in Buenos Aires the new viceroy, already suspicious of Romero and his pernicious influence in government, was overjoyed to discover that the owner of this ship caught engaging in contraband activity was none other than Romero himself. Further investigation brought forth much damaging evidence against the merchant, including instructions that Romero had secretly sent to his agent José Antonio Sanzetenea when the ship arrived in the area. In the trial that followed, Romero claimed that Sanzetenea had instructions to return to Buenos Aires with the ship in ballast but instead had allowed a Boston merchant, Thomas Halcey, to convince him to smuggle goods into the area. The viceroy was hardly swayed by Romero's rather weak defense. Aided by the fiscal de lo civil, one of the few bureaucrats who was not in Romero's pocket, he unearthed the details of Romero's purchase of the ship and his orders to outfit it for trade with the United States, Holland, England, and Brazil.[20]

Del Pino soon found that Romero's influence in local government was so widespread that the viceroy was forced to appoint a special investigator, Doctor José Pacheco, thereby bypassing his own legal machinery. Del Pino was eventually able to order the temporary house arrest of the merchant, holding him for eighteen days. While fiscal de lo civil drew up criminal charges against Romero, the viceroy attempted, unsuccessfully, to embargo the merchant's property. The fiscal de lo civil demanded that Romero be sentenced to death, but instead Romero was freed, although kept under close surveillance. Although implicated in a major scandal, Romero continued to exert influence over government officials. Shortly after Romero's arrest, for example, the Audiencia oidor Sebastián de Velasco, "forgetting what he owed to the nature of his position, visited Romero in broad daylight, during the morning, leaving his coach at the door, so that he could offer Romero his personal respect." [21] Pedro José Ballesteros and Juan Andrés Arroyo, high-ranking bureaucrats in the Tribunal de Cuentas, also visited the prisoner, and although they came at "more dissembling times," they also appeared more frequently. [22]

So strong was the influence of the Romero group that, according to del Pino, they had totally subverted the "good intentions" of his predecessor, Marqués de Avilés. Reporting on the situation under Avilés and detailing the last viceroy's inability to stop contraband, del Pino portrayed Avilés as a "good chief" who unfortunately was unable to control those opposed to his campaign against smuggling.

To what degree del Pino's report reflected his paranoia, to what degree he hoped to use the report as a self-serving vehicle to advance his ambitions and those of his sons, and to what degree his report reflected reality is difficult to determine. Del Pino claimed that he had not only "heard, among other rumors and information, of the disorder that ruled this capital" while still serving as governor of Chile, but that he had come to so distrust the bureaucrats surrounding him that he was forced to send his son to Spain personally to deliver the report and provide additional details to the crown. Indeed, long sections of the documentation sent to the crown were in the viceroy's own handwriting.

The list of those who were the object of the most scathing denunciations in del Pino's report is interesting both because of the rank of the individuals so named and the evidence presented against them. Although as a group they were all accused of participating in "sordid machinations," "criminal generosity," maintaining illegal influence at court, and reducing "most all of the branches of the administration to a most lamentable state," greatest condemnation was laid at the feet of the administrador of the Buenos Aires Aduana, Don Angel Izquierdo. Izquierdo, in charge of the storage of all shipments arriving in the port until their cargo manifests could be reviewed to determine whether or not illegal goods were included, was accused of brazenly declaring illegal goods to be legal, thereby directly defrauding the Royal Exchequer and indirectly injuring law-abiding merchants. Not only Izquierdo but all those working under him, including inspectors and members of the coast guard, were in the pay of the most notorious smugglers. Indeed, "although they received a limited salary, they are so busy putting up houses and keeping themselves and their families in such a fine state that, degenerating into luxury, they arouse everybody's attention." Even the commander of the coast guard, León Altolaguirre, who was at first believed to be an outstanding civil servant, was under suspicion, for so much corruption could not be going on around him without at least his tacit cooperation.

But this pernicious evil had gone farther than the Aduana. Del Pino claimed that the asesor general of the viceroyalty, Juan de Almagro, was another key member of the group dedicated to protecting the interests of the contraband traders. Almagro, an old personal friend of Romero, was responsible for providing legal council to the viceroys and could therefore subvert any attempt to prosecute his friend. Although there was no proof that Almagro had benefited directly from his actions, his brother, Manuel, had been transformed almost overnight from a poor minor bureaucrat posted to the subdelegation of Chucuito to a merchant deeply involved in neutral commerce and the *españolización* of foreign ships.[23]

Romero's influence had spread even further. During the Avilés viceroyalty both the personal advisers of the marqués and his personal chaplain had been bought off by the powerful merchant. Indeed, del Pino reported that the asesor general was now en route to Spain where he was planning to use Romero's connection and "heavy financing" to win an oidor position for himself.

According to del Pino, at least two judges of the Buenos Aires Audiencia were already implicated in this network dedicated to preserving the lucrative trade with neutral nations. Foremost was the regent, Benito de la Mata Linares, who was accused of interpreting royal legislation forbidding neutral trade in such a manner as to favor Spanish merchants bringing goods into the city in neutral ships. He had even himself claimed goods coming from Brazil that were detained in the Aduana. In addition to defending neutral commerce, the regent was always anxious to protect the position of "certain merchants who deserve special consideration from the government because of the usefulness of their business to both the treasury and the state."[24]

The oidor decano, Sebastián de Velazco, instead of receiving payoffs for his cooperation, had invested in several illicit ventures. Velazco, although eighty years old, was still "so tied to profit" that he could easily be bribed. Not only was he more than willing to sell favorable sentences for a price, his fellow oidores, fearing his rapacious nature, had refused to let him serve his turn as presiding judge of the *juzgado de bienes de difuntos* (probate court). According to the report of at least one Audiencia member, the regent successfully prevented Velazco from holding this office because he realized that a judge as unscrupulous as Velazco would easily devour all funds entrusted to him. When Velazco threatened that he would not continue as juez de provincia (provincial judge) if he did not also get the Difuntos post, the regent replied: "No to that matter about the difuntos because the dead cannot talk."[25] Furthermore, Velazco had invested his wealth in trade and was reported to have a part interest in the illegal cargo of Romero's ship, "La Mariana," as well as 4,000 pesos invested in goods aboard a French corsair, "El Valiente."

The three other oidores, Francisco Tomás Ansotegui, Joaquín Bernardo Campuzano, and Francisco Garasa, were believed by the viceroy to be honest men, but only the latter, Garasa, was clearly above suspicion. He was a man of "integrity, purity, and desire to fulfill all his obligations with punctuality," in spite of the fact that he frequented the weekend home *(quinta)* of Ventura Miguel Marcó, one of the principal merchants involved in clandestine trade. Ansotegui was thought to be a bit too indulgent on the contraband question because of "the family ties that he has with some of those involved in this trade" but was not obviously in Romero's pay.[26] Campuzano, "of friendly disposition and anxious to please," was also a close friend of Saenz Valiente and Pedro Andrés García, but there was no clear evidence that he had fallen directly under their influence.

At least one of the fiscales of the Audiencia, José Marqués de la Plata, was also believed to be an "upright, impartial, and zealous" defender of the royal interests, although his lack of speed in forwarding cases was notorious.[27] The other fiscal, Manuel Génaro Villota, was believed to be part of the "gang" because of his friendship with both Manuel Gallego, the viceregal secretary, who had housed him when he had first arrived in Buenos Aires, and with Pedro Andrés García. García, "one of those most involved in the forbidden trade," had provided Villota with the furnished house in which he was currently living.

Corruption extended beyond the Aduana and Audiencia. Manuel Gallego, the viceroy's secretary, in addition to being a most difficult personality ("he wants to give orders and not take them"), was believed to have strong connections with the merchants, an inordinate "fondness for profit," and to be deeply involved in smuggling. Gallego had access to a wide range of government documents and secret correspondence and was privy to the future actions planned by the viceroy. In addition, Gallego, who had been in Buenos Aires since 1795, was in charge of moving all official business through the bureaucratic maze and could therefore delay action on any legajo within his purview. The viceroy, already suspicious of Gallego because he was "an intimate friend of Don Tomás Romero," had his suspicions vindicated when he found Gallego purposely trying to slow investigation of the "Mariana" case. Del Pino was forced to turn to his two sons, both captains in the Real Cuerpo de Artillería, to draft important correspondence with the crown.

The Tribunal Mayor de Cuentas was also under suspicion, for at least three of its four top-ranking administrators were believed to be intimately linked to Romero and company. Pedro José Ballesteros, decano and the senior contador mayor, was accused of being little more than a business agent involved in all types of affairs, both inside and outside of the Tribunal, that added to his wealth. Furthermore, he was particularly well disposed toward Romero, who had recently helped him buy a house, furnished funds for costly repairs on the property, and provided one of his sons with a 6,000 peso capellanía. Juan Andrés de Arroyo, another of the contadores mayores, was accused of being directly involved in illicit commerce, storing contraband goods in his house, and of sending his son, Manuel, who had until recently been employed in the Tribunal as a meritorio, to Rio de Janeiro to deal in illegal monetary operations and trade. Ramón Oromí, another contador, was, according to del Pino, "a living copy of Ballesteros, formed in the same school, and more cut out for being a business agent than for being contador mayor of the Cuentas." Only the creole Martín José Altolaguirre, acting as interim contador mayor for his father-in-law, Francisco Cabrera, received a favorable judgment. "In spite of his personal connections, he comports himself judiciously and with tranquility." In sum, according to the viceroy, if "Ballesteros, Arroyo, and Oromí used their intelligence to fulfill their professional duties as they fulfill their private interests and business deals, the Tribunal de Cuentas would not be so plagued with delays nor would the Royal Exchequer be suffering so."

Even more venal than Pedro José Ballesteros was his brother Juan José, who was serving as contador of the Administración de Propios y Arbitrios. Although the viceroy could find no definite proof that the latter man was directly involved in the "gang," del Pino referred to him as "the more addicted brother," and went on to describe him as "one of the bureaucrats most given to intrigue." Furthermore, the viceroy accused both Ballesteros brothers of having stolen large quantities of money belonging to the accounts of Indios de los Pueblos de Misiones del Uruguay y Paraná while Juan José served as interim contador. These funds were later used to finance Juan José's trip to Madrid where he successfully petitioned for a permanent título in Propios y Arbitrios.[28]

The situation in the Royal Exchequer office itself was somewhat more hazy. Félix Casamayor, the factor, although not clearly a member of the *pandilla* (gang) was objectionable because of his personal habits, which included frequenting cafés and gaming houses, mixing with people of low and dishonorable social standing, refusing to wear his official uniform, preferring instead to dress like the masses, and running up considerable debts. Antonio Carrasco was felt to be a good civil servant, "zealous, faithful, and honorable." José María Romero, son of the infamous Tomás Antonio was suspected of aiding his father, although there was no direct proof.

Although del Pino could not document the younger Romero's involvement, proof of the merchant's influence, and of José María Romero's role in attacking his father's enemies, is contained in a secret letter that young Romero penned on 28 May 1803 to the secretary of state for finances, Miguel Cayetano Soler.[29] This letter, a scurrilous assault on his colleague Antonio Carrasco, accused the minister of waxing rich through his many projects, especially the Paraguayan wood venture undertaken by the Real Hacienda at Carrasco's instigation. Romero's attack was a response to Carrasco's earlier accusation that José María was little more than his father's stooge, a point all too dramatically demonstrated by Romero when he widened his barrage to include all his father's enemies. "The viceroy, Don Joaquín del Pino, the oidor, Don Francisco Garasa, the fiscal de lo civil, Don José Marqués de la Plata, the visitador de Real Hacienda, Don Diego de la Vega, . . . the director of the Real Renta de Tabaco, Don Francisco Barron, and the administrator of the Aduana, Don José Proyet, all form a chamber in which Carrasco is the main speaker, and they all blindly defend his ideas, whims, and intrigues." The accuracy with which Romero attacked those men who had been given clean slates in del Pino's secret correspondence raises grave questions about the viceroy's ability to preserve confidentiality in the world of the Buenos Aires bureaucracy and strengthens del Pino's claim that indeed he had found himself in the midst of a huge bureaucratic-commercial conspiracy. The ease with which the younger Romero was able to communicate with high-ranking ministers in Spain also suggests that his father had bought off more than just the local bureaucrats of Buenos Aires.[30]

Whether or not the charges and countercharges sent by del Pino and Romero were true, they do present a picture of viceregal bureaucracy deeply divided into warring camps. Furthermore, if we are to believe the viceroy's account, of eighteen high-ranking administrators half were clearly corrupt, four were possibly implicated, and only five were performing their duties in a fashion approaching the ideal of the disinterested civil servant. But it should be stressed that with the exception of the Aduana, corruption was limited to the highest reaches of the local bureaucracy. Indeed, it is striking that it was men earning salaries of 2,000 and 3,000 pesos, not their underlings with incomes of 300 to 800 pesos, who were the most corrupt. Put another way, there was much that the contadores mayores of the Tribunal de Cuentas could do for merchants such as Tomás Antonio Romero but little that an insignificant third or fourth clerk could do. Lastly, it is interesting to see that at least some of the local bureaucrats with close ties to the local aristocracy—Ansotegui and at least one of the Altolaguirre brothers—were, in the eyes of the viceroy, among the least corrupt bureaucrats. Although the crown believed that family alliances always twisted the "staff of accuracy and righteousness," there is some suggestion that some bureaucrats with close family links to the local oligarchy were especially careful to conduct themselves in a more disinterested manner.

Curiously, although the viceroy filed a long and damaging report against Romero and his bureaucratic accomplices, no successful official action was taken against either the merchants or the officials. Again, it seems that Tomás Antonio Romero's influence had spread well beyond Buenos Aires. The only government bureaucrats mentioned in del Pino's report who were publicly reprimanded were the Tribunal de Cuentas officials Andrés de Arroyo and Pedro José Ballesteros, who were relieved of their positions during the de la Vega visita the next year. The viceroy, realizing his own limitations in dealing with the matter, had decided to avail himself of the visitador in the hope that the latter would be more effective. But while de la Vega was able to temporarily relieve Ballesteros and Andrés de Arroyo of their posts (on the grounds of general incompetence, not on grounds directly connected with Romero), both men successfully pleaded their innocence and were reinstated by royal decree in 1807. By the first decade of the nineteenth century the crown was too weak to punish even the most blatantly corrupt of its civil servants in Buenos Aires.

In addition to the friendships that had developed between the high-ranking government officials mentioned in the del Pino report and a select group of prominent merchants engaged in slave and hide trade (Romero, Anselmo Saenz Valiente, García), ties of marriage and kinship also bound some of these bureaucrats to local society. Nonetheless, there is no evidence that those men married to local women were more prone to corruption than those who were not. While the Bourbons had attempted to curb the marriage patterns of their bureaucrats, they could not effectively stop friendship or greed. Furthermore, in spite of del Pino's harsh indictments of his fellow bureaucrats, one could argue that these men were more realistic in their appraisal of foreign trade and the impossibility of effectively controlling contraband. Although no doubt heavily influenced by money, either in the form of bribes or illegal participation in trade, many of the bureaucrats mentioned by del Pino clearly saw a continuation of the emergency regulations, that is, of free trade, as beneficial to themselves, to commerce, and to the region as a whole.

Finally, it is ironic that the few creole-born bureaucrats mentioned by del Pino in his report seemed to have conducted themselves in a far more exemplary manner than their Spanish-born counterparts. There was never any proof of scandal connected with León Altolaguirre or Martín José de Altolaguirre.[31] Whether their innocence was due to personal antipathy to Romero and other merchants or whether they were truly dedicated to carrying out the letter of the law and proving themselves to be exemplary civil servants is difficult to judge. They nonetheless emerged unscathed from a scandal that had touched virtually all of the high-ranking bureaucrats in Buenos Aires.

Although del Pino was credited with the purest motives in his attempt to root out corruption and attack Romero, the visitador, Diego de la Vega, who soon entered into a series of bitter controversies with the viceroy over de la Vega's jurisdiction, later questioned the viceroy's motives. De la Vega came to believe that the viceroy had detained the ship "La Mariana" in order to lay his hands on 124,000 pesos of Romero's money, money that was divided among the captors, informers, judges, and escribanos involved in the case. According to the visitador, among others who profited from the Romero scandal were Agustín de Pinedo, León Altolaguirre, the escribano José de Echevarria, and the viceroy himself.[32]

One last footnote to this incident concerns Tomás Antonio Romero. While del Pino continued the *pleito* (legal suit) against the merchant, Romero petitioned the Spanish government and lined up local support in the Buenos Aires Consulado. In 1804 Romero was vindicated. Although both his health and fortune had suffered, he remained as daring as ever. Shortly after Viceroy del Pino's sudden death in April 1804, the merchant brought a civil suit against his widow enjoining her to desist from touching any property in the viceroy's estate.[33] Romero planned to bring a suit against the viceroy's estate and wanted its assets kept in a form that would make them readily available.

Manuel Gallego, viewed as an anathema by Viceroy del Pino, went on to enjoy the full support of del Pino's successor, Viceroy Sobremonte. Gallego, a military man, had first come to Buenos Aires as a *subteniente* (sublieutenant) in the Burgos Infantry Regiment and returned to the Río de la Plata in 1795 to become chief of the viceroy's Secretaría. He held this post until 1808, the year of his death. In 1804 Sobremonte supported Gallego's request for promotion to an intendancy with the following words: "not only has he served in the army and seen battle several times . . . but his conduct has been, and is, the most correct . . . his breeding, his reputation, talent, and integrity have been well proven in the years that he has served as the secretary of this viceroyalty. The concerns of office and the multiplicity of important affairs have caused him a considerable amount of laudable hard work, but they have also brought about a new level of excellence and have confirmed his great aptitude for carrying out even more important duties."[34] Nevertheless, important sectors of the local elite had little use for the secretary, an attitude that was only hardened by his pusillanimous actions during the British invasions. In 1806, during del Pino residencia, several leading citizens, including merchants Antonio Pirán, Manuel Ortiz Basualdo, and Ignacio Rezabal, alluded to rumors that both Gallego and the viceregal asesor, Juan de Almagro, were deeply involved in the contraband trade.[35]

In 1807 the victorious Cabildo of Buenos Aires listed as one of its main requests that both Gallego and Almagro be removed from office, claiming "Gallego has abused all his power to an enormous extent, enriching himself extraordinarily, and causing grave harm to this city's citizens; Gallego and Almagro were among the first to flee and no doubt had a great role in the Viceroy Sobremonte's abandoning the city in June 1806 when the British entered."[36]

The correspondence of the victorious Cabildo with the crown in 1808 went even further than Viceroy del Pino in hurling charges of corruption in high places at most key bureaucrats. In a secret letter to the Consejo dated 13 September 1808, the Cabildo of Buenos Ares informed the royal government that

> corruption in all branches of government has reached its limit. The prostitution [of government officials] is both scandalous and intolerable. Justice is administered without following the laws; the political administration knows no rules; the Royal Exchequer is run without prudent management and with criminal indolence. . . . For many years America has made to suffer corrupt and despotic governors, ignorant and debased bureaucratic leaders, untrained and cowardly military men.[37]

Clearly, some of this rhetoric was the excited hyperbole of a Cabildo flushed with victory. But the letter also reflected a reality—growing disenchantment with a system that was perceived, rightly or wrongly, to have failed to provide good government.

Although they failed to remove Gallego from office, both the Cabildo and del Pino were right about his corruption. In his will, although Gallego complained that his wealth had diminished, it is clear that he had amassed a considerable fortune, one far greater than could be credited to either his inheritance or the salary paid him in Buenos Aires. Gallego owned a house, a quinta and chapel (bought and refurbished with money lent him by Ventura Miguel Marcó), ten slaves, two coaches, jewelry, books, clothing, and household goods worth a total of 65,012.2 pesos.[38] In addition to his sumptuous clothing, five trunks full of new clothing and textiles were found among his possessions, suggesting that either Gallego was attached to fine stuffs or was involved in some extralegal business dealings. Gallego's home was lavishly furnished and included a large selection of paintings, both sacred and profane. (Among the paintings were the traditional representations of Our Lord, San José, the Dolorosa, the Virgin of Conception, the Virgin of Soledad, and a guardian angel, as well as various Greek goddesses, Venus, Admiral Hood, and Lord Bridgeport.) In addition to a large collection of china, crystal, and silverware, several fine pieces of furniture and maps are listed in the Gallego inventory. Perhaps most outstanding was a library, furnished with a mahogany desk, three bookcases and a hardwood table, and boasting a large collection of books in Spanish, Latin, French, English, and Italian.[39]

In the face of such lax prosecution of high-ranking bureaucrats involved in illegal activities, it is noteworthy that low-ranking bureaucrats when apprehended for criminal action were sentenced and punished harshly for illegal activities. While all the contadores mayores of the tribunal suspended from office by the de la Vega visita were eventually returned to their former positions, lesser bureaucrats were treated with severity. Bernando Sánchez, a young man from Betanzos, Galicia, who arrived in Buenos Aires with Viceroy Loreto's retinue, was found guilty of selling falsified licenses to "harvest hides" in the Banda Oriental while he served as meritorio in the Secretaría de Cámara. He was sentenced to eight years of exile in the Malvinas for this blunder.[40]

As a general rule, the higher-ranking bureaucrats in each agency, especially those who took an active part in controlling the contraband trade or those who handled large sums of cash, continued to find ways to increase their incomes extralegally. The same phenomenon also held true for those bureaucrats stationed outside of the capital city, far from the gaze of viceroy, superintendent, and a large bureaucratic structure. There is no evidence however that the rank and file of the colonial bureaucracy, those clerks, escribientes, and contadores stationed in Buenos Aires, participated in graft on a large scale. Indeed, the weight of the evidence suggests just the opposite, for one must believe that their never-ending cries of penury reflected, at least in part, some economic reality. Even if they could escape the scrutiny of the massive bureaucracy and the jealous eyes of fellow clerks waiting for any pretext to move up the bureaucratic ladder, it is doubtful that most middle- and low-ranking bureaucrats had much influence to sell. For these men graft earned them at best a few more pesos per year. If we are to believe the evidence of marriage patterns, wills, and estate papers, it did not provide them with fabled riches.

Charges of corruption should not lead one to imagine that all, or even a majority, of the Buenos Aires bureaucrats became wealthy. Just as some bureaucrats amassed fortunes, others died in abject poverty. Perhaps typical of the economic situation of many local bureaucrats was the estate left by Félix Casamayor, factor of the Reales Cajas, the man accused by del Pino of being overly fond of the low life. At the time of his death in 1810 Casamayor left a widow and six surviving children. Although his goods were not assigned a total value, the inventory prepared by his widow gives a strong impression of bare comfort rather than luxury.[41] Among the furniture, kitchen utensiles, clothing, and personal ornaments listed are several pieces labeled "used" or "very worn." One of Casamayor's proudest possessions was "a rosewood walking stick with a gold head and a brass tip." Compared to Gallego's lavish wardrobe, that owned by Casamayor was poor indeed. Like Gallego, Casamayor also owned a personal library, although both the number and scope of titles included were far less exalted. Indeed the only works not in Spanish were two French dictionaries, one Italian-French grammar, and a copy of Virgil in the same two languages. Casamayor owned only three slaves, including a sixty-year-old man and a forty-eight-year-old woman. He owned no property in Buenos Aires, although he had inherited a house in Angaur, Baja Navarra, and a small *mayorazgo* (entailed estate) in Madrid. While a total of thirteen ounces of gold (208 pesos) were owed to Casamayor, he in turn owed more than 2,500 pesos to local merchants. Still another outstanding debt was for the expenses incurred in providing room and board to Casamayor's only son, twenty-five-year old Felipe, who was in Madrid trying to obtain a bureaucratic post for himself. At best the style of life of the factor was equivalent to that of a middle-ranking wholesale merchant.

Beyond corruption, favoritism, and factionalism, there was also a surprising degree of laxity demonstrated by the bureaucrats of Buenos Aires. The archive of the Tribunal de Cuentas, for example, that repository of the most important documents concerning the fiscal administration of the colony, was in a state of "total discomposition and abandon" by 1803.[42] Things had in fact gotten so bad that sometime in 1802 a newly named peon in the archive ("an indecent but salaried lad who was supposed to help move papers up and down") had taken advantage of his position and lack of supervision to extract "innumerable papers and documents . . . and to sell them in the confectioner's shops and other stores of this city." Although the ministers of the Tribunal later argued that nothing of worth was missing, their rather cavalier attitude toward the theft of government documents is somewhat surprising.

Royal official bureaucrats were always in the public eye, but there is little surviving evidence of how the people of Buenos Aires viewed their public officials, with perhaps one exception. This is the 1779 "anonymous seditious papers," a satire circulated among the leading citizens of Buenos Aires.[43] Included among those forty-seven individuals who were the butt of the satire were at least twenty bureaucrats ranging from the contador mayor of the Tribunal de Cuentas to the fiel administrador of the Almacenes de Tabaco.[44] While the level of the satire was rather infantile ("the imaginary beauty of the son of the vista [de Aduana, Juan de Vilanova], the eyeglasses of his father" or "the mouth and temperament of [Contador of Aduana Ignacio] Torrado"), some of the jokes were both pointed and cruel ("the toadying of [Francisco de Paula] Castellanos, [visitador of the Administración General de Tabacos]" or "the vanity of the army accountant [Francisco Cabrera] and the nostrils of his wife.") Historians have suggested that this parody was a reaction to a rise in the alcabala rate from four to six percent, but it should be noted that the largest group of bureaucrats ridiculed were tobacco monopoly employees. Viceroy Vértiz reacted strongly to the satire, probably because it made fun of so many public officials, and hunted down the culprits. Nevertheless, the inclusion of so many bureaucrats in the piece also attests to a degree of familiarity between these bureaucrats and the local elite. Some of those bureaucrats mentioned were native-born, and others had married local women. References to them, along with barbs at local merchants and military men, indicate that at least during the early days of the viceroyalty the bureaucrats were an integral part of local society. This sense of belonging lessened later in the period.

Although they never perceived their duties as going beyond providing efficient administration for the crown, colonial bureaucrats were in a very real sense public relations men for the metropolitan government. As representatives of the crown and as Spaniards of a certain class, racial purity, and birth, stringent norms of conduct were required of all. Unfortunately, those in positions of local power tended to become haughty, sometimes neglecting the day-to-day relationship with the inhabitants of Buenos Aires. Francisco Cabrera, contador mayor of the Tribunal de Cuentas from 1777 to 1796, acted with complete disregard for his neighbor, the widow María Magdalena de Vargas, when he persisted in having a drainage ditch built from the corral and stable of his home through an adjoining wall into the señora's property. The waters that flowed through this ditch were so foul and evil smelling that Doña María Magdalena's boarders were forced to seek other living arrangements, thus threatening her economic survival. She approached Cabrera but to no avail, and when in desperation she stopped up the ditch on her side of the dividing wall, the contador mayor lost no time in dispatching two fellow bureaucrats to her home. These gentlemen explained that if the widow failed to reopen the ditch, they would quickly bring the necessary men and wagons to the scene to restore Cabrera's draining system. Although she attempted to appeal to viceregal justice, Doña María was ineffective against Cabrera's clout.[45]

At times private disagreements exploded into public scandals, although in general bureaucrats attempted to keep their personal conflicts quiet so as not to endanger their careers. When these conflicts did erupt, verbal fireworks ensued, not only spewing invectives, but producing interesting insights into the bureaucratic mentality. Such a conflict existed between Antonio José Escalada, porteño-born canciller of the Real Audiencia, and merchant Manuel Antonio Warnes. Warnes, who had served as *alcalde de segundo voto* (vice-mayor) of the Buenos Aires Cabildo in 1786, has the distinction of being perhaps the most irascible citizen in colonial Buenos Aires.[46] Warnes was outspoken, arrogant, and willing to tangle with authority when he believed he was right (which seems to have been frequently) and his past dealings with Antonio José's late father, the merchant Manuel de Escalada, had produced a lasting animosity between him and all members of the Escalada family. In 1791 Antonio José and Joaquín Mosquera, an engineer commissioned to undertake a survey of lands belonging to the Temporalidades, were greeted by a wrathful Warnes when they attempted to step on his adjoining property. Warnes, the old merchant, not only seized the staff that Mosquera carried as a symbol of his authority, but attempted to strike Escalada with the weapon while hurling invectives against the canciller's lineage, upbringing, and personal conduct.[47]

Warnes's verbal attacks were not without foundation, for Antonio José was indeed an illegitimate child. Furthermore, Warnes, who had been sitting as *regidor* (town councilman) of the Buenos Aires Cabildo at the time that Antonio's father began proceedings to legitimize his two sons, was privy to much unflattering personal information about the family. His willingness to confront Escalada with some unpleasant truths "in front of a magistrate and so many other people" called for strong action. Escalada proceeded to press criminal charges against his detractor.

Escalada charged Warnes with attempting physical injury and with "wounding my honor, my person, and my very office." He argued that as "sealer, keeper of the secrets, deliberations, and mandates" of the Audiencia, he was due the privileges and honor of the position as stated in his royal título. Warnes had done more than attack him personally; Warnes had also attacked the honor of his position and, therefore, the honor of the king. Moreover, Warnes who had served as municipal magistrate and as such had received privileged information about the senior Escalada, had publicly betrayed the trust that had been given to him. "A judge must be prudent, politic, have good sense, and be subordinate to his superior, but we see in him insubordination, incivility, and offensiveness. How can anyone except justice, retribution according to law, or harmony between citizens, all things that a judge should work for, from this man?" Warnes had not only betrayed the Escalada confidence, he had forgotten that a "judge is obliged to set a good example. . . . [H]is private conduct might be one thing, but his public conduct must be prudent." Both Escalada's rights as a royal official and Warnes's duties as a local judge had been damaged by the latter's "monstrous actions."

As long as conflict was limited to a few individuals and corruption was kept within acceptable limits, there was little public hostility expressed toward the government and the crown. But by 1810 the bureaucrats themselves reflected a growing disenchantment with Spanish government. Fifty-two bureaucrats were invited to attend the Cabildo Abierto meeting, and forty-six remained at the sessions long enough to cast a vote.[48] The general summary of the bureaucratic vote was very similar to that of other participants. Seventeen bureaucratic participants (33 percent) supported the viceroy (as compared to 25 percent for the general population); and twenty-nine (or 56 percent) opposed his continued rule (compared to 60 percent for all participants). As a whole, bureaucrats showed slightly more support for the viceroy than the city's other outstanding citizens, but like the latter, a majority of bureaucrats voted publicly for an end to Cisneros's authority.

As table 8.1 illustrates, bureaucratic support for this first step toward independence varied greatly according to rank. High-level bureaucrats were in the majority loyal to the viceroy, although not quite as loyal as one

Table 8.1   Cabildo Abierto Vote of Porteño Bureaucrats

	Royalist	Independence	Abstain	Total
High-level bureaucrats	13	6	3	22
Low-level bureaucrats	2	12	0	14
Ancillary bureaucrats	2	11	3	16
Total	17	29	6	52
	(33%)	(56%)	(11%)	(100%)

would have expected. These men, heads of government agencies, contadores, and treasurers, had benefited both legally and extralegally from
Spanish control and wished to see it continue. They also realized that the
continued security of their social and professional position depended directly on a victory for Viceroy Cisneros. Nevertheless, more than 40 percent of the high-level officials chose either to support an end to Cisneros's
power or to refrain from voting.

Among low-level bureaucrats, clerks and escribientes, the voting pattern was markedly different. These men overwhelmingly opted for an end
to viceregal government. These were the men who had gained little from
the promise of the Bourbon reforms and who now showed themselves
willing to gamble that a change in government might better their fortunes.
The third group of government employees, composed of ancillary bureaucrats or contract employees, including escribanos, legal advisors, and purchased positions, adopted an attitude somewhere between the two groups
of bureaucrats. Although clearly supporting independence, as a group they
were not quite as ready as the low-level bureaucrats to end the system that
had employed them. A larger percentage of these men instead abstained
from voting. The vote of the ancillary bureaucrats is especially interesting
when compared to that of the low-level bureaucrats, for the former group
contained a higher percentage of native-born men than the latter. While
birthplace correlated with vote among the bureaucrats as a whole, this correlation was not particularly strong. In fact, Spanish-born low-level bureaucrats tended to vote against Cisneros, while native-born high-level bureaucrats supported him.

Although one could hardly expect the crown's bureaucrats to arm
themselves and take to the streets to defend royal government, the feeble

resistance to this first step toward independence offered by the loyal servants of the crown resulted, in part, from a growing disillusionment with the bureaucratic career. The ease with which porteños ended viceregal rule was both a demonstration of growing creole power and a reflection of the tenuous links between the royal bureaucracy and the local society. Those who had been most closely identified with the royal government were in an untenable position after May 1810, and the chief officials of all government agencies were forced to resign in the days following the establishment of the provisional junta.

Because of the ambivalent nature of the initial stages of Buenos Aires independence, the results of the Cabildo Abierto meeting of May 1810 did not produce a dramatic dismantling of the entire viceregal bureaucracy. While the viceroy and four members of the Real Audiencia were exiled within one month of the May meeting, several other bureaucrats remained in place for the next year or two. Indeed, the early revolutionary governments maintained both the form and nomenclature, as well as the staff itself, of several branches of the bureaucracy.[49] Not until late 1811 did the revolutionary junta feel itself firmly enough in command to begin dismissing more former viceregal bureaucrats. In that year Juan de Andrés de Arroyo, the contador mayor of the Tribunal de Cuentas, was exiled to Tucumán, and José Barrera, oficial primero of the Secretaría, was retired.[50] Rufino de Cárdenas, administrador general of the Real Renta de Tabaco, was dismissed by February 1812.[51]

Most of the Spanish-born bureaucrats departed Buenos Aires by 1813, for by then it had become evident that independence was a fait accompli that would not be easily reversed. The independence government, faced with the threat of a counterrevolution, had also begun to take on a more strident anti-Spanish tone. Nonetheless, some Spaniards remained in Buenos Aires loyal to the new government. For example, Francisco de Paula Saubidet, a native of Osuna, Seville, who had first come to the area with Francisco de Paula Sanz in 1777 and had subsequently been employed as oficial meritorio, oficial amanuense, and contador interventor in the tobacco agency, was promoted to administrador general of the same agency in February 1812. Within five months Saubidet took on American citizenship. He later was transferred to the Intendancy, where he served as secretary (1812), and then to the Tribunal de Cuentas, where he was employed as *contador séptimo de resultas* (seventh accountant for resolving accounts).

By 1821 Saubidet, an experienced bureaucrat who had had a lackluster career both before and after Independence, was charged with setting up the Archives of the Province of Buenos Aires.[52]

Other middle- and lower-ranking Spanish-born bureaucrats also stayed on after 1810, but even those who sympathized with the revolutionary movement or those married to local women often found that their birthplace automatically cast suspicion on their loyalty to the new government. Not only were many removed from office during the years following Independence, but they were increasingly seen as a fifth column by the porteño population. At times this suspicion was unfounded. In other instances, Spanish bureaucrats gave the new governments enough evidence to accuse them of treason. The most famous treason case in the years immediately following the 1810 Cabildo Abierto meeting was the Alzaga-Tellechea conspiracy, which resulted in the execution of, among others, Francisco de Valdepares, contador ordenador of the Tribunal de Cuentas from 1807 to 1812.[53] The discovery of this conspiracy and the harsh punishment meted out by the government served as a fair warning to other Spaniards that continued security did not lie in government service.

As late as 1817 criminal charges were brought against Tomás Saubidet, a "Spanish European" who had served as oficial tercero in the hacienda section of the Secretaría de Gobierno until 1810, for supposedly expressing traitorous words during a public gathering in San Isidro. According to informants, Saubidet had "accused the people of America of infidelity toward the man that he called their legitimate sovereign and lord, Don Fernando VII."[54] Only the personal intervention of José María Riera, a porteño-born merchant who testified that Saubidet was only jesting, saved the ex-bureaucrat from punishment.

It is not surprising that those porteños who had risen within the viceregal bureaucracy also continued to advance their careers after Independence. Indeed, the succession of local governments that followed the events of 1810 were sorely in need of a corps of experienced bureaucrats to take over the day-to-day running of the province. The local-born bureaucrats, although few in number, found that they now were able to progress rapidly within the bureaucratic structure. An example illustrative of the gains that porteños could and did make within the bureaucracy after Independence is provided by the career of José Joaquín Araujo. Araujo, born in Buenos Aires in 1762, attended the Colegio de San Carlos and then, at age seventeen, began work as a *meritorio* in the Real Hacienda. By 1786 the young man had gained the regular salaried position of *oficial escribiente* in the Tesorería General of the Reales Cajas. For the next twenty-six years Araujo continued to work in the Reales Cajas, following the general path of slow promotion to *primer escribiente* of the Contaduría (1792), *oficial tercero* of Contaduría (1799), and then *oficial segundo* (1808).[55] A more than adequate civil servant, Araujo also ghost-authored the 1803 *Guía de Forasteros*, which was published as the work of the *visitador general* Diego de la Vega.

In 1810 Araujo, a forty-eight-year-old lower-level bureaucrat threw in his lot with the Independence government. He was quickly promoted to *oficial mayor* of the treasury (1810) and then to interim treasurer of the Reales Cajas, a post he continued to hold when the "royal" was removed from the institution's title.[56] Clearly, a loyal patriot could make more career progress under the new regime.

Justo Pastor Lynch was another *porteño* who profited directly from Independence, although in Lynch's case it is interesting to note that he did not support independence at the Cabildo Abierto meeting. Lynch, who had already showed ability and political shrewdness, had experienced great career upward-mobility during the viceroyalty. More than any other *porteño* of his generation, Lynch, who had risen to the post of *contador* of the Aduana and interim administrator, had reason to maintain his loyalty to the crown. This loyalty was clearly expressed in his vote; he publicly stated that he could see no reason to end the rule of Viceroy Cisneros at the present time.[57] But regardless of his Cabildo Abierto vote, Lynch was a highly trained *porteño*, and in his case the revolutionaries were more than willing to overlook his support of Spanish governance, for Lynch was also the brother-in-law of Juan José Castelli, an outspoken revolutionary leader. By 1811 Lynch was appointed *administrador* of the Buenos Aires Aduana, a post he held until his death in 1830.

Although the Bourbons envisioned an efficient bureaucracy composed of honest civil servants, the reality fell short of the ideal. Bureaucrats, especially those high-ranking ones with expensive tastes and the opportunity to sell their influence and power, seem to have increasingly engaged in corrupt practices with impunity. Although corruption and malfeasance never reached the levels of previceregal days, the Bourbon attempt to staff local government with salaried, loyal civil servants was less than successful. How much of this corruption was due to greed, how much due to the increasing perception on the part of bureaucrats that they were underpaid and lacking in opportunities for advancement, and how much due to the gradual tarnishing of the Caroline dream of reform is difficult to say. Clearly, the factionalism that also increased in the later years of the viceroyalty was as much a product of increasing frustration as it was of the overlapping layers of colonial bureaucracy.

Still, the concentration of corruption, although not factionalism and general malfeasance of office, in the higher ranks of the Buenos Aires bureaucracy is striking. The rank-and-file clerks and minor officials were never deeply involved in selling favors or in embezzling government funds. No doubt the highly stratified system of ranked positions and the competitive ambience generated by the almost total lack of professional mobility tended to keep contadores and clerks relatively honest. Paradoxically, those who most needed additional funds to live in a manner befitting their ranks were the least able to supplement their incomes in the traditional, honored Hispanic manner. They would eventually voice their discontent in the fateful Cabildo Abierto meeting, sealing their fate and that of the viceroyalty.

9. Conclusion

THE BUREAUCRATIC REFORMS THAT THE Bourbon monarchs introduced into the Río de la Plata at the end of the eighteenth century produced a public administration that combined elements of traditional bureaucracy with strikingly modern features. Spanish administrative reforms were based on French Bourbon models. Like the French, the aim of the reformation of the bureaucracy was to increase fiscal efficiency. In the most general terms the Bourbons were trying to institute a modern fiscal bureaucracy, a corps of government servants who followed general rules and prescribed routines of organized behavior.[1] Indeed, the various agency codes drawn up under the intendancy of Fernández stress a methodical division of the integrated activities of each agency and provided continuously operating offices, clearly defined spheres of competence, and a precise enumeration of official responsibilities and prerogatives. The system under which the fiscal bureaucrat worked was based in theory on a clear hierarchy of position, logical promotion, and reward for competence and longevity. Moreover, government administration was to be in the hands of a standing army of salaried employees.

Nonetheless, not all bureaucrats came under this reform, and the net result was a combination of modern officeholders with traditional ones. The new bureaucrats were the salaried employees of agencies such as the Real Hacienda, the Tribunal de Cuentas, and the Aduana, who were subject to specific royal instructions regulating their functions and duties, to disciplinary controls, and at least in theory, to transfer or promotion. The old bureaucrats were the escribanos, Audiencia canciller and staff, and special revenue collectors, offices that were ancillary to government agencies.

These men continued to purchase a proprietary title to their office, to transfer their offices at will (usually from father to son), to be virtually irremovable and largely unaccountable to the crown, and to maintain strong regional and local attachments.

This dichotomy between bureaucrats who were appointed to salaried positions and those who held purchased office was not always clearly reflected in their respective behavior patterns. New bureaucrats often acted like their more traditional colleagues. Although in theory members of the new bureaucracy were chosen according to personal qualifications, nepotism and favoritism continued to play a role in the recruitment and promotion patterns of bureaucrats. Furthermore, among both old and new bureaucrats the concept that office was the property of an individual continued to be respected.

The idea of office as property led to an absence of any coherent retirement system, for an individual could not be forced to surrender his property. It was also the root of much inefficiency if not outright corruption. The same concept also produced infinite numbers of interinos and substitutes who held precarious positions, receiving little or no salary while the incumbent, the rightful owner of the position, absented himself or returned to Spain to seek an even more important título. Indeed, not only the bureaucrats, but the crown itself displayed a great degree of ambivalence in structuring the new bureaucracy. While striving to reform the way in which they governed, the Bourbons were always bound, on one hand, by a bureaucracy traditional in its very nature and, on the other, a society conservative in its very essence.

Nonetheless, the bureaucrats of viceregal Buenos Aires serve in many ways as an example of government officials in early modern society. Like the model of the "pure" bureaucrat outlined in the work of Max Weber, they governed fixed jurisdictional areas, were engaged in regular activities, and functioned with a bureaucracy organized along the principles of office hierarchy and levels of graded authority.[2] Moreover, as part of the Bourbon reforms, Buenos Aires bureaucrats, like those in other areas of the Spanish empire, came to be dependent on fixed salaries as their official activity demanded their full working capacity. By the end of the eighteenth century, government officials received a regular pecuniary compensation that consisted of a salary based not on work done, but rather on status and function within a government agency. While old age security was not yet provided to them in the form of a pension, the government had included at least some members of the civil bureaucracy within a system that guaranteed widows' benefits to their families.

In other respects the internal functions of the bureaucrat also conformed to the Weberian model. The crown sought to base office management on principles of specialized training and the use of written documents or files. The general rules that governed the daily activities of any office were increasingly made more stable and more exhaustive; they were inculcated in all incoming trainees. Colonial bureaucrats accepted the duties, responsibilities, and discipline of their jobs in exchange for a secure existence.

But while the bureaucrats increasingly conformed to the modern ideal, it is doubtful that they succeeded in bringing the supposed advantages of bureaucratic organization to local government. Precision, speed, unity of purpose, and the elimination of the purely personal were never achieved with the degree of success predicted by Weber's model, if they were achieved at all. It is also doubtful that the new bureaucracy increased administrative efficiency, perhaps because efficiency was antithetical to a more strongly held goal of the Spanish crown, the protection of a model of government that preserved both authority and flexibility.[3]

The problem of personnel proved to be still another impediment to the ideal of administrative efficiency. Although in theory merit was to govern both the selection and professional advancement of the bureaucrat in Buenos Aires, the basic criteria soon became seniority coupled with influence back at court. The failure to devise a workable compromise between the principle of promotion by merit and that of promotion by seniority eventually proved to be more disillusioning than any other aspect of the system.

Although an individual's merit and training were theoretically important in obtaining a position within the bureaucracy, the Bourbons allowed merit to be transferred from one individual to another. A prestigious or important relative could transfer merit to a brother or nephew, helping a young man to gain entrance into the system. In Weberian terms, ascriptive values, that is, family connections, were openly recognized as a reason for bureaucratic appointment. Although papered over by the insistence on a more efficient bureaucracy, a modified patronage system continued to exist in appointing new bureaucrats to entry-level positions throughout the colonial period.

The Buenos Aires bureaucracy was not only undergoing reform, it was also increasing in size. Even with an ever-enlarged bureaucracy, demand for government positions in the viceroyalty always outstripped supply, hence the development and perpetuation of the meritorio system. But while an enlarged bureaucracy did attempt to provide some jobs for new aspirants, because of the lopsided nature of this bureaucracy's growth, advancement remained difficult as a greater number of low-ranking individuals competed for the same number of middle- and top-level appointments.

The establishment of the Buenos Aires viceroyalty not only increased the number of bureaucrats in this city, it also produced a profound and lasting change in the relationship of these bureaucrats to the local society. Before 1778 the few bureaucrats posted to the city had tended to be incorporated into local society, often through marriage to local women. The most important bureaucrats were thus allied to merchants and other local elites through marriage. This was a continuation of a pattern that dated back to the seventeenth century, when merchants often purchased bureaucratic posts making them and local bureaucrats virtually indistinguishable one from another. The old relationship had been mutually advantageous, for the bureaucrats gained a father-in-law and kin who could supply strong local connections. In addition, these kin often served as partners in the bureaucrats' commercial transactions, as well as providers of a mercantile network and information. The merchants, on the other hand, welcomed the addition of one member of the family who could exert subtle pressure on the local bureaucracy just in case they fell afoul of the law.

This alliance changed dramatically after 1778. There are several causes for the decline in marital alliances between bureaucrats and other local elites. First, the viceregal bureaucracy was larger, and its members formed more of a self-sufficient community because of their very numbers than the handful of officials who had found themselves in Buenos Aires in the earlier days. Second, this larger bureaucracy was composed in the main of poor clerks who had little influence, few connections, and no family ties. They could therefore offer little to either the merchants or other local elites as marriage partners for their nubile daughters. In addition, the low salaries of the vast majority of bureaucrats made marriage a financial impossibility. This was especially true for the Spaniards, who lacked a local support network that could supplement their meager incomes. Lastly, with the establishment of the platense viceroyalty, stronger royal control was exerted over all phases of government, including internal regulations con-

trolling the marriage of bureaucrats. The royal ideal of a disinterested bureaucracy was seen as directly threatened by local marriage, and legislation
attempted, at least in theory, to limit these alliances.

By the end of the viceregal period fewer bureaucrats were allied to
local elite families, but whether this affected the level of government corruption is difficult to determine. Throughout the Hispanic world the improvements promised by the reformist zeal of the Bourbons had miscar-
ried. In Buenos Aires professional frustration, low salaries, the rising cost
of living, and merchants eager to continue the 1790s era of true free trade
had no doubt created conditions propitious for corruption in at least the
top levels of local bureaucracy. The ideal of an uncorrupted, salaried bureaucracy failed to take Spanish fiscal reality, local mercantile pressure, and
human nature into consideration. High-ranking bureaucrats who were able
to enrich themselves had done so; their underlings caught in the web of
low salaries, little advancement, and high prices had gradually become dis-
affected. Few voices would be raised to defend Spain in the fateful Cabildo
Abierto meeting of May 1810.

The goal and effect of the Bourbon reforms in local societies in the New
World, a subject of research and debate for the last twenty years, is still far
from clear. The view of these reforms range from that of D. A. Brading, who
sees in these reforms a "revolution," an attempt to transform the government, economic structure, and society, to that of Jacques Barbier, who finds
that the reforms were essentially moderate if not conservative.[4]

Just as there is no clear consensus on the nature of the reforms, there
is no agreement on their effect. Brading views the reforms as having produced cataclysmic controversies in Mexico and sees the reforms as disastrous for local creole power.[5] Early reforms such as the ousting of the
Jesuits, were answered by urban riots. Later reforms split the colonial bureaucracy. Agencies created by the arch Bourbon reformer, José de Gálvez
(the excise bureaucracy and the tobacco monopoly), reflected Gálvez's mis-
trust (or hatred) of creoles. There Spaniards were used to fill the growing
cadre. On the other hand, the Hapsburg institutions, the treasuries, Audiencias, and the court of audit, embodied a creole resistance to these ill-
conceived reforms. In Mexico the reforms produced an uneasy relationship
between the two groups of institutions, as the Bourbon agencies sought to
render the Hapsburg ones either powerless or less creole. Brading sees the
Audiencia of Mexico, for example, becoming both more Spanish in com-

position and less powerful, as military men and fiscal officers shear off its traditional power. Even the viceroy was threatened by the Bourbon intendancy and superintendency. Nonetheless, "old men" and new institutions seemed ultimately to sabotage the Bourbon reforms as the creole-controlled Junta Superior de Real Hacienda successfully rendered both local and regional reform impotent.

Linda Salvucci, in her study on the José de Gálvez visita and the excise bureaucracy in Mexico, finds serious weaknesses in Gálvez's vision of imperial reform.[6] She faults him for rotating his protégés throughout the empire, failing to enforce the prohibition on marriage to local women, maintaining a fianza system that encouraged an alliance between bureaucrats and merchants, and keeping salaries so low that corruption was inevitable. Her view of the Gálvez reforms is that they were far less revolutionary than Brading has suggested. According to Salvucci, the reforms were weakened less by creole sabotage than by their initial limitations.

Jacques Barbier goes even further, seeing the reform program as an essentially moderate one and, at least in the case of Chile, one that produced no lasting change.[7] Behind the political struggles that the reforms initially generated he finds a continuation of the traditional power groups of Santiago. Instead of Brading's "new men," Barbier presents a Bourbon bureaucracy co-opted by a local elite and tied to the local power structure through marriage, kinship, economic interest, and corruption. While certain reforms also threatened to produce riots, the power of the Santiago elite was not threatened by the reforms. To Barbier political events in Chile during the supposed apogee of the Bourbon reforms are little more than business as usual, the same struggles between a local audiencia, a local cabildo, and the governor, all tied in some degree to the same cliques.

Part of the radical difference in the interpretation of the aims and goals of the reform program itself lies in the region studied by each historian. For Brading, looking at the reforms within the Mexican context, they were revolutionary indeed for Mexico had an entrenched elite that controlled Indian tribute and that was directly threatened by the new Bourbon system's fiscal and intendancy reforms. Santiago, on the other hand, was a smaller provincial society, further from the direct hand of a viceroy and a full-blown bureaucracy. Here the local elite successfully used direct and indirect influence to render the reforms meaningless.

In Buenos Aires the Bourbon reforms, although still pursuing the same aims of instituting a cohesive fiscal policy under more direct control from Spain, produced still another effect. Unlike both Mexico City, the center of the Spanish colonial empire, and provincial Santiago, there was only a weak local elite in place before the reform period. Indeed, although both Mexico City and Santiago boasted Audiencias, high courts that were often the focus of creole economic and political power, this institution did not exist in Buenos Aires before the reforms. Furthermore, Buenos Aires did not have a university, a strong clerical establishment, a strong *hacendado* group, or titled nobility, all natural foci of creole power. The only elite in Buenos Aires was a commercial one, and this group benefited greatly from the economic and commercial features of the reform package.

Although not always united on certain aspects of imperial and local trade policy, compared to the elite of either Mexico or Santiago, that of Buenos Aires was a cohesive group, a group with few aspirations outside of the commercial sphere. While it never hurt to have friends in high government office, the merchants were only interested in challenging those administrative policies that endangered their commercial profits. To the merchants of Buenos Aires the Bourbon reforms, be they "revolutionary" or "moderate," did not represent a threat but rather a new commercial opportunity.

Because the bureaucracy in place in Buenos Aires before the era of Bourbon reforms was so small, the crown could effectively create a new, larger, and isolated bureaucracy with limited ties to the local elite. No bureaucratic institution in Buenos Aires could be called a product of the Hapsburg era with the one possible exception of the Cabildo, but the Buenos Aires Cabildo was by the mid-eighteenth century little more than a council of merchants. Because a full bureaucracy was put in place, the viceroy was always the commanding figure of government, even during the internal struggle between viceroy and superintendent.

This isolation of the Buenos Aires bureaucracy did not prevent the emergence of power struggles within and between agencies or between individual bureaucrats, but these struggles rarely concerned the local elite to any great degree. Unlike Mexico or Chile, there was never any uprising in Buenos Aires, or any hint of mass dissatisfaction. Neither did the isolation prevent corruption of certain members of the bureaucracy, both those acting alone and with merchants; in Buenos Aires the corruption seems to have been motivated more by monetary gain than by personal or family loyalty. In Buenos Aires, like Mexico and Chile, the Bourbon reforms were limited, but unlike those other areas of the colonies, the limitations came more from changes in Spanish policy and the local frustrations of a complex and often unwieldy system than from active local opposition.

The preceding study of the Buenos Aires bureaucracy presents a view of the reforms and their impact on the bureaucracy and on local society that echoes neither that of Brading nor of Barbier. It suggests the great variation that metropolitan legislation had on the diverse worlds of colonial Spanish America. In the case of Buenos Aires, because the relationship between the bureaucrats and the local elite had changed, the viceregal officials were increasingly isolated. In one sense royal policy had in fact been too successful. When the breakdown of imperial ties began in Buenos Aires with the successful ousting of the British invaders in 1806, there were few powerful family or kin groups anxious to protect the bureaucratic offices of their members and few personal loyalties to soften the growing demands for more autonomy.

The expansion of the bureaucracy that followed the creation of the Viceroyalty of Río de la Plata engendered new employment opportunities for educated young men, but many soon came to realize that their entry and advancement in this system was severely limited. Instead of being able to demonstrate their capabilities and receive suitable monetary and career rewards, they came to see their path blocked by older men increasingly accused of widespread corruption. Perhaps the unfulfilled promise was ultimately more disheartening than no promise at all. When the cries of independence triggered by Peninsular events were heard in the Río de la Plata, a group of frustrated officials and ex-meritorios were only too eager to listen.

Appendixes

A   Viceroys and Intendants of the Río de la Plata

VICEROYS

1777–78	Pedro de Cevallos
1778–84	Juan José Vértiz y Salcedo
1784–89	Francisco Cristóbal del Campo, Marqués de Loreto
1789–95	Nicolás de Arredondo
1795–97	Pedro Melo de Portugal y Vilhena
1797–99	Antonio Olaguer Feliú (interim)
1799–1801	Gabriel de Avilés y del Fierro, Marqués de Avilés
1801–4	Joaquin del Pino y Rosas
1804–7	Rafael de Sobremonte, Marqués de Sobremonte
1807	Pascual Ruíz Huidobro
1807–9	Santiago Antonio María de Liniers y Bremont (interim)
1809–10	Baltasar Hidalgo y Cisneros

INTENDANTS

1778–83	Manuel Ignacio Fernández
1783–88	Francisco de Paula Sanz (superintendent)
1803–10	Domingo de Reynoso

B   Selected Bureaucratic Genealogies

1   THE ANDONAEGUI CLAN

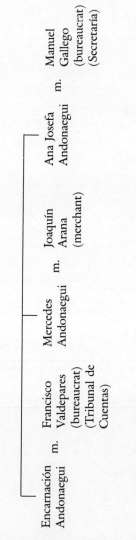

Encarnación Andonaegui m. Francisco Valdepares (bureaucrat) (Tribunal de Cuentas)

Mercedes Andonaegui m. Joaquín Arana (merchant)

Ana Josefa Andonaegui m. Manuel Gallego (bureaucrat) (Secretaría)

2   THE BASAVILBASO CLAN

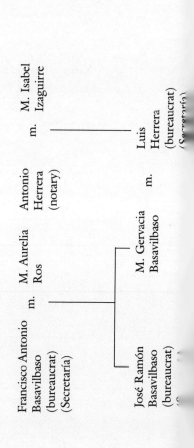

Francisco Antonio Basavilbaso (bureaucrat) (Secretaría) m. M. Aurelia Ros

José Ramón Basavilbaso (bureaucrat)

M. Gervacia Basavilbaso m. Antonio Herrera (notary)

Luis Herrera (bureaucrat) (Secretaría) m. M. Isabel Izaguirre

Agustín Pinedo (military; governor of Paraguay) m. M. Bartolina Arce

Juana Albizuri m. [Agustín José Pinedo]

Agustín José Pinedo (bureaucrat) — Juan Pablo Pinedo (lawyer) — Ana Gertrudis Pinedo m. Juan Andrés y Arroyo (superintendancy, Tribunal de Cuentas) — Rafaela Pinedo m. (1) Antonio José Pinedo Montufar (bureaucrat) (Real Hacienda); m. (2) José de Mendinyeta (bureaucrat) (Real Hacienda)

Ana Andres y Arroyo m. Juan Almagro de la Torre (military)

Agustín Pinedo (lawyer) m. Juana Irigoyen

José Pinedo (lawyer) — M. Damasia Pinedo m. Juan Isidro Casamayor (bureaucrat) (Secretaría) — Ambrosio Pinedo (lawyer) — Felipe Pinedo (priest)

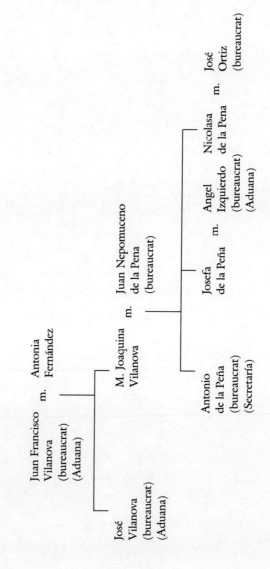

4 THE VILANOVA CLAN

Juan Francisco Vilanova (bureaucrat) (Aduana) m. Antonia Fernández

José Vilanova (bureaucrat) (Aduana)

M. Joaquina Vilanova m. Juan Nepomuceno de la Peña (bureaucrat)

Antonio de la Peña (bureaucrat) (Secretaría)

Josefa de la Peña m. Angel Izquierdo (bureaucrat) (Aduana)

Nicolasa de la Pena m. José Ortiz (bureaucrat)

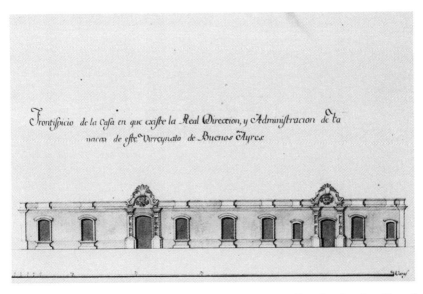

C.1 Front view of the Real Renta de Tabaco building, Buenos Aires, housing the offices of the Dirección General and the Administration of the Buenos Aires district, 1779. (AGI, Mapas y planos, Buenos Aires 125.)

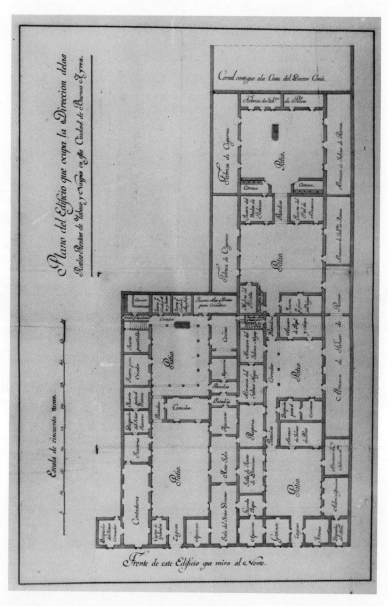

C.2   Floor plan of the Real Renta de Tabaco building, Buenos Aires (AGI, Mapas y planos, Buenos Aires 124-A.)

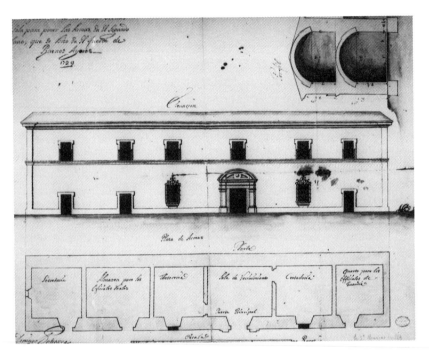

C.3 Front view and floor plan of an administrative wing within the Buenos Aires fort, constructed to house the Reales Cajas, 1729. (AGI, Mapas y planos, Buenos Aires 43-A.)

D Government Agencies

Real Hacienda

The Real Hacienda was the major fiscal agency of the Spanish crown. Before 1778 the Buenos Aires branch of the Real Hacienda, a so-called caja real, consisted of five employees (a contador, tesorero, and factor oficial who were the chief officials, an alguacil mayor, and one *oficial real*). Until 1767 Buenos Aires served as a caja principal, which in addition to preparing its own accounts also forwarded accounts and income from local suboffices (cajas subordinadas) on to Lima.[1] In that year, with the creation of a contaduría general in Buenos Aires, Buenos Aires accounts and income, along with those of Tucumán and Paraguay, began to be reviewed by the new local accounting agency and then dispatched directly to Spain. With a contaduría de cuentas now sitting in the same city as a caja, Buenos Aires treasury officials found themselves under more direct bureaucratic scrutiny.

As Buenos Aires emerged as a more autonomous financial unit within the Spanish colonial world, an attempt was made to improve the quality and appointment of caja officials. Prior to 1750 *ministro* appointments (i.e., contador, tesorero, and factor oficial) were either openly purchased from the Royal Treasury, for sums ranging from 2,000 to 4,000 pesos or awarded to repay outstanding royal debts. Purchase of appointment to government office, especially that of local treasury ministro, was a frequent investment made by *porteño* merchants for themselves and their sons. As such it was clearly expected to produce a handsome profit. After taking office ministros continued to engage in commerce, sometimes being prosecuted for smuggling while they held their posts. After 1750 these posts were no longer sold but were rather awarded to individuals for service to the crown. Nonetheless, corruption continued.

At the same time as a contaduría general was put in place, an attempt was made to reform the cajas and to force the most profligate ministros out of office. In 1770 Governor Francisco de Paula Bucareli moved against the three highest-ranking cajas bureaucrats, Martin José Altolaguirre, Pedro Medrano, and Juan de Bustinaga, suspending them from their offices for "suspected fanaticism."[2] As with many other Bourbon attempts at house-cleaning, initial results were ambiguous, in part because the crown, while supporting reform, was loathe to ignore the legal rights of its bureaucrats.

Bucareli's suspension was in effect for only two years, for the men so unceremoniously removed from office were able to appeal successfully to the new governor, Juan José Vértiz, who reinstated them. Back in office these ministros continued to press for royal censure of Bucareli's actions and for receipt of the salaries withheld while they were out of office. The ministros were finally vindicated by a Royal Order of 15 November 1791, which approved Viceroy Nicolás de Arredondo's earlier decision to pay the salaries withheld during the suspension. Furthermore, "because of the fact that the said ministers suffered greatly in faithfully carrying out the duties of their offices, and [because of] the huge expenses incurred as a result of the unjust persecution to which they were subjected," special consideration was to be given to both the surviving ministers and the children of any now deceased in obtaining employment in the Real Hacienda.[3] Nevertheless, new standards of professionalism demanded of Hacienda employees were made clear from 1776 on.

In 1776 the final step in raising the cajas of Buenos Aires to a full-fledged Real Hacienda occurred as part of the creation of the La Plata Viceroyalty when the cajas were split off from the Contaduría de Cuentas. Now called the tesorería de reales cajas (or the tesorería general de ejército y Real Hacienda) the cajas staff ballooned from five to twenty paid employees by 1779. The staff was responsible for collecting, accounting, and disposing of revenue within the viceroyalty.[4] The expanded tesorería consisted of a contador, a tesorero, a factor, and an ensayor mayor on the managerial level. All other employees worked in one of four sections: a mesa de real hacienda (with four oficiales), the veedoría (with another seven oficiales), the mesa de ejército (employing two staff members), and the contaduría de intervención (with another two clerks). One portero was also employed.

Some minor shifting of managerial personnel occurred between 1779 and 1785, and a three-man section charged with Patagonian accounts was also added. In 1788 another managerial post, that of contador interventor agregado, was temporarily added. By 1790 the Hacienda was reorganized into three sections (contaduría, tesorería, and almacenes) and some personnel was shifted to other agencies. The next year royal permission was granted for the creation of two new positions, those of contadores de dinero.[5] In 1798 three positions previously part of the Temporalidades were annexed to the Real Hacienda. In addition the retasas section of the Tribunal was shifted to Hacienda and its staff increased from one to five. Other minor clerkships were also added. By 1803 the Hacienda employed twenty-seven salaried bureaucrats. Nevertheless, Hacienda officials echoed their colleagues in the Tribunal de Cuentas by requesting additional personnel to handle the ever-growing accounts.

Aduana

The Real Aduana (Royal Customs Agency) was an agency that benefited from the increased importance of the Río de la Plata to the Spanish crown and the new commercial importance of the platense region. The founding of the viceroyalty in 1776 was quickly followed by an extension of comercio libre to the port of Buenos Aires in 1778. Prior to 1778 customs functions had been exercised by the Real Hacienda, which was charged with inspecting cargo and collecting revenues on the ships that called in the port. After 1778, with Buenos Aires now a port legally permitted to engage in trade with the rest of the Spanish world, a separate branch of bureaucracy, the Aduana, was created. Within three months of the issuing of the royal order that expressed the royal intention to establish a Buenos Aires Customs House, five officials were dispatched from Spain to take over the new institution and an employee of the local reales cajas was moved to the new division.[6]

At the time of the creation of the Aduana the intendant of Buenos Aires, Manuel Fernández, was charged with drawing up a list of customs duties to be administered by the Aduana, "for one of the most important responsibilities of the Aduana has to be evaluating goods in order to decide what percentage of value should be charged in duties."[7] By mid-February of 1779 Fernández issued this list, contained in his reglamento. This document, in addition to setting forth the rules governing the local customs service, spelled out in great detail the procedures to be followed in dispatching or receiving goods via land or sea.[8] At the same time Fernández also issued his instrucciones, governing the conduct and responsibilities of all Aduana employees.[9]

Although chiefly a customs tax collecting agency, the Buenos Aires Aduana from its creation in 1778 also had key policymaking functions. The Aduana was to be consulted by viceroy and intendant in important financial matters affecting the Royal Exchequer. Although not the only source of government revenue, the Aduana was expected to generate a profit from which a large portion of the funds expended on viceregal administration would come.[10] More than any other local agency the Aduana seems to have met this expectation. Before 1777 customs revenue never exceeded 20,000 pesos per year. From 1778 to 1804 customs revenues grew from approximately 54,000 to 1,000,000 pesos per year, a reflection of the growing Río de la Plata trade.

The Royal Aduana's most important role was collecting a series of taxes for the Royal Treasury, some of which were perceived as belonging to the treasury's general fund, while others were earmarked for special government funds. Those taxes included in the first category were part of the "masa comun" of viceregal finances and were turned over to the Royal Treasury, which was in charge of their dispersal. The latter group of funds, further subdivided into "ramos particulares" and "ramos ajenos," were reserved for specific ends, either in the colony or in Spain.[11]

The Aduana not only collected customs duties, it also was responsible for exacting fines levied against merchants found participating in illicit or clandestine operations. These fines comprised the ramo de comisos. In addition, merchants were required to pay the Aduana for its services, especially for drawing up official documentation on legal shipments (*producto de guías*) and for storing goods in its warehouse (*producto de eslingajo*).[12] The growth of the Aduana's overseeing ramos particulares reflect the attempt made during the first decade of the nineteenth century to generate increased royal revenues through new taxes while also transferring the collection of several local duties to one viceregal agency.

Following the creation of the Aduana in Buenos Aires and the free trade laws of 1778, the crown had initially attempted to rationalize tariffs through the institution of uniform rates. The reglamento enforced by the newly created Aduana not only lowered several duties, but unified the hodgepodge of different taxes that were slapped on any one good. Unfortunately, this uniform rate proved difficult to preserve as Bourbon administrators fell back on the old remedies of special tariffs, levies, and taxes when faced with economic exigencies either in the viceroyalty or at home.[13] In addition to the adverse effect that these taxes had on commerce, the amount of paperwork required of the Aduana staff became ever more formidable. In general, throughout the entire viceregal period the tendency was to increase the number of small accounts that were under the supervision of the Aduana staff.

Collection and accounting of these taxes comprised only part of the duties under the Aduana's jurisdiction. In addition, the Aduana was in charge of moving goods from shipboard to its warehouses and thence into the hands of individual merchants. Goods had to be inspected and documented as they moved through the Aduana, thus creating additional paperwork for the agency. Aduana employees prepared the guías and tornaguías that accompanied merchandise and kept track of merchandise on which duty was to be paid at some inland destination, as well as those accounts being paid in installments. In addition to keeping accounts of the various ramos under its supervision, from 1779 to 1803 the Aduana was also charged with keeping four major sets of books: administración, contaduría, tesorería, and alcaide, divided into yearly entries.

In 1804, in an attempt to reorganize bookkeeping practices and better accounting for its overall activity, the Aduana was ordered to discontinue keeping books by these four major categories and instead reorganize their accounts along more general lines. Most important of these newer books was the libro mayor, kept in original and duplicate, a chronological listing of all funds entering the Aduana that specified the ramos to which the funds were credited. Another book, the libro manual, also kept in duplicate, recorded all movement of funds either into or out of the Aduana, including salaries, rent, and transfer of funds to the Royal Treasury. Less inclusive than either of these two books were the two auxiliary books, one used to note the import of merchandise and the other the export, with their corresponding payments. In addition, four books were to be used to record individual shipments entering or leaving the city by either land or sea. Like all government agencies, personnel ledgers, including a book of tomas de razón, recording all official bureaucratic appointments was to be kept. Copies of all codes governing the organization of the Aduana and its tariff structure were also to be on hand, as were all royal orders and cédulas concerning the administration or tax policy of the customs bureau. Furthermore, the Aduana, like all viceregal institutions was also commissioned to keep a series of books relating to its internal organization and staff.

Early plans had called for a small Aduana staff consisting of an administrator who was to work with one accountant, one customs inspector, one treasury clerk, and a two-man accounting staff. These men were quickly overwhelmed by the amount of work placed under their jurisdiction by the Aduana reglamento, for the Aduana had to keep the aforementioned series of ledgers detailing revenue and expenses in addition to inspecting cargo, assessing duties, and collecting them. By 1779 two more men were added to the accounting staff, and the same number joined the treasury section. In addition, three mozos de confianza and a receptor de alcabalas were employed. By 1780 an additional staff member, an alcaide, was added to the Aduana. The same year a receptor de sisa was named along with an escribiente de alcabalas. So desperate was the Aduana for additional help that, while they awaited the arrival of another new tesorería official, a temporary appointment was made. Another two contaduría clerks and a fourth mozo de confianza were added before the end of the year.

Like almost all viceregal bureaucratic agencies, regardless of the delay in salary raises, the Aduana's duties and its need for personnel continued to grow. From the beginning it was clear to Intendant Fernández that a strong branch office had to be established in Montevideo, the principal ocean port of the region. Although faced with local pressure to name a bureaucrat employed by the Montevideo cajas who was also related to the principal commercial families of the city, Fernández was able by 1780 to complete his own staffing of the Montevideo customs house. In addition, a resguardo de mar charged with policing the local harbors and intercepting ships engaged in contraband activity was created in Montevideo. Both institutions remained under the jurisdiction of the Buenos Aires Aduana until 1794, but in general there was little movement of personnel from one agency to another.

A war-caused slowdown in legal trade produced a slacking of Aduana transactions in 1781, but the Aduana administrator continued to call for an increase in the number of personnel employed in the customs division. After receiving a request to present complete accounts to the Tribunal de Cuentas for the first two years of operation, Aduana Director Francisco Ximénez de Mesa appealed to the intendant to increase his staff by naming oficiales de pluma of "sufficient instruction and capacity in the necessary number" to the Aduana staff. Ximénez de Mesa admitted that he himself lacked the necessary experience to provide a full accounting to the Tribunal and then proceeded to detail the work load of his clerks, which made it impossible for them to attend to the required reporting.[14]

The Aduana director's request to increase the size of his staff, similar to all never-ending pleas from those in charge of the other branches of the colonial bureaucracy, was reviewed by the Junta General de Real Hacienda, which unanimously decided to deny his request. Instead, the Junta General suggested a modification in the internal organization of the Aduana. All oficiales were now to be assigned to one of two branches, either contaduría or administración y tesorería. Contaduría was clearly the more important internal division and was to be staffed by five clerks. Administración y tesorería, by contrast, was to have only two oficiales.

In 1788 a major scandal directly involving Ximénez de Mesa, chief of the Aduana, was uncovered. Ximénez de Mesa was found to be embezzling Aduana revenues and investing them in illegal commercial transactions.[15] The scandal was followed by a lengthy investigation of Aduana personnel, procedures, and organization. As a result, a minor shake-up of Aduana personnel was carried out and a more thorough restructuring of the customs bureaucracy was begun. The reform centered on the Resguardo de Mar for its chief, Ortega, had been deeply involved in the Ximénez case. Indeed, it was because of lax Resguardo supervision that Ximénez and his cohorts had been able to introduce large shipments of contraband goods into the area.[16] Royal determination to tighten its control on the Resguardo was thus strengthened. On 14 July 1794 a new instrucción was issued governing the Resguardo; this reform unified the Resguardo de Mar with the Resguardo de Tierra.[17] Two semi-independent agencies thus became one, to be known henceforth as the Rentas Unidas; the new agency still fell under the Royal Aduana.

Unfortunately, the Rentas Unidas soon proved to be an unwieldy agency. In addition, the new chief, Antonio Rute, was hardly more satisfactory than the old one. In 1802 Rute was removed from his post, and a new set of regulations again setting up a separate Resguardo de Mar were enacted.[18] Further internal modifications were made the next year, mainly concerned with the adjustment in the multiplicity of books that the Resguardo was required to keep.[19] Regardless of these reforms, the Resguardo never effectively controlled contraband and smuggling during the viceregal period.

One additional result of the Ximénez de Mesa embezzlement was a renewed attempt to rationalize the different departments within the Aduana. New regulations clearly established which oficiales were to be involved in which transactions. In 1789 the contaduría section was subdivided into accounting and copying departments; the former section continued to employ five clerks while the latter consisted of four men designated oficiales escribientes de contaduría. Soon after, a second customs inspector, a receptoría with two clerks, and an accountant of cash money (contador de plata) were created. By 1790 the staff of the Aduana had grown to twenty-four, but the most important division beneath the administrative section continued to be that of contaduría.[20] In 1798 the Temporidades staff was incorporated into the Real Hacienda. One further administrative adjustment was made in 1798 when administración y tresorería, which had been one division, was divided into two.

Although undergoing repeated internal reorganization, the number and quality of employees continued to be a constant problem for the Aduana administrator, or at least a readily seized justification for the delays that plagued the Aduana in keeping up with its mounting paperwork. In 1804 the new director, José Proyet, wrote to the viceroy that while reorganizing the agency's bookkeeping he had discovered "a multitude of papers," export lists, that had yet to be transferred to their respective books and canceled. Some of these lists were more than ten years old.[21] Proyet blamed the lack of trained personnel (there were too few employees, and those on hand were generally incompetent) and the lack of specific instructions given to the treasurer, Pedro Nolasco Vigueras, who seemed to be guiding himself by rules that he made up as he went along. Responding to this state of affairs, Viceroy Sobremonte named two temporary clerks to the Aduana. An enlarged staff coupled with new bookkeeping methods allowed Proyet to improve Aduana accounting at least temporarily.

Contaduría de Propios

The Contaduría was charged with supervising the collection and expenditure of municipal funds, and in turn reporting periodically to the Junta Superior de Propios y Arbitrios, which supervised the Contaduría. The agency, although small, was among the most unpopular branches of the royal bureaucracy. It was much resented by local Cabildos, which, although lacking financial autonomy and severely limited in the taxes they could impose, had traditionally supervised their own accounts.[22] Municipal finances tended to improve after the establishment of the intendancy system, with Buenos Aires showing especially impressive growth, but the existence of an agency that monitored yearly Cabildo receipts was a constant bone of contention.

Between its separation from the Tribunal de Cuentas in 1783 and its reincorporation into the Tribunal de Cuentas in 1791, the Contaduría de Propios in Buenos Aires employed one contador and two to four oficiales. In addition, because they were also to supervise Cabildos throughout the reign, receptores were appointed in the major provincial cities, who in return for a commission were responsible for collecting and transferring funds from local Cabildos to the Contaduría. Of special interest to both the receptor and the Contaduría was the collection of a tax on the Cabildo's total receipts payable to the Contaduría and thence to the Royal Treasury.

The Secretarías

The Viceroy's Secretaría, the agency that performed his clerical tasks, experienced great growth after 1778, although it existed in an attenuated form under the rule of the governors.[23] Throughout the early eighteenth century, governors of the Río de la Plata had used individuals, usually members of their personal staff, to help in the conduct of administrative tasks. In addition, a series of individuals were employed as asesores generales y auditores de guerra, a dual position awarded to trained lawyers who provided legal and military advice to the governor. While both private secretaries and asesores made up a skeleton administrative staff, only the latter received a fixed salary from the Royal Exchequer. The governor's secretary was paid whatever amount the governor settled upon him; in addition, he was paid out of the governor's pocket, a condition that encouraged several governors to reward their secretary with minor government commissions that could provide alternate sources of funding.[24]

With the creation of a viceroyalty in Buenos Aires, this embryonic secretariat was converted into a full-fledged government agency staffed by a secretary and clerks. The Royal Order of 30 July 1776 set up a Secretaría de Cámara y del Virreinato modeled on the same agency created in Mexico in the 1750s. The secretariat was to consist of five individuals—a secretary and three oficiales, as well as the asesor general, all appointed and paid by the crown. This agency, functioning although still not fully staffed by October 1777, was charged with aiding the viceroy in managing the growing paperwork generated by his administrative duties: the correspondence, consultas (written reports), licencias (requests for special licenses), and petitions that daily passed across the chief executive's desk.[25]

From the earliest days of the La Plata viceroyalty the crown sought to professionalize this institution. The crown's goal was to create an independent secretariat, more dependent on the crown than on any individual viceroy, while also limiting the viceroy's ability to place friends and family in colonial government. Governors had always named their own secretaries, and because of the close working relationship between the secretary of the viceroyalty and the viceroy, the latter hoped to nominate his own candidate for this job as well as other Secretaría staff posts. The crown, anxious to increase government efficiency and to limit the degree to which a viceroy could function as a satrap, was equally determined that both secretary and staff should become regular line positions filled by a royal nominee who would hold office during the tenure of several viceroys. This divergence of views produced a twofold conflict over the nominations of secretary and staff that began with Viceroy Cevallos and was not fully resolved until the nomination of a permanent secretary in 1790.[26]

The easier of the two issues to solve was that of professionalizing the secretariat's staff. Although Viceroy Cevallos had staffed the Secretaría with his appointees, as soon as Vértiz took office he dismissed all of Cevallos's people and replaced them with his own men. (Vértiz uniformly chose men who had served under him during his governorship, men who had been dismissed when Cevallos had taken office.) Some of those who had come to power with Cevallos attempted to challenge Vértiz's actions, but although unsuccessful in obtaining their old positions, they did provide the crown with the opportunity to declare the staff to be fixed in the future. From Viceroy Loreto on, the secretariat was served by an office staff (oficiales and archivero) that did not change with the arrival of each new viceroy. In essence, those bureaucrats below the rank of secretary who were appointed by Vértiz formed the core of the secretariat staff for much of the viceregal period.

The secretariat took form under Viceroy Cevallos, but it was the second viceroy to the Río de la Plata, José Juan Vértiz, who, goaded by the crown's desire to improve administration, concentrated on improving the secretariat's efficiency. Four months after his secretario, Rafael Sobremonte, arrived in Buenos Aires, the viceroy asked him to report on the state of the agency. Sobremonte's brief report outlined a series of defects that he had encountered.[27]

Sobremonte's first duty as secretary had been to review all correspondence between governors and viceroys and the crown. Vértiz was especially interested in locating and ordering all royal orders, which had up to then been filed in a rather chaotic form; Gálvez had recently sent instructions on how royal cédulas were to be stored—"by title and subject to make things clearer and easier to find."[28] Sobremonte located existing indexes within the Secretaría and then recommended that a major effort be undertaken to keep all royal orders together and to produce a comprehensive index, thereby facilitating the use of these important documents. The only problem was the "lack of people who write in this secretariat."[29] In fact, "there is no one who can work exclusively on the indexing task because everyone is busy just trying to keep all the papers in some sort of order."[30] Of course, the Secretaría needed more personnel. After reviewing the staff of the Lima secretariat, Sobremonte suggested that a total of five clerks (four oficiales and an archivero) be employed in Buenos Aires. "These positions never seem more necessary here than when we have to duplicate, triplicate, and even quadruplicate oficios and documents in our correspondence with the Ministry."[31] Although Vértiz had already detailed a loyal military officer to help in the Secretaría ("a man without whose help this job would have been impossible"[32] according to Sobremonte), still more positions were needed. Furthermore, the Secretaría had no portero to assure the necessary formality and order in carrying out the Secretaría's business with the public. "Those who come to request licencias or enter the Secretaría for any sort of business can march right into the room in which we work, bother those who have their desks right there, and, even more, observe things that should be secret. There is no one to take care of the entrance, clean the rooms, nor do any of the other duties of this job."[33]

Viceroy Loreto's secretario and nephew, Andrés de Torres, although later accused of being a rather inept administrator, continued Sobremonte's efforts to maintain some order among the ever-growing stacks of official papers. Sobremonte had turned over the government files complete with an inventory and an alphabetical index of reales disposiciones, and Torres now amplified the system by producing a new index for matters that were not included in specific legajos.[34] Torres was also interested in the conservation of the official papers and made several efforts to preserve all records already on hand. Many of the files that had become humid because of storage conditions in the offices of the Secretaría were aired out and recovered. All royal letters patent and duplicates of royal orders (reales cédulas y reales ordenes duplicadas) were also bound in leather.

The crown had little trouble staffing the Secretaría with career bureaucrats but found it more difficult to implement this same policy when it came to the Secretaría's chief administrator, the viceregal secretary. Although the secretary was now to be a salaried government employee, early viceroys followed the precedent established during the days of the captaincy-general. The governor's secretary had always been a man chosen by the governor, a close and trusted acquaintance who was paid by the governor himself. In 1779 Viceroy Vértiz, who had earlier served as governor of the Río de la Plata, attempted to name his candidate, the interim secretary, Antonio de Aldao to the permanent post. The crown refused to approve this appointment and instead named the Marqués de Sobremonte, a Spanish military officer, to serve as secretary.[35] But once the crown successfully established its jurisdiction over the choice of viceregal secretary, it failed to consistently maintain this policy. In 1784 Viceroy Loreto was allowed to name his nephew to the post of secretary instead of being forced to accept a crown candidate. Only in 1790, with the unification of the secretariats and the naming of Manuel Gallego as permanent secretary, was crown jurisdiction again established, but because Gallego did not take office until 1795, Viceroy Arredondo, like his predecessor Loreto, also named a personal favorite to the secretary's position.

While professionalizing the post and providing continuity between viceregal reigns, this change, which in essence placed the secretario on the same permanent footing as all other agency chiefs, destroyed the special confidential relationship that had existed up to then between the governor or viceroy and his secretary. From 1795 to 1808 any viceroy who distrusted Gallego had only one course of action: bypass the Secretaría in communicating with the crown. This seems to have been the route followed by Viceroy Avilés who employed Miguel José Lastarria, a Peruvian-born lawyer, as private secretary and advisor, and his successor Viceroy Joaquín del Pino, who preferred to use his two sons as informal secretaries.[36] According to local reports, del Pino so distrusted Gallego that he refused to give him knowledge of several matters that should have been under his jurisdiction.[37] Paradoxically, the end result of the crown's control of the secretario position was to force viceroys to return to the older system of using non-official employees paid out of private funds as the true viceregal secretary.

Shortly after the establishment of the viceregal Secretaría, another separate but parallel agency, the Secretaría de la Intendencia (later Superintendencia) de la Real Hacienda was also created in Buenos Aires. This secretariat, also consisting of a secretary and three clerks, served the intendant (later superintendent) in the same fashion as the Secretaría del Virreinato served the viceroy. Specifically, this secretariat was charged with providing aid to the intendants as he oversaw the development of the local economy, maintained contact with the crown and local agencies on the state of viceregal finances, and administered those aspects of institutional life under his jurisdiction. Correspondence about agencies under the superintendent's supervision, such as the Real Renta de Tabaco, the Aduana, the Real Renta de Azogues (Royal Mercury Monopoly), and development projects such as the colonization of the Patagonian coast, made up a major portion of the work of this secretariat.

Viceroys fought to name their own secretaries because of the supposed need for trust and secrecy between these close-working collaborators, but no such demand was made by the superintendent on his secretary. This post was professionalized from its inception, and one man served as secretary of the Superintendencia y Real Hacienda from its founding in 1777 to its disbandment in 1788. Perhaps this is why the superintendent's secretariat not only found it easier to get royal approval for additional staff positions but was provided with funds for general expenses.[38] Interestingly, all three officials appointed to the secretariat by Intendant Fernández transferred to other agencies during his last year in office. As all three had accompanied the first intendant when he arrived in Buenos Aires as Cevallos's comisario de guerra (and indeed one of them was a close blood relative), it is probable that Fernández used his influence to promote them before his successor took office.

In addition to staff, the secretariat also needed money, for in setting up the office the crown had failed to provide funds for the everyday "office expenses" such as paper, ink, and wax that were necessary to transact business. Sobremonte requested 400 pesos for these expenses, the same amount paid to the secretariat in Lima. He stressed that "there is absolutely no way in which the secretary can cover these expenses and still keep himself decently clothed and housed."[39] Although Viceroy Vértiz forwarded Sobremonte's report to Jose de Gálvez, minister of the Indies, no action was forthcoming on his recommendations until 1793. In 1797 the secretaría finally got permission to employ an archivero.

The development of the secretary of the superintendent and secretary of the viceroyalty is an excellent example of the escalation of bureaucratic staffing and salary in the years following the founding of the viceroyalty. A department originally employing one or two individuals who enjoyed the confidence of the governor and who were paid from the governor's pocket had evolved by 1784 into two Secretarías, one of Cámara and another of Real Hacienda, staffed by nine bureaucrats receiving salaries totaling more than 9,500 pesos per year from the Royal Exchequer, plus two legal staffs.[40] The two Secretarías existed as completely autonomous units, each one serving its respective master until 1788. When the Superintendency was disbanded by Royal Order of 9 May 1788, the Secretaría de Superintendencia was transferred to the viceroy's direct jurisdiction. But this did not result in a more streamlined organization. The same year an oficial quinto was added to the Secretaría de Real Hacienda, joining the oficial cuarto who had been authorized in 1784. For the next four years two secretariats, both staffed independently by secretarios and oficiales, labored under the viceroy's direction.

In 1792 the crown moved to improve the efficiency of the secretariats: by Royal Order of 19 May 1792 one unified Secretaría was created from the two institutions. Actually unification occurred only at the top of the agency, with one secretary instead of the two who had previously been in charge overseeing all employees. Under this secretary came all matters dealing with the colonial bureaucracy, be it hacienda, justicia, gobierno, or guerra. The clerks now found themselves working in one of two departments, Gobierno y Guerra or Hacienda. Although now a unified agency, the separation of personnel of these two departments was maintained as were separate pay scales. Until the end of the viceroyalty, the department of Gobierno employed three clerks while that of Hacienda was staffed by five men. In addition, an officially sanctioned post of archivero was added to the unified Secretaría in 1797, although such functions had been filled informally by military men on special assignment since 1778.[41]

Although unification of the two Secretarías resulted in the elimination of the position of secretario de Real Hacienda, the number of men working in the unified secretariat continued to grow. By 1809 twenty-one officials were employed in the Secretaría, including ten permanent staff members, seven bureaucrats or military men on special assignment, and four trainees.[42] The Secretaría, like all colonial agencies, believed itself perpetually short of help, but because of its proximity to the viceroy it was in a better position to remedy this shortage. It was the only agency that could either draft military men or transfer *agregados con sueldo* (salaried assistants) from other agencies when additional help was needed. While these solutions allowed the viceroy to meet his administrative duties without straining his budget, they tended to further exacerbate the difficulties felt by those agencies losing manpower to the Secretaría.

Both secretariats also had despachos judiciales charged with providing legal guidance and expertise in all matters before the viceroy or superintendent. The despacho judicial of the Secretaría de Cámara was headed by a lawyer who held the position of asesor general. To the extent that the viceroy exercised judicial power in matters pertaining to government, church, and the treasury, his asesor general actually served as a judge, deciding or at least drafting the viceroy's opinion. From the beginning of the eighteenth century all those appointed asesores generales also served as *auditores de guerra* (military legal advisors). Before 1776 the asesor general had also acted as interim governor. In effect, the creation of the viceroyalty and that of the Audiencia deprived the asesor general of this seldom-used but nonetheless important political power, relegating him to purely legal and judicial matters. But while the more highly articulated viceregal bureaucracy limited the asesor general's immediate opportunity to exercise power, the creation of an Audiencia enhanced future career opportunities for those legal advisors with ambition. The post of asesor general provided an eager lawyer with the opportunity to demonstrate both his legal expertise and judicial maturity and could under optimum conditions lead to an Audiencia judgeship.

Another member of the viceroy's legal office was the escribano mayor de gobierno y guerra, a position purchased at public auction like all other escribanía posts. For the entire viceregal period, the escribanía mayor was in the hands of the Basavilbaso family—first porteño-born Francisco Antonio de Basavilbaso and then his son, José Ramón. Chief among his duties was supervising and witnessing all official viceregal acts, including the transfer of power from one viceroy to another. Although the viceroy ostensibly attempted to improve the level of public service, neither of the Basavilbasos who had been awarded this position were qualified escribanos. More important than personal qualifications had been their willingness to pay 6,000 pesos into the Royal Treasury.[43] The escribano mayor was aided by an escribano de diligencías, who actually did much of the day-to-day notary paper work. This escribano was usually one of the owners of a public register who took on this additional role to earn extra fees for his services.

The superindent's despacho judicial was set up along the same lines as that of the viceroy, but differing jurisdictions produced modifications in the basic staff. In addition to an asesor who was charged with handling all civil and criminal litigation for the Superintendent and an escribano actuario to do the necessary paperwork, the legal office of the Superintendency also made use of the services of a fiscal for advice in financial matters. From 1779 to 1784 the fiscal employed by the despacho judicial also served as a fiscal in the Real Hacienda; after that date the Audiencia's fiscal became a member of the superintendent's legal staff. The legal office of the Secretaría of the Superintendency survived the suppression of the Superintendency itself, although the posts of asesor general in two secretariats was combined.

Audiencia

The final step in creating a fully developed bureaucratic machine in Buenos Aires was the reintroduction of an Audiencia (High Court) into the capital city. An Audiencia had existed briefly in the seventeenth century in the port city, but by 1671 the king and his councilors disbanded the porteño high court. For the next 112 years all cases originating in the jurisdiction of the city of Buenos Aires were brought to the Audiencia of Charcas. Although inconvenient for those citizens who had dealings with the high court, the lack of an Audiencia in Buenos Aires enhanced the power of the city's governors and early viceroys.

By the beginning of the 1780s the absence of an Audiencia in the new viceregal capital, a bustling commercial city, had become too inconvenient to ignore.[44] In 1783 the High Court of Río de la Plata was founded. The Audiencia's jurisdiction extended from the litoral northward to Paraguay and Córdoba. Its original staff of judges consisted of one regent, four oidores, and one fiscal. Like other branches of porteño colonial bureaucracy, the Audiencia grew in numbers during the following years. In 1787 the position of fiscal del crimen was added to the bench; a new position of fiscal de hacienda was decreed in 1811 but was never instituted because of the 1810 revolution.

In addition to the judges named to the high court, the Audiencia employed a staff of clerks, lawyers, and associates who were in charge of keeping the court calendar, preparing transcripts, assessing fines and legal costs, and running the day-to-day affairs of the high court. By 1790 the six Audiencia judges and two fiscales were assisted by a high court staff of seven. In addition to two escribanos de cámara, the Audiencia employed two lawyers as court reporters and two assistant attorneys, one for criminal and civil cases, respectively. This staff was headed by a chancellor who oversaw the smooth functioning of the court. By the late eighteenth century Audiencia judges themselves were salaried government officials, but at least half of their staff members purchased their positions from the Royal Treasury. Both the judges and the crown expected these staff members to profit from their investment by charging the public for their services. In 1792 another staff position, *alguacil mayor* (chief bailiff), was added. Although the first incumbent, Miguel Garcia de Tagle, was salaried, the post was auctioned after Tagle's retirement.[45]

Santa Cruzada

The Ordenanza de Intendentes created a junta de santa cruzada charged with overseeing the sale of papal bulls and collection of funds for the Santa Cruzada. This board, composed of five officers and a notary, was under joint clerical-secular leadership. The junta was headed by a comisario, a high-ranking churchman who was also a member of the local cathedral chapter. Aiding the comisario were an asesor and a fiscal who were also ordained priests, but this group was balanced by two high-ranking secular authorities, the treasurer and accountant of the Royal Treasury, who also served fiscal posts on the junta.

Not content with overseeing the collection of the Santa Cruzada funds, the Ordenanzas de Intendente went even further, legislating changes in the way in which church funds were collected and limiting the general use of tax farming. The Ordenanzas specifically called for the end of private collection of all *mandas forzazas* (mandatory bequests), including the funds for the Santa Cruzada.

Inquisición

Another religious institution placed under crown control by the Ordenanzas de Intendente was the comisaria de la Santa Inquisición, the investigatory arm of the church and the defender of colonial society against religious heresy. The Inquisition throughout Spanish America had grown weak by the latter decades of the eighteenth century, and in Buenos Aires, where the Inquisition had never wielded much power, participation in the Inquisition had become almost wholly honorific. Because of its slight economic and political importance, the crown chose to allow the two members of the comisaria, both of whom had inherited their posts from their respective fathers, to continue in office. More profitable for the royal fisc was the transference of the sale of papal bulls from the church to Royal Hacienda.

Temporalidades

Temporalidades, an agency that predated the founding of the platine viceroyalty, embodies an early Bourbon attempt to control religious property and tap ecclesiastical wealth. This branch of royal government, officially entitled La administración de temporalidades de los bienes de la Compañía de Jesús, was set up in 1767 to oversee the property and goods left in the region after the expulsion of the Jesuits.[46] According to the pragmática that established the Temporalidades, all viceroys, presidents, or governors in the Spanish colonies were to occupy "the temporal possessions of the Company of Jesus, including the property and assets such as movable goods, as well as landed property and ecclesiastical revenues that they legitimately possess."[47]

In the Río de la Plata, an area encompassing the famed Jesuit missions, both the embargoing of Jesuit property and the creation of an agency to oversee these holdings fell to Governor Francisco de Paula Bucareli. While local commissions were formed to take over Jesuit holdings and prepare inventories of the property and papers that they now seized, a three-man Administración de Temporalidades for the provinces of Río de la Plata, Tucumán, Paraguay, and Cuyo was put into place in Buenos Aires. Bucareli charged this new agency with the safe deposit and administration of the funds and property furnished, noting and examining the accounts of the individual commissioners and administrators, dividing according to type the various funds, income, pensions, and belongings of each colegio and chapter house, providing separate sheets detailing accounts and outstanding debts, and filling out with the necessary form, clarity, and detail all the respective books that such a vast undertaking require.[48]

In addition, the royal cédula of 2 May 1767 outlined the creation of a depositaria general of Temporalidades to collect Jesuit assets. Initially, the new agency was to be separate and independent of the Royal Treasury, but Bucareli's haste in carrying out the royal orders forced him to turn to local treasury officials, the only men with talent and training to undertake this major operation. He chose Martín José de Altolaguirre, factor oficial real, and Juan de Asco, veedor of the local Real Hacienda, to occupy the posts of Temporalidades treasurer and accountant. The third office, that of defensor was awarded to Antonio Aldao, a local lawyer. The Temporalidades took up quarters in the Buenos Aires fort, alongside the governor's offices.

Corruption and poor administration of the fabled Jesuit properties soon led to a series of piecemeal reorganizations. Two years later in 1769 another royal cédula created ten Juntas Superiores de Temporalidades throughout the Spanish American colonies. These juntas were charged with deciding to what use the houses, residential colleges, and missions run by the Jesuits were to be put. One of these juntas, that with jurisdiction over the areas of Tucumán, Paraguay, and Buenos Aires, was headquartered in Buenos Aires. The junta, which in effect oversaw the work of the Administración de Temporalidades, was originally composed of five members: the governor, the bishop, the local asesor de gobierno, a town councilman named by the Cabildo, and the procurador síndico general of the Cabildo.

Royal desire to keep Jesuit assets separate from those of the treasury was short-lived. By 1774 the Junta Superior de Temporalidades surpressed the independent Temporalidades and reconstituted the agency as a branch agency (dependencia) of the Royal Treasury. This reorganization reflected the governor's suspicion of the Temporalidades officers and presented a solution that placed those handling ex-Jesuit funds under the supposedly watchful eye of the director of the Royal Treasury. The failure of the Temporalidades to realize expected profits, the very failure that had caused the governor to doubt the probity of Altolaguirre and company, also made it uneconomical to maintain a separate staff of well-paid, high-ranking bureaucrats. Instead, one or two clerks within Real Hacienda were now charged with overseeing Temporalidades affairs.

Although the junta had no qualms about disbanding the original agency it was to oversee, the junta itself proved to be no more competent than the original Temporalidades. A more far-reaching reform of the entire agency was clearly needed, especially since wrangling, intrigue, and mismanagement continued to reduce the expected profit flowing into the royal coffers. In 1783, declaring that although "several active and vigorous orders have been issued and dispatched to the Indies . . . the results have not, up to now, fully met my kingly intentions, in part because of the very nature of the dealings, in part because of the poor way in which things are being handled," the king issued a new plan reorganizing both Temporalidades and juntas throughout the empire.[49]

The first item of importance contained in this lengthy reorganization was the complete and total disbandment of the Junta Superior. Instead a Junta Provincial composed of the intendant, the asesor general, three members of the Real Audiencia and the Cathedral Chantry, but lacking Cabildo representation, were named to oversee Temporalidades. In addition, an administrative office was again created to deal with matters pertaining to all ex-Jesuit property.

This administrative office, the Administración de Temporalidades, was now headed by an administrador principal who also served as the agency's treasurer. Although the viceroy was empowered to name the administrador, he was cautioned to exact a considerable guarantee from the individual because of the large amount of property that would fall into his hands. The viceroy was also to name a contador and other "indispensably necessary" staff. Temporalidades accounts were now transferred from the Real Hacienda back to Temporalidades, and the agency's administrador was given powers to collect funds as do "the chief officers, accountants, and treasurers of my Royal Exchequer." The administrador was also given a seat in the junta superior of Real Hacienda directly below that of the Hacienda ministros.

In addition to viceregal controls, the Temporalidades administrator was also subordinate to the Dirección General de Temporalidades in Madrid, receiving all instructions on cobro y distribución de caudales from that agency. The actual collection of funds was farmed out to local agents who worked on commission and who accounted to the contador within the Buenos Aires Temporalidades office; the latter in turn submitted general accounts to Madrid. In addition to the principal administrator and an accountant, the Buenos Aires office was staffed by two salaried clerks and employed a legal counselor.

Even this reformed Temporalidades failed to produce revenues close to the levels originally imagined, in part because many of the most valuable Jesuit properties had already been sold at outrageously low prices before the reorganization, in part because Temporalidades even in its new form had neither the personnel nor the ability to pay close attention to property administration.

On 15 January 1789 still another plan attempting to make efficient use of ex-Jesuit property was issued, a plan that called for the creation of an independent Administración y Contaduría de Temporalidades.[50] According to the royal cédula, "one principal administrator of Temporalidades, who would at the same time serve as treasurer," was to be appointed in each viceregal capital. The administrator would be aided by an accountant and the clerks who are needed to carry out the dual tasks of administration and accounting. The administrator was now given the same economic power as any principal administrator, accountant, or treasurer of the Royal Exchequer, including the specific power to collect outstanding debts due on royal accounts. He was also empowered to attend local meetings of the Junta Superior de Temporalidades, reporting to this group and to the Dirección General de Temporalidades back in Madrid. Six years later, on 7 February 1796, a detailed instrucción spelled out in great detail the specific duties that came under the re-created Temporalidades officers.

These further modifications proved no more successful than earlier attempts, and by the end of the eighteenth century European warfare and economic pressures forced the crown to once again restructure the Temporalidades. In 1798, in an attempt to streamline finances making cash more readily available to the beleaguered Spanish crown, separate accounting for Temporalidades was ended (thus ending the need for a contador), and Temporalidades' funds were absorbed into the Hacienda's general accounts.[51] Four years later visitador Diego de la Vega convinced both king and viceroy to disband the office of Administración. It was suggested that the agency be disbanded immediately, but wartime and the hope that Temporalidades could be used as a vehicle to collect clerical funds called in by the crown under the ley de consolidación de bienes prolonged the institution's life for another two years. The Temporalidades staff, consisting now of an administrador and two oficiales, was finally dissolved in 1804, and all unfinished administrative work concerning financial matters was subsumed by the treasury. Other related administrative matters were transferred to a variety of local agencies. Funding of the salaries of teachers at the Colegio de San Carlos (formerly the Colegio Grande of the Jesuits), for example, fell to the Buenos Aires Cabildo.[52]

Tobacco Monopoly

The Real Renta de Tabaco, first created to oversee the collection of royal tax on the sale of tobacco, was greatly expanded during the years 1760–80 throughout Spanish America as its jurisdiction was enlarged to encompass the planting, processing, and sale of all tobacco products in the colonies. From a small tax-collecting organization, the Renta grew into the colonial equivalent of a vertically integrated industry, controlling all aspects of production from the planting of the tobacco crop to the marketing of cigarettes through a system of specially licensed shops. Moreover, although the tobacco monopoly turned its receipts into the Royal Treasury, it functioned outside of the local branch of the Royal Exchequer in day-to-day transactions. As the roles of the Renta grew, so did its bureaucracy.

Before the creation of the viceroyalty, the tobacco monopoly in the Río de la Plata had come under the jurisdiction of the Peruvian monopoly set up in 1752. In 1776 an independent Real Renta (headquartered in Buenos Aires) was created for the La Plata viceroyalty. By 1778 four separate but related divisions of the Real Renta were established in Buenos Aires: the Dirección General of the entire viceregal tobacco administration; the General Storehouses of the Dirección General; the Contaduría General for the entire viceroyalty; and the Administración General of the Real Renta in Buenos Aires. The first three divisions were in charge of the Real Renta operations throughout the viceroyalty, while the Administración General in Buenos Aires was only one of several district offices under the central bureaucracy. Because of the proximity of central and branch office, positions in the Administración General, which carried a good deal of local influence in cities such as Asunción, Córdoba, or Cochabamba, were far less prestigious in Buenos Aires.

Although conceived of as separate branches of the Real Renta, there was a definite hierarchial relationship between the branches of the tobacco monopoly. The Contaduría General came under the direct jurisdiction of the Dirección General, although its chief administrative officer (the contador general) sat on the Dirección General's board. The same was true for the Administración General, whose chief officer also sat on the same board.

Growth in the tobacco monopoly, as in so many other viceregal bureaucratic institutions, consisted not only of an ever-increasing number of staff positions, but also of an ever-enlarged number of subagencies. By 1790 a separate Tesorería General had split off from the Contaduría General; although its staff was smaller than that of Contaduría and its chief officer was not a member of the Dirección General, it nevertheless formed a separate wing of the monopoly. In addition, the local tobacco factory was placed under a new subagency, the Dirección General de Nuevas Labores. The tobacco monopoly, originally envisioned as encompassing four agencies, had grown to six within approximately twelve years.

In spite of both agency and personnel growth, the Buenos Aires Real Renta de Tabaco failed to generate revenues on the same scale as those produced in other parts of the Spanish colonial world. Before its separation from the Peruvian viceroyalty, the Río de la Plata tobacco monopoly had produced between 9,000 and 20,000 pesos per year.[53] In an attempt to increase tobacco revenues, the first director general, Francisco de Paula Sanz, undertook an extensive tour of the entire viceroyalty within a year of his appointment.[54] Sanz, a protégé of José de Gálvez, investigated both tobacco production and consumption and returned to Buenos Aires prepared to undertake wide-reaching changes in both. Before leaving Asunción, the major tobacco-producing area of the La Plata viceroyalty, Sanz set up a Paraguayan office of the Real Renta and decreed that all tobacco producers were henceforth to sell their product only to the Renta. Local unhappiness with Sanz's original system, a plan that called for growers to draw up annual contracts with the Renta stipulating the amount of tobacco they could deliver each year, soon forced Sanz to modify his plans, allowing unlimited production and free trade in tobacco within the province of Paraguay. Nevertheless, grower dissatisfaction continued because of the price offered by the only legal purchaser of tobacco, the Renta. Clandestine smuggling of tobacco produced in Paraguay undermined the state's ability to control tobacco sales throughout the viceroyalty.[55]

Paraguay was not the only source of contraband tobacco entering the Río de la Plata. Another source was Brazil, which continued to supply the much sought after and illegal "tabaco negro" to local markets in spite of numerous prohibitions and the efficacy of the coast guard. Unable to completely shut off the flow of illegal tobacco, the Renta decided to approach the problem from another angle. While still concentrating on production of the leaf, the Renta became increasingly interested in tobacco processing. A plan was drawn up to provide local markets with good-quality, inexpensive tobacco products (primarily cigarettes), thus reducing the market for contraband tobacco. In 1782 Ramón de Oromí arrived in Buenos Aires charged with overseeing "nuevas labores," setting up a new model cigarette factory in Buenos Aires, which it was hoped would significantly increase local manufacture. Oromí's role was considered so important to the revitalization of the tobacco industry and its income that he was given the same rank and salary as the director general of tobacco and awarded membership into the Order of Charles III.

Although Oromí remained in Buenos Aires as the director general de Nuevas Labores until 1797 (and was later promoted to the post of contador mayor of the Tribunal de Cuentas), the expected revitalization of tobacco income was not forthcoming. To reduce expenditures, the model factory was disbanded, but tobacco revenue fell even further. Between 1798 and 1802, for example, the average annual tobacco monopoly profit for the entire viceroyalty was 173,533 pesos, a profit far short of that generated in Mexico, Peru, Chile, or Colombia.[56] Low profit caused in part by the Renta's inexplicable failure after 1798 to provide the local market with enough black tobacco to produce puro cigarettes, the product in most demand, forced the Renta to take the drastic step of adulterating its so-called "puros negros" with one-third lighter Havana tobacco. These cigarettes proved to be in even less demand than those made of inferior grades of tobacco, and Renta income continued to plunge, while shipments of unsalable cigarettes were set to the torch.[57] By 1804 the entire Renta's revenues totaled only 438,921 pesos, while the next year revenue declined to 419,166. Contraband in black tobacco continued to prosper.

Despite its failure to meet the hoped-for levels of economic performance, the tobacco monopoly did increase its revenues during the viceregal period by more than twentyfold. The Real Renta also displayed the same growth in the number of employees seen in other branches of the bureacracy. The original plan for the establishment of a Buenos Aires Renta provided for a total of twelve bureaucrats to staff the four offices within the Renta.[58] By 1790 that staff had grown to twenty-five; by 1802 the entire staff numbered thirty-six.

While the Renta bureaucracy grew through the addition of low-ranking clerks (the Contaduría, for example, was expanded from a staff of three oficiales to six in 1789), adjustments were continually being made in the agency's internal divisions. In 1786 a contador interventor in charge of the almacenes generales was added to the office of the Administración General. In 1783 a cigarette factory was set up and administratively staffed by an inspector (sobrestante), an interventor, and a portero. Two years later the fábrica de nuevas labores was established in Buenos Aires and was soon staffed by a director general, an amanuense, an interventor de fábrica, and a celador de fábrica. Other internal reorganization occurred as the office of treasurer, initially created on a par with that of accountant, was gradually subsumed by the latter. By 1790 the treasurer of the Renta had ceased to be a member of the central dirección general that oversaw all Renta activities.

In addition to growth of Renta divisions located in Buenos Aires, the Renta continually added new offices and increased personnel throughout the viceroyalty. By 1797 the Real Renta of the Viceroyalty of Río de la Plata consisted of the Dirección General, Contaduría General, Tesorería General, Almacenes Generales, and a Fábrica de Cigarros all in Buenos Aires; the Administración General of Buenos Aires, also in the capital city; a Buenos Aires resguardo; and administraciones generales and resguardos in Montevideo, Corrientes, Santa Fé, Paraguay, Mendoza, Córdoba, Salta (with branches in Tucumán and Jujuy), Potosí, Chuquisaca, and La Paz. Another administración general had been set up in Puno. In addition, three other factories—in Paraguay, Salta, and Cochabamba—produced tobacco products for local consumption.[59] The employees of all these branches of the Real Renta were on the government payroll. The Renta also commissioned a network of agents throughout the cities and countryside of the viceroyalty, the fieles estanqueros, who were the only licensed agents empowered to sell tobacco products to consumers. These individuals did not receive any salary from the Renta but rather earned commissions that represented the difference between the price at which they purchased their product from the Renta and the price at which they were legally allowed to sell the same product.[60]

E Posts Sold or Auctioned

Sale of office (auction)

Before 1776:
regidor of Cabildo
alguacil mayor of Cabildo
escribano público
escribano de Real Hacienda, minas y registros
depositario de Cabildo

After 1776:
escribano público
escribano de provincia
alcalde provincial
alguacil mayor de Cabildo
escribano de Cámara de la Audiencia
tasador general de costas de la Audiencia
procurador de la Audiencia
receptor numerario de la Audiencia
canciller y registrador de la Audiencia
receptor de penas de Cámara de la Audiencia
procurador de número de la Audiencia
alguacil mayor de la Audiencia
escribiente mayor de gobierno y guerra del virreynato

Sale of appointments

Before 1765:
tesorero de reales cajas
alguacil mayor de reales cajas
contador de reales cajas
defensor de naturales

Notes

1. Introduction

1. Susan Migden Socolow, *The Merchants of Buenos Aires, 1778–1810: Family and Commerce* (New York, 1978).
2. The term "elite" is used in its widest sense and includes all people of pure Spanish blood, some formal education, and moderate wealth. Specifically excluded from this group are all those who worked with their hands.
3. No one has successfully measured the rate of economic growth in the area, although there have been some attempts to determine levels of exports, imports, and taxes flowing into the Real Hacienda. Ricardo Levene, ed., *Historia de la nación argentina,* 2d. ed. (Buenos Aires, 1940), vol. 4:296; Juan Carlos Garavaglia, "Diferenciaciones regionales y crecimiento económico: El Río de la Plata a fines del siglo XVIII y comienzos del XIX," paper presented at the Americanistas meeting, Manchester, England, 1982; Herbert S. Klein, "Structure and Profitability of Royal Finance in the Viceroyalty of Río de la Plata in 1790," *Hispanic American Historical Review* (hereinafter referred to as *HAHR*) 53 (1973): 440–69; Herbert S. Klein and John J. TePaske, *The Royal Treasuries of the Spanish Empire in America,* vol. 3, *Chile and the Río de la Plata* (Durham, N.C., 1982). Although the economic growth of the region never approached that of Mexico, between 1785 and 1796 Buenos Aires was probably the third most important Spanish American port in terms of exports from Cádiz. John Fisher, *Commercial Relations Between Spain and Spanish America in the Era of Free Trade, 1778–1796* (Liverpool, 1985), 55.
4. John Lynch, *Spanish Colonial Administration, 1782–1810: The Intendant System in the Viceroyalty of the Río de la Plata,* 2d ed. (Westport, Conn., 1969), 95–107.
5. D. A. Brading, *Miners and Merchants in Bourbon Mexico, 1763–1810* (Cambridge, 1971), 33–34; Mark A. Burkholder, "From Creole to Peninsular: The Transformation of the Audiencia of Lima," *HAHR* 52, no. 3 (1972): 395–415; Leon G. Campbell, "A Colonial Establishment: Creole Domination of the Audiencia of Lima during the Late Eighteenth Century," *HAHR* 52, no. 1 (1972): 1–25.
6. Jean Sarrailh, *L'Espagne éclairée de la seconde moitié du XVIIIe siècle* (Paris, 1954); Richard Herr, *The Eighteenth Century Revolution in Spain* (Princeton, N.J., 1958); Juan Beneyto

Pérez, *Historia de la administración española e hispanoamericana* (Madrid, 1958), chaps. 46–51; Magnus Morner, "La reorganización imperial en Hispanoamerica, 1760–1810," *Ibero-Romanskt* 4, no. 1:1–33.

7. See, for example, Christon I. Archer, *The Army in Bourbon Mexico, 1760–1810* (Albuquerque, N.M., 1977); Asunción Lavrin, "The Execution of the Laws of Consolidación in New Spain: Economic Aims and Results," *HAHR* 53, no. 1 (1973): 27–49; Brian R. Hamnett, "The Appropriation of Mexican Church Wealth by the Spanish Bourbon Government: The Consolidation of *Vales Reales,* 1805–1809," *Journal of Latin American Studies* 1 (1969): 85–113; Klein, "Structure and Profitability"; Jacques Barbier, "The Culmination of the Bourbon Reforms, 1787–1792," *HAHR* 57, no. 1 (1977): 51–68; Miles L. Wortman, *Government and Society in Central America, 1680–1840* (New York, 1982), 111–211.

8. Jacques Barbier, *Reform and Politics in Bourbon Chile, 1755–1796* (Ottawa, 1980); Brading, *Miners and Merchants in Bourbon Mexico;* Linda K. Salvucci, "Costumbres viejas, 'hombres nuevos': José de Gálvez y la burocracia fiscal novo-hispana (1754–1800)," *Historia mexicana* 32, no. 2 (1983): 224–64; Linda Arnold, "Bureaucracy and Bureaucrats in Mexico City, 1808–1822" (master's thesis, University of Texas at Austin, 1975). For a review of the scholarship on the bureaucracy in colonial Latin America, see Linda Arnold, "Political, Social and Economic Status in the Mexico City Central Bureaucracy, 1808–1822," in *El trabajo y los trabajadores en la historia de México,* ed. E. C. Frost et al. (Mexico City and Phoenix, Ariz., 1979), 281–310.

9. Socolow, *The Merchants of Buenos Aires,* 120–34.

10. *Porteño* is used throughout this book to refer to the port city of Buenos Aires and, more specifically, to a person born in that city.

2. The Leadership: Viceroys and Intendants

1. Ricardo Zorraquín Becú, *La organización política argentina en el período hispánico* (Buenos Aires, 1959), 150–51.
2. Zorraquín Becú, *La organización política,* 153.
3. Zorraquín Becú, *La organización política,* 149.
4. AGNA, Reales Cédulas, 1775–76, Libro 22, IX-24-8-2.
5. Sigfrido Radaelli, *Los virreyes del Plata* (Buenos Aires, 1959), for brief biographies of these men. For more detailed information on specific viceroys, see Enrique M. Barba, *Don Pedro de Cevallos, Gobernador de Buenos Aires y Virrey del Río de la Plata* (Buenos Aires, 1978); Hialmar Edmundo Gammallsson, *El Virrey Cevallos* (Buenos Aires, 1976); José Torre Revello, "El testamento del virrey Pedro de Cevallos," *Boletín del Instituto de Investigaciones Históricas* 12 (1931): 163–83; José Torre Revello, *Juan José de Vértiz y Salcedo, Gobernador y Virrey de Buenos Aires* (Buenos Aires, 1932); J. M. Gutiérrez, "El vireinato del Río de la Plata durante la administración del Marqués de Loreto," *Revista del Río de la Plata* 8 (1874): 212–40; Vicente G. Quesada, "Noticias sobre el gobierno del Virey Arredondo," *Revista de Buenos Aires* 7 (1869): 139–66; José María Mariluz Urquijo, *El Virreinato del Río de la Plata en la época del Marqués de Avilés* (Buenos Aires, 1964); Ricardo R. Caillet-Bois, "Un informe reservado del Virrey Joaquín del Pino," *Boletín del Instituto de Investigaciones*

Históricas II (1930): 67–90; José Torre Revello, *El Marqués de Sobre Monte, Gobernador intendente de Córdoba y Virrey del Río de la Plata* (Buenos Aires, 1946); Paul Groussac, *Santiago de Liniers, Conde de Buenos Aires, 1753–1810* (Buenos Aires, 1907).

6. For a full discussion of the intendancy system in the Río de la Plata, see Lynch, *Spanish Colonial Administration*. John Fisher, *Government and Society in Colonial Peru: The Intendant System, 1784–1814* (London, 1970), studies the Peruvian attempt at instituting the same reform.

7. *Memorias de los Virreyes del Río de la Plata*, introduction by Sigfrido A. Radaelli (Buenos Aires, 1945).

8. For the capital and dowries of two of these future viceroys, see AGNA, Registro 3, 1788–89, Folios 107–9v, Capital y dote de Dn Antonio Olaguer Feliú; Registro 2, 1780–82, Folios 52v–56, Escritura de promesa de Dote y Arras de Dn Marcos Jph Larrazabal y su esposa y el S.r Marques de Sobre Monte a D.a Juana Maria Larrazabal; Registro 2, 1782–83, Folios 24–29v, Capital de Dn Raphael de Sobre Monte; Registro 2, 1782–83, Folios 23–23v, 30–31, Carta de dote del Señor Marqués de Sobre Monte a favor de D.a Juana de Larrazabal, y Quintana su lejitima esposa; Registro 2, 1782–83, Folios 1–2v, Poder del S. Marqués de Sobre Monte a Dn Agustin Casimiro de Aguirre para percevir la dote de D.a Juana Larrazabal su futura esposa; Registro 2, 1782–83, Folios 60–64v, Capital del S.n Marqués de Sobre Monte.

9. See Susan Migden Socolow, *The Merchants of Viceregal Buenos Aires: Family and Commerce* (New York, 1978), 142–43, for the example of merchant Gaspar de Santa Coloma, brother-in-law of Antonio Olaguer Feliú.

10. AHN, Consejos 20412, Residencia del Virrey Joaquin del Pino (finado), 1806.

11. AGI, Lista de la familia del Exmo Señor Theniente gral Dn Francisco de Bucarely y Ursua, gobernador y capitan general de la Provincia del Río de la Plata, Buenos Aires 180.

12. AGI, Buenos Aires 39. Governors had earlier arrived with large retinues, but compared to those later introduced by the more prestigious viceroys, their numbers pale. Governor Bucareli, for example, arrived in Buenos Aires accompanied by a nine-member household and at least one family of *dependientes*. AGI, Buenos Aires 180.

13. Mariluz Urquijo, *Avilés*, 33–36.

14. These figures have been reconstructed from the facsimile edition of Loreto's accounts, Andrés de Torres, *Diario de Gastos del Virrey del Río de la Plata Marqués de Loreto* (Bilbao, 1977).

15. Governor Bucareli, for example, was paid 12,000 pesos a year while he was governor of Buenos Aires, but his replacement, Juan José de Vértiz, initially earned only 6,000 pesos when he took on the governorship in 1770. His salary was later raised to 9,000 pesos (in March 1771), and eventually to 12,000 pesos, but this only occurred after repeated requests to the crown. Torre Revello, *Juan José de Vértiz*, 15–16.

16. AGI, Buenos Aires 58, Letter from Vértiz to Gálvez, 5 February 1779.

17. Ibid.

18. Vértiz to Arriaga, 8 November 1770, in Torre Revello, *Juan José de Vértiz*, 16. By the end of 1778, after serving as viceroy for two years, Vértiz complained that he was in debt for more than 20,000 pesos. AGI, Buenos Aires 58, Vértiz to Gálvez, 5 February 1779.

19. Mariluz Urquijo, *Avilés*, 26.
20. Torres, *Diario de Gastos*, 56, 75, 102, 133, 139.
21. Mariluz Urquijo, *Avilés*, 36.
22. One observer described the viceroy as "Sullen, laborious, and suspicious of all those around him; as a result he wants to oversee everything and do all the work himself." Marie Helmer, "Une lettre inédite de Victorian de Villava," *Revista de Indias* II, nos. 43–44 (January–June 1951): 278.
23. Lynch, *Spanish Colonial Administration*, 95.
24. AHN, Consejos 20410, Residencia de Superintendente Francisco de Paula Sanz, 1789.
25. See chap. 8 for additional information.
26. Lynch, *Spanish Colonial Administration*, 95—107.
27. Lynch, *Spanish Colonial Administration*, 77–78.
28. Torres, *Diario de Gastos*, 122; for Loreto's position in this dispute, see *Memorias de los Virreyes*, 339–42.
29. Lynch, *Spanish Colonial Administration*, 56–57.
30. AGNA, Royal Cédula of 21 March 1778, *Documentos referentes a la guerra de la independencia y emancipación política de la República Argentina* (hereinafter referred to as *DRGI*) I:27.
31. See Lynch, *Spanish Colonial Administration*, 65–67, for details on the geographical dimension of the new intendancies. The *Real Ordenanza de Intendentes* has been published in *DRGI* I:31–96.
32. Lynch, *Spanish Colonial Administration*, 223.
33. See ibid., 109, for details.
34. AGNA, Reales Ordenes, 1786, Libro 16, Foja 237, IX-25-1-9.
35. AGNA, Reales Ordenes, 1785, Libro 63, IX-25-4-9.
36. Lynch, *Spanish Colonial Administration*, 69.
37. AGI, Audiencia de Buenos Aires 85, Reynoso to the Minister of Grace and Justice, 10 April 1804.
38. AGNA, Reales Ordenes, 1798, Libro 29, Foja 105–6, IX-25-2-7. González de Bolaños was the same merchant who also supplied funds to Sanz's bete noire, Viceroy Loreto. In 1798 González de Bolaños received royal permission to have the treasury garnish the salary then being paid to Sanz as governor and intendant of Potosí.
39. AHN, Consejos 20414, Residencia del Virrey Marqués de Avilés, 1802.
40. The following residencias are extant: AHN, Consejos 20411, Residencia del Marqués de Loreto, 1789; Consejos 20412, Residencia del Virrey Joaquín del Pino (finado), 1806; Consejos 20414, Residencia del Virrey Marqués de Avilés, 1802; and Consejos 20410, Residencia de superintendente Francisco de Paula Sanz, 1789.
41. AHN, Consejos 20411, Residencia del Marqués de Loreto.

3. Growth of the Bureaucracy

1. Ricardo Zorraquín Becú, *La organización judicial argentina en el período hispánico* (Buenos Aires, 1952), 158–65.

2. The first of these, the gobernación of Montevideo, was set up in 1749 in an effort to strengthen Spanish control of the Banda Oriental in the face of increased expansion by England's ally, Portugal. The second gobernación was that of Malvinas, created in 1766 to stop the English from moving into the area. The third gobernación, created in 1767, was Misiones, charged with governing the area bordering Brazil, which had formerly been under the tutelage of the Jesuits.

3. Ricardo Zorraquín Becú, *La organización política argentina en el período hispánico* (Buenos Aires, 1959), 195.

4. John Lynch, *Spanish Colonial Administration, 1782–1810: The Intendant System in the Viceroyalty of Río de la Plata,* 2d ed. (Westport, Conn., 1969), 124.

5. Ibid., 53, 58–59.

6. Buenos Aires' population in 1810 was officially 42,500, producing a ratio of bureaucrats to total population of 1 : 299. Mexico City with an official population of 168,846 in 1812 had 505 civil bureaucrats or a ratio of 1 : 334. For the 1810 census of Buenos Aires, see AGNA, Padrón de habitantes de la ciudad de Buenos Aires, IX-10-7-7. The Mexican figures are from Arnold, "Bureaucracy and Bureaucrats," 25.

7. "La contaduría de Buenos Aires y la Instrucción de 1767," *Revista del instituto de historia del derecho* 19 (1968): 267–80. From the beginning of the seventeenth century when a Reales Cajas, or branch Royal Exchequer was set up in Buenos Aires, this office had reported to the Royal Exchequer located in Lima, the viceregal capital. Since the staff of the Buenos Aires Reales Cajas came under the Lima Real Hacienda, the yearly accounts of the office were sent to the Tribunal de Cuentas of Lima.

8. José M. Mariluz Urquijo, "El Tribunal Mayor y Audiencia Real de Cuentas de Buenos Aires," *Revista del instituto de historia de derecho* 3 (1951): 118.

9. Real Ordenanza para el establecimiento e instrucción de intendentes de exércitos y provincia en el virreinato de Buenos Aires, 28 January 1782, printed in *Documentos referentes a la guerra de la independencia y emancipación política de la República Argentina,* vol. 1 (Buenos Aires, 1914), 21–95. Those articles that specifically refer to the functions of the Tribunal de Cuentas include 188, 208, 214–16. Perhaps the most important change in the Tribunal's jurisdiction was the removal from its purview of Cabildo accounts (propios y arbitrios). AGNA, Reales Ordenes, Tomo 52, IX-25-3-15, Royal Order of 7 January 1783.

10. AGNA, Títulos y nombramientos de Contadores Mayores, 1768–1813, IX-14-7-15.

11. Mariluz Urquijo, "El Tribunal Mayor," 118.

12. AGNA, Tribunal de Cuentas, Fojas de servicio del personal, IX-14-7-13.

13. AGNA, Biblioteca Nacional 282, document 4261.

14. AGNA, Hacienda, 1726–1807, IX-26-2-2, Letter from Tribunal de Cuentas to Intendente Sanz, 13 February 1784.

15. AGNA, Reales Ordenes, 1791, Libro 69, IX-25-4-15, Royal Order of 3 January 1791.

16. AGNA, Reales Ordenes, 1798, Tomo 76, IX-25-4-22; AGI, Audiencia de Buenos Aires 147, Junta Superior de la Real Hacienda de Buenos Aires to Don Miguel Soler; AGNA, Tribunal de Cuentas, Fojas de servicio del personal, IX-14-7-13.

17. AGNA, Reales Ordenes, 1796, Tomo 26, IX-25-2-4, Royal Order of 31 July 1796.

18. AGS, Inventario 2, 82-87, 17 May 1798.

19. Lynch, *Spanish Colonial Administration,* 137.

20. Mariluz Urquijo, "El Tribunal Mayor," 52. Backlogs seemed to plague all Tribunals throughout the Spanish empire. That of Mexico has 2,272 accounts outstanding in 1753. Brading, *Miners and Merchants,* 43.

21. AGNA, Hacienda, 1790–91, Legajo 61, Expediente 1580, IX-33-7-3, Secret Royal Order (*real orden velada*) of 24 December 1803.

22. Ibid.

23. AGS, Inventario 2, 86-76, 24 February 1802.

24. AGNA, Hacienda, 1790–91, Legajo 61, Expediente 1593, IX-33-7-3.

25. For information on the attempt to institute double-entry bookkeeping, see AGI, Buenos Aires 99, Letter 68, Loreto to Valdes, 6 March 1788; Letter 69, Loreto to Valdes, 6 March 1788; "Nuevo método de cuenta y razón para la Real Hacienda de las Indias," *Revista de la biblioteca nacional* (Buenos Aires) 4 (1940): 267–318.

26. AGNA, Hacienda, 1790–91, Legajo 61, Expediente 1588, IX-33-7-3.

27. For the Real Hacienda's questioning the Tribunal de Cuentas' right to review the mayor-domo de fábrica accounts, see AGNA, Hacienda, 1790–91, Legajo 61, Expediente 1580, IX-33-7-3. The same document also contains information on the 1803 complaint from the Hacienda on the style of address received from the Tribunal. For additional bickering over the payment of *libranzas,* see AGNA, Hacienda, 1790–91, Legajo 61, Expediente 1593, IX-33-7-3.

28. Lynch, *Spanish Colonial Administration,* 139.

29. Ibid., 142; Mariluz Urquijo, "El Tribunal Mayor," 121–22.

30. AGNA, Justicia, 1808–13, Legajo 54, Expediente 1561, IX-31-9-4.

31. In Spanish America as a whole between 1751 and 1808, a position as legal adviser (*teniente asesor*) to an intendant proved to be a major route of advancement, followed by *asesores generales* and protectors of the Indians. Mark A. Burkholder and Dewitt Samuel Chandler, *From Impotence to Authority: The Spanish Crown and the American Audiencias* (Columbia, Mo., 1977), 126–27.

32. AGNA, Biblioteca Nacional 282, Document 4261, Reglamento . . . [de] la contaduría mayor y de Exército del Virreynato de Buenos Aires, con expresión de los ramos en que ban de ser distribuidos y de las reglas de conducta y gobierno que se les impone para desempeño de sus encargos.

33. Emilio Ravignani, "El Virreinato del Río de la Plata (1776–1816)," in *Historia de la nación argentina,* ed. Ricardo Levene, 4 : 133–37.

34. Ironically, the owner of this property was Doña Ana María de Herrera, wife of Juan Tomás de Echeverz, contador mayor of the Tribunal de Cuentas in Lima. She had inherited the property from her grandfather Don Juan Antonio Jijano, a government bureaucrat earlier employed by the Buenos Aires Reales Cajas. AGNA, Hacienda, 1781–82, Legajo 22, Expediente 515, IX-33-2-1.

35. AGNA, Reales Cedulas, 1789–92, Tomo 26, Folios 344–45, IX-24-8-6; AGI, Buenos Aires 99, Carta 166 from Loreto to Valdés, 1 July 1788; AGI, Buenos Aires 364, Carta 94 from Sanz to Valdés, 1 July 1788.

36. For a contemporary drawing of this building, see AGNA, Frontispicio de la casa en que existe la Real Dirección y Administración de Tabacos de este Virreynato de Buenos Aires, Carpeta de planos 4, pieza 55, 1791. A copy of this drawing has been reproduced in Muni-

cipalidad de la Capital, *Documentos y planos relativos al período colonial de la cuidad de Buenos Aires* (Buenos Aires, 1910) 3 : 96–97.

37. AGI, Buenos Aires 481, Letters from the Crown to the Viceroy of Buenos Aires dated 9 September 1802 and 31 October 1802.

38. AGI, Buenos Aires 39. Arredondo was told that the king had decided that each viceroy was responsible for replacing any broken glass in the lanterns as well as window and door panes, and that each viceroy, as he vacated the official living quarters, was to make sure that all the glass was in order. Arredondo was also ordered to pay 42 pesos for the glass already replaced.

4. The Bureaucrats: Recruitment and Appointment

1. On the first transfer (*primer renuncia*), from the original purchaser to his chosen successor, half of the purchase price went to the crown and the other half to the office's owner. The second transfer, from the second owner to third, was even less profitable for the crown, as only one-third of the purchase price had to be turned over to the Royal Treasury. The fourth and last renuncia brought one-forth of the purchase price into crown coffers. All purchased offices then reverted back to the crown.

2. Mark S. Burkholder and Dewitt Samuel Chandler, *From Impotence to Authority: The Spanish Crown and the American Audiencias* (Columbia, Mo., 1977), 18–19.

3. AGS, Inventario 24, 183, Folios 193, 26 March 1757.

4. AGS, Inventario 24, 180, Folios 57, 13 June 1740.

5. In calculating these totals the fianza has not been included, since at the end of an incumbent's service, it would theoretically be returned.

6. The distinction between these two groups of royal bureaucrats was not that one group received a salary while the other did not, but rather that the "new" employees achieved their positions through prior service in the bureaucracy not through purchase of office.

7. Burkholder and Chandler, *From Impotence to Authority*, 83.

8. AHN, Consejos 20411, Residencia del Marqués de Loreto. For the sale of appointment to Zamudio see AGS, Inventario 2, 35-16, 1745.

9. AHN, Consejos 20411, Residencia del Marqués de Loreto.

10. Martín José de Altolaguirre was the son of Martín de Altolaguirre, a prosperous merchant who had purchased the post of factor in 1751. In 1767, shortly after the young man had begun to work in the Reales Cajas, his father renounced the factor position in his favor. Martín José continued to hold the post after the founding of the viceroyalty and retired only in 1789. The crown was reluctant to grant Altolaguirre his retirement because the original purchase agreement that his father had entered into with the crown guaranteed the payment of a salary to the factor oficial even after retirement.

11. AGNA, Montepío, Pensiones, 1781–1818, IX-12-1-8.

12. José de Galvez, secretary of state for the Indies, advised Intendant Fernández that tobacco monopoly bureaucrats be exempted from posting a bond so that "these ministers have no reason to be grateful to the merchants of that city, who are the only ones who are able to afford a bond and who will perhaps exact payment or special treatment because of the

money that they have put forth." AGNA, Comunicaciones y resoluciones reales, 1776–80, Folios 171–172, IX-25-5-5.

13. AGNA, Tribunal de Cuentas, Instrucciones y Reglamentos, Libro 4, IX-14-7-7, Reglamento de los dependientes que desde oy deven quedar en la Tesoreria de esta capital . . . 1779.

14. AGNA, Reales Ordenes, 1790, Libro 21, IX-25-1-14.

15. AGNA, Solicitudes Civiles, 1781, Libro 2, Letra C-E, IX-12-9-5, Manuel de la Colina y Escudero expone hallarse de Receptor de Real Derecho de Sisa.

16. Angel Antonio Henry, *El oficinista instruido o práctica de oficinas reales: obra elemental, necesaria a todas las clases de empleados en ellas, y útil a las demás del estado* (Madrid, 1815), 55; José María Mariluz Urquijo, *Orígenes de la burocracia rioplatense* (Buenos Aires, 1974), 77–78.

17. Burkholder and Chandler, *From Impotence to Authority*, 287–88.

18. AGNA, Contaduría de Buenos Aires, Registro de empleados, IX-9-3-10; Juan Carlos Arias Divito, "Establecimiento de la Renta de Tabacos y Naipes en el Virreinato del Río de la Plata," *Historiográfia rioplatense* 1 (1978): 8.

19. See, for example, AGI, Buenos Aires 307, Fernández to Gálvez, 26 June 1778, in which the intendant explains that nine staff members of the Cevallos expedition will shortly be returning to Spain (thus saving the crown 16,000 pesos per year in salaries) but that three of the officials of the *contaduría* (Matías Bernal, Juan José Núñez, and Manuel de Véliz) will remain in Buenos Aires and form the staff of the intendant's office.

20. AGI, Buenos Aires 417, Nómina de los Empleados en la Renta del Tabaco del nuevo Virreynato de Buenos Aires, con expresión de sus Destinos y Sueldos.

21. Antonio de Prado, *Reglas para Oficiales de Secretarías y Catálogo de los Secretarios del Despacho, y del Consejo de Estado, que ha habido desde los Señores Reyes Católicos, hasta el presente: junto con las Plantas dadas a las Secretarías* (Madrid, 1755).

22. Prado, *Reglas*, vi–viii.

23. Ibid., 72–73, 75.

24. Ibid., 76.

25. Ibid., 79–80.

26. Ibid., 81.

27. Ibid., 82–83.

28. Ibid., 83.

29. Henry, *Oficinista*, 51.

30. Ibid., 21.

31. Ibid., 22.

32. Ibid., 33–34.

33. Ibid., 40.

34. Ibid., ii.

35. Ibid., iii.

36. Ibid., 34.

37. Ibid., 42.

38. Ibid., 43.

39. Ibid., 47.

40. Ibid., 89.

41. Ibid., 90.
42. Ibid., 91.
43. Ibid., 85–86.
44. Ibid., 88.
45. Ibid.
46. Ibid., 92.
47. Ibid., 98.
48. Ibid., 103.
49. Ibid., 98.
50. Ibid., 102–3.
51. AGNA, Reglamento del Tribunal de Cuentas, IX-14-7-48.
52. Ibid.
53. Ibid.
54. Ibid.
55. Ibid.
56. Ibid.
57. Ibid.
58. Ibid.
59. These instrucciones have been published in the *Boletín de la dirección general de aduanas* 1 (October–December 1938): 1035–38, 1045–47 and II (January–June 1939): 31–34, 125–29, 218–20, 311–14, 440–42, 554–57.
60. Ordenanza de Aduana, *1779, Boletín de la dirección general de aduanas* 2 : 442.
61. AGNA, Tribunal de Cuentas, Instrucciones y Reglamentos, Libro 4, IX-14-7-7.
62. AHN, Consejos 20411, Residencia del Marqués de Loreto, 1789.
63. Ibid., for the charge of insubordination against Félix Francisco Sánchez de Celis.
64. AGNA, Hacienda, 1781–82, Legajo 22, Expediente 502, IX-33-2-1, Instancia del Administrador de la Real Aduana de esta Capital sobre el aumento de oficiales de pluma que expone ser necesarios para el cabal desempeño de las operaciones y trabajo de dicha Aduana.
65. AGNA, Tribunal de Cuentas, Nombramientos de Meritorios, 1786–1812, IX-14-7-12. Probably the first man to serve as meritorio in this agency was Justo Pastor Lynch who was listed as "entretenido o meritante en la contaduria mayor" from July 1778 to January 1779. AGNA, Contaduría de Buenos Aires, Registros de empleados, IX-9-3-10.
66. AGS, Inventario 24, 176, Folio 26, 16 December 1716.
67. Hugo R. Galmarini, "Comercio y burocracía colonial: A propósito de Tomás Antonio Romero," *Investigaciones y ensayos* 28 (1980): 414–15.
68. AGS, Inventario, 82, Folio 6.
69. AGNA, Reales Ordenes, 1797, Libro 27, Folios 86 and 129, IX-25-2-5.
70. AGNA, Solicitudes Civiles, Libro 7, Letra S-Z, IX-12-9-10.
71. AGI, Buenos Aires 145.
72. AGS, Inventario 2, 80, Folio 257.
73. AGI, Buenos Aires 500, Nicolás de Arredondo to Fray Antonio Valdés, 9 April 1790.
74. AGS, Inventario 24, 184, Folio 381, 8 May 1763.
75. In seventeenth-century Lima, members of the viceroy's personal staff were "perhaps the safest, swiftest social climbers in the colony." Fred Bronner, "Elite Formation in Seven-

teenth-Century Peru," *Boletín de estudios latinoamericanos y del Caribe* 24 (1978): 3. Bronner documents cases in which a captain of the guard and a secretary were both named corregidor and married to local heiresses. Ibid., 20.

76. Torres, *Diario de Gastos,* xxxiii.

77. AGNA, Dirección General de Tabacos y Naipes, Fojas de servicio, 1800–1807, IX-14-8-17.

78. *D.H.A.,* vol. II, *Territorio y población: Padrón de la ciudad de Buenos Aires (1778)* (hereinafter called *Padrón [1778]*), 137–38.

79. AGI, Buenos Aires, 147.

80. AGNA, Comunicaciones y Resoluciones Reales, 1785–88, Libro 5, Foja 372, IX-25-5-7.

81. AGNA, Reales Ordenes, 30 August 1790, Libro 21, Foja 42, IX-25-1-14. Francisco Urdaneta was not the only member of his family to achieve a position of importance in the Spanish colonial bureaucracy. His brother, Martín José Urdaneta, was treasurer of the Royal Cajas of Santa Fé de Bogotá. Francisco had had two children by his first wife Rosalia de la Cueva, who died in San Lucar de Barrameda shortly before her family was about to depart for America. In addition to José Joaquín, a daughter also survived this marriage. She was sent to Bogotá to stay with her father's family. By 1794 she was married to her uncle Martín José.

82. AGNA, División Colonia, Sección Gobierno, Montepío, Pensiones, 1776–1820, IX-13-1-7.

83. AGNA, Dirección General de Tabacos y Naipes, Fojas de servicio, 1795–1809, IX-14-8-15. By 1796 the young Urdaneta decided that his future in Buenos Aires was bleak but that perhaps he could advance back in Bogotá where his uncle (who was also his brother-in-law) had been promoted to contador mayor supernumerario of the Tribunal de Cuentas. Claiming that "because of the well-known integrity of my father's professional conduct, I have been left without any assets," he requested and received permission to transfer to Bogotá. In 1797 José Joaquín traveled to Montevideo and from there embarked for New Granada. Unfortunately, Spain at that moment was involved in war with Great Britain, and before arriving in Bogotá José Joaquín was taken prisoner by the enemy twice, losing all of his baggage and sent as a prisoner to "different islands." Two and a half years after leaving Montevideo, he finally arrived in Bogotá, only to find that both his uncle's influence and a royal recommendation had failed to achieve a post higher than the one he had held in Buenos Aires. In 1799 a desperate José Joaquín again petitioned the crown, underscoring his previous twelve years of service, and requested that he be named to the vacant post of oficial primero segundo of the local Contaduría de Tabacos. The crown's response was to name José to the post of oficial tercero of the Contaduría de Tabacos in Santa Fé, a post that he probably never accepted, choosing to remain in Bogotá. See AGI, Buenos Aires 147, and AGNA, Reales Ordenes, 18 May 1801, Libro 79, Foja 10, IX-25-4-25.

84. Burkholder and Chandler, *From Impotence to Authority,* 105.

85. Among the oidores only José Cabeza Enriquez had already served in Quito (oidor from 1776–78) and Lima (alcalde del crimen from 1778–83), while Alonso González Pérez had been oidor of Charcas (1778–83).

86. The three porteños named to the Audiencia posts were Julián de Leyba (oidor), Manuel Mariano de Irigoyen de la Quintana (oidor), and Manuel Ignacio de Molina (fiscal). Other Americans whose appointments came too late for Buenos Aires service were Miguel José Lastarría, a native of Arequipa (appointed fiscal de la hacienda in 1811 and fiscal

in 1813), and José de Alvárez de Acevedo y Salazar, a native of Chile (appointed oidor in 1811). Andrés José de Iriarte, a native of Bogotá, had been named fiscal for Buenos Aires in 1798.

87. Burkholder and Chandler, *From Impotence to Authority,* 104.

88. Burkholder and Chandler, *From Impotence to Authority,* 98–104.

89. See Mark A. Burkholder, *Politics of a Colonial Career: José Baquíjano and the Audiencia of Lima* (Albuquerque, N.M., 1981), for an example of a limeño attempting to get royal appointment to the Audiencia of Lima.

90. *Padrón (1778),* 635–36.

91. BNM, Relación de méritos de Dn Manuel Martínez de Mansilla, 1812–14.

92. Ibid.

93. DRGI, "Real Ordenanza . . . de intendentes," capítulo 215, vol. 1 : 84.

94. AGNA, Dirección General de Tabacos y Naipes, Empleados, 1785–1812, IX-19-s/a-4, Testimonio [de] todos los documentos relativos a el oficial primero de esta Administración D. Manuel de Obarrio.

95. AGNA, Tribunal de Cuentas, Nombramientos de Meritorios, 1786–1812, IX-14-7-12.

96. Mariluz Urquijo, *Orígines,* 75–75.

97. AGNA, Tribunal de Cuentas, Nombramientos de Meritorios, 1786–1812, IX-14-7-12.

98. AGNA, Tribunal de Cuentas, Nombramientos de Meritorios, 1786–1812, IX-14-7-12, 28 September 1802.

99. AGNA, Tribunal de Cuentas, Nombramientos de Meritorios, 1786–1812, IX-14-7-12, 11 July 1799.

100. AGNA, Criminales, 1788–89, Legajo 33, Número 46, IX-32-4-5.

101. Mariluz Urquijo, *Orígines,* 75; AGNA., Reales Ordenes, 1790, Libro 20, Foja 232, IX-25-1-13.

102. AGNA, Solicitudes Civiles, 1782, Libro 3, Letra F-G, IX-12-9-6.

103. AGNA, Comunicaciones y Resoluciones Reales, 1791–93, Libro 7, Foja 189, IX-25-5-9.

104. AGNA, Reales Ordenes, 8 April 1794, Libro 24, Foja 75, IX-25-2-2. Finally achieving the position of oficial tercero did not end Fuentes's frustration. In 1794 he was surprised to find that José de Rebollar, *contador de dinero* of the Buenos Aires Reales Cajas, had received an interim appointment to the newly created archivero post within the Secretaría. Fuentes complained to the viceroy, arguing that he should have been preferred for this appointment, which because of its higher salary was a definite professional advancement. In turn, the viceroy supported Fuentes's request, expressing his predilection for the young man. In 1797 a royal order named him archivero, citing his "aptitude and application" for the job. (AGNA, Reales Ordenes, 1797, Libro 75, IX-25-4-21.) This was the highest position that Fuentes was to achieve in the colonial bureaucracy.

105. AGNA, Dirección General de Tabacos y Naipes, Fojas de Servicio, 1795–1809, IX-4-8-15.

106. AGNA, Dirección General de Tabacos y Naipes, Empleados, 1785–1812, IX-19-s/a-4, Testimonio [de] todos los documentos relativos a el oficial primero de esta Administración D. Manuel de Obarrio.

107. Ibid.

108. Ibid.

109. Ibid.

110. Ibid.

111. Ibid.

112. Ibid.

113. AGNA, Dirección General de Tabacos y Naipes, Tomas de razón de reales cédulas, órdenes y decretos, 1778–1807, IX-15-1-8; AGNA, Dirección General de Tabacos y Naipes, Administración de Buenos Aires, Fojas de servicios, 1795–1809, Folio 14, IX-14-8-15.

114. AGNA, Reales Ordenes, 1796, Libro 74, Foja 34, IX-25-4-20.

115. AGNA, Reales Ordenes, 1807–8, Libro 38, Foja 76, IX-25-3-1.

116. Carlos Calvo, *Nobiliario del antiguo Virreynato del Río de la Plata* (Buenos Aires, 1936–43), vol. 6 : 139–40. For information on the Lezica family, see Socolow, *The Merchants of Buenos Aires,* 147, 182–83.

117. Ramón de Oromí was moved to a post as contador mayor supernumerario of the Tribunal de Cuentas when his agency, the Fábrica de Nuevas Labores, was disbanded by the Real Renta de Tabaco.

118. In 1803, for example, the receptor was Bernardo Gregorio de las Heras, a local merchant; Juan Antonio de Lezica, another merchant, was tasador. Araujo, *La guía de forasteros del virreynato de Buenos Aires para el año de 1803* (Buenos Aires, 1908), 363.

119. The actual price paid was 400 pesos of 9½ reales each. AGS, Inventario 24, 182, Folio 182.

120. AGS, Inventario 24, 183, Folio 219.

121. AGS, Inventario 2, 58, Folio 300.

122. Zenzano's register, because of its importance, was worth over 6,000 pesos. AGS, Inventario 24, 184, Folio 365, and Inventario 2, 69, Folio 70.

123. According to José Zenzano, these costs had raised the true price of his escribanía from 6,360 to over 8,000 pesos. AGS, Inventario 2, 69, Folio 70.

124. AGNA, Escribanía Mayor de Gobierno y Guerra, Títulos, Despachos, Provisiones, etc., 1783–85, IX-8-3-14.

125. AGNA, Escribanía Mayor de Gobierno y Guerra, Títulos, Despachos, Provisiones, etc., 1783–85, Folios 102–5, Número 115, IX-8-3-14.

126. AGNA, Tribunales, Legajo 53, Expediente 44, IX-35-9-3, Sobre el título de Escribano público librado a Dn Josef Luis Cabral en virtud de renuncia hecha por la viuda de Dn Francisco Xavier Conget.

127. For examples of these fees, see AGNA, Comerciales, 1790–91, Legajo 15, Expediente 3, 1790, IX-31-1-1, Recivos de las costas del Penque portugues; AGI, Buenos Aires 239.

128. AGNA, Reales Cédulas, 1782–92, Libro 26, IX-24-8-6, Real Cédula of 9 September 1789.

129. The three candidates who presented themselves in the oposición held in 1788, for example, were all native-born lawyers. AGS, Inventario 2, 72, Folio 17.

130. *Genealogia: Hombre de Mayo,* 22–24.

131. Lavarden was the son and namesake of Juan Manuel Lavarden, a graduate of the University of Chuquisaca who had served as auditor de guerra in Buenos Aires from 1761 until his death in 1777. He was the nephew of Antonio Aldao, a porteño-born lawyer who had held the post of Defensor of Temporalidades from 1767 and was unsuccessfully nominated for "some Audiencia post or at least Audiencia honors and half salary" by Governor Bucareli. Aldao, who also served as interim secretary of the viceroyalty in 1778–79, died in 1788. For information on both Aldao and on Lavarden, father and son, see Enrique Udaondo, *Diccionario biográfica colonial argentino* (Buenos Aires, 1945), 47–48, 485–87.

132. Bandos, Libro 7, Fojas 324–29, IX-8-10-7; Despachos y nombramientos civiles y eclesiásticos, 1799, A-I, IX-12-6-3.

133. AGNA, Reales Ordenes, Libro 81, Foja 32, IX-25-4-27.

134. AGI, Buenos Aires 282.

135. See AHN, Consejos 20412, Residencia del Virrey Joaquin del Pino (finado), 1806, Testimony of Cornelio Saavedra. Saavedra, a middle-ranking merchant turned bureaucrat, testified that he had done everything possible to get his brother named to a post in "any of the agencies" that were under the viceroy but had met with no success. Saavedra later became one of the leaders in the Buenos Aires independence movement.

136. AGI, Audiencia de Buenos Aires 500.

5. The Bureaucrats: Advancement

1. Mariluz Urquijo, *Orígines*, 81.

2. For suggested use of military fojas in social history, see Leon G. Campbell, "The Military Service Record as a Source for the Study of Latin American Social History," *Manuscripta* 19 (1975): 147–58.

3. AGNA, Tribunal de Cuentas, Fojas de servicio del personal, IX-14-7-12.

4. AGNA, Despachos y Nombramientos Civiles y Eclesiásticos, J–Z, IX-12-6-4.

5. See, for example, the Royal Order of 17 October 1786 (AGNA, Reales Ordenes, Libro 64, Foja 57, IX-25-4-10), naming Francisco Valdepares to the oficial position vacated by Miguel de Lizarazu and moving Martín José de Medrano into Valdepares's slot.

6. AGNA, Hacienda, 1781–82, Legajo 22, Expediente 502, IX-33-2-1. The internal controversy reflected in the testimony of Ximénez de Mesa and Torrado was brought to an abrupt halt with the death of Torrado in September 1782. But troubles were far from over for the Aduana's administrador, for within three years Ximénez de Mesa was to become the central figure in the most important administrative scandal of the entire viceregal period.

7. The signees were José de la Barreda, Pedro Francisco Arteaga, and Manuel Moreno, first, second, and third oficiales of the Secretaría de Cámara; Matías Bernal, Juan Lustu, Tomás Saubidet, and Antonio de la Peña, first through fourth oficial of the Superintendencia Department; Lorenzo de Fuentes, archivero; and Francisco Díaz de Orejuela, salaried assistant. AGI, Buenos Aires 505; Mariluz Urquijo, *Orígines, 95–96.*

8. Manuel Moreno, *Vida y memorias de don Mariano Moreno*, in AGNA, *Biblioteca de Mayo*, vol. 2 (Buenos Aires, 1960), 1238. Mariluz Urquijo, *Orígines*, 106.

9. AGNA, Dirección General de Tabacos y Naipes, Fojas de servicio, 1800–1806, IX-14-8-17. The same year Goycoechea unsuccessfully petitioned the crown to be named the permanent minister contador of the Royal Treasury in Córdoba. AGI, Buenos Aires 149.

10. AGNA, Dirección General de Tabacos y Naipes, Contaduría General, Fojas de servicio, 1800–1806, IX-14-8-17.

11. AGNA, Dirección General de Tabacos y Naipes, Empleados, 1785–1812, IX-19-s/a-4.

12. AGI, Buenos Aires 145.

13. Agustín, a native of Burgos, served as a member of the Buenos Aires Cabildo and later was named *maestre de campo* and *general de los reales ejércitos*. Married to María Bartolina de

Arce y Baz de Alpoin, a porteña from one of the city's most important families, he went on to serve as governor of Paraguay (1772–78) and was president of the Real Audiencia of Charcas at the time of his death in 1780.

14. AGNA, Reales Ordenes, 1747–51, Libro 3, Foja 95, IX-24-10-11.

15. AGNA, Registro de Escribano 2, 1798, Folios 313–19, Testamento del Señor don Antonio de Pinedo.

16. *Padrón (1778)*, 128.

17. AGNA, Comunicaciones y resoluciones reales, 1789–90, Libro 6, Foja 413, IX-25-5-8. For Moreno's service on the Boundary Commission (1783–88), see AGNA, Reales Ordenes, 5 August 1784, Libro 14, Foja 73, IX-25-1-7; José Torre Revello, "Documentos relativos a Antonio Valle y Manuel Moreno Argumosa, abuelo materno y padre, respectivamente, de Mariano Moreno," *Boletín del instituto de investigaciones históricas* 27 (1942–43): 309–34.

18. AGNA, Reales Ordenes, 22 November 1790, Libro 68, Foja 90, IX-25-4-14.

19. AHN, Consejos 20411, Residencia del Marqués de Loreto.

20. Mariluz Urquijo, *Orígenes*, 59–61.

21. AGNA, Reales Ordenes, 1793, Libro 23, Foja 199, IX-25-2-1.

22. AGI, Buenos Aires, 307. AGNA, Contaduría de Buenos Aires, Registro de empleados, Folio 81, IX-9-3-10.

23. AGNA, Reales Ordenes, 1791, Libro 69, IX-25-4-15.

24. AGNA, Reales Ordenes, 1804, Libro 82, Foja 30, IX-25-4-28.

25. Medrano was the son of Pedro Medrano, contador of the Reales Cajas and the grandson of Francisco Cabrera, contador mayor of the Tribunal de Cuentas from 1777 to 1796. Ortiz was also well connected within the Buenos Aires bureaucracy. His sister, Josefa Ortiz, was the abovementioned Cabrera's wife. Ortiz also married into the bureaucracy, wed to Nicolasa Peña y Vilanova, daughter of Juan Nepomuceno de la Peña, a lawyer who served as relator of the Junta Superior of the Real Hacienda, and granddaughter of Juan de Vilanova, *vista de Aduana*. Lynch's connections were the least impressive of the trio. The son of Patricio Lynch, a merchant who had died in 1765, in 1786 he married Ana María Roo, daughter of the contador ordenador interino of the Tribunal de Cuentas from 1790 to 1796, Cornelio Matías Roo. Lynch made far more professional progress than this *cuñado*, José María Roo, oficial primero of the Real Aduana in Montevideo, further indication that his career progress was in part the result of talent and intelligence.

26. AGNA, Montepío, Pensiones, 1776–1820, IX-13-1-7.

27. See Mariluz Urquijo, *Orígenes*, 82, for the details of these complaints.

28. AGNA, Reales Ordenes, 1800, Libro 78, Folio 6, IX-25-4-24.

29. Mariluz Urquijo, *Orígenes*, 82.

30. AGI, Buenos Aires 505.

31. AGI, Buenos Aires 505.

32. Araujo, *Guía de foresteros*, 361.

33. These were given to Fermín de Aois, ministro de real hacienda in Potosí, and Lamberto de Sierra, *ministro tesorero* of the Reales Cajes of Potosí. Araujo, *Guía de foresteros*, 365; AGS, Inventario 24, 77-68.

34. Miguel Sánchez Moscoso had been named honorary oidor in 1784; the later group consisted of José Medeiros, asesor of the Intendancy of Salta, Miguel Gregorio Zamalloa,

asesor jubilado of Montevideo, and Victoriano Rodriguez, *teniente asesor letrado* of the Intendancy of Córdoba. Simancas, Inventario 24, 77-68, 189-138, 189-285; Inventario 2, 92-255; *Guía de foresteros*, 362.

35. Araujo, *Guía de foresteros*, 367. For another honorary treasury post see AGNA, Toma Razon de Títulos, 1801–7, IX-7-5-5 (1804).

36. Mariluz Urquijo, *Orígenes*, 79. Any bureaucrat who held a title (título) appointment was guaranteed permanent employment. Linda Arnold, "Apprenticeship, Permanency, and Free-lancing: Bureaucratic Career Patterns in Late Colonial Mexico City" paper presented at the Pacific Coast American Historical Association meeting, 1981, 4–6. For the position of bureaucrats in the seventeenth century, see John Leddy Phelan, *The Kingdom of Quito in the Seventeenth Century: Bureaucratic Politics in the Spanish Empire* (Madison, Wis., 1967), 327.

37. Mariluz Urquijo, *Orígenes*, 80.

38. See Linda K. Salvucci, "Costumbres viejas, 'hombres nuevos': José de Gálvez y la burocracia fiscal novohispana, 1754–1800," *Historia mexicana* 33 (1983): 234–43, for José de Galvez's unsuccessful attempt to dismiss corrupt Aduana officials in Mexico city.

39. AGNA, Dirección General de Tabacos y Naipes, Fojas de servicio, 1800–1806, IX-14-8-17.

40. AGNA, Dirección General de Tabacos y Naipes, Fojas de servicio, 1800–1806, IX-14-8-17. Marqués de la Plata was promoted to fourth oficial only in 1799. AGNA, Reales Ordenes, 17 February 1799, Libro 77, Foja 13, IX-25-4-23.

41. AGNA, Dirección General de Tabacos y Naipes, Empleados, 1785–1812, IX-19-s/a-4. For the Reyna family, see *Padrón (1778)*, 533.

42. AGNA, Dirección General de Tabacos y Naipes, Empleados, 1785–1812, IX-19-s/a-4.

43. Ibid.

44. Ibid.

45. AGNA, Dirección General de Tabacos y Naipes, Fojas de servicio, 1800–1806, IX-14-8-17.

46. Ibid.

47. Ibid.

48. Ibid.

49. AGNA, Toma Razón de Títulos, 1801–7, Folios 373v–376, IX-7-5-5.

50. AGNA, Tribunal de Cuentas, Títulos y Nombramientos de Contadores Mayores, 1768–1812, IX-14-7-5, and Reales Ordenes, 1807–8, Tomo 38, Foja 19, IX-25-3-1.

51. AGNA, Reales Ordenes, 1 July 1795, Libro 25, Foja 320, IX-25-2-3.

52. Mariluz Urquijo, *Orígenes*, 72; AGI, Buenos Aires 354.

53. For the effect of Gálvez's favoritism in Mexico, see D. A. Brading, *Miners and Merchants in Bourbon Mexico* (Cambridge, 1971), 37; Salvucci, "Costumbres viejas," *Historia mexicana* 33 (1983): 256.

54. One of the three American-born was from Buenos Aires, the other two from Maracaibo and Lima.

55. *Padrón (1778)*, 536; AGNA, Dirección General de Tabaco y Naipes, Fojas de servicio, 1800–1807, IX-14-8-17.

56. José Antonio Pillado, *Buenos Aires Colonial* (Buenos Aires, 1910), 237; Mariluz Urquijo, *Orígenes*, 47–48; AGI, Buenos Aires 308.

57. Aldao had also impressed ex-governor Bucareli, who in a letter to the Conde de Aranda

recommended that he be named to some American Audiencia. Enrique Udaondo, *Diccionario biográfico colonial argentino* (Buenos Aires, 1945), 47–48.

58. AGNA, Reales Ordenes, 1779, Tomo 9, IX-25-1-2.

59. Mariluz Urquijo, *Orígenes*, 48; AGNA, Correspondencia Loreto-Gálvez, 1785, IX-8-1-16, Letter of 24 May 1785.

60. Although they were of the same prestige, salary, and rank as high-level administrators, judges on the Audiencia are not included in this group because of special education and professional requisites of their position. They are discussed below.

61. Enrique M. Barba, *Don Pedro de Cevallos,* 2d ed. (Buenos Aires, 1978), 254–66.

62. Iglesia de la Merced, Libro de Matrimonios 6, 1760–1808, Folio 268.

63. Socolow, *The Merchants of Buenos Aires,* 180.

64. AGNA, Reales Ordenes, 1799, Libro 77, Foja 12, IX-25-4-23.

65. AGI, Buenos Aires 147.

66. AGI, Buenos Aires 149.

67. AGI, Buenos Aires 502.

68. See, for example, the request of the secretary of the viceroyalty, Manuel Gallego, that he be considered for a post of intendant. In his letter the rumor that the intendants of Cochabamba and La Paz are ready to retire is passed on to the crown, and Gallego suggests himself for one of these posts. AGI, Buenos Aires 502. The same legajo also contains information on Manuel Carvallo, portero of the Real Audiencia, and his quest to grab the post of recaudador del ramo de arbitrios for Santa Fé from Miguel Geronimo Garmendia, its interim occupant.

69. Manuel de Velazco y Camberos, oidor of the Buenos Aires Audiencia, received his appointment after suggesting to the crown that he share one salary with his father, soon-to-be-retired oidor decano of the same Audiencia. AGI, Buenos Aires 316.

70. AGNA, Hacienda, 1797, Legajo 82, Expediente 2135, IX-33-9-7.

71. AGNA, Hacienda, 1786, Legajo 35, Expediente 910, IX-33-3-7, Denuncia que haze el Director de la Real Renta de Tavacos sobre haver fallas en la Thesoreria de ella.

72. AGI, Buenos Aires 148.

73. AGNA, Hacienda, 1790–91, Legajo 61, Expediente 1580, IX-33-7-3, Sobre haber llegado a noticia del Rey que en algunos destinos de Indias se trata de los Ministros en terminos inpersonales, Real Orden, 14 May 1791 and 8 February 1793.

74. AGNA, Hacienda, 1790–91, Legajo 61, Expediente 1580, IX-33-7-3, Félix de Casamayor, Antonio Carrasco and José María Romero to Viceroy Sobremonte, Buenos Aires, 24 April 1806.

75. AGNA, Reales Ordenes, 1799, Libro 77, Número 89, IX-25-4-23.

76. AGNA, Reales Ordenes, 1803, Libro 33, Foja 117, IX-25-2-11.

77. AGNA, Reales Ordenes, 1803, Libro 34, Foja 225, IX-25-2-12.

78. AGNA, Reales Ordenes, 1803, Libro 34, Folios 229–30, IX-25-2-12. Another innovative bureaucrat was Juan Francisco Antonio de Vilanova, vista primero of the Buenos Aires Aduana who at age seventy-five suggested a reform in the way tasks were assigned to the contadores of the Tribunal de Cuentas. Vilanova's proposal was ignored. AGI, Buenos Aires 149.

79. AGNA, Dirección General de Tabacos y Naipes, Contaduría General, Fojas de servicios, 1800–1806, IX-14-8-17.
80. AGNA, Reales Ordenes, 1790, Libro 21, Foja 152, IX-25-1-14.
81. See, for example, the petition of Andrés de Somellera asking that his salary be raised and that his son-in-law be named to his post upon retirement. AGI, Buenos Aires 502.
82. See, for example, the case of José Tirado y Merino, son of the late Antonio Tirado y Villalba, director general of the Real Renta de Tabaco in Buenos Aires, and grandson of José Gómez Merino, factor general of the Real Renta de Tabaco of Cochabamba, asking for royal appointment. AGI, Buenos Aires 502.
83. AGNA, Tribunal de Cuentas, Títulos y nombramientos de Contadores Mayores, 1768–1812, IX-14-7-15; Reales Ordenes, 1796, Libro 74, Foja 32, IX-25-40-20, and Reales Ordenes, 1802, Libro 80, Foja 24, IX-25-4-26.
84. AGNA, Comunicaciones y resoluciones reales, 1789–90, Libro 6, Foja 344, IX-25-5-8. The viceroy had justified shutting the tobacco production experiment on the grounds that the factory was losing money.
85. AGNA, Licencias y pasaportes, Letra N-Pe, Libro 12, Foja 235, IX-12-8-11.
86. AGNA, Montepío, Pensiones, 1776–1820, IX-13-1-7.
87. AHN, Consejo, Libro 1490, Número 57.
88. AGI, Buenos Aires 500, Letter from del Pino to Soler, 19 June 1802. Carrasco's wife was described as originally suffering from "copious menstruation." Treatment had resulted in a definite worsening of her condition, and she now had "obstructions in the viscera of her stomach, heaviness, tiredness, swelling in her lower limbs, delayed and extreme indigestion with dry intestines, excessive obesity, and lastly a syndrome of symptoms that threatened an infarction of the vein discharging from the liver, and a resulting case of dropsy." His daughter suffered from epilepsy.
89. AGNA, Reales Ordenes, 1794, Tomo 72, Folio 1, IX-25-4-18.

6. Salary, Retirement, and Montepío

1. AHN, Consejos 20380, Don Martín de Altolaguirre, oficial real de Buenos Aires con Dn Alonso de Arze y Arcos, tambien oficial real de las cajas sobre dever ser comprehendidos en el Repartimiento de varios comisos.
2. *Recopilación de leyes de los reynos de las Indias*, Ley 44, Book 8, Título 14, Libro 8.
3. AGI, Buenos Aires 179, Número 35, Expediente respondido por el Señor Fiscal sobre el aumento de sueldo que solicitan los oficiales reales de Buenos Aires.
4. An example of the type of fees paid to the superintendent can be seen in AGNA, Comerciales, 1790–91, IX-31-1-1. Among other costs incurred in a contraband case involving a Portuguese ship were 19 pesos paid to Francisco de Paula Sanz for his signatures. The superintendent (or intendant) also replaced the Hacienda ministros as the judge in contraband cases and was therefore awarded a percentage of the diminishing comisos. He probably used this income to underwrite his secretariat's office expenses. See "Real Ordenanza para el establecimiento e instrucción de intendentes de exército y provincia en el

virreinato de Buenos Aires, 28 enero 1782," published in Archivo General de la Nación, Argentina, *Documentos referentes a la guerra de la independencia y emancipación política de la República Argentina* (hereinafter referred to as *D.R.G.I.*) (Buenos Aires, 1914), capítulo 77, I, 45; capítulo 212, I, 84. See also AGI Buenos Aires 516, El intendente de Buenos Aires informe sobre el comiso de dos sacos de hilo. . . , 1786.

5. "Real Ordenanza . . . de intendentes," *DRGI*, I, 21–95.

6. "Real Ordenanza de intendentes," capítulo 92; *DRGI* 1:50.

7. "Real Ordenanza de intendentes," capítulo 83; *DRGI* 1:47–48.

8. "Real Ordenanza de intendentes," capítulo 84; *DRGI* 1:48–49.

9. AGNA, Tribunal de Cuentas, Instrucciones y Reglamentos, Libro 4, IX-14-7-7.

10. AGNA, Reales Ordenes, Libro 77, Número 86, IX-25-4-23, Royal Order of 20 October 1799.

11. In 1800, for example, 4,624 pesos (34 percent of the total of 13,448 pesos charged to the account) was used for bureaucratic salaries. The remaining 8,932 was at least equal to those bureaucrats' salaries not covered by any of these accounts.

12. Herbert S. Klein and John J. TePaske, eds., *The Royal Treasuries of the Spanish Empire in America*, vol. 3, *Chile and the Río de la Plata* (Durham, N.C., 1982), 184–208. My thanks to John J. TePaske for generously providing this information before publication.

13. "Because of the uprising in Peru, funds are short, even for military expenses. I have found it necessary to put all government employees on half salary, starting with myself and the intendant." AGI, Buenos Aires 62, Letter 566, Vértiz to Gálvez, 24 December 1781.

14. The tendency of the government to view bureaucrats' salaries as an emergency fund to be tapped in times of dire necessity did not change with Independence. In December 1811 a decree published by the revolutionary government enacted a forced salary reduction of all civil employees based on a sliding scale. AGNA, Consulado de Buenos Aires, Tomas de Razón de Títulos de Empleados, Resoluciones, Formularios, etc., 1802–18, IX-7-5-10.

15. Tulio Halperin Donghi, *Guerra y finanzas en los orígenes del estado argentino (1791–1850)* (Buenos Aires, 1982), 51–68.

16. Alejandro de Humboldt, *Ensayo político sobre el Reino de la Nueva España,* ed. Juan A. Ortega y Medina (Mexico, 1973), Libro VI, Capítulos XIII and XIV, 539–545.

17. Klein, "Structure and Profitability," 456. The ratio of expenditure on bureaucratic salaries to monies collected by that bureaucracy for both Buenos Aires and Mexico are far from those produced by a modern bureaucracy. According to figures of the U.S. Internal Revenue Service for the fiscal year 1983, for example, the ratio of obligations of personnel to total tax collections was .01. See *Statistical Abstract of the United States* (Washington, D.C.: USGPO, 1985), 315, and *Budget of the United States Government* (Washington, D.C.: USGPO, 1985), appendix.

18. AGNA, Reales Ordenes, 1787, Tomo 65, IX-25-4-11, Royal Order of 28 October 1787; AGI, Buenos Aires 99, Marqués de Loreto to Antonio Valdés, 6 March 1788.

19. AGNA, Reales Ordenes, 1787, Tomo 17, IX-25-1-10, Royal Order of 20 November 1787; AGI, Buenos Aires 99, Marqués de Loreto to Antonio Valdés, 6 March 1788. The two men who suffered most from this new regulation were Pedro Medrano who lost his supplement of 700 pesos per year and his son-in-law Francisco Cabrera who lost payments of 500 pesos yearly.

20. AGI, Buenos Aires 99, Marqués de Loreto to Antonio Valdés, 31 October 1787 and 1 March 1788.
21. AGI, Buenos Aires 99, Marqués de Loreto to Antonio Valdés, 6 March 1788.
22. Eduardo Martiré, *Los regentes de Buenos Aires: La reforma judicial indiana de 1776* (Buenos Aires, 1981), 24–25.
23. The canciller post was created in 1791 (AGS, Inventario 32, 75-19); receptor de penas in 1792 (AGS, Inventario 2, 76-3); and *alcalde provincial* in 1804 (AGS, Inventario 2, 88-20). In addition, a salaried alguacil mayor of the Audiencia was named in 1796, with the proviso that after the incumbent's retirement the post was to be auctioned (AGS, Inventario 2, 80-257).
24. Klein, "Structure and Profitability," 440–69; Halperin Donghi, *Guerra y finanzas*.
25. Klein, "Structure and Profitability," 440–69.
26. "Presupuesto colonial de comienzos del siglo XIX (1801–1804)" *Boletín del instituto de investigaciones históricas* 1 (1922): 122–23.
27. AGNA, Montepío, Pensiones, 1776–1820, IX-13-1-7.
28. For the earlier report of plenitude, at least to European eyes, see Concolorcorvo, *El lazarillo de ciegos caminantes desde Buenos Aires hasta Lima (1773)* (Buenos Aires, 1942). One of the myriad complaints about the high cost of living in the viceregal capital is found in APBA, "Carta del Regente y oidores de Buenos Aires al Rey, 11 August 1787," *Libro de informes y oficios de la Real Audiencia de Buenos Aires* (La Plata, 1929), 12–13.
29. José M. Mariluz Urquijo, *El Virreinato del Río de la Plata en la época del Marqués de Avilés, 1799–1801* (Buenos Aires, 1964), 356; AGNA, Tribunales 234, Expediente 32, IX-39-1-3.
30. This salary increase, decreed in the Royal Order of 11 February 1809, was to take place "as soon as the nation's turbulence is over." AGNA, Reales Ordenes, 1809–10, Tomo 85, IX-25-4-31.
31. Tomás Diego Pacheco, for example, held the post of contador ordenador interino from 1791 until his death in 1796. Pacheco was barely in his grave when Lorenzo Figueroa and Pascual Cernadas, two oficiales employed by the Tribunal, began a dispute over who would succeed to this interim appointment. The case was decided by the king in favor of Figueroa. AGNA, Reales Ordenes, 1617–1796, Tomo 86, Fojas 99, IX-25-4-32; 1796, Tomo 74, Foja 56, IX-25-4-20; Tomo 26, Foja 92, IX-25-2-4.
32. AGNA, Reales Ordenes, 1781–82, Libro 11, Foja 58, IX-25-1-4, Gálvez to Fernández, 16 March 1781.
33. Emilio Ravignani, "El Virreinato del Río de la Plata (1776–1816)," in Ricardo Levene, ed., *Historia de la nacion argentina*, vol. 4, *El momento histórico del Virreinato del Río de la Plata*, 135.
34. For examples of loans against future salary, see AGNA, División General de Tabacos y Naipes, Lista de sueldos, 1778–1809, IX-46-4-6, and Certificaciones de Sueldos, Asignaciones de Empleos civiles, militares y eclesiásticos, 1769–1807, IX-10-1-6. The most exaggerated case of a local bureaucrat who habitually depended on these loans to make ends meet was Vicente Caudevilla y Escudero, the second oficiale segundo of the Dirección General de Tobacos. Caudevilla, whose salary was 600 pesos per year, borrowed the same amount from the Real Renta in 1793, thereby reducing his monthly salary of 50 pesos to 33 pesos 2½ reales. The original debt was repaid by 1798 when Caudevilla, now earning a yearly

wage of 800 pesos, borrowed another 800 pesos from his employer. During 1798 and 1799 he was granted a further emergency loan of 400 pesos. As a result of these debts, Caudevilla's salary, which should have totaled 66 pesos 5¼ reales per month, came to only 22 pesos 1⅝ reales. By 1804 Caudevilla, now promoted to oficial mayor of the accounting section of the Real Renta de Tabaco, was earning 1,400 pesos per year, but a year earlier he had been permitted to borrow another 1,300 pesos from government funds. As a result, he received only 87 pesos 3½ reales per month instead of a full salary of 116 pesos 5½ reales. Having repaid this latest debt, Caudevilla once again turned to the government in 1808 for still yet another advance of 1,300 pesos, a sum he was still paying off at the time of Independence.

35. AGNA, Tomas de Razón, 1778–1810, Tomo 17, IX-8-5-17.

36. By Royal Order of 28 June 1796 the king decreed that when an employee had to be transferred to a "lower paying post" because of the needs of the Royal Service he was to continue enjoying the higher salary. AGNA, Reales Ordenes, 1796, Tomo 74, IX-25-4-22. In 1788 the viceroy of Buenos Aires was advised by the crown that in those cases when an employee was asked to take on an interim appointment, if the resulting half salary was less than the employee's regular salary, he was to receive the greatest payment. AGI, Buenos Aires 99, Marqués de Loreto to Antonio Valdés, 1 May 1788.

37. AGNA, Reales Ordenes, 1792, Tomo 70, IX-25-4-16, Royal Dispatch of 6 June 1792 and Royal Order of 23 May 1792.

38. AGNA, Interior, 1793–94, Legajo 34, Expediente 19, IX-30-5-1.

39. AGI, Buenos Aires 127; José M. Mariluz Urquijo, *Orígenes de la burocracia rioplatense,* 86.

40. AGNA, Títulos de Contadores de Retasas, IX-8-5-17.

41. Lyman L. Johnson, "Wages, the Organization of Work and Prices in Colonial Buenos Aires, 1770–1815," unpublished paper, 1982.

42. A maestro mayor in the construction trades earned 400 pesos per year in the 1790s; by 1810 this wage had risen to 720 pesos per year. Journeymen bricklayers received an average wage of 375 pesos per year by the latter date. Johnson, "Wages, the Organization of Work and Prices."

43. Marcelo Urbano Salerno, "Aplicación en el Virreinato del Río de la Plata del auto acordado del 31 de julio de 1792 sobre arrendamiento de casas de Madrid," *Revista de la facultad de derecho de México* 26, nos. 101–2 (January–June 1976): 780.

44. AGNA, Montepío, Pensiones, 1781–1818, IX-12-1-8. Da. María Josefa Aldao, viuda del Auditor de Guerra Dn. Juan Manuel de Labarden.

45. Ravignani, "El Virreinato del Río de la Plata," 133.

46. AGI, Buenos Aires 316, Liniers to the Crown, 17 March 1808.

47. See, for example, the royal title granted to Manuel José de la Valle in 1788 giving him possession of the post of contador general of the Real Renta de Tabaco. "[E]ach year that you serve in the aforementioned post you will receive a salary of 2,500 pesos, and in addition 30 pesos per month for the rental of a house until you can be given the adequate housing that you should be given in the tobacco monopoly quarters." APBA, 7-5-14, Expediente 53.

48. AGNA, Dirección General de Tabacos y Naipes, Empleados, 1785–1812, IX-19-s/a-4.

49. AGNA, Hacienda, Legajo 14, Expediente 292, IX-32-9-7.

50. AGNA, División General de Tabacos y Naipes, Lista de Sueldos, 1778–1809, IX-46-4-6.

51. Of the first nine men appointed to the Real Renta de Tabaco, four borrowed funds for habilitación. The average sum borrowed in this case was 74 percent of an individual's annual salary. AGNA, División General de Tabacos y Naipes, Lista de sueldos, 1778–1809, IX-46-4-6.

52. See, for example, the appointment of Manuel Ortega Espinosa as asesor to the viceroy of the Río de la Plata. AGS, Inventario 24, 186-308, 1778.

53. AGS, Inventario 2, 62-45.

54. Halperin Donghi, *Guerra y finanzas*, 55–58.

55. AGI, Buenos Aires 149.

56. Klein and TePaske, *The Royal Treasuries*, vol. 3.

57. AGNA, Certificaciones de Sueldos, 1767–1807, IX-10-1-6. García de Tagle's post, which had been purchased from the treasury, was not included in those salaried positions being taxed.

58. A Royal Cédula dated 26 August 1794 required all bureaucrats employed in justicia or hacienda and earning 600 pesos or more annually to pay this new tax. AGNA, Reales Cédulas, 1786 94, Tomo 49, IX-24-10-2.

59. Klein and TePaske, *The Royal Treasuries*, vol. 3.

60. "Lista de los Donativos Patrioticos," Buenos Aires, Imprenta de los Niños Expósitos, 1809, John Carter Brown Library, Providence, R.I.

61. AGS, Inventario 2, 88-123, 2 June 1804.

62. Mariluz Urquijo, *Orígenes*, 93.

63. AGNA, Reales Ordenes, 1805, Tomo 36, Folio 153, IX-25-2-14.

64. For a study of the Montepío in eighteenth century Mexico, see Dewitt Samuel Chandler, "Pensions and the Bureaucracy of New Spain in the Late Eighteenth Century" (Ph.D. diss., Duke University, 1971).

65. Ricardo R. Moles, *Historia de la previsión social en Hispanoamérica* (Buenos Aires, 1962), 103–150.

66. Bureaucrats also had to hold their posts through a royal título to qualify for membership in the pension fund. Chandler, "Pensions and the Bureaucracy," 95.

67. For a list of the documents required before receiving a military pension, see AGNA, Montepío, Pensiones, 1776–1820, Documento 1, Instrumentos que deven presentarse para obtener pensión en el Montepío Militar, IX-13-1-7.

68. AGNA, Montepío, Pensiones, 1776–1820, IX-13-1-7.

69. AGNA, Montepío, Pensiones, 1781–1818, IX-12-1-8.

70. Moles, *Historia de la previsión social*, 121–122.

71. AGNA, División Colonia, Montepío-Hacienda, Varios, 1700–1815, IX-21-3-4.

72. *Cedulario de la Real Audiencia de Buenos Aires*, vol. 4 : 103.

73. Mariluz Urquijo, *Orígenes*, 94.

74. *Cedulario de la Real Audiencia de Buenos Aires*, vol. 1 : 256, Royal Order of 21 February 1789.

75. The Montepío hoped to have a total of 21,000 pesos awarded to it. This request was based on a calculation of 3,000 pesos per year for the past eight years (since 1778) minus one payment of 3,000 pesos that the Royal Branch Treasury of La Plata had sent in 1784. See AGNA, División Colonia, Montepío, 1762–1810, IX-23-3-2.

76. AGNA, Montepío, Pensiones, 1776–1820, IX-13-1-7.

77. AGNA, Montepío, Pensiones, 1781–1818, IX-12-1-8.
78. AGI, Indiferente General 1810, Número 4, Buenos Aires, 1790–1811, Montepíos, Informes, Oficios y Declaraciones de Pensiones, sobre los de dicho Virreynato y Cádiz, 8 March 1811.
79. José María Goñi Moreno, *Derecho de la previsión social* (Buenos Aires, 1956), vol. 1:77.
80. *Registro Oficial de la República Argentina* (Buenos Aires, 1879), 1:194.

7. Local Ties, Marriage, and Family

1. John L. Phelan, "El auge y la caída de los criollos en la Audiencia de Nueva Granada, 1700–1781," *Boletín de historia y antigüedades* (Bogotá) 59 (1972): 598.
2. Ibid., 600.
3. Burkholder and Chandler, *From Impotence to Authority,* 110.
4. The relatively short duration of the Bourbon's anticreole policy has been stressed by John Phelan. "The tendency [to replace creoles with Spaniards in the Bogotá Audiencia] suffered a complete reversal during the reign of Charles IV, the Regency, and Fernando VII." Phelan, "El auge y la caída," 603.
5. APBA, Disensos, Legajo 4, 7-5-17-3, Royal Order of 13 July 1789.
6. APBA, Disensos, Legajo 4, 7-5-17-3, Royal Order of 20 March 1791.
7. AGNA, Reales Ordenes, 1791, Libro 69, IX-25-4-25.
8. Ibid.
9. AGNA, *Comunicaciones y Resoluciones Reales,* Libro 9, Folio 173, IX-25-5-11. This right also extended to military personnel.
10. *Recopilación de leyes de los reynos de las Indias,* Ley 8, Título 2, Libro 8, Prohibe los casamientos de Contadores de Cuentas con hijas, y parientas de Oficiales Reales: y de Oficiales Reales con hijas, parientas de los contadores, and Ley 62, Título 4, Libro 8, Que los Oficiales reales no se puedan casar con parientas de sus compañeros, como se ordena.
11. *Recopilación de leyes de los reynos de las Indias,* Ley 63, Título 4, Libro 8, Que por tratar, y concertar el casamiento de palabra, o por escrito, o promesa, o esperanza de licencia, incurran en la pena.
12. AGNA, Reales Cédulas, 20 January 1775, Tomo 22, IX-24-8-2; Reales Ordenes, 5 May 1785, Tomo 63, IX-25-4-9; Reales Ordenes, 24 September 1799, Tomo 77, IX-25-4-23 (*real rescripto*).
13. APBA, Disensos, Legajo 4, 7-5-17-3.
14. Enrique Udaondo, *Diccionario biografico colonial argentino* (Buenos Aires, 1945), 573–74.
15. Iglesia de la Merced, Libro de Matrimonio 6, 1760–1808, Folio 65.
16. Victoria Cabrera's dowry can be found in AGNA, Registro de Escribanos 2, 1764, Folios 245–49v.
17. APBA, Disenso, Legajo 4, 7-5-17-3. Specifically mentioned among her "very close kinfolk, people of great glory and distinction in this country," were Don Pedro Saavedra, married to Doña Clara Gutiérrez, daughter of Don Juan Gutiérrez Humanes who served as lieutenant general in this city, and Doña Ana de Paz. Juan Gutiérrez was in turn the son of Don Pedro Gutiérrez, one of the founders of Buenos Aires. Ana de Paz had founded the Convent of Santa Catalina in the city. Another Gutiérrez de Paz daughter, Doña Juana, was the mother of two of the city's bishops, Fray Gabriel and Don Juan de Arregui.

18. AGNA, Reales Ordenes, 1774—77, Libro 7, Foja 165, IX-24-10-15, 20 March 1776.
19. AGNA, Reales Ordenes, 1774—76, Libro 46, Foja 203, IX-25-3-9, 30 July 1776.
20. AGNA, Comunicaciones y resoluciones reales, 1776—80, Libro 3, Foja 66, IX-25-5-5, 12 October 1777.
21. *Padrón (1778)*, 512.
22. AGNA, Reales Ordenes, 1786, Libro 64, Foja 15, IX-25-4-10, 4 October 1785.
23. AGNA, Intendente de Buenos Aires, 1778—81, IX-20-10-4; Mariluz Urquijo, *Orígenes,* 42.
24. AGNA, Reales Ordenes, 1792, Libro 70, Foja 65, IX-25-4-16, 24 August 1792.
25. APBA, Disensos, Legajo 4, 7-5-17-3.
26. Medrano's will, dated 1795, mentions accounts that he had pending with Tomás Romero and states that "whatever state Romero reports these accounts to be in, is not to be questioned, as he [Medrano] was greatly satisfied with the dealings of the abovementioned Romero." AGNA, Registro de Escribano 5, Folios 255v—58, Testamento en virtud del poder del Señor Don Pedro Medrano por su esposa Doña Victoriana Cabrera y su hijo el Doctor Don Mariano.
27. AGNA, Permisos para edificar, March—July 1785, Legajo 2, IX-10-10-7.
28. AGNA, Registro de Escribano 5, 1795, Folios 255v—258, Testamento en virtud del poder del Señor Don Pedro Medrano, and Registro de Escribano 1, 1773, Folios 209v—16, Venta de chacra de Don Domingo y Don Manuel de Basavilbaso a Don Pedro Medrano. The *chacra* (form) measured 1,800 *varas* (.93 miles) along the riverfront by 6,000 *varas* (3.11 miles) in depth.
29. AGNA, Reales Ordenes, 1794, Libro 24, Foja 75, IX-25-2-2, 8 April 1794. This order probably reached Buenos Aires three months later.
30. Iglesia de la Merced, Libro de Matrimonios 5, 1747—96, Folio 561.
31. AGNA, Reales Ordenes, 1790, Libro 68, Número 70, IX-25-4-14, 19 September 1790.
32. Three of these men (Olaguer Feliú, Sobremonte, and Liniers) held interim appointments.
33. Iglesia de la Merced, Libro de Matrimonios 6, 1760—1808, Folio 230.
34. Palomeque married the criollo María Andrea Albizuri without prior royal permission in 1785, causing a local scandal. He was saved from viceroy Loreto's wrath by the intervention of the church and quickly moved to a post as oidor of the Charcas Audiencia. Iglesia de la Merced, Libro de Matrimonios 6, 1760—1808, Folio 196; AGNA, Criminales, 1786, Legajo 101, Expediente 22, IX-32-4-2; Comunicaciones y resoluciones reales, 1786, Libro 5, Foja 113, IX-25-5-7; Reales Ordenes, 1786, Libro 16, Foja 61, IX-25-1-9. In 1805 Campuzano married María Josefa de Warnes in spite of the fact that his request for a royal license had been turned down. He was immediately transferred to the Audiencia of Guatemala. AGNA, Reales Ordenes, 1804, Libro 35, Foja 100, IX-25-2-13; Mark A. Burkholder and Dewitt Samuel Chandler, *Bibliographical Dictionary of Audiencia Ministers in the Americas, 1687—1821* (Westport, Conn., 1982), 69—70.
35. The wives of the bureaucrats were comparatively old at the time of marriage. There was a greater disparity between husband's age and wife's age at marriage for other groups such as the merchants. The average age of women marrying merchants was 18.76. Susan M. Socolw, "Marriage, Birth and Inheritance: The Merchants of Eighteenth-Century Buenos Aires," *HAHR* 60, no. 3 (1980): 390.
36. *Padrón (1778)*, 146—47, lists María Ventura Morales as a thirty-four-year-old widow; among the boarders living in her house is eighteen-year-old Pedro Martínez de Velazco.

37. Iglesia de la Merced, Libro de Matrimonios, 1760–1808, Folio 213.

38. Pinedo lost more than 10,000 pesos in the uprisings; although he still had more than 13,000 pesos in outstanding debts owed to him by residents of the area, he also owed 18,000 pesos to local citizens. AGNA, Registro de Escribano 6, 1792, Folios 237–40v, Testamento de Don Antonio de Pinedo y Montufar.

39. APBA, Disensos, 7-5-18-115, Expediente solicitando contraer matrimonio, Don Manuel de la Valle sobre disenso de matrimonio.

40. APBA, Disensos, 7-5-15-53.

41. AGNA, Registro de Escribano 1, 1792–1793, Folios 418v–19v, Poder para testar de Don Juan González Bordallo a su mujer y yerno.

42. For a more detailed discussion of late-eighteenth-century marriage legislation, see Susan M. Socolow, "Acceptable Partners: Marriage Choice in Colonial Argentina, 1778–1810," unpublished paper, 1985.

43. APBA, Disensos 1794, Legajo 4, 7-5-17-3, Doña Pascuala Iraola a fin de contraer matrimonio con Don Martín Medrano, oficial de la Contaduría Mayor de Cuentas.

44. AGNA, Reales Ordenes, 1799, Libro 77, Fojas 13 and 52, IX-25-4-23.

45. Pragmática sanción para evitar el abuso de contraer matrimonios desiguales, published in Richard Konetzke, Colección de documentos para la historia de la formación social de hispanoamérica (Madrid: 1962) vol. 3:406–13.

46. AGNA, Tribunales, Legajo E-6, Expediente 11, IX-40-9-2, Expediente formado por parte de Don Julián Gregorio Espinosa, menor de hedad demandando que su abuelo, tutor y curador Don Domingo Belgrano Pérez le de el consentimiento correspondiente para contraer matrimonio con Doña María Candelaria Somellera, y en su defecto se supla por la Real Autoridad.

47. AGNA, Reales Ordenes, July–December 1786, Tomo 16, Folios 271–72, IX-25-1-9.

48. AGNA, Sucessiones 5903, Testamentaria de Don Manuel de Gallego.

49. AGNA, Registro de Escribano 3, 1811, Folios 56v–57.

50. AGNA, Tribunales Administrativos, Expedientes, 1810–12, Expediente 934, IX-23-8-2.

51. AGI, Buenos Aires 308.

52. AGI, Buenos Aires 145.

53. AGNA, Registro de Escribano 6, 1782, Folios 328v–36v, Testamento en virtud de poder de Doña Josefa del Rincon por el finado su marido Don Nicolas Torrado; Sucesiones 8558, Testamentaría de Don Nicolas Torrado; and Montepío, Pensiones, 1776–1820, IX-13-17.

54. AGI, Buenos Aires 60.

55. AGNA, Registro de Escribano 2, 1813, Folios 388v–91v, Testamento del Señor Don Martín José de Altolaguirre.

56. Genealogia: Hombres de mayo (Buenos Aires, 1961), 22–24.

57. AGNA, Permisos para matrimonios, 1774–1809, IX-12-3-2. Mendinueta was distantly related to his new bride through consanguinity of the fourth degree. He was fifty-nine at the time of marriage; Rafaela was fifty-three.

58. AGNA, Registro de Escribano 2, 1780–82, Folios 47v–52v, Testamento de Don Martín Altolaguirre.

59. AGNA, Sucesiones 3864, Testamento de Martín Altolaguirre.

60. Padrón (1778), 568.

61. Laurio H. Destefani, "Jacinto de Altolaguirre, Primer Gobernador criollo de la Islas Malvinas (1781–83), *Investigaciones y ensayos* 14 (1973): 205–21.

62. León Altolaguirre was one of the few Buenos Aires bureaucrats to be honored with membership in the Order of Carlos III. Guillermo Lohmann Villena, *Los americanos en las ordenes nobiliarias* (Madrid, 1947), vol. 2:268–69. For Altolaguirre's lengthy fight with the *visitador,* Diego de la Vega, see AGI, Buenos Aires 148 and 149.

63. Iglesia de la Merced, Libro de Casamientos 6, 1760–1808, Folio 175v.

64. AGNA, División Colonia, Sección Gobierno, Montepío, Pensiones, 1776–1820, IX-13-1-7.

65. Iglesia de la Merced, Libro de Casamientos 6, 1760–1808, Folio 268.

66. Exact details on who María Luisa was are scarce. She is listed in the 1778 census as an eighteen-year old unmarried *española,* living with her mother, two younger siblings, and six slaves. Although there is no occupational information given for her family, all neighbors are artisans. *Padrón (1778),* 469. Another viceroy, Santiago de Liniers, had a liaison with Ana de Périchon, daughter of a French-born shopkeeper and wife of Edmundo O'Gorman, Groussac, *Santiago de Liniers,* 283 passim.

67. Iglesia de la Merced, Libro de Bautismos 14, 1775–79, Folio 176.

68. José Torre Revello, "El testamento del Virrey Pedro de Cevallos," *Boletín del instituto de investigaciones históricas* 12 (1931): 163–83.

69. AGNA, Criminales, 1789, Legajo 33, Número 6, IX-32-4-5.

70. AGNA, Criminales, 1786, Legajo 30, Expediente 27, IX-32-4-2.

71. AGNA, Criminales, 1789, Legajo 33, Número 6, IX-32-4-5.

72. AGNA, Criminales, 1789, Legajo 33, Número 6, IX-32-4-5.

73. Manuel de Labarden, son of Juan Manuel Labarden, lawyer and asesor de gobierno, was sent to Spain where he entered a colegio mayor at age seventeen. After completing a three-year course of studies, Manuel was awarded a degree of bachelor of laws from the University of Granada. María Lourdes Díaz-Trecheula López-Spinola, "Españoles americanos en los colegios mayores del Sacromonte y de San Bartolomé y Santiago de la Universidad de Granada: Siglos XVIII y XIX," in *Quinto congreso internacional de historia de América* 3:497–534.

74. AGI, Buenos Aires 500.

75. See, for example, the case of José María de Roo, son of Cornelio Roo and Petrona Cabezas, who after spending approximately four years in the Buenos Aires Reales Cajas and one year in the Tribunal de Cuentas was sent to Montevideo as oficial primero in 1779. Twenty-four years later José María was still in the same job, in spite of a real order signed in 1792 suggesting his promotion. "He has seen with the greatest pain that instead of paying attention to his claims for promotion, the agency heads have forgotten completely about him whenever an opening for an administrator or accountant has occurred in this customs office." AGI, Buenos Aires 502.

76. For another example of discrimination against native sons, see Mark Burkholder, *Politics of a Colonial Career: José Baquíjano and the Audiencia of Lima* (Albuquerque, N.M., 1980), 121.

77. AGNA, Reales Ordenes, Tomo 26, IX-25-2-4, Royal Order of 31 July 1796.

78. APBA, Disensos 1790, Legajo 1, 7-5-14-53, Manuel José de la Valle con María de las Mercedes González y Ros.

79. AGNA, Sucesiones 8821, Testamentaria de Ambrosio Zamudio.

80. AGNA, Comerciales, 1788–89, Legajo 14, Expediente 1, IX-30-9-9, and Reales Ordenes, 1779, Libro 9, Folios 156–57, IX-25-1-2.

81. AGNA, Hacienda, 1760–1805, Legajo 68, Expediente 1831, IX-33-8-2, 1793, Expediente promovido por don Josef Ignacio Taybo en nombre del Marqués de Carvallo contra Don Juan Francisco Antonio de Vilanova y su hijo Don Josef. . . .

82. AGNA, Registro de Escribano 4, 1813, Folios 82v–85v, Testamento de Don Juan Francisco Vilanova en virtud de su poder.

83. AGNA, Registro de Escribano 2, 1798, Folios 313–19, Testamento del Señor Don Antonio de Pinedo Montufur.

84. AGNA, Registro de Escribanos 2, 1780–82, Folios 32v–34, Poder para testar de Don Juan Francisco Navarro, Contador del Tribunal de Cuentas, and Registro de Escribanos 2, 1780–82, Folios 49–53v, Testamento de Don Juan Francisco Navarro.

85. Enrique Udaondo, *Crónica histórica de la Venerable Orden Tercera de San Francisco en la República Argentina* (Buenos Aires, 1920).

86. AGNA, Hermandad de la Caridad, 1792–93, Legajo 3, Folios 289–292v, IX-6-8-2.

87. For details on the use of capellanías by the local merchants, see Socolow, *The Merchants of Viceregal Buenos Aires*, 100–104.

88. María Baéz y Alpoin, for example, wife of Alonso de Arce y Arcos, treasurer of the Reales Cajas from 1726 to 1760, founded a capellanía with 12,000 pesos of principal at the time of her death. AGNA, Registro de Escribanía 6, 1756, Folios 495v–96v, Poder para testar de Doña María Baéz y Alpuyn, and Registro de Escribanía 6, 1757–58, Folios 102v–6, Testamento de Alonso de Arce y Arcos como apoderado del finado María Baéz de Alpoin su esposa.

89. The two porteños who gained entry into the Order of Charles III were Manuel de Basavilbaso, son of the merchant Domingo de Basavilbaso, who inherited the post of administrador principal (chief) of the Real Renta de Correos from his father (1788); and León de Altolaguirre, member of the powerful and well-connected Altolaguirre family, who was admitted in 1798 while serving as chief of the Aduana Resguardo. See Lohmann Villena, *Los americanos en las ordenes nobiliarias* 2:268–69, 282–83. Those Spanish-born bureaucrats who gained admittance were Manuel Ignacio Fernández, admitted while serving as superintendent of Buenos Aires (1780); Francisco de Paula Sanz, admitted the same year while serving as director of the Real Renta de Tabacos; and Francisco de Cabrera, contador mayor of the Tribunal de Cuentas (1785). At least four other top-ranking bureaucrats—the Marqués de Sobremonte (1786), intendant of Córdoba; Lorenzo Blanco Cicerón (1789), oidor of the Audiencia of Buenos Aires; Juan José Núñez, contador and administrador of the Aduana; and Manuel Gallego, secretary of the viceroyalty also applied for membership but were turned down. See José Torre Revello, "La Orden de Carlos III en el Buenos Aires colonial," *Boletín del instituto de investigaciones históricas* 20 (1936): 27–34.

90. Hugo Raúl Galmarini, "Comercio y burocracia colonial: A propósito de Tomás Antonio Romero," *Investigaciones y ensayos* 28 (January–June 1980): 419.

91. AGI, Buenos Aires 120.

8. Corruption, Scandal, and Political Reaction

1. AGNA, Comunicaciones y Resoluciones Reales, 1776–80, Folios 171–72, IX-25-5-5.
2. AGI, Buenos Aires 355, Letter 383, Fernández to Gálvez, 20 October 1780.
3. Galmarini, "Comercio y burocracia colonial: A propósito de Tomás Antonio Romero," pt. 1, *Investigaciones y ensayos* 28 (January—June 1980): 413.
4. Zacarías Motoukias, "Le Río de la Plata et l'espace peruvien au XVIIème siècle: Commerce et contrebande par Buenos Aires, 1648–1702," unpublished thesis de 3ème cycle, Ecole des Hautes Etudes en Sciences Sociales (Paris, 1983), 176–77, 291–96; AGI, Escribanía de Cámara 903B, Legajo 35, Folios 181–82; Escribanía de Cámara 883A, Legajo 6, Comisión de Buenos Aires, Número 1; and Charcas 28, Governor to the Crown, 12 July 1678 and 14 July 1678.
5. AGI, Buenos Aires 57, Secret letter (*carta reservada*) from Cevallos to Gálvez, 9 May 1777. Bucareli was accused of having engaged in large-scale trade with Francisco San Ginés and having created general disorder in government throughout the area.
6. AGI, Buenos Aires 39, Crown to Melo, 1795.
7. AGNA, Criminales, 1788, Legajo 32, Expediente 6, Número 1, IX-32 4 4, Ximénez y Ortega sobre giro y utiles.
8. Lynch, *Spanish Colonial Administration,* 147; Loreto, "Memoria de gobierno, 10 Feb. 1790," in Sigfrido A. Radaelli, ed., *Memorias de los virreyes del Río de la Plata* (Buenos Aires, 1945), 259–62.
9. Mariluz Urquijo, "El Tribunal Mayor," 140–41.
10. AGNA, Criminales, 1788, Legajo 32, Expediente 13, IX-32-4-4, Diligencias practicadas en la ciudad de Corrientes sobre descubrimiento de bienes de Don Francisco Ximénez de Mesa y complices que incidió en otros cargos para Pérez por pagos reales en efectos. See also Jorge Daniel Gelman, "Un 'repartimiento' de mercancias en 1788: Los sueldos 'monetarios' de las milicias de Corrientes," *Cuadernos de Historia Regional* (Argentina) 2 (1985): 3–17.
11. For examples of corruption in the Mexico City alcabalas, a branch of the Aduana of that city, see Salvucci, "Costumbres viejas," *Historia mexicana* 33 (1983): 237–42. Salvucci describes the way in which officials, in return for bribes from merchants, either permitted goods to leave the Aduana without paying taxes or undervalued goods. She also finds cases of customs officials engaged in outside business and in embezzling by failing to repay cash advances and loans in collusion with treasury officials.
12. AGI, Buenos Aires 500, Crown to Viceroy, 20 July 1802.
13. AGNA, Hacienda, 1798, Legajo 28, Expediente 702, Foja 110, IX-33-2-7; AGI, Buenos Aires 147. See also Mariluz Urquijo, "El Tribunal Mayor," 54; Radaelli, ed., *Memorias de los virreyes del Río de la Plata,* 259–62.
14. D.H.A., vol. 7, *Comercio de Indias,* 134–35. For a discussion of trade during and after this period, see Jerry W. Cooney, "Neutral Vessels and *Porteño* Slavers: Building a Viceregal Merchant Marine," *Journal of Latin American Studies* 18 (1986): 25–39.
15. The first cédula was issued on 20 April 1799 and followed by another on 18 July 1800.
16. See Socolow, *The Merchants of Viceregal Buenos Aires,* 125–29.

17. AGI, Buenos Aires 500. The three bureaucrats accused of "injustices and robbery" were Juan Almagro, asesor of the viceroyalty, Manuel Gallego, viceregal secretary, and Francisco Caballero, a military officer temporarily assigned to Gallego's office.

18. AGI, Buenos Aires 39, del Pino to the Prince of Peace, 15 March 1802. Much of the document is reproduced in Ricardo R. Caillet-Bois, "Un informe reservado del Virrey Joaquín del Pino," *Boletín del instituto de investigaciones históricas* 11 (1930): 67–90.

19. See Galmarini, "Comercio y burocracia colonial: A propósito de Tomás Antonio Romero," pt. 2, *Investigaciones y ensayos* 29 (July–December 1980): 415–16.

20. Among other things, Romero's ship had loaded goods in London for export to the Río de la Plata at a time when Spain was at war with Great Britain.

21. Caillet-Bois, "Un informe reservado," 86.

22. Ibid., 88.

23. According to del Pino, Manuel de Almagro had neither "credit nor money" when he returned to Buenos Aires and still owed, among other outstanding debts, the 800 pesos that he had borrowed to travel to Potosí.

24. Caillet-Bois, "Un informe reservado," 83. The regent was also charged with having protected Romero's lawyer, Mariano Saravia, who had left his wife in Santiago de Chile fourteen years earlier and was now carrying on "a scandalous liaison" with a young woman from one of the principal families of Buenos Aires in spite of her mother's repeated attempts to take legal action.

25. Ibid., 70.

26. Ansotegui had made a habit of serving as compadre to several merchants implicated in Romero's dealings.

27. Del Pino, aware that over 1,500 cases were being delayed by Marqués de la Plata, the fiscal de lo civil, investigated and found that his lack of speed was due to the large number of cases brought to his attention, his precarious health, and the care with which he handled all matters.

28. Caillet-Bois, "Un informe reservado," 88.

29. AGI, Buenos Aires 147.

30. José María Romero's letter makes mention of at least one other secret letter sent in July 1797 to the Prince of Peace and of a letter of November of the same year delivered to Francisco Saavedra "during my stay at the court."

31. See chapter 7, pp. 217–19, for the posts held by other members of the Altolaguirre family. In addition, Martín José's niece, Maria Francisca de Sarratea Altolaguirre, was married to Lázaro de Rivera, governor of Paraguay (1797–1806), while her sister Martina became the bride of Santiago de Liniers, military officer and future viceroy of Buenos Aires (1807–9). The scion of a prosperous local family, Martín José could well afford to maintain himself pure in the face of Romero's attempts at corrupting the local bureaucrats. At the time of his marriage (1787) Martín José was worth the rather magnificent sum of 136,294 pesos, most of which had been inherited from his late father. See Marcos Estrada, "La casa de Altolaguirre," *Genealogia* 12 (1957): 139–51; Laurio H. Destefani, "Jacinto de Altolaguirre, primer gobernador criollo de las islas Malvinas (1781–1783)," *Investigaciones y ensayos* 14 (1973): 205–21; AGNA, Registro de Escribano 4, 1784–88, Folios 480v–82v, Instrumento de capital y dote: El señor Don Martin José de Altolaguirre.

32. Galmarini, "Comercio," 2:414. For de la Vega's report see AGI, Buenos Aires 371, Visita de Diego de la Vega, Report of 27 February 1804.

33. AGNA, Tribunales Administrativos, Expedientes, 1804, Expediente 365, Legajo 13, IX-23-6-1, Tomás Romero solicita que la Exma. Señora Doña Rafaela de Vera, viuda del Exmo. Señor Don Joaquín del Pino no disponga de los bienes, dinero y alajas de la testamentaria de su cargo, y tambien de 3530 onzas de oro que pocos dias antes del fallecimiento de S.E. se cambiaron en estas Reales Cajas.

34. AGNA, Sucesiones 5903, Testamentaría de Don Manuel Gallego.

35. For an inventory of Gallego's books, see Mariluz Urquijo, *Orígenes,* appendix IX, 126–32.

36. AGI, Buenos Aires 502.

37. AGI, Buenos Aires 316.

38. AHN, Madrid, Consejos 20412, Residencia del Virrey Joaquín del Pino (finado).

39. AGI, Buenos Aires 316.

40. Mariluz Urquijo, *Orígenes,* 103.

41. AGNA, Sucesiones 4838, Quaderno de inventario de los bienes que quedaron por fallecimiento de Don Félix de Casamayor, 1811.

42. AGI, Buenos Aires 500, Crown to Visitador Diego de la Vega, 26 May 1803.

43. Socolow, *The Merchants of Viceregal Buenos Aires,* 86.

44. AGNA, Criminales, 1779, Legajo 15, Expediente 20, IX-32-2-4; Pillado, *Buenos Aires Colonial,* 207–23.

45. AGNA, Solicitudes Civiles, S–Z, Libro 7, Folio 486, IX-12-9-10. It should be noted that Cabrera often had trouble being agreeable to his fellow bureaucrats, even to his superior, Intendant Manuel Ignacio Fernández. His repeated lack of the required subordination in his dealings with Fernández earned him a stern warning from both the viceroy and the crown. AGI, Buenos Aires 62, Vértiz to Gálvez, 30 June 1781.

46. See AGI, Buenos Aires 364, for Intendant Sanz's report on Warnes.

47. AGNA, Criminales, Legajo 36, 1791–92, IX-32-4-8, Don Antonio José Escalada causa criminal contra Manuel Antonio Warnes por injurias.

48. An absentee rate of 11 percent for the bureaucrats was not unlike that for the entire population attending the meeting. Of a total of 261 inhabitants invited to the Cabildo Abierto, forty, or 15 percent, failed to vote.

49. In the case of Mexico Arnold argues that Independence did not cause the collapse of either the structure or staff of the Spanish bureaucracy but only produced some modifications. Linda Arnold, "Bureaucracy and Bureaucrats in Mexico City: 1808–1824" (master's thesis, University of Texas at Austin, 1975).

50. *Genealogía: Hombres de Mayo* (Buenos Aires 1961), 34–35, 63.

51. AGNA, Dirección General de Tabacos y Naipes, Títulos y Nombramientos, Tomas de Razón, 1799–1812, Tomo 2, IX-14-8-14.

52. Jacinto R. Yaben, *Biografías argentinas y americanas* (Buenos Aires, 1939), vol. 5:598–99.

53. Francisco Tellechea, a merchant deeply implicated in the conspiracy, also had bureaucratic connections. At the time of his execution Tellechea was married to María Ana Ballesteros, daughter of Pedro José Ballesteros, contador mayor of the Tribunal de Cuentas up to 1809. Ballesteros and his wife had sought refuge from the revolution in the nearby haven of

Montevideo. Valdepares, contador ordenador since 1807, had continued in his post until denounced to the government in 1812.

54. AGNA, Criminales, 1816–36, Legajo 62, IX-32-7-8.
55. Araujo did file a formal complaint in 1799 because while the first and second oficiales of the Contaduría had received salary increases, he had not. AGI, Buenos Aires 147.
56. Yaben, *Biografías argentinas* 1:288–89.
57. Lynch's loyalty to Cisneros might also have been caused by personal gratitude. In 1809 an anonymous letter sent to the court had accused both Lynch and the Aduana treasurer Pedro Vigueras of grave irregularities in the Aduana accounts and of being protected by Cisneros. *Genealogía,* 231.

9. Conclusion

1. Much of the following discussion on "old" and "new" bureaucracies is based on Hans Rosenberg, *Bureaucracy, Aristocracy and Autocracy: Prussian Experience, 1660–1815* (Cambridge, 1958), 2–25. For the classical discussion of the evolution of the modern bureaucratic state, see Max Weber, "Bureaucracy," in *Economy and Society* (New York, 1968), 3:956–1005. For specific discussion of Latin American bureaucracy, see John Leddy Phelan, "Authority and Flexibility in the Spanish Imperial Bureaucracy," *Administrative Science Quarterly* 5 (1960): 47–65; Frank Jay Moreno, "The Spanish Colonial System: A Functional Approach," *Western Political Quarterly* 20 (1967): 308–20; Richard M. Morse, "Toward a Theory of Spanish American Government," *Journal of the History of Ideas* 15 (1954): 71–93; Frederick B. Pike, "The Municipality and the System of Checks and Balances in the Spanish American Colonial Administration," *The Americas* 15 (1958): 139–58.
2. For Weber's model of bureaucracy, see *From Max Weber: Essays in Sociology,* ed. and trans. H. H. Gerth and C. Wright Mills (New York, 1946), 196–244. An abridged version is also published in *Bureaucracy in Historical Perspective,* ed. Michael T. Dalby and Michael S. Werthman (Glenview, Ill., 1971), 3–16.
3. John Leddy Phelan, "Authority and Flexibility in the Spanish Imperial Bureaucracy," *Administrative Science Quarterly* 5, no. 1 (June 1960): 47–64.
4. D. A. Brading, *Miners and Merchants in Bourbon Mexico, 1763–1810* (Cambridge, 1971), 31–34; Jacques A. Barbier, *Reform and Politics in Bourbon Chile, 1755–1796* (Ottawa, 1980), 6–7.
5. Brading, *Miners and Merchants,* 33–92.
6. Linda K. Salvucci, "Costumbres viejas, 'hombres nuevos': José de Gálvez y la burocracia fiscal novohispana, 1754–1800," *Historia mexicana* 33 (October–December 1983): 224–64.
7. Barbier, *Reform and Politics,* 190–94.

Appendix D. Government Agencies

1. Klein, "Structure and Profitability," 442.
2. AGNA, Comunicaciones y resoluciones reales, Libro 2, Foja 100, IX-25-5-4. For the origi-

nal appointments, see AGS, Inventario 24, 182–544, 1750 (Altolaguirre); Inventario 42, 184–760, 1763 (Medrano); Inventario 24, 184–381, 1763 (Bustinaga).

3. AGNA, Reales Ordenes, 1791, Libro 69, IX-25-4-15, Royal Order of 15 November 1791.

4. Arnold, "Bureaucracy and Bureaucrats," 45. For a list of the four major categories into which these revenues could fall see Ibid., 43.

5. AGNA, Reales Ordenes, 1791, Libro 69, IX-25-4-15, Royal Order of 8 July 1791.

6. AGNA, Reales Ordenes, 1778, Libro 8, IX-25-1-1.

7. Ibid., Viceroy Vértiz to Intendente Manuel Fernández, 10 December 1778.

8. AGNA, Reglamento de Real Aduana, 15 February 1779, IX-14-2-3, also published in *Boletín de la dirección general de aduanas* (Buenos Aires), 1, nos. 1–12 (October–December 1938) and 2, nos. 1–6 (January–June 1939).

9. AGNA, Biblioteca Nacional Manuscritos, Legajo 49, Documento 39.

10. Lynch, *Spanish Colonial Administration*, 121.

11. Among those taxes originally collected by the Aduana for the *masa comun* of the treasury were *almojarifazgo de entrada, almojarifazgo de salida, alcabala marítima, alcabala terrestre,* and *alcabala de cabezón.* In addition, during the decade of 1790, when prolonged European warfare forced Spain to liberalize the colonial trade allowing neutral nations to participate in Buenos Aires' commerce, a series of new duties were added to the Aduana's roster. These included the *derecho do extracción de negros* (1791), *extracción al comercio de frutos* (1795), and *derecho de círculo.* César García Belsunce, "La Aduana de Buenos Aires en las postrimerias del Regimen Virreinal," *Investigaciones y ensayos* 19 (July–December 1975): 471; Klein, "Structure and Profitability," 442–43.

12. Other funds collected by the Aduana and turned over to the Royal Treasury included the *alcance de cuentas donativos* (voluntary and forced loans to the Royal Treasury) and the media anata on Aduana staff salaries. Among the ramos particulares collected by the Aduana, at one time or another during the viceregal periods were the montepío de ministros, the ramo de vacantes mayores, the ramo municipal de guerra, and the derecho de sisa. Other ramos particulares that fell to the Aduana to supervise were the *depósitos particulares y decomisos* (collected from 1802), the *bienes de contrabando,* the *cuartas partes* (one-fourth of contraband fines collected for the Supreme Council of the Indies from 1802), the *contribución de hospital,* the *arbitrio de Santa Fé* (1806), the *almirantazgo* (1807), the *contribución patriotica* (1808), and the *nuevo impuesto de Córdoba* (1809). Garcia Belsunce, "La Aduana," 463–86, contains a full discussion of the books maintained by the Aduana and the Resguardo.

13. For example, by 1795 three different duties on hides exported from Buenos Aires were being paid into the Aduana: the *almojarifazgo de salida,* an export tax of 3 percent; the *extracción al comercio de frutos,* an additional duty of 2 percent; and the *ramos municipales de guerra,* 2 reales per hide earmarked for the Cabildo to maintain frontier troops.

14. AGNA, Hacienda, 1781–82, Legajo 22, Expediente 502, IX-33-2-1, Instancia del Administrador de la Real Aduana de esta Capital sobre el aumento de oficiales de pluma que expone ser necesarios para el cabal desempeño de las operaciones y trabajo de dicha Aduana.

15. AGNA, Criminales, 1788, Legajo 32, Expediente 6, IX-32-4-4.

16. AGNA, Instrucción de los Resguardos del 12 de enero de 1787, Document 70, IX-14-7-7.

17. AGNA, Instrucción de los Resguardos del 14 de julio de 1794, Document 74, IX-14-7-7.

18. AGNA, Administrativos, 1802–3, Legajo 10, Expediente 280, IX-23-5-5.

19. García Belsunce, "La Aduana," 464–70.

20. *Guía de forasteros en la ciudad y virreynato de Buenos Aires para el año de 1792* (Buenos Aires, Imprenta de Niños Expósitos, 1791), 2–21.

21. García Belsunce, "La Aduana," 464.

22. Lynch, *Spanish Colonial Administration*, 207–8.

23. For an excellent discussion of this agency, see Mariluz Urquijo, *Orígenes*.

24. Ibid., 44.

25. According to the Real Cédula of 28 August 1757 that established the Secretaría in Mexico, the duties of the oficiales were to be divided as follows: the oficial mayor, as the head of the oficiales, had under his special care directing and overseeing all the work, opening the correspondence received, editing the drafts of all letters, consultas, and representaciones to be issued, helping to get all mail (*pliegos* and *despachos*) ready, overseeing the storing and binding of all consultas and royal orders, and drawing up an index for all letters sent to the crown. He was also in charge of three books: the first used to note all important information that could be helpful to the office such as the date of arrival of ships; the second containing a list of all government employees and their corresponding royal titles; the third containing information on all expedientes sent to other agencies of government. The second and third oficiales were in charge of specific geographical zones and offices and were to oversee all viceregal business related to those regions and administrative divisions. Mariluz Urquijo, *Orígenes*, 24–25.

26. Ibid., 47–49, 69.

27. AGNA, Correspondencia Vértiz-Gálvez, 1780, IX-8-1-9. The same Sobremonte, after his stint as Vértiz's secretary, went on to become intendant of Córdoba (1784–97) and viceroy of Río de la Plata (1804–7).

28. Torres, *Diario de gastos*, xxiv. Some crown agents, such as Viceroy Cevallos, seem to have systematically removed all royal orders and other papers from the files before their departure, believing these to be part of their personal correspondence.

29. AGNA, Correspondencia Vértiz-Gálvez, 1780, IX-8-1-9, Letter of 30 April 1780, Sobremonte to Vértiz.

30. Ibid.

31. Ibid.

32. Ibid.

33. Ibid.

34. Torres, *Diario de gastos*, xxiv–xxv.

35. Torre Revello, *Juan José de Vértiz*, xvi.

36. Mariluz Urquijo, *Orígenes*, 64.

37. See ibid. for this rumor contained in a letter of August 1801 from Francisco Antonio de Letamendi to Ambrosio Funes.

38. AGNA, Correspondencia de Arredondo con los ministros de la Corona, 1791, Número 19, IX-8-2-8, letter of 18 March 1791 to Conde del Campo de Monge; Mariluz Urquijo, *Orígenes*, 123–24.

39. AGNA, Correspondencia Vértiz-Gálvez, 1780, IX-8-1-9, Letter of 30 April 1780, Sobremonte to Vértiz.
40. AGNA, Contaduría de Buenos Aires, Registro de empleados, IX-9-3-10.
41. See the Royal Order of 29 January 1797 creating the post of archivero. AGNA, Reales Ordenes, 1797, Libro 75, Número 5, IX-25-4-21. Earlier futile attempts to set up this position can be found in AGNA, Correspondencia Vértiz-Gálvez, IX-18-1-9, Letter of 30 April 1780 from Juan José de Vértiz to José de Gálvez; and AGNA, Correspondencia de Arredondo con los ministros de la Corona, 1791, IX-8-2-8, Nicolás de Arredondo to the Conde del Campo de Alange. These two latter documents are reproduced in Mariluz Urquijo, *Orígenes,* 120–24.
42. AGI, Buenos Aires 505; Mariluz Urquijo, *Orígenes,* 66.
43. AHN, Residencia del Marqués de Loreto. Included in the charges made by Francisco Cabrera, contador mayor of the Tribunal de Cuentas, against Viceroy Loreto is a lengthy denuncia of Basavilbaso. For the purchase of the escribanía mayor by José Ramon, see AGS, Inventario 2, 85–94, 1801.
44. Santiago de Chile, the capital of a new captaincy-general but by no means a viceregal capital, had an Audiencia that had been functioning since 1609.
45. AGS, Títulos, Inventario 2, Legajo 80–257. Título of Miguel García de Tagle as alguacil mayor of the Audiencia of Buenos Aires.
46. The Jesuits were banished from Spanish possessions by Royal Order of 27 February 1767. Explicit instructions for the takeover of Jesuit holdings and the creation of a Temporalidades was contained in the *pragmática sanción* of 2 April of the same year. Luis María Torres, *La administración de temporalidades en el Río de la Plata* (Buenos Aires, 1971) 511, 516. To insure the quick implementation of this new royal policy, a real cédula, dated 5 April, was issued, and additional information detailing Jesuit holdings in America was dispatched to the New World. Torres, *La administración,* 517.
47. Torres, *La administración,* 516.
48. Francisco de Paula Bucareli y Ursua. "Memoria del governador a su sucesor D. Juan José de Vértiz," *Revista de la biblioteca pública de Buenos Aires* 2 (1880): 301–98; Torres, *La administración,* 518.
49. AGNA, Tribunal de Cuentas Instrucciones y Reglamentos, Libro 4, IX-14-7-7, Testimonio de la Real Cédula e Instrucción para la administración y contaduría de Temporalidades de Buenos Aires.
50. Ibid.
51. Torres, *La administración,* 528.
52. Juan Probst, "La enseñaza primaria desde sus orígenes hasta 1810," in *Historia de la nación argentina,* ed. Ricardo Levene, vol. 9:504–6.
53. David Lorne McWatters, "The Royal Tobacco Monopoly in Bourbon Mexico, 1764–1810" (Ph.D. diss., University of Florida, 1979); Guillermo Céspedes del Castillo, "La Renta de Tabaco en el Virreinato de Peru," *Revista histórica* 21 (1954): 160.
54. Francisco de Paula Sanz, *Viaje por el Virreinato del Río de la Plata: El camino de tabaco* (Buenos Aires, 1977).

55. Jerry W. Cooney, "Tobacco and Defense: A Dilemma of the Intendencia of Paraguay," paper delivered at the 1975 Southern Historical Association meeting.

56. Klein, "Structure and Profitability," 449; for Mexican profits, see McWatters, "The Royal Tobacco Monopoly," 254–55; for Peru, see J. R. Fisher, *Government and Society in Colonial Peru* (London, 1970), 102–11; Chilean profit figures are presented by Agnes Stapff, "La renta del tabaco en Chile en la época virreinal," *Anuario de estudios americanos* 18 (1961): 2; Columbian profits are found in John P. Harrison, "The Colombian Tobacco Industry from Government Monopoly to Free Trade, 1778–1876" (Ph.D. diss., University of California, 1951).

57. Juan Carlos Arias Divito, "Auge y decadendia de la Renta del Tabaco en Buenos Aires," *Nuestra Historia* 22 (1978): 195–201.

58. AGI, Audiencia de Buenos Aires, 417.

59. AGNA, Dirección General de Tabacos y Naipes, Listas de Sueldos, 1778–1809, IX-46-4-6.

60. For lists of *fieles estanqueros,* see AGNA, Dirección General de Tabacos y Naipes, Empleados, 1785–1812, IX-19-s/a-4.

Bibliography

I. Primary Sources

A. ARCHIVES

1. Archivo General de la Nación, Buenos Aires, Argentina (AGNA)
2. Archivo existente en la Iglesia de la Merced, Reconquista y Cangallo, Buenos Aires, Argentina
3. Archivo de la Provincia de Buenos Aires, La Plata, Argentina (APBA)
4. Archivo General de Indias, Sevilla, Spain
5. Archivo General de Simancas, Simancas, Spain (AGS)
6. Archivo Histórico Nacional, Madrid, Spain (AHN)
7. Biblioteca Nacional, Madrid, Spain (BNM)
8. Archivo de la Real Academia de la Historia, Madrid, Spain (Colección Mata Linares) (RAH)

B. ARCHIVAL GUIDES

Archivo General de la Nación, Argentina. *Indice temático general de unidades archivonómicas del período colonial: Gobierno*. Buenos Aires: Archivo General de la Nación, 1978.

Archivo Histórico de la Provincia de Buenos Aires "Ricardo Levene." *Catálogo del Archivo de la Real Audiencia y Cámara de Apelación de Buenos Aires*. La Plata: Provincincia de Buenos Aires, 1974.

Contreras, Remedios. *Catálogo de la Colección Mata Linares*. 5 vols. Madrid: Real Academia de la Historia, 1977.

Furlong, Guillermo, S. J. *Cartografía histórica argentina: Mapas, planos y diseños que se conservan en el Archivo General de la Nación*. Buenos Aires, 1963.

Magdaleno, Ricardo, ed. *Catálogo XX, Archivo General de Simancas: Títulos de Indias*. Valladolid: Casa Martín, 1954.

Ministerio de Relaciones Exteriores y Culto (Argentina). *Catálogo de documentos del Archivo General de Indias de Sevilla referentes a la historia de la República Argentina*. 3 vols. Buenos Aires, 1901.

Musso Ambrosi, Luis Alberto. *El Río de la Plata en el Archivo General de Indias de Sevilla: Guía para investigadores*. 2d ed. Montevideo, 1976.

Paz, Julián. *Catálogo de manuscritos de América existentes en la Biblioteca Nacional*. Madrid: Patronato de la Biblioteca Nacional, 1933.

Torre Revello, José. *Adición a la Relación descriptiva de los mapas, planos, etc. del Virreinato de Buenos Aires existentes en el Archivo General de Indias*. Buenos Aires: Instituto de Investigaciones Históricas, Universidad de Buenos Aires, 1927.

———. "Catálogo de las relaciones impresas de méritos y servicios, relativos al período colonial de la Argentina, que se conserven en el Archivo General de Indias," *Boletín del Instituto de Investigaciones Históricas* 19 (1935), 259–96; 21 (1936–37), 173–207; 22 (1938), 177–84; 23 (1938–39), 94–107; 24 (1939–40), 137–60; 25 (1940–41), 203–52; 26 (1941–42), 202–12.

———. *Documentos referentes a la historia argentina en la Real Academia de la Historia de Madrid*. Buenos Aires, Instituto de Investigaciones Históricas, Universidad de Buenos Aires, 1929.

———. *Mapas y planos referentes al Virreinato del Plata conservados en el Archivo General de Simancas*. Buenos Aires: Peuser, 1938.

Torres Lanzas, P. *Relación descriptiva de los mapas, planos, etc. del Virreinato de Buenos Aires, existentes en el Archivo General de Indias*. 2d ed. Buenos Aires: Talleres Casa Jacobo Peuser, 1921.

C. PRINTED DOCUMENTS AND CONTEMPORARY WORKS

Acuerdos del extinguido Cabildo de Buenos Aires. Serie III. Buenos Aires: Archivo General de la Nación, 1928.

Angelis, Pedro de. *Colección de obras y documentos relativos a la historia antigua y moderna de las provincias del Río de la Plata*. 2d ed. 5 vol. Buenos Aires, 1910.

"Apuntes sobre el trabajo de Manuel Fernández Hortelano, oficial tercero de Secretaría, 1777." In Jonathan Costa Rego Monteiro, *A Côlonia de Sacramento: 1680–1777*. Porto Alegre, 1937. Vol. 2, 183–92, document 73.

Arancel general de los derechos de los Oficiales de esta Real Audiencia, de los Jueces Ordinarios, Abogados, y Escribanos Públicos, y Reales de Provincias, Medidores y Tasadores, y de las visitas y examenes del Proto-medicato de este Distrito. Buenos Aires: Real Imprenta de los Niños Expósitos, 1787.

Araujo, José Joaquín de. *La guía de forasteros del virreynato de Buenos Aires para el año de 1803*. Buenos Aires: Biblioteca de la Junta de Historia y Numismática Americana, 1908.

Archivo General de la Nación, Argentina. *Documentos referentes a la guerra de la independencia y emancipación política de la República Argentina*. 3 vols. Buenos Aires, 1914–26.

Archivo Histórico de la Provincia de Buenos Aires, Argentina. *Cedulario de la Real Audiencia de Buenos Aires*. 3 vols. La Plata: Taller de Impresiones Oficiales, 1929–38.

———. *Libro de informes y oficios de la Real Audiencia de Buenos Aires (1785–1810)*. La Plata: Taller de Impresiones Oficiales, 1929.

Aviles, Virrey Marqués de. "Informe." *Revista de la Biblioteca Pública de Buenos Aires* 3 (1881): n.p.

"Bando . . . comunicando la creación del Estanco de Tabaco y Naipes," In Facultad de Filosofa y Letras, *Documentos para la historia del virreinato del Río de la Plata.* Buenos Aires, 1912. 1:236–37.

Bucareli y Ursúa, Francisco de Paula. "Memoria del gobernador a su sucesor D. Juan José de Vértiz," *Revista de la biblioteca pública de Buenos Aires* 2 (1880): 301–98.

Concolorcorvo. *El lazarillo de ciegos caminantes desde Buenos Aires hasta Lima (1773).* Buenos Aires: Ediciones Solar, 1942.

Cortesao, Jaime, ed. *Manuscritos da Coleçao De Angelis.* Vol. 8. *Do Tratado de Madrid a conquista dos sete povos.* Rio de Janeiro, 1969.

Escalona y Aguero, Gaspar de. *Gazofilacia real del Perú: tratado financiero del coloniaje.* Madrid, 1775.

Facultad de Filosofía y letras, Universidad de Buenos Aires. *Documentos para la historia argentina.* Vol. 6. *Comercio de Indias. Comercio libre (1778–1791).* Buenos Aires: Compañía Sudamericana de billetes de banco, 1915.

———. *Documentos para la historia argentina.* Vol. 7. *Comercio de Indias. Consulado, comercio de negros y de extranjeros (1791 1809).* Buenos Aires: Compañía Sud americana de billetes de banco, 1916.

———. *Documentos para la historia argentina.* Vol. 11. *Territorio y población: Padrón de la ciudad de Buenos Aires (1778).* Buenos Aires: Compañía Sud-americana de billetes de banco, 1919.

———. *Documentos para la historia del virreinato del Río de la Plata.* 3 vols. Buenos Aires: Compañía Sud-Americana de Billetes de Banco, 1912–13.

Fernández-Burzaco y Barrios, Hugo. "La Venerable Orden Tercera de Santo Domingo en Buenos Aires: Libro primero de ingresos: Libro segundo de ingresos," *Historia* 12 (1958): 121–44.

Guía de forasteros en la ciudad y virreynato de Buenos Aires: Para el año de 1792. Buenos Aires: Imprenta de los Niños Expósitos, 1791.

Helmer, Marie. "Une lettre inédit de Victorian de Villava," *Revista de Indias* 11 (1951): 275–79.

Henry, Angel Antonio. *El oficinista instruido o práctica de oficinas reales.* Madrid, 1813.

"Instrucción de los Resguardos de 12 de enero de 1787," *Boletín de la dirección general de aduanas* (Buenos Aires), 4 (1941): 900–901, 1012–14.

"Instrucción para precaver las funestas consecuencias del contrabando e ilícito comercio." In *Boletín de la dirección general de aduanas* (Buenos Aires), 3:610–12; 710–13.

"La Contaduría de Buenos Aires y la Instrucción de 1767," *Revista del instituto de historia del derecho* 19 (1968): 267–80.

Lista de los donativos patrióticos. Buenos Aires: Imprenta de los Niños Expósitos, 1809.

Moreno, Manuel. *Vida y memorias de don Mariano Moreno.* In *Biblioteca de Mayo,* Buenos Aires: Archivo General de la Nación, 1960.

Municipalidad de la Capital (Buenos Aires). *Documentos y planos relativos al período edilicio colonial de la ciudad de Buenos Aires.* 4 vols. Buenos Aires, 1910.

"Nuevo método de cuenta y razón para la Real Hacienda de las Indias . . . 9 de mayo de 1784." *Revista de la biblioteca nacional* (Buenos Aires), 4 (1940): 267–318.

Pérez del Barrio Angula, Gabriel. *Dirección de secretarios de señores y las materias, cuidados y obligaciones que les tocan, con las virtudes de que se han de preciar, estilo y orden del despacho y expediente, manejo de papeles de ministros, formularios de cartas, provisiones de oficios.* Madrid, 1613.

Prado y Rozas, Antonio de. *Reglas para oficiales de secretarias y catálogo de secretarios del despacho y del Consejo de Estado que ha habido desde los Señores Reyes Católicos hasta el presente.* Madrid: Antonio Marín, 1755.

"Presupuesto colonial de comienzos del siglo XIX." *Boletín del instituto de investigaciones históricas* 1 (1922): 122–23.

Radaelli, Sigfrido A., ed. *Memorias de los virreyes del Río de la Plata.* Buenos Aires, 1945.

"Real Ordenanza para el establecimiento e instrucción de intendentes de exército y provincia en el virreinato de Buenos Aires, 28 de enero de 1782." In Archivo General de la Nación Argentina, *Documentos referentes a la guerra de la independencia y emancipación política de la República Argentina.* Buenos Aires, 1914. 1:21–95.

Recopilación de leyes de los reynos de las Indias (1681). 4 vols. Facsimile edition. Madrid, 1973.

Registro oficial de la República Argentina. Vol. 1. Buenos Aires, 1879.

"Reglamento de Aduana de 15 de febrero de 1779." *Boletín de la dirección general de aduanas* (Buenos Aires), 1 (1938): 1035–38, 1045–47; 2 (1939): 31–34, 125–29, 218–20, 311–14, 440–42, 554–57.

"Relaçao de papeis existentes num arquivo de Buenos Aires por meados do século XVIII." In Jaime Cortesao, *Manuscritos da Coleçao De Angelis.* Rio de Janeiro, 1969. 8: 301–18.

Semanario de agricultura, industria y comercio (1802–1807). Facsimile edition. Buenos Aires, 1928.

Telégrafo mercantil, rural, político, económico e historiográfico del Río de la Plata. Facsimile edition. Buenos Aires: Junta de Historia y Numismática, 1914.

Tomas de Razón de despachos militares, cédulas de premio, retiros, empleos civiles y eclesiásticos, donativos, etc. (1740–1821). Buenos Aires: Kraft, 1925.

Torres, Andrés de. *Diario de gastos del Virrey del Río de la Plata, Marqués de Loreto, 1783–1790.* Bilbao: Publicaciones de la Disputación Foral del Señorío de Vizcaya, 1977.

II. Selected Secondary Sources

Acevedo, Edberto. "El viaje del contador Navarro entre Lima y Buenos Aires en 1779." *Revista de historia americana y argentina* (Mendoza), 3:5–6 (1960–61): 257–330.

Alden, Dauril. "The Undeclared War of 1773–1777: Climax of Luso-Spanish Platine Rivalry." *Hispanic American Historical Review* 41 (1961): 55–74.

Amaral, Samuel. "Public Expenditure Financing in the Colonial Treasury: An Analysis of the Real Caja de Buenos Aires Accounts, 1789–1791." *Hispanic American Historical Review* 64, no. 2 (May 1984): 287–95.

Amparo Ros, María. "La Real Fábrica de Tabaco: apuntes acerca de la organización del trabajo." In Seminario de Historia Urbana, *Investigaciones sobre la historia de la ciudad de México* 2 (1976): 97–103.

Andrien, Kenneth J. "The Royal Treasury and Society in Seventeenth Century Lima." Ph.D. diss., Duke University, 1977.

Arias Divito, Juan Carlos. "Auge y decadencia de la renta del tabaco en Buenos Aires," *Nuestra historia* 22 (1978): 195–201.

———. "Breve noticia de la factoría del Paraguay." *Nuestra historia* 21 (1978): 180–82.

———. "Dificultades para establecer la renta de tabaco en Paraguay." *Anuario de estudios americanos* 33 (1976): 1–17.

————. "El gusto de los consumidores de tabaco en Santa Fé y la Real Hacienda." *Res gesta* (Rosario), 10 (1981): 20–25.

————. "Establecimiento de la renta de tabacos y naipes en el virreynato del Río de la Plata." *Historiografía rioplatense* (Buenos Aires), 1978, 7–56.

————. "La Real Ordenanza de Intendentes y la renta de tabaco," *Revista de historia del derecho* 11 (1983): 341–76.

Armas, Fernando de. "Los oficiales de la Real Hacienda en las Indias." *Revista de historia* 16 (1963): 11–34.

Arnold, Linda. "Administrative Appeals and Government Wages: The Bureaucrats of Mexico City, 1761–1808." Paper presented at the Southern Historical Association Conference, November, 1983.

————. "Apprenticeship, Permanency and Free-lancing: Bureaucratic Career Patterns in Late Colonial Mexico City." Paper presented at the Pacific Coast American Historical Association meeting, 1981.

————. *Breve compendio sobre la historia de la secretaría de cámara del virreinato en Nueva España, 1750–1800.* Mexico: Archivo General de la Nación, 1980.

————. "Bureaucracy and Bureaucrats in Mexico City, 1808–1822." Master's thesis, University of Texas at Austin, 1975.

————. *Directorio de burócratas en la ciudad de Mexico, 1761–1832.* Mexico: Archivo General de la Nación, 1980.

————. "La audiencia de México durante la fase gaditana." *Memorias del II congreso de historia del derecho mexicano* (UNAM, Mexico), 1981, 361–75.

————. "Political, Social and Economic Status in the Mexico City Central Bureaucracy, 1808–1822." In *El trabajo y los trabajadores en la historia de México*, ed. Elsa Cecilia Frost, Michael C. Meyer, and Josefina Zoraida Vázquez. (México and Phoenix: El Colegio de México and University of Arizona Press, 1979), 281–310.

Avellá Cháfer Francisco. "La situación económica del clero secular de Buenos Aires durante los siglos XVII y XVIII (Primera parte)." *Investigaciones y ensayos* 29 (July–December 1980): 295–318.

Azarola Gil, Luis Enrique. *Apellidos de la patria vieja.* Buenos Aires, 1942.

Bandelier, Adolf F. "The Siege of La Paz." *Historical Records and Studies of the United States Historical Society* 4 (1906): 243–64.

Barba, Enrique M. *Don Pedro de Cevallos, gobernador de Buenos Aires y virrey del Río de la Plata.* 2d ed. Buenos Aires, 1978.

Barba, Fernando Enrique. "Personal empleado en el Puerto de San Julián, 1780–1784." In Academia Nacional de la Historia (Argentina), *Bicentenario del virreinato del Río de la Plata,* Buenos Aires, 1977. 2:141–55.

Barbier, Jacques A. "Elite and Cadres in Bourbon Chile," *Hispanic American Historical Review* 52 (1972): 416–35.

————. *Reform and Politics in Bourbon Chile, 1755–1796.* Ottawa: University of Ottowa Press, 1980.

————. "The Culmination of the Bourbon Reforms, 1787–1792." *Hispanic American Historical Review* 57 (1977): 51–68.

————. "Toward a New Chronology for Bourbon Colonialism: The 'Depositaria de Indias' of Cadiz, 1722–1789." *Ibero-Amerikanisches Archiv* 6 (1980): 335–53.

———. "Tradition and Reform in Bourbon Chile: Ambrosio O'Higgins and Public Finances." *The Americas* 34 (1978): 381–99.

———. "Venezuelan 'Libranzas', 1788–1807: From Economic Nostrum to Fiscal Imperative." *The Americas* 37 (1981): 457–78.

Beneyto Pérez, Juan. *Historia de la administración española e hispanoamericana.* Madrid, 1958.

Bernard, Gildas. *Le Secrétariat d'Etat et le Conseil Espagnol des Indes (1700–1810).* Geneva: Libraire Droz, 1972.

———. "Liste des Secretaires d'Etat Espagnols de l'Avenement des Bourbons Jusqu'en 1808." *Revista de archivos, bibliotecas y museos* (Madrid), 62 (1956): 387–94.

Bierck, Harold A. "Tobacco Marketing in Venezuela, 1798–1799: An Aspect of Spanish Mercantilist Revisionism." *Business History Review* 39 (1965): 489–502.

Brading, D. A. "Bourbon Spain and Its American Empire." *The Historical Journal* 24 (1981): 961–69.

———. *Miners and Merchants in Bourbon Mexico, 1763–1810.* Cambridge, England: Cambridge University Press, 1971.

Bronner, Fred. "Elite Formation in Seventeenth-Century Peru." *Boletín de estudios latinoamericanos y del Caribe* 24 (1978): 3–26.

———. "Peruvian Encomenderos in 1630: Elite Circulation and Consolidation." *Hispanic American Historical Review* 57, no. 4 (November 1977): 633–59.

Budget of the United States Government. Washington, D.C.: USGPO, 1985.

Burkholder, Mark A. "Bureaucratic Patronage: The High Courts of Spain and the Indies, 1751–1808." Paper presented at the American Historical Association meeting, Washington, D.C., 1980.

———. "From Creole to Peninsular: The Transformation of the Audiencia of Lima." *Hispanic American Historical Review* 52 (1972): 395–415.

———. *Politics of a Colonial Career: José Baquíjano and the Audiencia of Lima.* Albuquerque: University of New Mexico Press, 1980.

———. "The Council of the Indies in the Late Eighteenth Century: A New Perspective." *Hispanic American Historical Review* 56 (1976): 404–23.

———, and Dewitt S. Chandler. "Creole Appointments and the Sale of Audiencia Positions in the Spanish Empire Under the Early Bourbons, 1701–1750." *Journal of Latin American Studies* 4 (1972): 187–206.

———. *Biographical Dictionary of the Audiencia Ministers in the Americas, 1687–1821.* Westport, Conn.: Greenwood Press, 1982.

———. *From Impotence to Authority: The Spanish Crown and the American Audiencias, 1687–1808.* Columbia, Mo.: University of Missouri Press, 1977.

Bushnell, Amy. *The King's Coffer: Proprietors of the Spanish Florida Treasury, 1565–1702.* Gainesville: University Presses of Florida, 1981.

Caillet-Bois, Ricardo R. "Un informe reservado del virrey Joaquín del Pino." *Boletín del instituto de investigaciones históricas* 11 (1930): 67–90.

Calvo, Carlos. *Nobiliario del antiguo virreynato del Río de la Plata.* 6 vols. Buenos Aires: Editorial La Facultad, 1936–43.

Campbell, Leon G. "A Colonial Establishment: Creole Domination of the Audiencia of Lima during the Late Eighteenth Century." *Hispanic American Historical Review* 52 (1972): 1–25.

————. "Los peruanos en la Audiencia de Lima a fines del siglo XVIII." In *Quinto congreso internacional de historia de América*. Lima, 1972. 2:393–405.

————. "Recent Research on Andean Peasant Revolts, 1750–1820." *Latin American Research Review* 14 (1979): 3–49.

————. "Recent Research on Bourbon Enlightened Despotism, 1750–1824." *New Scholar* 7 (1978): 29–49.

————. "The Military Service Record as a Source for the Study of Latin American Social History." *Manuscripta* 19 (1975): 147–58.

Carril, Bonifacio del. *La expedición Malaspina en los mares americanos del Sur*. Buenos Aires: Emecé, 1961.

Céspedes del Castillo, Guillermo. "La Renta de Tabaco en el Virreinato de Peru." *Revista histórica* 21 (1954): 138–63.

————. *Lima y Buenos Aires: Repercusiones económicas y políticas de la creación del virreinato del Plata*. Sevilla: Escuela de Estudios Hispanoaméricanos, 1947.

————. "Reorganización de la hacienda virreinal peruana en el siglo XVIII," *Anuario de historia del derecho español* 23 (1953). 329–69.

Chandler, Dewitt Samuel. "Pensions and the Bureaucracy of New Spain in the Late Eighteenth Century." Ph.D. diss., Duke University, 1971.

————. "The *Montepíos* and Regulation of Marriage in the Mexican Bureaucracy, 1770–1821." *The Americas* 43 (July 1986): 47–68.

Cignoli, Francisco. "Providencia del Virrey Cevallos sobre presentación y revisión de títulos del arte de curar y visita de bóticas (Buenos Aires, 1777)." In Academia Nacional de la Historia (Argentina), *Bicentenario del virreinato del Río de la Plata*. Buenos Aires, 1977, 1: 271–82.

Cooney, Jerry W. "Neutral Vessels and *Porteño* Slavers: Building a Viceregal Merchant Marine." *Journal of Latin American Studies* 18 (1986): 25–39.

Cornblit, Oscar, "Levantamientos de masas en Perú y Bolivia durante el siglo dieciocho." *Revista latinoamericana de sociologia* 6 (1970): 100–143.

Correa Luna, Carlos. *Don Baltasar de Arandia*. 2d ed. Buenos Aires, 1918.

Cortes, María del Carmen. "Benito de la Mata Linares, juez y testigo en la rebelión de Tupac Amaru." In *Quinto congreso international de historia de América* Lima, 1972 1:431–65.

Cuello Martinell, María Angeles. "La Renta de los Naipes en Nueva España." *Anuario de estudios americanos* 22 (1965): 231–335.

Cútolo, Vicente Osvaldo. "Los abogados en la revolución de Mayo." In *Tercer congreso internacional de historia de América*. Buenos Aires, 1961. 5:199–212.

————. "Los abogados del congreso graduados en Chuquisaca," In *Cuarto congreso internacional de historia de América*. Buenos Aires, 1966. 195–215.

Dalby, Michael T., and Michael S. Werthman, eds. *Bureaucracy in Historical Perspective*. Glenview, Ill., 1971.

Destefani, Laurio H. "Jacinto de Altolaguirre, primer gobernador criollo de la Islas Malvinas (1781–1783)." *Investigaciones y ensayos* 14 (1973): 205–21.

Díaz-Trecheulo López-Spinola, María Lourdes. "Españoles americanos en los colegios mayor del Sacromonte y de San Bartolomé y Santiago de la Universidad de Granada: Siglos XVIII y XIX." In *Quinto congreso internacional de historia de América*. Lima, 1972. 3: 497–534.

Donoso, Ricardo. *Un letrado del siglo XVIII: Don José Perfecto de Salas*. 2 vols. Buenos Aires, 1967.

Escudero, José Antonio. *Los orígenes del consejo de ministros en España*. 2 vols. Madrid, 1979.

Estrada, Marcos. "La casa de Altolaguirre." *Revista genealógica* 12 (1957): 139–51.

Feliú Cruz, Guillermo. "Un bibliógrafo español del siglo XVIII: José de Rezabal y Ugarte: estudio biográfico, bibliográfico y crítico." *Boletín de la academia chilena de la historia* 74 (1966): 74–121.

Fisher, J. R. *Commercial Relations Between Spain and Spanish America in the Era of Free Trade, 1778–1796*. Liverpool: Centre for Latin American Studies, 1985.

———. *Government and Society in Colonial Peru: The Intendant System, 1784–1814*. London: Athlone Press, 1970.

———. "Imperial 'Free Trade' and the Hispanic Economy, 1778–1796." *Journal of Latin American Studies* 13 (1981): 21–56.

Flusche, Della M. "A Study of the *Cabildo* in Seventeenth Century Santiago, Chile, 1609–1699." Ph.D. diss., Loyola University of Chicago, 1969.

Funes, Dean. *Ensayo de la historia civil del Paraguay, Buenos Aires y Tucumán*. 3 vols. Buenos Aires, 1816–17.

Furlong, Guillermo, S. J. *Historia social y cultural del Río de la Plata: El trasplante cultural: Ciencia*. Buenos Aires: Tipográfica Editora Argentina, 1969.

———. *Historia y bibliografía de la primeras imprentas rioplatenses*. 4 vols. Buenos Aires, 1953–75.

Galmarini, Hugo Rául. "Comercio y burocracia colonial: A propósito de Tomás Antonio Romero." *Investigaciones y ensayos* 28 (January-June 1980): 407–39; 29 (July–December 1980): 387–424.

Gammalsson, Hialmar Edmundo. "El Callejon de Ibáñez." *Investigaciones y ensayos* 20 (1976): 361–75.

———. *El Virrey Cevallos*. Buenos Aires: Plus Ultra, 1976.

———. "Tribulaciones del Virrey de la luces." In Academia Nacional de la Historia (Argentina), *Bicentenario del virreinato del Río de la Plata*. Buenos Aires, 1977. 2:157–69.

Gandia, Enrique de. "Economic Growth and Regional Differentiations: The River Plate Region at the End of the Eighteenth Century." *Hispanic American Historical Review* 65 (1985): 51–89.

Garavaglia, Juan Carlos. "Diferenciaciones regionales y crecimiento económico: El Río de la Plata a fines del siglo XVIII y comienzos del XIX." Paper presented at the Americanistas meeting, Manchester, England, 1982.

García Belsunce, César A. "La Aduana de Buenos Aires en las postrimerías del regímen virreinal." *Investigaciones y ensayos* 19 (1975): 463–86.

Gelman, Jorge Daniel. "Un 'repartimiento de mercancias' en 1788: Los sueldos 'monetarios' de las milicias de Corrientes." *Cuadernos de historia regional* (Argentina), 2 (1985): 3–17.

Genealogia: Hombres de mayo. Buenos Aires: Instituto Argentino de Ciencias Genealógicas, 1961.

Gil Munilla, Octavio. *El Río de la Plata en la politica internacional: Genesis del virreinato*. Sevilla: Escuela de estudios hispanoaméricanos, 1949.

Gómez Gómez, Amalia. *Las visitas de la Real Hacienda novohispana en el reino de Felipe VI. 1710–1733*. Sevilla: Escuela de estudios hispanoaméricanos, 1979.

Goñi Moreno, José María. "Antecedentes históricos de la previsión social argentina," *Revista de la facultad de derecho y ciencias sociales* (Buenos Aires), 8 (1953): 1449–65.

———. *Derecho de la previsión social.* Buenos Aires: Ediar, 1956.

Groussac, Paul. *Santiago de Liniers, Conde de Buenos Aires, 1753–1810.* Buenos Aires, 1907.

Gutiérrez, J. M. "El virreinato del Río de la Plata durante la administración del Marqués de Loreto." *Revista del Río de la Plata* 8 (1874): 212–40.

Halperin-Donghi, Tulio. *Guerra y finanzas en los orígenes del estado argentino (1791–1850).* Buenos Aires: Editorial Belgrano, 1982.

Hamnett, Brian R. "The Appropriation of Mexican Church Wealth by the Spanish Bourbon Government: The Consolidation of *Vales Reales,* 1805–1809." *Journal of Latin American Studies* 1 (1969): 5–113.

Harrison, John P. "The Colombian Tobacco Industry from Government Monopoly to Free Trade, 1778–1876." Ph.D. diss., University of California at Berkeley, 1951.

Heredia Herrera, Antonia M. "La carta como tipo diplomático indiano." *Anuario de estudios americanos* 34 (1977): 65–95.

———. *La renta del azogue en Nueva España, 1709–1751.* Sevilla: Escuela de estudios hispano américanos, 1978.

———. "Organización y descripción de los fondos de la Audiencia de Quito del Archivo General de Indias." *Historiografía y bibliografía americanistas* 21 (1977): 139–65.

Hernández Palomo, José Jesús. *La renta del pulque en Nueva España, 1663–1810.* Seville: Escuela de estudios hispanoaméricanos, 1980.

Herr, Richard. *The Eighteenth Century Revolution in Spain.* Princeton: Princeton University Press, 1958.

Holguin Callo, Oswaldo. "Las actividades lucrativos del doctor Diego de Salinas, letrado de Lima (1558–1595)." *Revista de Indias* 153–54 (1978): 617–51.

Johnson, Lyman L. "Recent Contributions to the History of Eighteenth-Century Spanish America." *Latin American Research Review* 17 (1982): 222–30.

———. "Wages, the Organization of Work and Prices in Colonial Buenos Aires, 1770–1815." Paper given at the Americanista Meeting, Manchester, England, 1982.

———, and Susan M. Socolow. "Population and Space in Eighteenth Century Buenos Aires." In *Social Fabric and Spatial Structure in Colonial Latin America,* ed. David J. Robinson. Syracuse, N.Y., and Ann Arbor, Mich.: Syracuse University and University Microfilms, 1979. 339–68.

Kicza, John E. "The Legal Community of Late Colonial Mexico: Social Composition and Career Patterns." Paper delivered at the Latin American Studies Association meeting, Washington, D.C., 1982.

Klein, Herbert S. "Structure and Profitability of Royal Finance in the Viceroyalty of Río de la Plata in 1790." *Hispanic American Historical Review* 53 (1973): 440–69.

———, and John J. TePaske. *The Royal Treasuries of the Spanish Empire in America.* Vol. 3. *Chile and the Río de la Plata.* Durham, N.C.: Duke University Press, 1982.

Konetzke, Richard, ed. *Colección de documentos para la historia de la formación social de His-panoamérica.* 1493–1810. 3 vols. Madrid, 1953–62.

———. *Descripción de la provincia del Río de la Plata.* Buenos Aires, 1947.

Kuethe, Allan J. and G. Douglas Inglis, "Absolutism and Enlightened Reform: Charles III,

344 THE BUREAUCRATS OF BUENOS AIRES

the Establishment of the *Alcabala,* and Commercial Reorganization in Cuba." *Past and Present* 109 (November 1985): 118–43.

Labougle, Raúl de. *Litigios de antaño.* Buenos Aires: Imprenta y Casa Editora Coni, 1941.

Lang, James. "Imperial Reorganization in the Americas," Paper delivered at the Wilson International Center for Scholars, Washington, D.C., 1978.

Lanning, John Tate. "Legitimacy and *Limpieza de Sangre* in the Practice of Medicine in the Spanish Empire." *Jahrbuch für Geschichte von Staat, Wirtschaft und Gesellschaft Lateinamerikas* 4 (1967): 37–60.

Lavrin, Asunción. "The Execution of the Laws of *Consolidación* in New Spain: Economic Aims and Results." *Hispanic American Historical Review* 53 (1973): 27–49.

Levaggi, Abelardo. "La fundamentación de las sentencias en el derecho indiano." *Revista de historia del derecho* 6 (1978): 45–73.

———, ed. *Los escritos del fiscal de la Audiencia de Buenos Aires Manuel Genaro de Villota.* Buenos Aires: Fundación para la Educación, Ciencia y la Cultura, 1981.

Levene, Ricardo. *Ensayo histórico sobre la revolución de mayo y Mariano Moreno.* 3 vols. 4th ed. Buenos Aires: Ediciones Peuser, 1960.

———, ed. *Historia de la nación argentina (desde los orígenes hasta la organización definitiva en 1862).* 2d ed. Buenos Aires, 1940.

———. *Historia del derecho argentino.* 3 vols. Buenos Aires, 1946.

Lewis, James A. "The Royal Gunpowder Monopoly in New Spain, (1766–1783): A Case Study of Management, Technology, and Reform under Charles III." *Ibero-Amerikanisches Archiv* 6 (1980): 355–72.

Lira González, Andrés. "Aspecto fiscal de la Nueva España en la segunda mitad del siglo XVIII." *Historia mexicana* 17 (1968): 361–94.

Lockhart, James. "The Social History of Colonial Latin America: Evolution and Potential." *Latin American Research Review* 17 (1972): 5–45.

Lohmann Villena, Guillermo. *Los americanos en las ordenes nobiliarias (1529-1900).* 2 vols. Madrid: Instituto Gonzalo Fernández de Oviedo, 1947.

———. *Los ministros de la audiencia de Lima (1700–1821).* Sevilla: Escuela de estudios hispanoaméricanos, 1974.

Lynch, John. "Intendants and Cabildos in the Viceroyalty of La Plata, 1782–1810." *Hispanic American Historical Review* 35 (1955): 337–62.

———. *Spanish Colonial Administration, 1782–1810: The Intendant System in the Viceroyalty of the Río de la Plata.* 2d ed. Westport, Conn.: Greenwood Press, 1969.

———. *The Spanish American Revolutions, 1808–1826.* New York: W. W. Norton, 1973.

Macmillan, Mary Maloy. "The King's Hammer: Francisco Bucareli y Ursúa, Governor of the Provinces of Río de la Plata and Buenos Aires, 1766–1770." Ph.D. diss., Washington State University, 1977.

Mariluz Urquijo, José María. "Elenco de los contadores mayores de la Contaduría Mayor de Cuentas y del Tribunal Mayor de Cuentas de Buenos Aires. *Investigaciones y ensayos* 16 (1974): 139–44.

———. *El Virreinato del Río de la Plata en la época del Marqués de Avilés (1799–1801).* Buenos Aires: Academia Nacional de la Historia, 1964.

————. "El tribunal mayor y audiencia real de cuentas de Buenos Aires." *Revista de la facultad de derecho y ciencias sociales* (Buenos Aires), 6 (1951): 25–54. Also published in *Revista del instituto de historia de derecho* (Buenos Aires) 3 (1951): 112–41.

————. *Ensayo sobre los juicios de residencia indianos.* Sevilla: Escuela de estudios hispanoaméricanos, 1952.

————. "La biblioteca de un oidor de la Real Audiencia de Buenos Aires." *Revista del instituto de historia de derecho* 7 (1955–56): 140–46.

————. "La organización militar del virreinato en la época del Marqués de Avilés." *Trabajos y comunicaciones* (Universidad Nacional de la Plata), 3 (1953): 117–51.

————. "La situación del mitayo en las glosas de Benito de la Mata Linares al código carolino." *Jahrbuch für Geschichte von Staat, Wirtschaft und Gesellschaft Lateinamerikas* 14 (1977): 161–98.

————. "Las memorias de los Regentes de la Real Audiencia de Buenos Aires Manuel Antonio de Arredondo y Benito de la Mata Linares." *Revista del instituto de historia del derecho* 1 (1949): 19–26.

————. *Orígenes de la burocracia rioplatense.* Buenos Aires: Ediciones Cabargon, 1974.

Martiré, Eduardo. *El código carolino de ordenanzas reales de las minas de Potosí y demás provincias del Río de la Plata (1794) de Pedro Vicente Cañete.* Buenos Aires: Universidad de Buenos Aires, 1973.

————. "El estatuto legal del oficial de la administración pública al crearse el Virreinato del Río de la Plata: Notas para su estudio." *Revista de la facultad de derecho* (Universidad Nacional de México), 26 (1976): 417–36.

————. *Los regentes de Buenos Aires: La reforma judicial indiana de 1776.* Buenos Aires: Universidad de Buenos Aires, 1981.

Mendiburu, Manuel de. *Diccionario histórico biográfico del Perú.* Lima, 1874–90.

Mayer Arana, Alberto. *La caridad en Buenos Aires.* 2 vols. Buenos Aires, 1911.

Molina, Raúl A. "El primer arancel de gastos de justicia del Río de la Plata." *Revista del instituto de historia del derecho* 4 (1952): 196–204.

————. "Las finanzas municipales en la colonial." *Revista de derecho administrativo municipal* 166: 1169–91.

————. "Los primeros oficiales reales del Río de la Plata: Hernando de Montalvo: El juicio de la historia." *Boletín de la academia nacional de historia* (Buenos Aires), 35 (1964): 181–225.

————. *Regimen financiero de la ciudad de Buenos Aires: historia, naturaleza y jurisprudencia de sus recursos ordinarios.* Buenos Aires: Editorial Bernabé, 1941.

————. "Una historia ínedita de los primeros ochenta años de Buenos Aires: El 'Defensorio' de D. Alonso de Solorazano y Velazco, Oidor de la Real Audiencia (1667)." *Revista de historia de América* (Mexico) 52 (1961): 429–97.

————. "Une plieto célebre en el siglo XVII." *Revista penal y penitenciaria* 14 (1949): n.p.

Morazzani de Pérez Enciso, Gisela. *Las ordenanzas de intendentes de Indias (cuadro para su estudio).* Caracas: Universidad Central de Venezuela, 1972.

————. "Observaciones sobre las Ordenanzas de Intendentes de Indias de 1782 y 1786." In *Tercer congreso del instituto internacional de historia del derecho indiano.* Madrid, 1973. 633–53.

Moreno, Frank Jay. "The Spanish Colonial System: A Functional Approach." *Western Political Quarterly* 20 (1967): 308–20.

Moreyra y Paz Soldán, Manuel. "Valor histórico de los libros de contabilidad hacendaria colonial." *Revista histórica* 22 (1955–56): 311–35.

Morner, Magnus. "La reorganización imperial en hispanoamérica." *Ibero-Romansk* (Stockholm), 4:1–33.

Morse, Richard M. "Toward a Theory of Spanish American Government." *Journal of the History of Ideas* 15 (1954): 71–93.

Moutoukias, Zacarías. "Le Río de la Plata et l'espace peruvien au XVIIème siècle: commerce et contrebande par Buenos Aires, 1648–1702." Thesis de 3ème cycle, Ecole des Hautes Etudes en Sciences Sociales, Paris, 1983.

Navarro Garcia, Luis. "El real tribunal de cuentas de México a principios del siglo XVIII." *Anuario de estudios americanos* 34 (1977): 517–35.

———. *Intendencias en Indias.* Sevilla: Escuela de estudios hispanoaméricanos, 1959.

Oss, A. C. van. "Comparing Colonial Bishoprics in Spanish South America." *Boletín de estudios latinoamericanos y del caribe* (Amsterdam), 24 (1978): 27–66.

Ots Capdequi, José María. *El derecho de familia y el derecho de sucesión en nuestra legislación de Indias.* Madrid, 1920.

———. *La condición jurídica de la mujer en la legislación de Indias.* Madrid, 1922.

———. *Las instituciones sociales de la América española durante el período colonial.* La Plata, 1934.

———. *Manual de historia de derecho español en América y del derecho propiamente indiano.* Madrid, 1966.

Phelen, John Leddy. "Authority and Flexibility in the Spanish Imperial Bureaucracy." *Administrative Science Quarterly* 5 (1960): 47–65.

———. "El auge y la caída de los criollos en la audiencia de Nueva Granada, 1770–1781." *Boletín de historia y antigüedades* (Bogotá), 59 (1972): 597–618.

———. *The People and the King: The Comunero Revolution in Colombia, 1781.* Madison: University of Wisconsin Press, 1978.

Pike, Frederick B. "The Municipality and the System of Checks and Balances in Spanish Colonial Administration." *The Americas* 15 (1958): 139–58.

Pillado, José Antonio. *Buenos Aires colonial: Edificos y costumbres.* Buenos Aires: Compañía Sud-Americana de billetes de banco, 1910.

Probst, Juan. *Juan Baltasar Maziel, el maestro de la generación de Mayo.* Buenos Aires: Instituto de didáctica, 1946.

———. "La enseñanza primaria desde sus orígenes hasta 1810." In *Historia de la nación argentina (desde los orígenes hasta la organización definitiva en 1862),* ed. Ricardo Levene. Vol. 4. *El momento histórico del virreinato del Río de la Plata.* 2d ed. Buenos Aires, 1940. 155–87.

Quesada, Vicente G. "Noticias sobre el gobierno del Virey (sic) Arredondo." *La revista de Buenos Aires.* 1869. 139–66.

Radaelli, Sigfrido A. *Blasones de los Virreyes del Río de la Plata.* 2d ed. Buenos Aires, 1945.

———. "La institución virreinal en las Indias." *Revista de Indias* 15 (1954): 37–56.

———. *Los virreyes del Plata.* Buenos Aires: Editorial Perrot, 1959.

Ratto, Hector R., ed. *La expedición Malaspina en el virreinato del Río de la Plata.* Buenos Aires: Biblioteca del oficial de marina, 1936.

Ravignani, Emilio. *Constituciones del Real Colegio de San Carlos*. Buenos Aires: Talleres gráficos del Ministerio de Agricultura de la Nación, 1917.

———. "El virreinato del Río de la Plata (1776–1816)." In *Historia de la nación argentina (desde los orígenes hasta la organización definitiva en 1862)*, ed. Ricardo Levene. Vol. 4. *El momento histórico del virreinato del Río de la Plata*. 2d ed. Buenos Aires, 1940.

———. *El virreinato del Río de la Plata (1776–1810)*. Buenos Aires, 1938.

Real Díaz, José Joaquín. *Estudio diplomático del documento indiano*. Sevilla: Escuela de estudios hispanoaméricanos, 1970.

Reyna Almandos, Alberto. *Los primeros escribanos de Buenos Aires*. La Plata, 1963.

Ringrose, David R. "Perspectives on the Economy of Eighteenth Century Spain." *Historia ibérica* 1:59–81.

Rodríguez Crespo, Pedro. "Sobre parentescos de los oidores con los grupos superiores de la sociedad limeña (a comienzos del siglo XVII). *Mercurio peruano* 450 (1964): 49–63.

Rodríguez Molas, Ricardo. *Historia de la previsión social en Hispanoamérica*. Buenos Aires, Editorial Depalma, 1962.

Rodríguez Vicente, María Encarnación. "La contabilidad privada como fuente histórica." *Anuario de estudios americanos* 32 (1975): 303–27.

———. "La contabilidad virreinal como fuente histórica." *Anuario de estudios americanos* 23 (1966): 1523–42.

———. "La Real Hacienda en Perú a comienzos del siglo XIX." In *Quinto congreso internacional de historia de América*. (Lima, 1972), 3:292–301.

Rosenberg, Hans. *Bureaucracy, Aristocracy and Autocracy: The Evolution of Governmental Bureaucracy in Prussia, 1660–1815*. Cambridge, Mass.: Harvard University Press, 1958.

Ruiz Guinazú, Enrique. *La magistratura indiana*. Buenos Aires, 1916.

Salvucci, Linda K. "Costumbres viejas, 'hombres nuevos': José de Gálvez y la burocracia fiscal novohispana, 1754–1800." *Historia mexicana* 33 (October–December 1983): 224–64.

Sánchez Bella, Ismael. *La organización financiera de las Indias (siglo XVI)*. Sevilla: Escuela de estudios hispanoaméricanos, 1968.

Sánchez Ramírez, Antonio. "Notas sobre la Real Hacienda de Cuba (1700–1760)." *Anuario de estudios americanos* 34 (1977): 465–86.

Sánchez Ramos, Ignacio. *En el virreinato del Río de la Plata: Don Rafael de Sobremonte, Intendente, Gobernador, Inspector de Armas, Virrey, Mariscal de Campo, Consejero de Indias: Contribución a su revindicación histórica*. Buenos Aires: Casa Jacobo Peuser, 1929.

Santos Martínez, Pedro. "Reforma a la contabilidad colonial en el siglo XVIII: El método de partida doble." *Anuario de estudios americanos* 17 (1960): 525–36.

Sarrailh, Jean. *L'Espagne éclairée de la seconde moitié du XVIIIe siècle*. Paris: Imprimerie Nationale, 1954.

Schwartz, Stuart B. *Sovereignty and Society in Colonial Brazil: The High Court of Bahia and its Judges, 1609–1751*. Berkeley: University of California Press, 1973.

———. "State and Society in Colonial Spanish America: An Opportunity for Prosopography." In *New Approaches to Latin American History*, ed. Richard Graham and Peter H. Smith. Austin, Texas: University of Texas Press, 1974. 3–35.

Socolow, Susan Migden. "Acceptable Partners: Marriage Choice in Colonial Argentina, 1778–1810." Unpublished paper, 1985.

———. "Buenos Aires at the Time of Independence." In *Buenos Aires: 400 Years,* ed. Stanley R. Ross and Thomas F. McGann. Austin, Texas: University of Texas Press, 1982. 18–39.

———. "Marriage, Birth and Inheritance: The Merchants of Eighteenth-Century Buenos Aires." *Hispanic American Historical Review* 60, no. 3 (1980): 387–406.

———. *The Merchants of Buenos Aires, 1778–1810: Family and Commerce.* Cambridge: Cambridge University Press, 1978.

Stapff, Agnes. "La renta del tabaco en Chile de la época virreinal." *Anuario de estudios americanos* 18 (1961): 1–63.

Statistical Abstract of the United States. Washington, D.C.: USGPO, 1985.

Stein, Barbara H. and Stanley J. "Concepts and Realities of Spanish Economic Growth, 1759–1789." *Historia ibérica* 1 (1973): 103–19.

Tanzi, Hector José "La Contaduría de Buenos Aires y la instrucción de 1767." *Revista del instituto de historia del derecho* (Buenos Aires), 19 (1968): 267–80.

TePaske, John. "La crisis del siglo XVIII en el virreinato del Perú." In *Historia y sociedad en el mundo de habla española,* ed. Bernardo García Martínez. Mexico, 1970. 263–79.

Tjarks, Germán O. E. "Potosí y los situados de comercio." *Boletín del instituto de historia argentina 'Doctor Emilio Ravignani'* 4 (1961): 48–82.

Torre Revello, José. "Documentos relativos a Antonio Valle y Manuel Moreno Argumosa." *Boletín del instituto de investigaciones históricas* 27 (1942–43): 309–34.

———. *El Marqués de Sobre Monte, gobernador, intendent de Córdoba y Virrey del Río de la Plata.* Buenos Aires: Instituto de Investigaciones Historicas, Universidad de Buenos Aires, 1946.

———. "El testamento del virrey Pedro de Cevallos." *Boletín del instituto de investigaciones históricas* 12 (1931): 163–83.

———. *Juan José de Vértiz y Salcedo, gobernador y virrey de Buenos Aires.* Buenos Aires: Imprenta de la Universidad, 1932.

———. "La Orden de Carlos III en el Buenos Aires colonial." *Boletín del instituto de investigaciones históricas* 20 (1936): 27–34.

———. "Los gobernadores de Buenos Aires, 1617–1777." In Academia Nacional de la Historia, *Historia de la nación argentina.* Buenos Aires, 1937. 3:459–525.

Torres, Luis María. *La administración de temporalidades en el Río de la Plata.* Buenos Aires: Talleres gráficos del Ministerio de Agricultura de la Nación, 1917.

Udaondó, Enrique. *Crónica histórica de la venerable orden tercera de San Francisco en la República Argentina.* Buenos Aires, 1920.

———. *Diccionario biografico colonial argentino.* Buenos Aires: Editorial Huarpes, 1945.

Urbano Salerno, Marcelo. "Aplicación en el Virreinato del Río de la Plata del auto acordado del 31 de julio de 1792 sobre arrendamiento de casas de Madrid." *Revista de la facultad de derecho de México* 26 (1976): 773–84.

———. "Cajas de censos y bienes de comunidad: Evolución histórica en el Río de la Plata." In *Tercer congreso del instituto internacional de historia del derecho indiano.* Madrid, 1973. 869–91.

Weber, Max. "Bureaucracy." In *Economy and Society: An Outline of Interpretive Sociology,* ed. Guenther Roth and Claus Wittich. New York: Bedminister Press, 1968. 3:956–1005.

————. *From Max Weber: Essays in Sociology*. Ed. and trans. H. H. Gerth and C. Wright Mills. New York: Oxford University Press, 1946. 196–244.

————. *On Charisma and Institution Building: Selected Papers*. Chicago: University of Chicago Press, 1968.

Williams, Christopher T. "A Biographical Sketch of Francisco de Paula Sanz, Spanish Colonial Official." Ph.D. diss., Louisiana State University, 1977.

Yaben, Jacinto R. *Biografías argentinas y americanas*. 5 vols. Buenos Aires: Editorial Metropolis, 1938–40.

Zorraquin Becú, Ricardo. *La organización judicial argentina en el período hispánico*. Buenos Aires: Libreria del Plata, 1952.

————. *La organización política argentina en el período hispánico*. Buenos Aires: Emecé, 1959.

————. "Los cabildos argentinos." *Revista de la facultad de derecho y ciencias sociales* (Buenos Aires), 11 (1956): 95–156.

————. "Los grupos sociales en la Revolución de Mayo." *Historia* 6 (1961): 40–63.

Index

THE AUTHOR

Susan Migden Socolow is associate professor of history at Emory University. She is also the author, among other works, of *The Merchants of Buenos Aires, 1778–1810: Family and Commerce.*

Library of Congress Cataloging-in-Publication Data

Socolow, Susan Migden, 1941—
The bureaucrats of Buenos Aires, 1769–1810.
Includes index.
Bibliography: p.
1. Bureaucracy—Argentina—History.   2. Argentina—
Politics and government—To 1810.   I. Title.
JL2046.S66   1987   306'.24'0982   87-9211
ISBN 0-8223-0753-7